Mathematical Questions from the Classroom

Richard J. Crouse
University of Delaware

Clifford W. Sloyer
University of Delaware

Prindle, Weber & Schmidt, Incorporated
20 Newbury Street, Boston, Massachusetts   02116

Dedicated to

Our wives, Joann Crouse and Barbara Sloyer, without whose infinite patience and supreme understanding this book would not have been written.

Honorable mention goes to *Mary Hartman, Mary Hartman* and her chicken soup for the relief they provided.

© Copyright 1977
Prindle, Weber & Schmidt, Incorporated
20 Newbury Street, Boston, Massachusetts 02116.

Library of Congress Cataloging in Publication Data

Crouse, Richard J
    Mathematical questions from the classroom.

    Includes index.
    1. Mathematics–Study and teaching (Secondary)
I.   Sloyer, Clifford W., joint author.   II. Title.
QA11.C74   570'.7'12   76-53513
ISBN 0-87150-219-4

Second printing: August 1978

Printed in the United States of America.

Preface

After several years of teaching a methods course for college students preparing for secondary mathematics teaching, we found that these student teachers had great difficulty answering mathematical questions raised by their students. The authors began to collect the kinds of questions that puzzled these university students, as well as in-service teachers. This book is a compilation of those questions together with suggested solutions.

The majority of questions have come from actual classroom experiences. We feel that these questions and answers are valuable resource material for teachers and can be used in a variety of pre-service, inservice, undergraduate and graduate courses or seminars.

One way we have used this material is to tell the class that at the next meeting they will be asked questions on a particular topic. At the next meeting, questions from the given category are read and students are selected to answer them at the blackboard. If a student needs help, an effort is made to obtain it from others in the class. This gives the students practice in "thinking on their feet" and also allows the instructor to focus discussions in many directions; for example, how this concept might be taught in the schools, and what it is related to. Some of these questions are difficult to answer and may be given as homework assignments, and then discussed in class.

The questions are separated according to topic under a specific subject (e.g., Algebra I, Algebra II, Geometry, etc.) and are mainly of two types. Type I are those questions that teachers usually face when teaching a specific topic. Type II are those questions which occur occasionally, but are the type that many mathematics teachers would have a difficult time answering.

One of the qualities we feel all teachers should have is the ability to answer content questions from their students while "thinking on their feet." The questions in this book have been used in our methods courses for the past two years to help students develop this competence.

For many of the questions included, a dozen teachers would offer twelve different responses. The authors make no claim that our answers are the "best." The suggested answers are simply a means of stimulating teachers and future teachers to constantly look for better pedagogical techniques.

We would like to express our thanks to the people who assisted us in the preparation of this text. In particular we would like to thank the many student teachers and practicing teachers of mathematics who supplied us with many of the questions. We also particularly appreciate the constructive criticisms offered by reviewers, Willard Baxter (University of Delaware), Margariete Montague (Northern Illinois University), Robert Washburn (Southern Connecticut College), John G. Harvey (University of Wisconsin, Madison), and John Wagner (Michigan State University). We would also like to thank Cathy Chudzik, Alison Chandler, Dorothy Voorhees, Sarajon Martin and our wives, Joann Crouse and Barbara Sloyer, for doing a magnificent job in typing the original manuscript.

Richard J. Crouse

Clifford W. Sloyer

Contents

Chapter 2   Algebra I

QUESTIONS

ANSWERS

ANSWERS

1

Junior High

QUESTIONS

Q1.1   Absolute Value

1   We are often faced with some very hard content questions to explain even at the seventh and eighth grade levels. How would you help a student to answer the following question? "You said |a| = −a, but how can the absolute value of a number be negative?"

Q1.2   Decimals

1   A student asks you if it is possible to get all of the real numbers between any two real numbers by finding the average of these two numbers and continuing the averaging process indefinitely. What is your response?

2   When a student asks you if the set of irrational numbers is closed under addition, what is your reply?

3   A student asks you the following question. "When multiplying decimals, why do we count off decimal places from right to left in each factor and then add them in order to find out where to put the decimal point in the answer?" How do you respond?

4   A student asks, "We learned that if the denominator of a fraction in base ten has a factor of 2 or 5 then the decimal numeral is terminating. Will the same idea be true in other bases?" What is your response?

5   A seventh grade student asks you, "Why when multiplying or dividing decimals do we put the decimal point where we do." What is your response?

6   You make the statement that $1.\overline{9} = 2.0$. Some of your students protest, saying that the above statement is impossible because you have nines all the time after the decimal point. How do you handle this situation?

7 One student asks you the following question. "Why isn't 0.12½ equal to 0.62, since ½ = 0.5 and 0.12 + 0.50 = 0.62?" How would you answer this student?

Q1.3   Equality

1 In your eighth grade class, one of your students asks the following question. "Is there a difference between *equal* and *equivalent* in mathematics?" How would you answer him?

Q1.4   Exponents

tricky

1 In response to your question of how to define y^k, a student says that y is multiplied by itself k times. How do you reply?

2 A student asks, "Why is $x^0 = 1$?" How do you respond?

3 One of the students asks you what 0^{-7} is. How do you respond and why?

Q1.5   Fractions

1 A student asks, "Since we have defined multiplication as repeated addition, how is it possible that when you multiply two fractions you get a product smaller than either of the factors?" How do you reply?

2 A sixth grader asks why $3\frac{1}{3} \times \frac{3}{5} = 2$? What the student does not understand is that the answer, 2, is smaller than one of the factors, $3\frac{1}{3}$. How do you reply?

3 You put the problem $\frac{1}{5} + \frac{2}{3}$ on the board and ask one of your students to come to the board and demonstrate how to compute the answer. He writes the following: $\frac{1}{5} + \frac{2}{3} = \frac{3}{8}$. You tell him that it is wrong, but he gives you the following explanation. "If a baseball players is up at bat 5 times on the first day and gets one hit, and on the second day he gets 2 hits out of 3 times at bat, then altogether he has 3 hits out of 8 times at bat." How do reply?

4 One student asks the following question. "Can you divide fractional numbers by dividing the numerator of the top fraction by the numerator of the bottom fraction and likewise the denominator of the top fraction by the denominator of the bottom fraction?" For example,

$$\frac{14}{9} \div \frac{2}{3} = \frac{14 \div 2}{9 \div 3} = \frac{7}{3}$$

How do you reply?

5   One student makes the following assertion. "1/2 = 1/3 because my picture here shows it."

How would you explain to this student that he is incorrect?

6   A student says that there is something wrong with the definition of less than and shows you the following problem.

$$\frac{-3}{-4} < \frac{-2}{5} \quad \text{because} \quad (-3) \cdot (5) < (-2) \cdot (-4)$$

but $\frac{-3}{-4} = \frac{3}{4}$.

How would you answer this student?

7   An eighth grade student hands in the following solution when asked to reduce 64/16 to lowest terms.

$$\frac{\cancel{6}4}{1\cancel{6}} = \frac{1 \cdot 4}{1 \cdot 1} = \frac{4}{1} = 4 \,. \qquad \text{Is the student correct?}$$

8   There is ¾ of a pie left. Jane and Sue want to divide what is left in ½ so they each get an equal part. How much do each of them receive? A seventh grader's answer:

$$\frac{3}{4} \div \frac{1}{2} = \frac{3}{4} \times \frac{2}{1} = \frac{6}{4} = 1\frac{2}{4} = 1\frac{1}{2} \,.$$

What is your response?

9   You are teaching division of fractions. A seventh grader asks, "Why does multiplying by the reciprocal of the divisor give the correct answer?" What is your response?

10   A student in your class asks, "Why don't we need to get common denominators when multiplying fractions?" How would you respond?

11   In your seventh grade class, a student is doing the following problem.

$$\frac{3}{4} + \frac{5}{2}$$

The student writes $\frac{3}{4} + \frac{5}{2} = \frac{8}{4}$ and reasons as follows: "5 + 3 = 8 but since 2 will go into 4, then don't add the bottom numbers." How would you help this student?

12   A teacher asks a student the following question. "Which would you rather have, 20/35 of a cake or 4/7 of a cake?" The student says, "20/35 because there are then

more pieces." How would you respond if you were the teacher?

13   You have given your class the following problem. "If the selling price of a car is $3300 and the profit is 1/10 of the cost, then how much is the profit?" One student says that the profit is $330 because $330 is 1/10 of $3300. Is the student correct?

14   An eighth grade student asks, "You said that a rational number is one of the form p/q, p, q integers, q ≠ 0. What about:

$$\frac{\sqrt{3} \cdot 3}{\sqrt{3} \cdot 4} ?$$

Is this a rational number or not?" How do you reply?

15   You have given your class the following problem to solve: "A 20-foot board is to be cut into shorter pieces. If each piece is 4¾ feet long, how many pieces will there be?" One student hands in the following work:

$$\text{"} 20 \div 4\frac{3}{4} = 20 \div \frac{19}{4} = 20 \times \frac{4}{19} = \frac{80}{19} = 4\frac{4}{19}.$$

Thus there are 4 pieces and 4/19 of a foot left over." Is the student correct?

Q1.6   Geometry

(A)   ANGLES

1   You are teaching your students the idea of the degree measure of an angle and you have related it to the circle. One student makes the assertion that the degree will vary because the angle intercepts arcs of different lengths depending upon the size of the circle. Is the student right? If so, what explanation will you give to get around the difficulty presented? If the student is not right, then how will you resolve the student's misunderstanding?

2   A student asks the following question. "Since an angle is the union of two rays with a common endpoint and a triangle contains three angles, why doesn't the triangle look like this?"

How do you respond?

3   How would you respond to the following question? Since two lines are perpendicular if they form a 90° angle with one another, is it necessary for them to be in the same plane to be perpendicular?

4   How would you respond if a student in your class asks, "Why can't you measure the size of an angle in inches?"

5 We are often faced with some very hard content questions to explain even at the seventh and eighth grade level. How would you help a student to answer the following question. "Why isn't a straight angle considered to be an angle in our definition?"

(B)   *AREA*

1 You ask your eighth grade students to find the area of the circle with a radius of five inches. One of your students then gives the following answer. "You cannot find the area of a circle, you can only find its perimeter." What is your response?

2 While you are teaching your seventh grade class the formulas for areas of simple polygons (triangle, square, etc.), a student excitedly says that she has a formula that does it all. She says that the formula is: $A_p = \frac{1}{2}h \cdot (t + b)$ where:

> A_p is the area of the polygon you want;
>
> h is the length of the height of the polygon;
>
> t is the length of the top segment;
>
> b is the length of the bottom segment.

What do you tell the student?

3 A seventh grade student is trying to find the area of a rectangular lot 75 feet by 25 feet. The student reasons as follows: "I'll subtract 25 from 75 thus making it 50; then I'll add the 25 I subtracted to the other 25; then the problem reduces to 50 x 50 which is 2500. Therefore, the area of the lot is 2500 square feet." Is the student correct?

4 A student asks, "If two figures have the same area and the same perimeter, are the figures congruent?" What is your response?

(C)   *AXIOMS AND DEFINITIONS*

1 One of your seventh grade students asks, "You say that a point has no dimensions, i.e., in width or length. You also say that a line segment consists of an infinite number of points and that a line segment has a definite length. How can an infinite number of points each with no length considered separately, add up to a segment that has a definite length when considered all together. I don't understand." How can you help this student?

2 While beginning a unit on geometry with your junior high class, you make the statement that a point can be represented by a dot on the blackboard. You put the dot on the board and then erase it. One student then remarks that you have just erased the point. Is the student correct?

3 One student asks you the following question. "What is the difference between a ray and a half line?" How would you respond?

4 A student says, "Two half-lines make a line since $\frac{1}{2} + \frac{1}{2} = 1$." Is the student correct?

5   If a student asks the following question, "When working with rays such as $\overrightarrow{PQ}$, why is P called an endpoint rather than a beginning or starting point?" what response would you give?

6   A student is asked the definition of congruence and the reply is: "Congruence means equal." Is the student correct?

(D)   MEASUREMENT

1   One student makes the following comment. "Congruence and equal segments have the same relationship or meaning as equivalent and equal sets, right?" What is your response?

2   A student asks, "Why are there two different types of measures for weight, dry measure and liquid measure?" How do you reply?

3   An eighth grade student says: "36 in. = 1 yard, 9 in. = ¼ yard, $\sqrt{9}$ in. = $\sqrt{¼}$ yard, 3 in. = ½ yard." Is this student correct?

4   If a student asks, "Why are there two different measurements for the ton?" how do you reply?

5   A student asks you if there is a difference between the following terms: 2 square feet and 2 feet square? What response do you give?

6   How would you answer if a seventh grade student asks you why the abbreviation *lb* is used for pound?

(E)   POLYGONS

1   You ask a student to draw a polygon on the board. One of your pupils draws this figure on the board. What is your reaction?

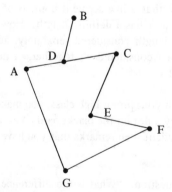

Could you modify your definition (if necessary) to include the above figure as a polygon?

2   A student in your class asks the following question. "What is the difference between a polygon and a polyhedron; is it that one just has sides and the other has
area?" What is your response?

3   You state the following definition. "A polygon is the union of three or more coplanar segments, each of which intersects at least two of the other segments."
After showing some examples of polygons, a student shows you the following figure and asks if it is a polygon. What do you tell this student?

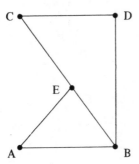

Q1.7   *Mean and Average*

1   A student in your eighth grade class is trying to solve the following problem. "A
man drives a car for one mile at 60 miles per hour and for another mile at 120 miles
per hour. What is his average speed?" The student reasons that the average speed
should be

$$\frac{60 + 120}{2} = \frac{180}{2} = 90 \text{ mph.}$$

Is this student correct?

2   A student asks, "Is a baseball average (hitter's batting average) really an average or
is it a probability since it is the number of successes over the number of trials?"
How do you respond?

3   If a student asks, "Why do we need three different types of averages? Wouldn't
one, like the mean, be good enough?" how do you reply?

4   Jack, a junior high student, is excited. "Miss Jones, I've found a new way to get the
average of two numbers. Take 12 and 18, for example. Subtract 12 from 18; that's
6. Divide the difference by 2, you get 3. Add 3 to 12, and you get the average,
15." If you were Miss Jones, what would you tell Jack?

Q1.8   *Numbers, Operations, Properties and Algorithms*

1   How do you handle the following situation? A student says, "You can't divide 2
by 3 because 2 is less than 3." All reasonable efforts to convince the student that
$2 \div 3 = 2/3$ fail.

2 A student asked to solve $\dfrac{7.2 \times 10^8}{1.2 \times 10^5}$ does the following.

$(7.2 - 1.2) \times (10^{8-5}) = 6 \times 10^3$.

Is the student correct?

3 A student asks, "Why is it when you subtract two negatives you have to change the sign of the subtrahend?" How would you respond?

4 Problem: $96 \div 6$.
Student Solution:

$$
\begin{array}{ll}
\begin{array}{r} 6 \\ +6 \\ \hline 12 \\ +12 \\ \hline 24 \\ +24 \\ \hline 48 \\ +48 \\ \hline 96 \end{array}
&
\left.\begin{array}{l} \text{two 6's} \\[8pt] \text{four 6's} \\[8pt] \text{eight 6's} \\[8pt] \text{sixteen 6's} \end{array}\right\} = \text{thirty 6's}
\end{array}
$$

So the answer to $96 \div 6$ is 30. What is your response?

5 While you are discussing multiplication, one student asks you if it makes a difference if you say "2 times 3" or "2 multiplied by 3"? What is your response?

6 Tony can't understand why division by zero is undefined. He wants $0 \div 0 = 0$. His explanation is: "If you have nothing in one hand and you divide it by nothing, why don't you still end up with nothing?" How would you respond?

7 You give your seventh graders a short quiz to do in class. Add the following:

(a) $(2 + 3) + (-6)$ (b) $2 + (3 + -6)$ (c) $2 + -5$
(d) $-5 + 2$ (e) $(-2 + -3) + -4$ (f) $(-2 + -3) + 0$

One of the students hands in the following work. Answer: -22. Is the student correct?

8 The student (sixth grade, top section) was asked to divide 16 by 3 by annexing zeros. She asks, "How can you divide 16 by 3 after you annex zeros, when you can not otherwise if adding zeros is the same as adding nothing?" What is your response?

9 A seventh grade student makes the following statement. "It doesn't make any sense to me that when you divide a number like -10 into -200 you get 20 because that means when you divided a small number into an even smaller number you get a great big answer." How would you answer this student?

10 While doing the problem $6 \div 0$, a student reasons as follows: "$6 \div 0$ equals nothing since you are dividing by nothing, you get nothing as a result." How will you help this student?

11 You are trying to teach the concept of dividing by zero, and you have just explained that $0 \div 0$ is undefined because the value could have too many answers. One of your students then asks, "Why can't we just define $0 \div 0$ to be equal to one and always use it that way?" How would you respond?

12 A seventh grader does the following problem.

$$
\begin{array}{r}
5\ 4 \\
3\,\overline{)1512} \\
\underline{15}\ \ \ \\
12 \\
\underline{12}
\end{array}
$$

How would you help this student?

13 In your seventh grade class, a student has devised a new subtraction algorithm and shows you the following work.

$$
\begin{array}{r}
2 \\
\cancel{3}4 \\
-\ 17 \\
\hline
17
\end{array}
$$

(1) $7 - 4 = 3$

$10 - 3 = 7$

(2) $2(10) - 1(10) = 1(10)$

Is the student correct?

14 While doing long division with your class, you observe that one of the students did this problem as follows:

$$
\begin{array}{r}
115 \\
25\,\overline{)625} \\
\underline{25}\ \ \ \\
37 \\
\underline{25} \\
125
\end{array}
$$

How can you help this student?

15 A seventh grade student says that zero is nothing and wants to know if he is mathematically correct. What is your response?

16 An eighth grader asks you the following question. "We have said that if a and b are integers, then $a - b = a + (-b)$. Now, subtraction is not commutative, but the expression on the right above $(a + (-b))$ is commutative; I don't understand." How would you handle this situation?

17 While studying a unit on the properties of zero and one, a student says that not only is zero an additive identity but it is also an identity with respect to subtraction. Do you agree?

18 In your seventh grade class, you are correcting a set of homework exercises, and you come across one student who is doing the following:

(a) $3 + 0 = 3$ (b) $4 + 0 = 4$ (c) $-1/2 + 0 = -1/2$

(d) $0 + 1/2 = 0$ (e) $0 + (-2/3) = 0$ (f) $0 + 1/4 = 0$

What concept is the student having trouble with?

19   You are showing a seventh grade student the standard method of dividing the following example.

$$
\begin{array}{r}
13 \\
25\overline{)3420} \\
25 \\
\hline
92 \\
75 \\
\hline
170
\end{array}
$$

You get to this point and tell the student that 25 does not go into 1 so look at 17; the student says that it does, since the 1 represents 100 and 25 goes into 100, the answer being 4 times. How do you respond to his answer?

20   While working on a unit covering negative integers, you make the statement that $-3 < -1$. However, a student raises his hand and says that he does not believe it. He says that if you have debt of three dollars then that is larger than a debt of one dollar. How do you respond to this student and how would you convince him that $-3 < -1$?

Q1.9   Number Theory

1   While studying a unit on divisibility rules for numbers expressed in base-ten numerals, a student asks you if the divisibility rules for numbers expressed in other bases are the same. What is your reply?

2   You make the following statement to your seventh grade class. "A counting number *a* is divisible by another counting number *b*, if *b* divides *a* evenly." What difficulty do you think students might have with this definition?

How would you help seventh and eighth grade students to answer the following content questions?

3   Isn't mod 7 arithmetic just like base 7?

4   "Why isn't 1 a prime number?"

5   An eighth grade student says that an even counting number is one which ends in 0, 2, 4, 6, or 8. Is this student correct?

6   A student rushes to your desk during class and tells you the following discovery, "If we take any two counting numbers, the greatest common factor multiplied by the least common multiple equals the product of the two numbers." Is this student correct?

7   A student in your eighth grade class asks, "What is the difference between the sym-

bols ÷ and | when used in the following ways: 4 ÷ 8 and 4|8?" How would you respond?

8. The subject is divisibility rules. The divisibility rule for 8 is: if 8 can be divided into the number formed by the last three digits of a numeral, then 8 can be divided into the whole numeral evenly. The rule for 4 is the same, except we use the last two digits Students know that if a number is divisible by 8 then it is also divisible by 4. A student tries the divisibility test for 8 and 8 doesn't work. He discovers that if the remainder is 4, then 4 is a divisor and he doesn't have to go through the test for 4. If the remainder is not 4, then 4 won't work either. Is the student right?

Q1.10   Numeration Systems

1. While studying different bases for numeration systems, one student asks if it is possible to have a negative number for a base. What do you tell this student?

2. An eighth grade student asks, "Is it possible to change 243_{seven} into a numeral in base three without first changing 243_{seven} into a numeral in base ten?" Can you help this student?

3. A student asks you if zero is a necessary element in our numeration system. What is your response?

4. In your seventh grade class, a student is trying to do the following problem.

$$35_{twelve} \text{ multiplied by } 46_{twelve} \text{ i.e.,} \qquad \begin{array}{r} 35_{twelve} \\ \times\ 46_{twelve} \\ \hline \end{array}$$

He knows that $5 \times 6 = 26_{twelve}$ but he can't figure out whether he should multiply 3×6 to get 16 and then add the 2, all in base twelve, or should he multiply 3×6 to get 18 and then add 2 to get 20 and then convert to base twelve. How would you handle this situation?

5. While studying a unit on different bases, a student asks you if it is necessary in, say, base 4 to use only the digits 0, 1, 2, 3, or can other digits be used. What is your response?

6. You are teaching a unit on ancient systems of numeration, to include Roman numerals. An eighth grade student asks, "Since IV represents 4, why doesn't IXX represent 19 instead of XIX?" How do you explain the answer?

7. One student asks you how the Roman numerals represented fractional numbers. How would you answer this question?

8. For writing Roman numerals, the pupils are told the principles of economy, which was to use as few symbols as possible for each number. Therefore, 9 was written IX instead of VIIII. Johnny writes IIX instead of VIII for 8 and CCD instead of DCCC

for 800. Do you tell him he is wrong, or right, and why?

9   Your class asks you why 148 cannot be written as CIIL. How do you respond?

Q1.11   *Percent*

1   You have just given your class the following problem to solve. "Find 28% of 50." You call on one of your students to put his solution on the blackboard. Below is the student's solution.

$$\begin{array}{r} 28 \\ \times\ .5 \\ \hline 14 \end{array}$$ 28% of 50 is 14.

Is this student correct?

2   A student in your class asks, "Why do banks, finance companies, loan sharks and credit unions all charge different interest rates on loans?" How do you respond?

3   If a student in your class asks, "Why is there no 100th percentile on standardized tests?" how would you answer?

4   "My father bought a house for $20,000 at 12% interest. He told me that by the time he finished paying for the house, it will have cost him more than $50,000. How is that possible? 12% of 20,000 is only $2400." If a student presented you with this question, how would you respond?

5   You ask the class to find 62% of 50. A student turns in the following solution.

$$\begin{array}{ccc} 9 \\ 1\!\!\not0\!0\% & 50 & 50 \\ -62\% & \times\ .38 & -\ 19 \\ \hline 38\% & 400 & 31\% \\ & 150 \\ & \overline{19.00} \end{array}$$

How do you help this student?

6   You ask your seventh grade class to find $\frac{1}{10}$% of 50. One student writes that $\frac{1}{10} = .1$, then $\frac{1}{10}$% of 50 equals $(.1)(50) = 5$. How would you help this student.

Q1.12   *Sets*

1   A seventh grade student says that he has another definition of subset: "If set A does not contain an element that is not also an element of set B, then A is a subset of B." Is the student correct?

2   A seventh grader says that $\{\emptyset\}$ is the notation that you should use for the empty set. What is your response?

3   "If $A = \{1, 2, 4\}$ and $B = \{1, 2, 3\}$, why isn't $A \cup B = \{1, 1, 2, 2, 3, 4\}$? Or, if $A =$ {science book, math book} and $B =$ {French book, math book}, isn't $A \cup B =$ {math book, math book, science book, French book}?" This question frequently arises in the classroom. What is your reply?

4   You are going over the following problem in class. "Indicate whether the following statement is true or false:

$$\text{If } A \cap B = A \cup B, \quad \text{then} \quad A \subseteq B.\text{"}$$

One student says that it is false because A would have to be equal to B, not a subset of B. Is the student right? How would you answer?

5   Your class is working on the following problem. "Analyze the data below and find out how many students are in the school. Assume that every student in the school takes one of the courses."

    28 students take English
    23 students take French
    23 students take German
    12 students take English and French
    11 students take English and German
     8 students take French and German
     5 students take all three courses

One of your students does the problem as follows.

    28
    23
    23
    ——
    74 students total if students took only one course.

but   12
       8
      11
      ——
      31 taking 2 courses
     −5 taking 3 courses
      ——
      26 taking more than one course. $74 - 26 = 48$ students in the school.

Is this student correct in the method used and answer given?

Q1.13   *Square Root*

1   After studying the extraction of square roots, a student asks, "Can we extract cube roots?" How would you answer this student?

2   A student asks, "If it is true that the square root of 25 is ±5, then why doesn't $\sqrt{25} = \pm5$?" How do you reply?

Q1.14   *Trigonometry*

1   A teacher of eighth grade mathematics put the following figure on the board to use for drill work on trigonometric ratios.

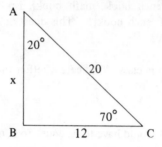

The students were told to solve for the unknown parts of $\triangle ABC$. The following was discovered:

$$\tan 20° = \frac{12}{x} \qquad x = 32.6$$

$$\tan 70° = \frac{x}{12} \qquad x = 32.9$$

$$\sin 70° = \frac{x}{20} \qquad x = 18.8$$

Also by the Pythagorean theorem $M(\overline{AB}) = x = 16$. What is wrong?

ANSWERS

A1.1   *Absolute Value*

1   The main difficulty here is with the notation. If $a < 0$, then $|a|$ = the additive inverse or opposite of a. Since a is a negative number, then the additive inverse or opposite of a negative number is positive. For example, if $a = -3$, then the additive inverse of -3 is denoted by $-(-3)$ and equals 3.

A1.2   *Decimals*

1   No, it is not possible. For example, if the numbers 3 and 4 are chosen, then since the averaging process will involve only rational numbers, one would never be able to get π or any other irrational number between 3 and 4 by this process. One would get rational approximations for these irrational numbers, but never the numbers themselves. One should emphasize that the set of rational numbers and the set of irrational numbers are disjoint.

2   The set of irrational numbers is not closed under addition. For example, $\sqrt{2}$ + $(-\sqrt{2}) = 0$ and 0 is a rational number. Another example is the following: $(3 + \sqrt{2})$ and $(-\sqrt{2})$ are irrational numbers, but $(3 + \sqrt{2}) + (-\sqrt{2}) = 3$ is a rational number. One should emphasize that the set of rational numbers and the set of irrational numbers are disjoint sets.

3   One way to respond would be to take a specific problem and show why the strategy works as follows. Suppose one multiplies the following using the traditional algorithm. The result is given below.

$$
\begin{array}{r}
3.24 \\
\times\ .35 \\
\hline
1620 \\
972\ \ \\
\hline
1.1340
\end{array}
$$

If one writes out each decimal as a fraction one would get the following:

$$3.24 = 3 + \frac{2}{10} + \frac{4}{100}$$

$$.35 = \frac{3}{10} + \frac{5}{100}$$

Thus

$$3.24 \times .35 = \left(3 + \frac{2}{10} + \frac{4}{100}\right)\left(\frac{3}{10} + \frac{5}{100}\right)$$

$$= \left(\frac{300 + 20 + 4}{100}\right)\left(\frac{30 + 5}{100}\right) = \left(\frac{324}{100}\right)\left(\frac{35}{100}\right)$$

$$= \frac{(324)(35)}{10^4} = \frac{11340}{10^4} = 1.1340.$$

One should notice that the exponent of the denominator is 4, which is the same number one gets by counting off decimal places in each factor and adding. Thus, the reason why the decimal algorithm works is because of the equivalency of the decimal and fractional notation in our numeration system.

4   The statement which the student made is imprecise. For example, the fraction 2/15 has a denominator with a factor of 5 but the fraction cannot be represented as a terminating decimal. The student meant to say the following: a fraction a/b (in lowest terms) can be expressed as a terminating decimal if and only if the prime factorization of b is of the form $b = 2^x \cdot 5^y$ where x and y are whole numbers.

   The same idea can be generalized to other bases as follows. The fraction a/b (in lowest terms) in base N can be expressed as a terminating decimal in base N if and only if the prime factorization of b in base N is of the form

$$b = c_1{}^{x_1} c_2{}^{x_2} \cdots c_k{}^{x_k}$$

where the c_i, i = 1, ... k are prime numbers (in base ten) and each c_i divides N.

5   For an answer, see the explanation for Section A1.2, Answer 3.

6   For an answer to this question, read the following article by L.T. Hall.* Also read: W. Peterson, "Beware of Persuasive Arguments," *The Mathematics Teacher*, December 1972, p. 709.

PERSUASIVE ARGUMENTS: .9999... = 1

By **LUCIEN T. HALL, JR.**

Richmond Public Schools
Richmond, Virginia

WHEN teaching high school students, prospective teachers, and in-service classes, I have used the usual method for changing the repeating-decimal format of a rational number to an a/b format where a and b are integers and $b \neq 0$. The usual method referred to is, using $.7272 \ldots$ as an example,

to let $\qquad N = .7272 \ldots,$
multiply both sides by 100 $\qquad 100N = 72.7272 \ldots,$
subtract equals from equals $\qquad 99N = 72.0000 \ldots,$
and divide both sides by 99 $\qquad N = 72/99.$

Thus, $.7272 \ldots = 72/99.$

Students readily accept this but balk when an example has repeating 9s—such as $.9999 \ldots$ or $.4999 \ldots$. Several arguments can be used to persuade students that, for example, $.9999 \ldots$ is exactly 1.

First Argument. Use the usual method:

$$N = .9999 \ldots,$$
$$10N = 9.9999 \ldots,$$
$$9N = 9.0000 \ldots,$$
$$N = 9/9.$$

So, $.9999 \ldots$ is 1. Ask the students emphatically, "Have I made a mathematical mistake?" The usual answer from students is "No, but . . . ."

Second Argument. Tell students that this argument is no proof but good intuitive reasoning. Ask them to express $.1111 \ldots$ in a/b form, express $.2222 \ldots$ in a/b form, express $.3333 \ldots$, and so on, and finally $.8888 \ldots$ in a/b form. The students answer 1/9, 2/9, 3/9, and so on, and finally 8/9. Then say, "Intuitively speaking, then, what is $.9999 \ldots$?" Students acknowledge that the answer is 9/9.

Third Argument. Tell students that if $.9999 \ldots$ is not 1, then it must be either larger or smaller than 1. Which is it? Students always answer, "Smaller." So ask, "How much smaller?" This question is met with silence. You might tell students that if they think the number is smaller than 1 they must be thinking about a *large but finite* number of 9s rather than an infinite number of 9s in the decimal expression.

Fourth Argument. Ask students if they agree that $1/3 = .3333 \ldots$. When they readily agree, then ask if you might multiply both sides by 3. Naturally you get $3(1/3) = 3(.3333 \ldots)$, or $1 = .9999 \ldots$ This seems to be the most persuasive argument.

Fifth Argument. Ask students if they agree that $4/9 = .4444 \ldots$ and $5/9 = .5555 \ldots$. When they agree, then ask if you might add equals to equals. Adding, we get $9/9 = .9999 \ldots$, or $1 = .9999 \ldots$

Sixth Argument. Sometimes a very good student will suggest that if $.9999 \ldots$ does equal 1 or 9/9, then you should be able to change 9/9 to $.9999 \ldots$ by dividing the denominator into the numerator. You must remind students that a division prob-

---

*From *The Mathematics Teacher*, December 1971, pp. 749-50. Reprinted by permission.

lem is correct when the quotient times the divisor plus the remainder equals the dividend. You must also admit that we usually require the remainder to be smaller than the divisor but that this is a matter of definition and not necessarily mandatory.

Start dividing.

$$\begin{array}{r} .9 \\ 9\overline{)9.0000} \\ 8.1 \\ \hline .9 \end{array}$$

Note that the quotient times the divisor plus the remainder equals the dividend.

Go several steps further.

$$\begin{array}{r} .9999\ldots \\ 9\overline{)9.0000\ldots} \\ 8.1 \\ \hline .90 \\ .81 \\ \hline .090 \\ .081 \\ \hline .0090 \\ .0081 \\ \hline .0009 \end{array}$$

At any point, the quotient times the divisor plus the remainder is equal to the dividend; 9 divided by 9 is producing the quotient .9999. . . .

7   The main problem here is one of determining what the symbol 0.12½ means. If the student was correct, then this would mean that a numeral such as .125 would mean .12 + 5, which it certainly does not. The symbol 0.12½ means

$$\frac{1}{10} + \frac{2}{100} + \frac{1}{2}\left(\frac{1}{100}\right).$$

Thus $0.12\frac{1}{2} = \frac{1}{10} + \frac{2}{100} + \frac{5}{1000} = .125.$

It is quite unfortunate and, at times, quite confusing when similar looking symbols mean different things. For example,

$$2\frac{1}{3} = 2 + \frac{1}{3}, \quad \text{but} \quad (a)\frac{1}{2} = a \cdot \frac{1}{2} \quad \text{and} \quad 2a = a + a, \quad \text{not } 2 + a.$$

You might want to point these out to the student and tell him that one of the skills that he must develop is the ability to understand what meaning to attach to different symbols in mathematics.

A1.3   *Equality*

1   Yes, there is a difference between *equal* and *equivalent* in mathematics. Usually equality is used to mean that whatever is on one side of the equals sign names the same object as that on the other side of the equals sign. Thus, 1 + 2 = 3 means that "1 + 2" and "3" are names for the same number. Thus we say that the expressions "1 + 2" and "3" are equivalent expressions, but the numbers that they stand for are equal. The expressions themselves are not equal since they are not identical expressions. Likewise, the numerals 5/2, 2½, 2.5 and 250% are equivalent numerals since they name the same number. Thus the numerals are equivalent but not equal; i.e., the symbol 5/2 is not the same symbol as 2½, etc. but the numbers represented by these numerals are equal.

Equivalency and equality are related but not the same concept. Equivalency is in many instances a generalization of equality and usually means that objects share a common property or attribute. Thus if A = {1, 2, 3} and B = {3, 4, 5}, then A is equivalent to B since there is a one-to-one correspondence between the elements of A and B. If C = {2, 3, 1}, then we say that A is equal to C since they contain exactly the same elements. Thus, in this illustration with sets, we can say that if two sets A and B are equal then they are equivalent; but the converse statement need not be true.

As another illustration consider the following equation $3y^2 + 5y + 4y + y^2 = 4y^2 + 9y$. If we replace y by any member of its replacement set we have a true statement. Thus the members of this equation are called equivalent expressions. For any value of y in the replacement set, the equivalent expressions represent the same number and thus the equation is called an identity. The expressions "$3y^2 + 5y + 4y + y^2$" and "$4y^2 + 9y$" are not equal expressions, i.e., the same expressions.

As a last example, consider the statements $p \rightarrow q$ and $\sim p \vee q$ where p and q are statements. These expressions are clearly not the same expressions. However, if a truth table is made for each expression, the truth tables are identical, i.e., equal, and thus the expressions are called logically equivalent statements.

Space limits us from considering other examples in detail, but it could be a very interesting exercise for the reader to go through secondary mathematics material to find many other different places where the idea of equivalence is used. The following is an incomplete listing to start you off.

Equivalent expressions	Equivalent polygons
Equivalent equations	Equivalent vectors
Equivalent inequalities	Equivalent matrices
Equivalent rational expressions	Equivalent polynomials
Equivalent systems of equations	Equivalent fractions
Logically equivalent statements	Equivalence classes
Equivalent triangles	

The name *equivalent* comes from the notion that when objects are equivalent, this relation usually turns out to be an equivalence relation. In many instances the distinction concerns the difference between an object (equality) and the names of the objects (equivalence). For an interesting article concerning equality and equivalence consult:

Walter Sanders, "Equivalence and Equality," *The Arithmetic Teacher*, April 1969, pp. 317-22.

A1.4   Exponents

1   This student is incorrect. Suppose that k = 3, then by the student's definition $y^3 = [\{(y \cdot y) \cdot y\} \cdot y] = y^4$. It would be much better to say that y is used as a factor k times.

2    $x^0 = 1$ mainly for our desire to maintain for the zero exponent the laws for positive integral exponents, i.e., $x^a \cdot x^b = x^{a+b}$ where a, b are positive integers. When we enlarge the domain to include zero, then we would wish the same law of exponents to hold. Thus,

$$x^0 \cdot x^a = x^{a+0} = x^a$$

Therefore, $x^0 = x^a/x^a = 1$, assuming that $x \neq 0$. If x = 0, then we encounter the undefined expression 0^0. An intuitive way of showing that $x^0 = 1$ is plausible is as follows:

$$2^6 = 64 \qquad\qquad 3^6 = 729$$
$$2^5 = 32 \qquad\qquad 3^5 = 243$$
$$2^4 = 16 \qquad\qquad 3^4 = 81$$
$$2^3 = 8 \qquad\qquad 3^3 = 27$$
$$2^2 = 4 \qquad\qquad 3^2 = 9$$
$$2^1 = 2 \qquad\qquad 3^1 = 3$$
$$2^0 = ? \qquad\qquad 3^0 = ?$$

3    $0^{-7} = 1/0^7$ is undefined. In general, 0^{-k}, where k is a positive integer, is undefined.

A1.5   *Fractions*

1   When we write $2 \cdot 3$, we usually mean $3 + 3$. Thus $\frac{1}{4} \cdot \frac{1}{2}$ should be the number that is $\frac{1}{4}$ of $1 \cdot \frac{1}{2}$ or $1 \cdot \frac{1}{2}$ divided by 4. Thus the result is smaller than the original factor $\frac{1}{2}$. Likewise, by the commutative law of multiplication $\frac{1}{4} \cdot \frac{1}{2} = \frac{1}{2} \cdot \frac{1}{4} = \frac{1}{2}$ of $1 \cdot \frac{1}{4}$ or $1 \cdot \frac{1}{4}$ divided by 2. Thus, the result is smaller than the original factor $\frac{1}{4}$. In general, $(a/b) \cdot (c/d)$, $(b, d \neq 0; a/b, c/d$ proper fractions), can be viewed as

$$\left[\frac{1}{b}\left(a \cdot \frac{c}{d} \right) \right].$$

Thus c/d is first multiplied by a, and the result is divided by b. Since $a < b$, then the resulting number is less than c/d. Using the commutative property for multiplication, one can use a similar argument for a/b.

2   If we write $3\frac{1}{3}$ as the improper fraction $\frac{10}{3}$, then the answer to this question is given in Answer 1.

3   For an answer to this question, read the following article by Van Engen and Cleveland.*

MATHEMATICAL MODELS FOR PHYSICAL SITUATIONS

By H. VAN ENGEN

University of Wisconsin
Madison, Wisconsin

and RAY W. CLEVELAND

Jersey City State College
Jersey City, New Jersey

RECENT attempts to improve the teaching of problem solving in mathematics have made it necessary to look carefully at physical situations and the way in which they are represented by conventional mathematics. Relatively recent interest in the newer studies in developmental psychology has focused attention also on the need for a closer examination of experiences' being provided ele-

*From *The Mathematics Teacher*, October 1967, pp. 578-81. Reprinted by permission.

mentary and secondary pupils in connection with certain mathematical ideas as they relate to problem solving. There are instances in the physical world where it is possible, and at times desirable, to represent a physical situation by using mathematical ideas and their properties which are quite different from those commonly used.

Consider, for example, the two categories of physical situations that are popularly known as "ratio" or "fraction" situations. In these cases, two numbers are present, and no mathematical operation is implied.

Category 1

a) Three apples for five cents.
b) Three miles in five minutes.
c) Three inches to five inches.
d) Three marbles out of five are red.

Category 2

a) A pie is cut into five equal parts, and three parts are under consideration.
b) A ribbon is marked off into five equal parts, and three parts are cut off.

To teach children how the pairs of numbers are used in each of the two categories, one would ordinarily present entirely different physical arrangements of objects. In fact, a knowledge of Piaget's developmental psychology would cause one to question whether children consider the instances mentioned in the two categories as similar in any respect. Certainly, it is unwise to insist on calling all such instances "fraction" situations, although this is frequently done.

It is easier to see that the two categories are different if we attempt to define an operation on the number pairs in each category. In Category 1, a purchase of three apples for five cents followed by a purchase of two apples for seven cents results in a total purchase of five apples for twelve cents. Using the symbolism for ordered pairs, we then have

$$(3, 5) + (2, 7) = (5, 12).$$

If we were to use the standard ratio symbolism, then we would write the following:

$$\frac{3}{5} + \frac{2}{7} = \frac{5}{12}.$$

In Category 2, three fifths of a cake and two sevenths of a cake, when considered as a total portion of one cake, result in $\frac{31}{35}$ of a cake, not $\frac{5}{12}$ of a cake.

$$\frac{3}{5} + \frac{2}{7} = \frac{21}{35} + \frac{10}{35} = \frac{31}{35}.$$

It is obvious that the rules for combining the pairs of numbers in Category 1 differ from the rules used in Category 2. The question now arises as to what mathematical model to use when the pairs of numbers are abstracted from each category. In Category 2, it is clear that the rules for computing with rational numbers enable us to find a satisfactory interpretation of the computational results. In other words, there is no deviation from commonly accepted practice. In Category 1, however, the pairs of numbers cannot be combined as if they were rational numbers if we are to interpret the result in a way that really represents the situation. This suggests that the rational numbers do not form a model for ratio situations. What, then, is the model?

In answering the question, we shall restrict our examples to pairs of integers. Furthermore, we shall use the symbols $\frac{2}{3}$ and $(2, 3)$ interchangeably to represent the pairs of numbers as they occur in the physical situations of Category 1. First we shall give interpretations for pairs with negative components as well as pairs with positive components. These interpretations can be made if one is allowed the same liberties first-year algebra teachers demand when they interpret such statements as $(^-2)(^-3) = {}^+6$ for their students.

$(2, 3)$ or $\frac{2}{3}$ means
a) Get 2 apples, pay 3 cents (buying)
b) Earn 2 dollars, put 3 dollars in the bank
c) Move 2 miles north in the next 3 hours
d) Take 2 reds, take 3 greens
e) Go 2 miles east, go 3 miles north

$(2, -3)$ or $\frac{2}{-3}$ means
a) Get 2 apples, get 3 cents
b) Earn 2 dollars, withdraw 3 dollars
c) Move 2 miles north in the past 3 hours
d) Take 2 reds, give 3 greens
e) Go 2 miles east, go 3 miles south

$(-2, 3)$ *a)* Give 2 apples, pay 3 cents
or $\dfrac{-2}{3}$ *b)* Give 2 dollars, put 3 dollars in the bank
means   *c)* Move 2 miles south in the next 3 hours
  d) Give 2 reds, take 3 greens
  e) Go 2 miles west, go 3 miles north

$(-2, -3)$ *a)* Give 2 apples, get 3 cents (selling)
or $\dfrac{-2}{-3}$ *b)* Give 2 dollars, withdraw 3 dollars
means   *c)* Go 2 miles south in the past 3 hours
  d) Give 2 reds, give 3 greens
  e) Go 2 miles west, go 3 miles south

We now proceed to define and interpret an operation "$+$" on ordered pairs (a, b) and (c, d), where a, b, c, and d are rational numbers. Remember that, in choosing our examples, we will use only integers.

Definition: $(a, b) + (c, d) = (a+c, b+d)$.
Interpretation: Two apples for three cents and five apples for eight cents is the same as seven apples for eleven cents.

$$(2, 3) + (5, 8) = (7, 11).$$

Obviously, the operation of addition of number pairs as defined above is closed, because $a + c$ and $b + d$ are rational numbers. Addition of number pairs has properties other than the closure property, and the properties are listed below.

P_1. *Closure:* $(a+c, b+d)$ is an ordered pair of rational numbers.

P_2. *Associative:* $[(a, b) + (c, d)] + (e, f) = (a, b) + [(c, d) + (e, f)]$.

P_3. *Identity:* $(a, b) + (0, 0) = (a, b)$.

P_4. *Inverse:* $(a, b) + (-a, -b) = (0, 0)$.

Interpretation: Buying two apples for three cents followed by selling two apples for three cents, or $(-2, -3)$, results in zero apples and zero cents or $(0, 0)$.

$$(2, 3) + (-2, -3) = (0, 0).$$

P_5. *Commutative:* $(a, b) + (c, d) = (c, d) + (a, b)$.

Next, let us define and interpret an operation of multiplying an ordered pair (a, b) by a rational number α.

Definition: $\alpha(a, b) = (\alpha a, \alpha b)$.
Interpretation: Two purchases of two apples for three cents is the same as a purchase of four apples for six cents.

$$2(2, 3) = (4, 6).$$

The properties of this multiplication are as follows:

P_6. *Closure:* $(\alpha a, \alpha b)$ is an ordered pair of rational numbers.

P_7. *Distributive:* $\alpha[(a, b) + (c, d)] = \alpha(a, b) + \alpha(c, d)$.

Interpretation: Two purchases of three apples for five cents and six apples for seven cents is the same as two purchases of three apples for five cents added to two purchases of six apples for seven cents.

$$2[(3, 5) + (6, 7)] = 2(3, 5) + 2(6, 7).$$
$$(\alpha + \beta)(a, b) = \alpha(a, b) + \beta(a, b).$$

Interpretation: $(4+6)$ moves, each move consisting of two units east and three units north, equals four moves of two units east and three units north, followed by six moves of two units east and three units north, as shown below:

$$(4 + 6)(2, 3) = 4(2, 4) + 6(2, 3).$$

P_8. *Associative:* $\alpha \cdot \beta(a, b) = \alpha \cdot (\beta a, \beta b)$.
Interpretation: Four repetitions of five purchases of two apples for three cents equals four purchase of ten apples for fifteen cents, as shown below:

$$4 \cdot 5(2, 3) = 4(10, 15).$$

P_9. *Identity:* $1(a, b) = (a, b)$.

The properties P_1 through P_9 are those of a vector space, where the elements (a, b) are pairs of rational numbers, and the elements α and β are scalars, in this case rational numbers. The ordered pairs, which are the elements of the vector space, are called vectors. However, the physical interpretations given in this article are commonly regarded as ratios. What has been shown is that ratios satisfy a vector-space interpretation. In short, ratios are vectors.

There are a few difficulties in such an interpretation. For example, when people are using ratios in elementary mathematics, science, or business, they often write $\dfrac{a}{b} = \dfrac{c}{d}$ for $(a, b) = (c, d)$. It is well known that two vectors (a, b) and (c, d) are equal if and only if $a = c$ and $b = d$. Thus, if we give a vector interpretation to ratio situations, it is incorrect to write $\dfrac{a}{b} = \dfrac{c}{d}$ unless it is actually true that $a = c$ and $b = d$. A similar difficulty arises in connection with cross products of ratios; that is, if $\dfrac{a}{b} = \dfrac{c}{d}$, then $ad = bc$. How do these ideas fit, if at all, into a vector-space interpretation?

Suppose that we look at the graph of the following set of ratios: *a)* two apples for ten cents, *b)* four apples for twenty cents, *c)* six apples for thirty cents, and *d)* eight apples for forty cents.

The graph suggests that in this instance we are dealing with a subspace of a two-dimensional vector space. A linear subspace of a two-dimensional vector space is the set of vectors, V, defined as follows:

$$\{\alpha(a, b) \mid \alpha,\ a,\ \text{and}\ b \in R\}.$$

This definition tells us that each vector in the same linear subspace as vector (a, b) is a scalar multiple of vector (a, b). Hence, the definition provides the clue for finding two vectors (ratios) that represent the same price. If the ratios represent the same price, they are in the same subspace. In solving problems like the following, therefore, we consider the ratios to be in the same subspace.

If two apples cost ten cents, how much will fifty apples cost?

We know that $(2, 10)$ determines the subspace in which we are interested; we want to find another ratio (vector) in the same subspace. Hence,

$$\alpha(2, 10) = (50, x).$$
$$(2\alpha, 10\alpha) = (50, x).$$

By our definition of equality of two ratios (vectors), we have

$$2\alpha = 50,\ \text{or}\ \alpha = 25,$$

and

$$10\alpha = x,\ \text{or}\ x = 250.$$

Hence, fifty apples cost 250 cents, or $2.50.

GRAPH OF $\{(2,10), (4,20), (6,30), (8,40),\ \dots\}$

It is, however, more convenient to solve such problems by using a theorem that pertains to ratios in the same subspace; namely, the theorem that (a, b) and (c, d) are in the same subspace if and only if $ad = bc$.

The proof of the theorem has two parts.

Part 1

$\alpha(a, b) = (c, d).$

$\alpha a = c$ and $\alpha b = d.$

$\alpha a d = \alpha b c.$

$\therefore\ ad = bc$ if $\alpha \neq 0.$

Part 2

$ad = bc.$

$\dfrac{d}{b} = \dfrac{c}{a} = \alpha.$

$\alpha b = d$ and $\alpha a = c.$

$\therefore\ \alpha(a, b) = (c, d).$

This is the well-known cross product of two "equal" ratios. The fact that this property holds for two ratios in the same subspace and also for two rational numbers may be the source of the confusion that often exists concerning ratios and rational numbers.

Mathematics educators agree that the elementary and secondary schools must provide experiences that help students to understand the properties of the rational numbers. The rational numbers under addition and multiplication are an example of an important mathematical structure. We feel that the vector-space model is another structure that should be included in the school program. True, it is debatable whether elementary school children should be asked to write the following:

$$\frac{2}{3} + \frac{5}{6} = \frac{7}{9}$$

$$(2, 3) + (5, 6) = (7, 9),$$

but the question is still an open one. Certainly, program planners should be well aware of the problem confronting them with respect to ratios and rational numbers.

We now turn our attention to a second issue. Since the interpretation of certain pairs, such as $(-3, 4)$, is rather awkward in the situations usually presented to elementary and junior high school students, it might be desirable to limit ratios as vectors to those pairs (a, b) for which $a > 0$ and $b > 0$; in other words, the vectors should be limited to the first quadrant of the plane. True, this limitation prevents one from exhibiting the entire vector-space structure, but this same limitation exists with respect to the rational numbers as taught in the elementary school. For example, the additive-inverse element is lacking in both instances.

In conclusion, we offer a few words about terminology. It makes little difference whether the pairs we have been considering are called ratios, rate pairs, or vectors. What an idea is called, after all, is only a name. Individual teachers may have various reasons for not liking a name, but these reasons are often personal, rather than mathematical or pedagogical. For instructional purposes, it matters very little what name is given to the pairs of numbers under consideration. Although a real case could be made for calling the pairs vectors, even in the elementary school, common practice in science and in the business world has to be considered.

To summarize, we have tried to show that ratios may be interpreted as vectors; that there are important curricular implications for a vector-space interpretation; and that there are instructional implications for this point of view. As a teacher, you should give the matter some thought.

4   Yes, you can.

$$\frac{a}{b} \div \frac{c}{d} = \frac{ad}{bc} \qquad b, c, d \neq 0$$

$$\frac{a}{b} \div \frac{c}{d} = \frac{ad}{bc} \cdot \frac{1/dc}{1/dc}$$

$$\frac{a}{b} \div \frac{c}{d} = \frac{ad \cdot (1/dc)}{bc \cdot (1/dc)}$$

$$\frac{a}{b} \div \frac{c}{d} = \frac{(ad/dc)}{(bc/dc)} = \frac{(a/c)}{(b/d)} = \frac{a \div c}{b \div d} .$$

Thus, $\dfrac{a}{b} \div \dfrac{c}{d} = \dfrac{a \div c}{b \div d}$.

5   The basic problem here is that the student is using different basic units for comparison purposes. The student must be made to realize that when comparing objects, the same units must be used in order to get a valid comparison. For example, if a student said that ½ = ¼, then one might ask this student if ½ of a dollar is equal to ¼ of a dollar.

6   The usual definition of less than for rational numbers is stated as follows: If a/b and c/d are expressions for rational numbers with b and d positive integers, then $a/b < c/d$ if and only if $a \cdot d < b \cdot c$. The definition requires that b and d both be positive, which is the condition violated in the student's example. The reason for requiring the condition is given as follows:

$$\text{If } \frac{a}{b} < \frac{c}{d}, \quad \text{then } \frac{ad}{bd} < \frac{bc}{bd}$$

as long as b and d have the same sign (i.e., either both are negative or both positive); otherwise the sign of the inequality changes. In order to ensure that this is always the case, then the condition follows since any natural number can be represented as a fraction with a positive denominator.

7 For an answer to this question, read the interesting article:

   Fred B. Thomas, "A Dialogue on $2\phi/\phi5 = 2/5$," *The Mathematics Teacher*, January 1967, pp. 20-23.

8 The basic problem here is one of language. It probably would have been better to state the problem as follows: "There is ¾ of a pie left. Jane and Sue want to divide what is left in two parts so they each get an equal part." Even if the problem is left as stated, the teacher might point out that the student's answer is wrong. How could each person get 1½ pies if they only started out with ¾ of a pie. Perhaps a good question to ask the student is the following: "How much should each of two people receive if they divide one dollar evenly between them?" The student should recognize that each person gets 50 cents and the student arrived at this answer by dividing by 2, not ½.

9 There are various ways of answering the student. Some of these ways are given below. A specific example is used in each case.

   (a) $\dfrac{2}{3} \div \dfrac{4}{5} = r \leftrightarrow \dfrac{2}{3} = \dfrac{4}{5} \cdot r$ by the definition of division

   $\dfrac{2}{3} = \dfrac{4}{5} r \leftrightarrow \dfrac{2}{3} \cdot \dfrac{5}{4} = \dfrac{5}{4}\left(\dfrac{4}{5} r\right)$

   $\dfrac{2}{3} \cdot \dfrac{5}{4} = \dfrac{5}{4}\left(\dfrac{4}{5} r\right) \leftrightarrow \dfrac{2}{3} \cdot \dfrac{5}{4} = \left(\dfrac{5}{4} \cdot \dfrac{4}{5}\right) r$

   $\dfrac{2}{3} \cdot \dfrac{5}{4} = \left(\dfrac{5}{4} \cdot \dfrac{4}{5}\right) r \leftrightarrow \dfrac{2}{3} \cdot \dfrac{5}{4} = 1 \cdot r = r$

   (b) $\dfrac{2}{3} \div \dfrac{4}{5} = \dfrac{\frac{2}{3}}{\frac{4}{5}} \cdot 1 = \dfrac{\frac{2}{3} \cdot \frac{5}{4}}{\frac{4}{5} \cdot \frac{5}{4}} = \dfrac{\frac{2}{3} \cdot \frac{5}{4}}{1} = \dfrac{2}{3} \cdot \dfrac{5}{4}$

10 The student is having trouble here with the way that addition of fractions is defined where, with the usual introduction, one *must* get common denominators. One way of answering this student would be as follows: It would be true that one could get common denominators when multiplying fractions. For example,

   $$\frac{1}{3} \cdot \frac{1}{2} = \frac{2}{6} \cdot \frac{3}{6} = \frac{6}{36} = \frac{1}{6}.$$

Notice, however, that there is no need to get a common denominator because of the way that multiplication of fractions is defined; i.e.,

   $$\frac{a}{b} \cdot \frac{c}{d} = \frac{a \cdot c}{b \cdot d}.$$

Thus, in the above problem

   $$\frac{1}{3} \cdot \frac{1}{2} = \frac{1 \cdot 1}{3 \cdot 2} = \frac{1}{6},$$

which is the same answer that we arrived at using common denominators.

11   The student seems to be using an incorrect algorithm for adding fractions. Most likely, the student is adding the numerators and/or denominators if these numbers are relatively prime (i.e., have greatest common divisor of 1); if the numerator and/or denominator are multiples of each other, then the larger of these multiples is used. One approach that might be used with this student is to ask the student to add $\frac{2}{2} + \frac{4}{4}$. Since $\frac{2}{2} = 1$ and $\frac{4}{4} = 1$, then $\frac{2}{2} + \frac{4}{4}$ should equal 2. However, by the algorithm that the student is using, $\frac{2}{2} + \frac{4}{4} = \frac{4}{4}$, which is certainly incorrect. Then, you might ask the student to add $\frac{2}{3} + \frac{3}{5}$. According to the algorithm that the student is using $\frac{2}{3} + \frac{3}{5} = \frac{5}{8}$. However, this algorithm is incorrect for adding rational numbers. See the article on page 19 for further information.

12   The teacher might respond as follows: "Yes, you would certainly have more pieces, but each piece that you would have would be smaller than each piece taken by the person who has 4/7 of the cake. In fact, five of your smaller pieces would be the same amount of cake as one of the pieces taken by the person who has 4/7 of the cake. Thus, since you have 20 of these small pieces, then you would have the same amount of cake as the person who took 4/7 of the cake." It would probably be beneficial to similate the cutting of two cakes or similar objects into the appropriate sizes and showing the student the physical objects.

13   No, the student is not correct. Since the selling price equals the cost plus the profit, then selling price = 1/10 cost + cost; i.e., $3300 = (1/10)c + c, and thus the cost is $3000. Therefore, the profit is (1/10) · 3000 = $300.

14   What the teacher should have said was that a rational number is a number that can be expressed in the form of $\frac{p}{q}$, p, q integers, q ≠ 0. Since $\frac{\sqrt{3} \cdot 3}{\sqrt{3} \cdot 4}$ can be expressed as $\frac{3}{4}$, then $\frac{\sqrt{3} \cdot 3}{\sqrt{3} \cdot 4}$ is a numeral that represents a rational number.

15   No, the student is not correct. There are $4\frac{4}{19}$ pieces each $4\frac{3}{4}$ feet long; i.e., there are 4 pieces and $\frac{4}{19}$ of a piece. Now, $\frac{4}{19}$ of a piece is $\frac{4}{19}$ of $4\frac{3}{4}$ feet, or 1 foot left over.

   Problem Find two different methods of showing the student that 1 foot is left over, not 4/19 of a foot.

A1.6   *Geometry*

(A)   *ANGLES*

1   One way of convincing the student that the degree measure of an angle will not vary is as follows: On a transparency construct a circle c with radius r. Using overlays with the same center as circle c, construct three or four other circles with

different radii. On each circle have the student construct angles of various degree measures such as 90°, 45°, 30°, etc., taken one at a time. When all the overlays are put together, the student should see the following (Figure 1.6.1) for say 30°:

FIGURE 1.6.1

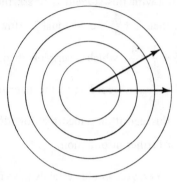

Thus, even though the angle intercepts arcs of different lengths in different circles, the angle being measured is still 30°.

2   The student is using imprecise language. The angles are *not contained* in the triangle, but the angles are *determined* by the triangle. Thus when we talk about the three angles of a triangle, we mean the three angles are determined by the three corners of the triangle.

3   Yes, it is. If two distinct lines l_1 and l_2 form a 90° angle with one another, then the lines intersect at the point, P, which is the vertex of the right angle. If we take any other point on l_1 except P and likewise any other point on l_2 except P, then we have the plane determined by these noncollinear points.

4   You might ask the student how this could be done. The student would probably suggest a method similar to the one shown in Figure 1.6.2. "Measure arc RS in inches as in the figure given, and use this number as the measure of angle ABC."

FIGURE 1.6.2

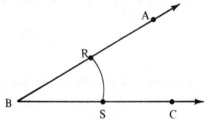

Of course, the basic problem here is that the measure of the angle will change depending upon how the points R and S are chosen. Since this is a highly unsatisfactory situation, measuring the size of angles in inches is not used. If one introduces the degree measure or radian measure at this level, one should certainly point out that these measures are independent of the "relative size" of the angle drawn.

5   Some texts do not consider a straight angle to be an angle because of the following limitations.

(a)   A straight line is impossible to distinguish from a line.

(b)   A straight line angle has no unique vertex, sides, interior or exterior.

(c)   These would be the only angles not contained in a unique plane.

When a straight angle is not considered to be an angle, then the idea of a linear pair is introduced to take care of the idea of supplementary angles; i.e., if two angles form a linear pair, then the angles are supplementary. However, whether a given text includes a straight angle as an angle in their definition is a matter of choice by the authors.

(B)   *AREA*

1   The student is correct. A circle is normally defined to be the set of points in a plane at the same distance from a fixed point called the center of the circle. Thus, a circle has no area but does have a perimeter called the circumference. The teacher meant to ask the students to find the area of the circular region with a radius of five inches.

2   A very good teaching strategy to use here is to first compliment the student for doing some excellent and creative thinking. Using positive reinforcement can be very beneficial to the student and the class. Then you might ask the student to demonstrate how the formula can be applied to the various polygons. Assuming that the student does this correctly for the simple polygons such as the triangle, square, rectangle, trapezoid, etc. you might ask her if the formula can be applied to figures such as the pentagon, hexagon, etc. You also might ask the student how the formula can be applied for the circle. She will have to do quite a bit of thinking in order to get the area of a circle, but it can be done.

However, for some polygons such as the regular hexagon, the student will get an incorrect answer. e.g. the area of a regular hexagon is ½ a • p, where a is the apothem of the hexagon and p is the perimeter. According to the student's formula, the area of the hexagon should be:

$$\frac{1}{2} \cdot 2a \cdot \left(\frac{p}{6} + \frac{p}{6}\right) = \frac{a \cdot p}{3}.$$

Thus, although the formula works for quite a number of polygons, it does not work for all polygons. Also consult:

Howard Fehr, *Secondary Mathematics: A Functional Approach for Teachers*, D. C. Heath & Co., Lexington, Ma., 1951, pp. 8-19.

Problem Although a *direct* application of the student's formula does not work in all cases, the student has discovered a very important principle. Can you modify the student's formula so that it will work? If you have trouble consult the reference above.

3   For an answer to this question, read the following article by M. Walter.*

*From *The Arithmetic Teacher*, April 1970, pp. 286-89. Reprinted by permission.

A common misconception about area

MARION WALTER*

Harvard University, Cambridge, Massachusetts

Marion Walter is an assistant professor at the Harvard University Graduate School of Education. Her concern is the education of teachers in the mathematics program. She conducts many in-service workshops and is particularly interested in the visual aspects of learning mathematics.

Can you help the bank manager?

Recently a friend of mine had her living room floor scraped. The cost was to be reckoned by the square foot. She measured the floor to be 19½ feet long and 12½ feet wide. In order to know how much the job was going to cost, she had to know how many square feet were going to be scraped. Thus, she had to calculate the area of the floor. She remembered that one could find the area of a rectangle by "multiplying the length by the width." How many square feet: 19½ ft. × 12½ ft.? So that she wouldn't have to multiply numbers involving halves, she decided to calculate 19 × 13 instead of 19½ × 12½. (She subtracted ½ from the 19½ and added it to the 12½.) Draw yourself a diagram.

She realized that the calculation would have been still simpler if she had rounded off the numbers the other way; instead of changing the 19½ × 12½ to 19 × 13, she could multiply 20 × 12. (Multiplying by 20 is easier than multiplying by 19.) To check her calculation, she calculated both products. What a surprise she got when the two answers did not come out to be the same! She "did it" several times. No, 19 × 13 = 247 and 20 × 12 = 240. She was stumped. "After all," she argued, "either way, I have taken off a half foot from one

side and put it on the other—it should give the same answer."

The next day she took the vexing problem to her friendly bank manager who is usually only too pleased to explain any intricacy of income tax, and even complications on incorrect gas bills. He too was mystified. He calculated 20 × 12 and 19 × 13—no, the two products were *not* the same. One was 240 and the other, 247. He even calculated the exact answer (19½ × 12½ = 243¾) on his desk calculator. It did not worry him that the two calculations did not give the *right* answer—only that the two estimates did not give the *same* answer.

Your students may want to explore other floors—for example, a room 25½ × 20½ feet or 14½ × 8½ feet, or 17½ ×

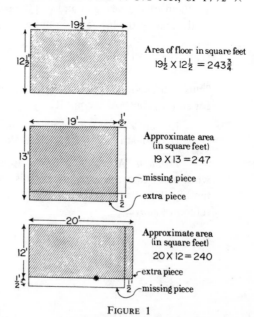

Area of floor in square feet
$19\frac{1}{2} \times 12\frac{1}{2} = 243\frac{3}{4}$

Approximate area (in square feet)
$19 \times 13 = 247$

— missing piece
— extra piece

Approximate area (in square feet)
$20 \times 12 = 240$

— extra piece
— missing piece

FIGURE 1

---

* Marion Walter is author of a booklet, *Boxes, Squares, and Other Things: A Teacher's Guide for a Unit in Informal Geometry.* The unit is available through the NATIONAL COUNCIL OF TEACHERS OF MATHEMATICS, 1201 Sixteenth Street NW, Washington, D.C. 20036, and the price is $1.80.

9½ feet, or 14¼ × 8¾ feet. Then ask your class to try to explain the dilemma of the bank manager. The drawings in figure 1, though not drawn to scale, may help.

Trouble with area and perimeter

The opening story is a true one. Many children and adults have trouble dealing with areas and perimeters. They often think that two patterns with the *same* perimeter, though *different* in shape, must have the *same* area. As can be seen from figure 1, the perimeters of all three shapes are the same—they are 2 (19½ + 12½) feet, 2 (19 + 13) feet, and 2 (20 + 12) feet, so each is equal to 64 feet. My friend probably realized intuitively that she was not changing the perimeter when she "took off ½ foot from one side and added it to the other," and concluded therefore that the areas should remain the same too. It is interesting to note that the bank manager *was* prepared to have the two estimates differ from the real answer but not from each other.

Let us look for a moment at the relationship between the estimates and the correct answer. Notice that in our case one approximation is too small and the other too large. We have

$$240 < 243\tfrac{3}{4}$$

and

$$247 > 243\tfrac{3}{4}$$

which can be written 240 < 243¾ < 247. The bank manager may have noticed that the average of the two estimates

$$\left(\frac{240 + 247}{2}\right)$$

is 243½ and that the actual area (243¾) differs from the average of the two estimates by only ¼. Cutting a transparent paper model of each piece shown in figure 1 (but drawn to scale), and placing all 3 models on top of each other (figure 2) will help one to see the relationship.

Fold the extra pieces over as shown to cover part of the model of the floor. The floor is now covered twice except for one small piece. The missing small piece has area ¼ square foot. Can you see how this

FIGURE 2

is related to the difference between the correct answer and the average of the two estimates?

Another example

Before making some suggestions, let us consider another example where misconceptions often creep in.

FIGURE 3

When someone is asked to find the area of a pattern like that in figure 3, a common first reaction is, "I have not been taught a formula for finding the area of such an irregular shape!" Often, after some thought, such a person takes a piece of string to measure the perimeter of that shape. Then he uses that length of string to

FIG. 4. The perimeter of each shape is 24 inches.

make a rectangle *R* or square *S* (see fig. 4). Then the area of such a rectangle (or square) is found by using the formula [$A = \ell \times w$], which he "knows." Great is the surprise when he finds out that the areas of *R* and *S* are not necessarily the same and that neither generally gives the area of *A*.

What can be done to prevent such misconceptions?

In order to try to prevent such misconceptions from taking hold permanently, first let children find perimeters and areas of figures without giving them any formulas. For example, let the children draw some irregular shapes as shown in figure 5.

FIGURE 5

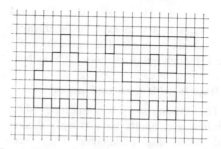

FIG. 6. The perimeter of each shape is 24 inches.

FIG. 7. The perimeter of each shape is 24 inches.

They can find the approximate perimeter of each by using string and laying it carefully on the figure. After straightening the string they can measure its length. You can also draw a large "park" on the floor or a playground and measure its perimeter by using a piece of string.

Work can be done with areas. Choose a small square as a unit. (For work preceding the use of square units see [2], for example.) Ask the children to find out approximately how many square units are needed to cover each of the shapes shown in figure 5. This can be done in a variety of ways:

> Children can cut out unit squares and lay them on the region and then estimate halves of squares to get a better approximation.
>
> Children can draw the shapes on graph paper of appropriate scale and count how many whole and how many half squares are inside the region.
>
> Can you think of another way?

Next ask the children to draw many shapes with a given fixed perimeter. They may create such shapes in a variety of ways. One way is to count edges of squares when the shape is drawn on graph paper. Using a perimeter of 24 inches, they may obtain numerous shapes. Some possible ones, drawn on 1-inch graph paper are shown in figure 4 (*R* and *S*) and in figure 6.

One can also make shapes with a perimeter of 24 inches by using a piece of thin string that is 24 inches long (after being tied). One can trace any shape that the string makes. Some possible shapes are shown in figure 7.

Many people will be surprised that with a given perimeter of 24 inches, shapes exist that have different areas. For example, we have made shapes with areas of 35 square inches, 36 square inches (see fig. 4), 17 square inches, 11 square inches, and 14 square inches (see fig. 6)—just to list a few. One can get a shape that has an area as small as one wants—for example, ½ square inch. (Can you describe such a shape?)

The areas of the shapes in figure 7 (each of which has a 24-inch perimeter) can be found approximately by counting squares and estimating half-squares. The shape in figure 7 that is roughly circular can be found to be approximately 45 square inches while shape 7*d* is approximately 4 square inches. What can you say about 7*b*? Can you make shapes with perimeter 24 inches that have an area of any number of square inches between 0 and 45? Figure 8 shows a shape whose perimeter is 24 inches and whose area is 34 square inches.

Investigate several such problems using different perimeters. What is the shape of

FIG. 8. 24-inch perimeter.

the largest area you can get for a given fixed perimeter?

Turn the problem around now. Suppose you have a shape that has an area of 20 square inches, for example. Some such shapes are drawn on 1-inch graph paper in figure 9.

FIG. 9. The area of each shape is 20 square inches.

Find the perimeter of each shape, either by counting edges of squares or by using string. Are the perimeters of all these shapes the same? Can two different shapes with the same area have the same perimeter? Draw other shapes with an area of 48 square inches. Which has the small-

est perimeter? Which has the largest? Is there a smallest? Is there a largest?

After several exercises like the ones described in this article, the children should no longer feel that shapes with the same perimeter always have the same area—or that shapes with the same area always have the same perimeter. You will find it useful to look at the references given below.

References

1. Biggs, Edith, and MacLean, James R. *Freedom to Learn: An Active Learning Approach to Mathematics.* Ontario & Reading: Addison Wesley, 1969.
2. Bourne, H. N. "The Concept of Area." THE ARITHMETIC TEACHER 15 (March 1968): 233–43.
3. Holloway, G. E. T. *An Introduction to the Child's Conception of Geometry.* London: Rontledge & Kagan Paul, 1967.
4. Members of the Association of Teachers of Mathematics. *Notes on Mathematics in Primary Schools.* Cambridge: University Press, 1967.
5. Page, David. *Ways to Find How Many.* University of Illinois Arithmetic Project. Education Development Center, 1965.
6. The Schools Council. *Mathematics in Primary Schools.* 2d ed. Curriculum Bulletin No. 1. Her Majesty's Stationery Office, 1967.
7. Strangman, Kathryn. "Grids, Tiles, and Areas." THE ARITHMETIC TEACHER 15 (December 1968): 668–72.

4   For an answer to this question, read:

(1)   Janet Jean Brougher, "Discovery Activities with Area and Perimeter," *The Arithmetic Teacher*, May 1973, pp. 382-85.

(2)   Robert W. Prielipp, "Are triangles that have the same area and the same perimeter congruent?", *The Mathematics Teacher*, February 1974, p. 157.

(C)   *AXIOMS AND DEFINITIONS*

1   This student is assuming that there is some kind of "infinite addition" of points. One must be extremely careful when dealing with infinite processes. Useful and intuitive properties of finite processes may not carry over. This idea becomes clearer once one has studied the calculus.

　　　The student might even be shown that it is possible to consider a square as an infinite collection of lines (a square has a positive area, a line does not) and that a cube can be considered as an infinite collection of squares (a cube has a positive volume, a square does not).

2   No, the student is not correct. A dot is a physical representation of the abstract

mathematical idea of a point just as a numeral is a written representation for a number. Since a point is an abstract idea, then it cannot be seen much less erased.

The main point for you to try to get across to the student is the difference between a geometric idea and the representation of that idea. The analogy of a number and its representation (a numeral) is a useful one to use in this situation. Another idea that might prove helpful is the distinction between a person and that person's name.

3   In many mathematics texts, there is no difference between the two. However, in some books such as those used in the elementary or middle schools, a half line is a ray $\overrightarrow{AB}$ with the endpoint or starting point "A" deleted. Thus one should look carefully at the definition in a particular book.

4   If the student is trying to get an intuitive grasp of the concepts involved, then it should be shown to the student that one can get a line from two half lines if the half lines include their endpoints as shown in Figure 1.6.3, but one could also get a figure such as shown in Figure 1.6.4.

FIGURE 1.6.3   *FIGURE 1.6.4*

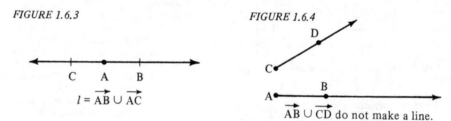

$l = \overrightarrow{AB} \cup \overrightarrow{AC}$

$\overrightarrow{AB} \cup \overrightarrow{CD}$ do not make a line.

However, if a half line is defined as a ray $\overrightarrow{AB}$ with the endpoint A deleted, then the student is incorrect.

It should also be pointed out to the student that one cannot mathematically identify ½ with either a ray or a half line since this does not make any sense; e.g., what would ½ of a line mean?

5   In reality P should be called a beginning or starting point, but through traditional use the name endpoint has been commonly used. Perhaps the name came about because if one allows movement in either direction on this ray, then one of the *endpoints* would be P since no further movement along $\overrightarrow{PQ}$ would be allowed in that direction.

6   The student is incorrect. Equality is reserved for identity; e.g., two triangles are equal if and only if they are precisely the same set of points. On the other hand, at this level, congruence means that objects have the same size and shape. Thus, two triangles could be congruent and not equal.

(D)   *MEASUREMENT*

1   Although the relationship is not precisely the same, there is a definite similarity. One can think of segments as being equivalent if and only if they are congruent; i.e., $\overline{AB}$ is equivalent to $\overline{CD}$ if and only if $\overline{AB} \cong \overline{CD}$. Also, sets are defined as equivalent if and only if the elements in the sets can be put in one-to-one correspondence. However, the notion of *equivalent* is used in two different senses and one cannot interchange the meaning. For example, one cannot use the word *equivalent* as used

for sets in the meaning for segments because there are segments that can be put in one-to-one correspondence with each other and yet the segments are not congruent as shown:

A   B

C   D

These segments are equivalent in the set theoretic meaning of the word equivalent (one-to-one correspondence) but not equivalent as congruent segments.

However, equal segments mean the same as equal sets, i.e., the same set of points or the same set of elements.

2   Dry weight is a measure of weight while liquid weight is really a measure of volume. Liquid measure is especially useful in certain situations such as in pharmacies. Druggists often have bottles that measure say 6 fluid ounces, and they can put in any liquid in these bottles and know that they thus have a certain volume. The liquid in these bottles is then equivalent in weight to 6 ounces of water. Dry measure on the other hand is measured by weight not volume. For example, cereal packages may not be filled to capacity (volume) due to settling, but you can be assured it weighs the required amount.

3   The student is incorrect. The problem here is one concerning dimensional analysis. The student could be corrected as follows:

$$36 \text{ in.} = 1 \text{ yard}$$
$$9 \text{ in.} = \tfrac{1}{4} \text{ yard}$$
$$\sqrt{9 \text{ in.}} = \sqrt{\tfrac{1}{4} \text{ yard}}$$
$$3 \sqrt{\text{in.}} = \tfrac{1}{2}\sqrt{\text{yard}}$$

This is the point where the student in incorrect. One cannot disregard $\sqrt{\text{in.}}$ and $\sqrt{\text{yard}}$. One might continue the problem as follows:

$$3\sqrt{\text{in.}} = \tfrac{1}{2} \sqrt{36 \text{ in.}}$$
$$3\sqrt{\text{in.}} = \tfrac{1}{2} \cdot 6\sqrt{\text{in.}}$$
$$3\sqrt{\text{in.}} = 3\sqrt{\text{in.}}$$

Also consult the answer given in Section A2.13, Answer 6.

4   Our system of weights and measures was carried over into the colonies from Great Britain. These weights and measures were not derived from any scientific basis, and thus there was considerable lack of uniformity in the units used.

In essence there are really three different systems used for measuring the ton: the long ton, the short ton and the metric ton. The long ton is derived from Great Britain and was formulated as follows: One stone = 14 pounds, 8 stones = a hundredweight = 112 pounds, 20 hundredweights = a ton = 2240 pounds. Thus the *long ton*, or the *net ton* as it is sometimes called, is a measure left over from our relation with Great Britain. This measure is still used today in some foreign countries and is used in our country mainly in the shipping and mining industries.

The short ton is the one commonly used in our country. It is derived from our desire to use 100 pounds = a hundredweight and thus 20 hundredweights = 2000 pounds.

The metric ton is also used and is equal to 1.102 short tons.

5   Yes, there is a difference between the terms. When one writes 2 square feet, one is

referrring to a unit of measuring area (1 square foot) and there are two of them as illustrated in Figure 1.6.5.

FIGURE 1.6.5

When one writes 2 feet square, one is referring to a square that has a length of 2 feet on each side as illustrated in Figure 1.6.6 and thus contains 4 square feet of area.

FIGURE 1.6.6

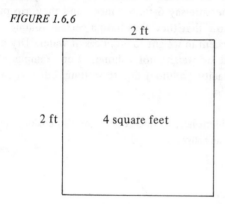

6   The abbreviation *lb* is derived from the Latin word *libra*, the ancient Roman word for pound.

(E)   *POLYGONS*

1   Most likely this figure is one that we would not ordinarily want to classify as a polygon. Usually, at this level, we consider only simple, closed figures as polygons. A definition of a polygon that is usually given at this level is: a polygon is the union of three or more coplanar line segments joined at successive endpoints to form a closed figure, but otherwise the segments have no points in common and successive segments do not lie on the same line. If the following restrictions were all removed, then the figure shown could be classified as a polygon: (1) figure is closed; (2) segments contain no points in common other than endpoints; (3) successive endpoints are joined.

2   A polygon is a two-dimensional figure consisting of line segments, and the region determined by this figure has area. A polyhedron is a three-dimensional figure whose surface consists entirely of polygonal regions. Thus a polyhedron has both surface area (the sum of the areas of the polygonal regions) and volume. See the definition in Answer 1 of this section.

3   According to the definition made by the teacher, the figure is a polygon. Most

likely, however, we would ordinarily not want the figure to be polygon. Thus, it would seem to be the case that the teacher might want to modify the definition given by saying that each segment intersect exactly two of the other segments at the endpoints, but otherwise the segments have no other points in common.

A1.7   *Mean and Average*

1   No, the student is not correct. This error is one that many students and teachers make. The formula which the student is using assumes that the same amount of *time* is spent traveling at each speed. However, this assumption is violated in this problem; the cars travel at the same *distance* (one mile), but they do not travel this distance in the same amount of time. Traveling at 60 mph for 1 mile takes 1 minute while traveling at 120 mph for 1 miles takes ½ minute. The correct formula to use is the following:

$$\text{average speed} = \frac{\text{total distance}}{\text{total time}} \tag{1}$$

Thus, in this problem the average speed would be $\frac{2}{1\frac{1}{2}} = \frac{4}{3}$ miles per minute or 80 miles per hour.

You might want to show the student that the formula he was using is a special case of (1), where the cars are traveling for the same time, as follows:

Let x = the amount of time that either car travels,
    y = distance traveled at 60 mph,
    z = distance traveled at 120 mph.

Thus,

$$\text{average speed} = \frac{y+z}{2x} = \frac{1}{2}\left(\frac{y+z}{x}\right) = \frac{1}{2}\left(\frac{y}{x} + \frac{z}{x}\right)$$
$$= \frac{1}{2}(60 + 120) = \frac{60 + 120}{2}.$$

2   A baseball average can be looked at either as an average or as a probability. For example, if we assign the numeral 0 for not getting a hit and the numeral 1 for getting a hit, then the arithmetic mean or average of the following 0 0 1 0 0 1 0 0 would be 2/8 or 1/4. Likewise a 0 can be deemed as not successful in getting a hit and a 1 as being successful in getting a hit. The above can then be interpreted as

$$\text{Probability of getting a hit} = \frac{2}{8} = \frac{1}{4}.$$

3   We will assume that the different kinds of "average" mentioned in this question refer to the three different kinds of measures of central tendency called the mean, median and mode. At a higher level one might be referring to the arithmetic, geometric and harmonic means, but these means are not usually studied in high school until an Algebra II course.

Each of the averages, mean, median and mode, has certain features that are useful to a person who would like a summary measure of a set of data. The choice of which of these three measures to use requires careful thought. For example, if four persons have incomes of $5000, $6000, $7000, and $8000, then one kind of average, the mean, would be $6500. If a fifth person, whose salary is $20,000, is added to the group, then the mean of this new group would be $9200. Now, if someone says that this last figure is the average salary in a company, would this measure be a good one to use in this situation? Obviously not, because it does not represent either group and is very misleading.

The problem here is that an extreme score affects the mean and can move the mean away from what would generally be considered the central area. In this case, the median would probably be a better measure to use. The main point here is that the choice of an average as a summary measure of a set of data depends on several factors. Two of these factors would be: (1) the shape of the distribution scores; (2) for what purpose will the summary measure be used. In either case, one of these averages might be better to use than another in order to get a useful interpretation of a set of data.

4   You might first commend Jack for devising this new method. Then you might ask him how he developed this process and if it works all the time or only with certain numbers. If it seems to work all the time, can he devise a justification or proof that it does. An algebraic proof, which shows that Jack is correct, is given in the following. Assume without loss of generality that $x \leqslant y$. Thus,

$$y - x = f, \quad f \geqslant 0 \quad \text{and} \quad x + \frac{f}{2} = x + \frac{y - x}{2} = \frac{2x + y - x}{2} = \frac{x + y}{2}.$$

A1.8   *Numbers, Operations, Properties and Algorithms*

1   One approach to handling this situation might be to ask the student what $2 \div 3$ means in terms of multiplication. Hopefully the student would respond that division is defined in terms of multiplication so that $2 \div 3 = c$ if and only if $2 = 3 \cdot c$. Then you would ask the student what number c would satisfy the latter equation. By direct substitution, the fraction $2/3$ is a solution of $2 = 3 \cdot c$.

Another approach to the question might be an intuitive one using geometry. You could show the student how to divide the rectangle shown in Figure 1.8.1 into three congruent parts. Since this rectangle can be thought of as two squares put together, the student could be shown Figure 1.8.2 where the rectangle is divided into three congruent parts (one of the parts is shaded).

FIGURE 1.8.1   *FIGURE 1.8.2*

Since the area of the whole rectangle is two units, the area of one of the congruent parts in Figure 1.8.2 (such as the shaded part) must be $2/3$ units. This is easily seen in Figure 1.8.2 because the shaded part in each square is $1/3$ unit and there are two shaded parts.

2   In this particular case, the student is correct. However, in general, the method that the student used is incorrect. For example,

$$\frac{12 \times 10^4}{2 \times 10^2} = \frac{12}{2} \times \frac{10^4}{10^2} = 6 \cdot 10^2,$$

not $(12 - 2) \times (10^{4-2}) = 10^3$.

   Problem   Under what conditions will the student's method work?

3   According to the definition of subtraction for integers, $a - b = a + (-b)$. Thus, if b is a negative number, $(-b)$, the additive inverse of b, is a positive number.
   Another approach to this question might be to ask the student to graph a problem such as $-2 - (-3)$ on the number line. If the student falters, ask the student to graph $(-2) + (-3)$ on the number line, which is illustrated as follows:

Then tell the student that since subtraction is the inverse operation of addition, the arrow representing $-(-3)$ must go in the opposite direction as illustrated:

Since this is exactly how $-2 + 3$ would be represented, it must be the case that $-2 - (-3) = -2 + 3$.

4   Ask the student to multiply 30 by 6. The student should realize that if $96 \div 6 = 30$ then $30 \cdot 6 = 96$. Assuming that the student multiplies correctly, he should realize that something is incorrect. Then you might point out that the mistake made was adding together all of the 6s, in which case, some 6s have been added more than once. The correct answer is simply the number of 6s recorded in the last line. A possible strategy to use with this student is to ask him to do the following problem: $24 \div 6$. The student should realize that $24 \div 6 = 4$, and he would get the answer using the algorithm that he developed as follows:

$$
\begin{array}{ll}
\left.\begin{array}{r} 6 \\ +6 \end{array}\right\} & \text{two 6s} \\
\left.\begin{array}{r} \overline{12} \\ +12 \end{array}\right\} & \text{four 6s} \\
\overline{24}
\end{array}
$$

Notice that the correct answer is the number of 6s recorded in the last line, not the total number of 6s (6 of them) recorded.

5   For an answer to this question, read the article by J. Weaver.*

A Nontrivial Issue of Symbolism in Multiplication

J. Fred Weaver

The University of Wisconsin, Madison, Wisconsin

Consistency is not necessarily a virtue in all things, and inconsistency in some things does not necessarily imply lack of virtue. But in the case of a deductive mathematical system, for instance, consistency is more than a virtue; it is a necessity. And inconsistency is more than lack of virtue; it is an intolerable condition.

There are other instances in mathematics, however, where inconsistency is not as damning and we are at least willing to tolerate it. For example, we can learn to live with alternative definitions of *trapezoid*,[1] providing we understand the logical consequences of each and are aware of which definition is intended within a given context.

But we should pause and reflect upon some of these tolerated inconsistencies within the framework of mathematical learning among young children at the elementary-school level. It is not unlikely that certain inconsistencies inhibit pupils' mathematical understanding. A case in point well may be the way in which we commonly interpret the symbol for the operation of multiplication [×], in contrast with the way in which we interpret the operational symbols for addition [+], subtraction [−], and division [÷].

AN INTERPRETATION OF +, −, ÷

Let us first consider the following illustrations:

(1) $12 + 4 = 16$ [12 *plus* 4 is equal to 16]

(2) $12 - 4 = 8$ [12 *minus* 4 is equal to 8]

(3) $12 \div 4 = 3$ [12 *divided by* 4 is equal to 3]

Virtually without exception, mathematics program for elementary-school children reflect a similar interpretation for each of these three instances: the first number, 12, is treated as the *operand* [the number operated on] and the second number, 4, is treated as the *operator* [which "acts" on the first number in accord with the operation specified (+ or − or ÷)]. The terms *operand* and *operator* are not used with elementary-school pupils, to be sure; but the *ideas* named by these technical terms clearly are in evidence.

---

[1] Under one definition a trapezoid is characterized as a quadrilateral with *at least* one pair of parallel sides, under another definition it is characterized as a quadrilateral with *exactly* one pair of parallel sides. In the first case, *parallelogram* is a proper subclass of *trapezoid;* in the second case, parallelogram and trapezoid are disjoint classes.

*From *School Science and Mathematics*, October 1968, pp. 629-30, 639-42. Reprinted by permission of the editor and the author.

Interpretations of ×

Now let us consider this illustration:

(4) $12 \times 4 = 48$

If we read "12×4" as "12 *multiplied by* 4," we are consistent with the preceding interpretation for addition, subtraction, and division: the first number, 12, is treated as the operand and the second number, 4, is treated as the operator [in this instance in accord with the operation of multiplication].

But suppose we follow a much more common practice at the elementary-school level and read "12×4" as "12 *times* 4." Then we are treating the first number, 12, as the *operator* and we are treating the second number, 4, as the operand.

These two interpretations clearly do *not* mean the same thing. For example, some persons suggest that we associate the multiplication of counting numbers with the union of equivalent disjoint sets. If this is the case, "12 *multiplied by* 4" is associated with equivalent sets of 12 things, and the product of 12 and 4 is the number of elements in the union of 4 such sets. On the other hand, "12 *times* 4" is associated with equivalent sets of 4 things, and the product of 12 and 4 is the number of elements in the union of 12 such sets. [In either instance, of course, the equivalent sets are disjoint.]

Material on multiplication in most professional books, articles, etc. for elementary-school teachers usually includes no mention of this ambiguous interpretation of the operational symbol, ×. A notable exception, however, is found in Fehr and Phillips' opening discussion of "Multiplication of Cardinal Numbers" in which the following point of view is expressed:

> "It might be well if the 'times' language were never introduced, since it makes the symbols for a multiplication the only ones children have to 'read backward.' Some of the new textbooks are not using it for this reason. However, it does have certain advantages, and it is widely used. When teachers use the language 'times' and 'multiplied by,' they should know which numeral refers to the operator and which to the operand and express the operation accordingly in any work they do with a class. Since multiplication is commutative, it is not a serious matter if a child gets an occasional example 'turned around.' "[2]

Looking Further

But let us look a bit further. In particular, let us look to certain mathematical sentences which relate the operations of multiplication and division. We shall do this, however, by first considering some mathematical sentences which relate the operations of addition and subtraction. The following properties are true for every real number a and every real number b:[3]

---

[2] Howard F. Fehr and Jo McKeeby Phillips, *Teaching Modern Mathematics in the Elementary School.* (Addison-Wesley, 1967). pp. 101–102.

[3] These properties also are valid for some but not all distinguished subsets of the real numbers. For instance, they continue to be valid if a and b are rational numbers, or if a and b are integers. But suppose that a and b are whole numbers $[W = \{0, 1, 2, 3, 4, 5, 6, \cdots \}]$. Sentence (5) remains valid for every $a \in W$ and every $b \in W$. Sentence (6), however, is meaningful and valid only when $a \geq b$. And sentence (7) is meaningless, since the concept of an additive inverse does not even apply within the set of whole numbers [i.e., for $b \in W$, $^-b \notin W$]. Notice also that sentence (6) is a logical consequence of the mathematical definition of subtraction in terms of addition: $a - b = c$ is true if and only if there exists a number c such that $c + b = a$. Also, sentence (5) is a logical consequence of the implication: if $a + b = c$, then $c - b = a$.

(5) $(a + b) - b = a$ $\left[\text{e.g., } (12 + 4) - 4 = 12\right]$

(6) $(a - b) + b = a$ $\left[\text{e.g., } (12 - 4) + 4 = 12\right]$

(7) $a - b = a + {}^{-}b$ $\left[\text{e.g., } 12 - 4 = 12 + {}^{-}4\right]$

In each of these cases it makes sense mathematically to treat a [or 12] as the operand and to treat b [or 4] as the operator at the outset. The remaining part of each sentence is consistent with this initial interpretation of operand and operator.

Now let us turn to the counterparts of properties (5), (6), and (7) for the operations of multiplication and division, where a is any real number and b is a real number such that $b \neq 0$:[4]

(8) $(a \times b) \div b = a$ $\left[\text{e.g., } (12 \times 4) \div 4 = 12\right]$

(9) $(a \div b) \times b = a$ $\left[\text{e.g., } (12 \div 4) \times 4 = 12\right]$

(10) $a \div b = a \times \dfrac{1}{b}$ $\left[\text{e.g., } 12 \div 4 = 12 \times \dfrac{1}{4}\right]$

The sense of each of these properties casts b [or 4], and not a, in the role of an *operator*, with the consequent interpretation of "$\times$" as "multiplied by" rather than "times."

Notice that if we read the left-hand side of sentence (8) as "(a *times b*) *divided by b*," then the intended sense of this "doing-undoing" property is *not* maintained. Similarly, the intended sense of (9) and (10) is *not* maintained if "$\times$" is read as "times" [and "$\div$" is read as "divided by."][5]

If we insist upon reading "$\times$" as *"times"* and still wish to maintain the intended sense of the property exemplified by sentence (8), *without involving the additional property of commutativity of multiplication*, we have two alternatives. If b is to be an operator, then we should write

(8.1) $(b \times a) \div b = a$ $\left[\text{e.g., } (4 \times 12) \div 4 = 12\right]$

On the other hand, if a is to be an operator, then we should write

(8.2) $(a \times b) \div a = b$ $\left[\text{e.g., } (12 \times 4) \div 12 = 4\right]$,

in which case we must apply the restriction that $a \neq 0$ rather than $b \neq 0$.

It should not be necessary to illustrate specifically the fact that we encounter similar problems with sentences (9) and (10) if we read "$\times$" as *"times"* and wish to maintain the intended sense of the property involved in each case.

---

[4] Observations analogous to those in footnote 2 apply here but are not stated explicitly. The reader may wish to do so for himself, however.

[5] At some mathematical levels we prefer to symbolize "a divided by b" as $\frac{a}{b}$ or as a/b rather than as $a \div b$. In each of these instances the operator is b, so that $a \div b = b = a/b$. These symbols,—particularly the last one,—should not be confused with the symbol $a \mid b$, which we may read as "a divides b" [i.e., a is a factor of b]. In the case of $a \mid b$, the operator is a rather than b.

ARRAYS

In an earlier article in this journal I advocated a basic character-
ization of the multiplication operation in terms of arrays.[6] In that
article I was concerned principally with some other issues and, to
avoid beclouding them, more or less followed the common practice
of treating *a* as the *operator* in expressions of the form *a*×*b* [read as
"*a times*" *b*]. Now, however, I wish to emphasize the desirability of
treating *b* as the operator in connection with an array characteriza-
tion of multiplication.

We commonly name an array with 5 rows and 7 columns, for instance, as a 5-*by*-7 array [Fig. 1]. This 5-by-7 array, and every 5-by-7
array has 5×7 or 35 elements.

```
o   o   o   o   o   o   o

o   o   o   o   o   o   o

o   o   o   o   o   o   o

o   o   o   o   o   o   o

o   o   o   o   o   o   o
```

FIG. 1. A 5-by-7 array.

More generally, an array with *a* rows and *b* columns is termed an
a-by-b array, and has *a*×*b* elements [where *a* and *b* are counting
numbers.][7]

When we speak of a 5-*by*-7 array, for instance, it seems sensible
and consistent to think of 5×7 as "5 *multiplied by* 7." In general,
when we speak of an *a-by-b* array, it seems sensible and consistent
to interpret *a*×*b* as "*a multiplied by b*."

Notice also that when a 5-by-7 array, for instance, is viewed as a
union of disjoint equivalent sets, it is preferable to think of the array
as being generated in the form of Figure 2 rather than in the form
of Figure 3 if we are to interpret "5×7" as "5 *multiplied by* 7."

FIG. 2   FIG. 3

[6] J. Fred Weaver, "Multiplication Within the Set of Counting Numbers." SCHOOL SCIENCE AND MATHE-
MATICS, 67: 252–70; March 1967.
[7] As indicated in the preceding article, the array interpretation of *a*×*b* for counting numbers may be extended
to whole numbers, to cover those instances in which *a*=0 or *b*=0, and *a*×*b*=0.

The sense of Figure 3 would lead to interpreting "5×7" as "5 *times* 7" rather than as "5 multiplied by 7," if we are thinking of the array as being generated in relation to the union of disjoint equivalent sets.

In Conclusion

It is true that the symbol for multiplication [×] may be interpreted ambiguously without affecting the product of two real numbers. Since multiplication is commutative [when applied to real numbers], "5 *times* 7" and "5 *multiplied by* 7," for instance,in dicate the same product, 35. In general, for every real number a and every real number b, "a times b" and "a multiplied by b" designate the same real number.

At certain stages of mathematical learning this ambiguity undoubtedly is of trivial consequence. But this is *not* a trivial matter for children's mathematical learning at the elementary-school level. If we tolerate an ambiguous interpretation of "12×4," for instance; if we are willing to accept either "12×4" or "4×12" as expressing the sense of a particular problem, etc.; and if we are just as free with "12+4" and "4+12,"—then we are inviting confusion on the part of children between expressions such as "12−4" and "4−12," and between "12÷4" and "4÷12."

Let us attempt to build for elementary-school pupils an unambiguous interpretation of the symbol, ×, for multiplication. And in the interests of advantages likely to be gained by consistency of interpretation in relation to the symbols for addition [+], subtraction [−], and division [÷], let us consider seriously the interpretation of "×" as *multiplied by* rather than as "times." This non-trivial issue at the elementary-school level deserves more than token attention in terms of empirical exploration and investigation.

A Postscript

The manuscript for this article was prepared and submitted before I read in the November 1967 issue of School Science and Mathematics Professor Rappaport's reaction to my previous discussion of "Multiplication Within the Set of Counting Numbers,"[8] in which he contends that I emphasized "logic at the expense of psychology."[9] This reaction has given me no cause to modify either the suggestion I advance in this present article or the position I advocated in my previous discussion.

I am intrigued by the fact that my emphasis upon "logical" [mathematical] considerations which Rappaport interprets to be at the "expense of psychology" can be viewed, instead, to have *support* from "psychology." For instance: In a recent discussion of meaningful verbal learning, Ausubel[10] states: "It is self-evident that before new ideas can be meaningfully learned, they must be adequately discriminable from similar established ideas in cognitive structure. If the learner cannot discriminate clearly, for example, between new idea A' and previously learned idea A, then A' enjoys relatively little status as a separately identifiable meaning in its own right, even at the very onset of its incorporation into cognitive structure."[11]

---

[8] David Rappaport, "Logic, Psychology and the New Mathematics." School Science and Mathematics, 67: 681–85; November 1967.

[9] *Ibid.*, p. 684.

[10] David P. Ausubel, "Facilitating Meaningful Verbal Learning in the Classroom." *Arithmetic Teacher*, 15: 126–32, February 1968.

[11] *Ibid.*, pp. 131–32.

Rappaport asks, "Is it not possible to develop mathematical principles in accordance with sound psychological principles?"[12] Certainly it is,—and I am very much interested in doing so. In view of the principle mentioned by Ausubel, I have both *psychological and mathematical* reasons to question Rappaport's contention that "Repeated addition serves as an excellent introduction to multiplication,"[13] and to favor an array interpretation independent of addition.

Finally, interested readers may wish to relate two articles from another journal to the issue in question:

Robert D. Bechtel and Lyle J. Dixon, "Multiplication—Repeated Addition?" *Arithmetic Teacher*, 14: 373–76, May 1967.

David Rappaport, "Multiplication—Logical or Pedagogical?" *Arithmetic Teacher*, 15: 158–60; February 1968.

---

[12] Rappaport, *ibid.*, pp. 681–82.
[13] *Ibid.*, p. 684.

6   One way of solving this problem is: Go back to the definition of "÷" where $a \div b = c$ if and only if $a = bc$. If $a = 0$ and $b = 0$, we have

$$0 \div 0 = c$$

if and only if

$$0 = 0 \cdot c. \tag{1}$$

Any number c will make (1) a true statement. When this situation develops, it is customary for mathematicians to say that the particular operation in question is undefined (or undetermined).

An alternate approach to the given problem is as follows. It is frequently the case that an expression such as $6 \div 2$ is intuitively presented as the number of times two objects can be subtracted from six objects before one encounters a negative number. In the case of $0 \div 0$, one would be asking, "How many times can one subtract zero objects from zero objects before one encounters a negative number?" This could be done once, twice, etc. Again, in this case, there is not a unique answer.

7   The problem is with the teacher and not the student. The question is very ambiguous, although the teacher probably wanted the answer to each individual part. What the student did was to find the answers to each individual part and add them together. Since the answer given by the student is correct under this interpretation, it would be unjust to mark the answer incorrect.

8   The student is not correct in saying that we cannot divide 16 by 3 without annexing zeros. This can be accomplished by two different methods as follows:

(1)   Since $16 \div 3 = \dfrac{16}{3}$, then $16 \div 3 = 5\dfrac{1}{3} = 5 + \dfrac{1}{3}$.

$$\frac{1}{3} = \frac{1}{10} \cdot \frac{10}{3} = \frac{1}{10}\left(3 + \frac{1}{3}\right) = \frac{3}{10} + \frac{1}{10} \cdot \frac{1}{3}$$

Thus $16 \div 3 = 5 + \dfrac{3}{10} + \dfrac{1}{10} \cdot \dfrac{1}{3}$.

$$\frac{1}{10} \cdot \frac{1}{3} = \frac{1}{100} \cdot \frac{10}{3} = \frac{1}{100}\left(3 + \frac{1}{3}\right) = \frac{3}{100} + \frac{1}{100} \cdot \frac{1}{3}$$

Thus $16 \div 3 = 5 + \frac{3}{10} + \frac{3}{100} + \frac{1}{100} \cdot \frac{1}{3}$ which can be written as $5.33\frac{1}{3}$. It is evident that this process can be continued as far as one would like to go.

(2)   Since $16 \div 3 = \frac{16}{3}$, then $16 \div 3 = \frac{16 \cdot 100/3}{100}$. We can find $\frac{1600}{3}$ by using the division algorithm for natural numbers.

$$\begin{array}{r} 533 \\ 3\,\overline{)1600} \\ \underline{15} \\ 10 \\ \underline{9} \\ 10 \\ \underline{9} \\ 1 \end{array}$$

Thus $\frac{1600}{3} = 533\frac{1}{3}$, and therefore $\frac{1600/3}{100} = 5.33\frac{1}{3}$.

In this situation, we can see that in order to get a decimal fraction we first move the decimal point in the numerator two places to the right (by multiplying by 100). Then we move the decimal point to the left two places by dividing by 100. The net result is to leave the decimal point where it was in the first place and supply zeros as needed. Then we carry through the division algorithm as if there were no decimal point present. The act of annexing zeros is thus simply the result of devising a shorter algorithm that accomplishes the same thing as the longer processes presented.

9   There are several ways of explaining this result to a student as follows:

(1)   Suppose that you owe someone \$200 represented by −200, and you are going to repay the loan by giving the person \$10 a day, represented by −10. Then, how many days will it take you to pay the debt? The main idea is to try to get the student to see division as repeated subtraction.

(2)   Division can be defined in terms of multiplication as follows: $a \div b = c$, $b \neq 0$, if and only if $a = b \cdot c$. Thus $-200 \div -10 = c$ if and only if $-200 = -10 \cdot c$; i.e., $c = 20$.

(3)   One could also show the result on a number line.

    Problem   Show $-200 \div -20$ on a number line.

10   One way of doing this problem is to go back to the definition of "÷". $6 \div 0 = b$ if and only if $6 = 0 \cdot b$. However, $0 \cdot b = 0$ and $6 \neq 0$. Thus, there is no number b such that $6 \div 0 = b$.

An intuitive way of looking at this problem is as follows: $6 \div 0$ can be thought of as repeated subtraction. Thus $6 \div 0$ asks the question, "How many times can you subtract zero from 6 until the six objects are gone." You can never do this, and thus $6 \div 0$ is not defined.

An alternate way of looking at the problem is to first look at related problems. For example, $6 \div 2$ asks the question, "How many times can you partition 6 objects into groups of 2." Thus $6 \div 2 = 3$. $6 \div 1$ likewise would be 6. Then $6 \div 0$ would ask, "How many times can you partition 6 objects into groups of 0." It can't be done.

11 If $0 \div 0$ were defined to be equal to one, then one would be led to make the following deduction. Since the fraction $a/b = a \div b$, then the fraction a/b would be equivalent to $0/0$, which is equal to 1. That is, every fraction would be equivalent to a fraction, which is a name for 1, and thus we would have just one equivalence class of fractions all of which are names for the number 1. Since the idea of equivalence classes of fractions is such an important idea when working with fractions, then it follows that defining $0 \div 0$ to be equal to 1 is not justified.

12 One way of helping this student is as follows: Ask the student to multiply 54 by 3. Assuming that the student does this correctly, it should be obvious that something is wrong. The following procedure may then be shown to the student.

$$
\begin{array}{r}
4 \\
500 \\
\hline
3\,|\overline{1512} \\
1500 \\
\hline
12 \\
12 \\
\hline
\end{array}
\quad \rightarrow 504
$$

By employing this procedure, the student should realize that 5 in the quotient refers to 500.

13 The student is correct. Intuitively, in the first step, the student is finding out how many objects are left over in the units place in the subtrahend $(7 - 4)$. Then the number 3 is subtracted from the minuhend in the form of $10 - 3$. Since the student has used up one ten in the first step, then, in the second step, the student must reduce the number of tens by one and then subtract the number of tens. In general, let the subtraction be represented by

$$
\begin{array}{r}
ab \\
-cd \\
\hline
\end{array}
\quad \text{where } b < d.
$$

Then the student would do the following:

$$
\begin{array}{r}
ab \\
-cd \\
\hline
\end{array}
$$

(1) $d - b = x$
    $10 - (d - b) = (10 + b - d)$
(2) $(a - 1) \cdot 10 - (c \cdot 10) = (a - 1 - c) \cdot 10$

14 This student has a problem with place value. Thus, one way of helping him would be to rewrite the way he has done the problem as follows:

$$
\begin{array}{r}
5 \\
10 \\
100 \\
\hline
25\,|\overline{625} \\
250 \\
\hline
370 \\
250 \\
\hline
125 \\
125 \\
\hline
\end{array}
$$

Then, ask the student if $25 \cdot 100 = 250$. The student should then see that the first

"1" is placed in the wrong place. If the student wants to do the problem in the manner illustrated, then the following should help.

$$
\begin{array}{r}
5 \\
10 \\
10 \\
25\overline{)625} \\
\underline{250} \\
375 \\
\underline{250} \\
125 \\
\underline{125}
\end{array}
$$

15   Mathematically, the student is not correct. For example, if one knows that it is zero degrees centigrade outside does this mean that there is no temperature? Likewise, in bowling, if a zero is placed on the scoreboard, then this would indicate that the person had a turn. If nothing is put on the scoreboard, then the person has not yet taken his turn. The student is trying to equate the empty set with the set containing zero. Mathematically, the two concepts are different although in normal everyday use we usually use the terms interchangeably with no resulting ambiguity.

16   The student is assuming that since addition is commutative, it should also be true that subtraction is commutative; i.e., if $a + (-b) = (-b) + a$, then $a - b = a + (-b)$. However, $b - a = b + (-a)$, and this is the point where the student is confused. The student thinks that $b - a$ should equal $-b + a$. Thus, the fact that addition is commutative just happens to be a property of addition that is an added bonus and has nothing to do with $a - b = a + (-b)$.

17   No, the student is not correct. For example, $2 - 0 = 2$, but $0 - 2 = -2$, not 2. Thus, 0 is a right-handed identity but not a left-handed identity with respect to subtraction. Remind students that if $a \in S$ and # is the binary operation in S, then i is an identity with respect to S and # if and only if $a \# i = i \# a = a$ for all $a \in S$.

18   The student does not seem to understand that zero is the additive identity; i.e., $a + 0 = 0 + a = a$ for all real numbers a. The student seems to be using the following:

$a + b = a$ where a, b are real numbers.

It would be interesting to find out if this student uses the same procedure on all addition problems.

19   The student is correct. The problem could be done as the student suggests.

$$
\begin{array}{r}
134 + 2 = 136 \\
25\overline{)3420} \\
\underline{25} \\
92 \\
\underline{75} \\
170 \\
\underline{100} \\
70 \\
\underline{50} \\
20
\end{array}
$$

When we show students the traditional algorithm, we usually gloss over this point.

20 One way of convincing the student that $-3 < -1$ would be as follows. Although it is true that a debt of three dollars is larger than a debt of one dollar, one might look at the situation in terms of how much money would be left over for oneself. Suppose that you had five dollars in your pocket. If you paid the person the three dollars that you owed that person, they you would have two dollars left over. If you paid the person the one dollar that you owed, then you would have four dollars left over for yourself.

  Another way to convince a student that $-3 < -1$ would be to use the definition of less than. $-3 < -1$ because you must add a positive integer to -3 to get -1.

  Another way to answer this question might be to think in terms of temperature. Three degrees below zero is colder than one degree below zero; i.e., there is less heat at three degrees below zero than at one degree below zero.

A1.9 *Number Theory*

1 For an answer to this question, read:

  R.F. Wardrop, "Divisibility Rules for Numbers Expressed in Different Bases," *The Arithmetic Teacher*, March 1972, pp. 218-20.

2 This definition might lead to the following difficulty. Students might say that 6 is not divisible by 2 because $6 = 2 \cdot 3$ and 3 is not an even counting number. It would be better to leave out the word *evenly* in the definition.

3 Although there are certain similarities between mod 7 arithmetic and base 7, there are fundamental and essential differences. In the first place, base 7 is a numeration system. (Numeration systems are the actual systems used in writing numbers and numeration systems differ from one another in the way that numbers are named.) Mod 7 is a number system just as the set of integers, rational numbers, etc. are number systems. Number systems differ from one another in the behavior of the objects under discussion.

  Mod 7 arithmetic consists of only a finite set of elements and no number is larger than 6; negative numbers and fractions are not needed. Base 7 consists of an infinite set of elements including negative and fractional numbers.

  Thus, although there are certain similarities (such as using the numerals 0, 1, 2, 3, 4, 5, 6; the addition and multiplication identities, 0 and 1, are the same; many properties such as commutative, associative and distributive properties are valid in both systems), base 7 and mod 7 are formally different entitites.

4 At one time in history, the number "1" was considered to be a prime number. A major reason why the number "1" is no longer considered to be a prime number is because of the Fundamental Theorem of Arithmetic, which states that every composite positive integer can be factored uniquely into a product of primes. If "1" is allowed to be prime, then the uniqueness property is violated. Consider factoring 36 into a product of primes:

$$36 = 2^2 \cdot 3^2 .$$

However, If "1" is considered a prime, then one can write

$$36 = 2^2 \cdot 3^2$$
$$= 2^2 \cdot 3^2 \cdot 1$$
$$= 2^2 \cdot 3^2 \cdot 1^2, \text{ etc.,}$$

and the uniqueness is lost.

5   If the statement means that an even counting number when represented in base ten is a numeral whose last digit is 0, 2, 4, 6, or 8, then the student is correct. However, the numeration system used is important in the question. For example, in base five or in any odd base, $11_{\text{odd base}}$ represents an even counting number.

6   Yes, this student is correct. This question lends itself nicely to an inductive exploration such as given below.

Table 1.9.1 is put up on the blackboard and each student is asked to complete one line of the table. Then you might ask the students what they observe.

TABLE 1.9.1

(1)	(2)	(3)	(4)	(5)	(6)
a	b	GCD (a, b)	LCM (a, b)	$(3) \times (4)$	$a \times b$
1	2				
2	3				
3	6				
4	12				
5	9				
8	16				
8	24				
16	84				
20	90				
30	120				
36	81				
etc.					

Most likely a formal proof that the GCD (a, b) multiplied by the LCM (a, b) equals the product of the two numbers, a and b, is beyond the grasp of your students, but an informal justification such as given below would not be.

Suppose we take $a = 36$ and $b = 162$ and factor each of them into prime representations.

$$36 = 2^2 \cdot 3^2$$
$$162 = 2 \cdot 3^4$$

$$36 \cdot 162 = (2^2 \cdot 3^2)(2 \cdot 3^4) = (2^2 \cdot 3^4)(2 \cdot 3^2)$$
$$= [\text{LCM}(36, 162)] [\text{GCD}(34, 162)]$$

One might then make the formal statement, using loose language, that the GCD takes care of those primes or powers of primes that are common to both numbers, while the LCM takes care of those primes or powers of primes that would be in the union of both numbers. Since in this process all the primes or powers of primes of the numbers are used up, then the result follows.

Problem   Construct a mathematical proof that LCM $(a, b) \cdot$ GCD $(a, b) = a \cdot b$.

7   The symbol "÷" in 4 ÷ 8 usually means a binary operation and the result (in this case) is represented by the fraction $\frac{4}{8}$. The symbol "|" in 4|8 usually means a binary relation and stands for the statement that 4 divides 8 because 8 = 4 · 2.

8   Yes the student is correct. When the number represented by the last three digits is divided by 8, then the possibilities are that the remainders will be 0, 1, 2, 3, 4, 5, 6, 7. If the remainder is 0, then the number is divisible by 8. The only other time that the number is divisible by 4 is the situation in which the remainder is 4; i.e., the number represented by the last three digits is of the form 8k + 4 = 4(2k + 1). Since every other value after the hundreds place is divisible by 4, then the whole number must be divisible by 4.

A1.10   **Numeration Systems**

1   For an answer to this question, read the following article by A.H. Nelson.* Also read:

> Pedersen and Armbruster, "Models for Rational Number Base," *The Mathematics Teacher*, February 1975, p. 113.

INVESTIGATION TO DISCOVERY WITH A NEGATIVE BASE

By ALLYN H. NELSON

Longwood High School
Middle Island, New York

CAN the elements of investigation and discovery that are so exhilarating to the research mathematician have ·the same effect on a high school student? I believe so. In fact, Professor G. Polya says, "A great discovery solves a great problem, but there is a grain of discovery in the solution of any problem. Your problem may be modest; but if it challenges your curiosity and brings into play your inventive faculties, and if you solve it by your own means, you may experience the tension and enjoy the triumph of discovery."[1] The challenge generally is to find a problem or area of investigation that might simulate in some small way the work of the research mathematician, and yet remain within the ability of the secondary student. I believe that an exploration into base negative two offers the student an opportunity to have some of these stimulating and illuminating experiences.

Why base negative two? The answer is very simple—more interesting things happen with base negative two than in other bases, interesting things that are within

---

[1] *How to Solve It* (Garden City: Doubleday Anchor Books, Doubleday & Co., 1957), Preface to the First Printing, p. v.

*From *The Mathematics Teacher*, November 1967, pp. 723-26. Reprinted by permission.

$$\ldots \;(-2)^4 \quad (-2)^3 \quad (-2)^2 \quad (-2)^1 \quad (-2)^0 \;\cdot\; (-2)^{-1} \quad (-2)^{-2} \quad (-2)^{-3} \quad (-2)^{-4} \ldots$$

$$\ldots \;+16 \qquad -8 \qquad +4 \qquad -2 \qquad +1 \;\cdot\; -1/2 \qquad +1/4 \qquad -1/8 \qquad +1/16 \ldots$$

FIGURE 1

the grasp of junior and senior high school students. Aside from two very good articles in THE MATHEMATICS TEACHER[2] of February 1963, which delved into counting and addition in base negative two, I have found nothing to indicate any extensive work done in this area. I am especially indebted to Harry Foxwell, formerly a senior at Longwood High School and presently a student at Franklin and Marshall College, who was the first of my students to really dig into base negative two. He did such an excellent job and his results were so exciting that a paper he did on it won a first-place gold medal in the Long Island Mathematics Fair. Many of the examples and illustrations that follow are taken from the work he did and illustrate vividly the main point of this paper, i.e., base negative two is an excellent topic for student investigation.

The values of the positions in base negative two are shown in Figure 1. The first basic operation is counting, and in base negative two many very fascinating outcomes occur that can be observed by any youngster who has worked with negative numbers.

An example of the first few positive and negative numerals is shown in Table 1.

The patterns that unfold in base negative two numeration can be discovered by most junior high students. In the units place, note the alternating order of one, zero, one, zero, etc., for both the positive and negative numbers. In the second position the pattern is one, one, zero, zero, one, one, etc. The pattern continues, doubling the number of repeating digits each time. Essentially a similar thing happens in base ten, of course, but the pattern is not nearly so evident. Another sig-

[2] Richard D. Twaddle, "A Look at the Base Negative Ten," LVI, 88–90, and Chauncey H. Wells. Jr., "Using a Negative Base for Number Notation," LVI, 91–93.

TABLE 1

POSITIVE		NEGATIVE	
Base Ten	Base (−2)	Base Ten	Base (−2)
1	1	− 1	1 1
2	1 1 0	− 2	1 0
3	1 1 1	− 3	1 1 0 1
4	1 0 0	− 4	1 1 0 0
5	1 0 1	− 5	1 1 1 1
6	1 1 0 1 0	− 6	1 1 1 0
7	1 1 0 1 1	− 7	1 0 0 1
8	1 1 0 0 0	− 8	1 0 0 0
9	1 1 0 0 1	− 9	1 0 1 1
10	1 1 1 1 0	−10	1 0 1 0
11	1 1 1 1 1	−11	1 1 0 1 0 1
12	1 1 1 0 0	−12	1 1 0 1 0 0
13	1 1 1 0 1	−13	1 1 0 1 1 1
14	1 0 0 1 0	−14	1 1 0 1 1 0
15	1 0 0 1 1	−15	1 1 0 0 0 1
16	1 0 0 0 0	−16	1 1 0 0 0 0
17	1 0 0 0 1	−17	1 1 0 0 1 1
18	1 0 1 1 0	−18	1 1 0 0 1 0
19	1 0 1 1 1	−19	1 1 1 1 0 1
20 etc.	1 0 1 0 0	−20 etc.	1 1 1 1 0 0

nificant pattern is the number of digits in the positive numbers and the negative numbers. The positive numbers are represented by numerals with an odd number of digits and the negative numbers are represented by numerals with an even number of digits. A bit of exploration will quickly give the reason for this. The fact that the negative numbers are represented without the need of additional symbols raises some interesting possibilities and also some vexing problems. Explorations into "one-to-one correspondence" and "isomorphism" prove to be interesting for the more advanced student.

The operation of addition is relatively simple, but leads to some new methods. Since most problems in base negative two involve "carrying," the example in Table 2 should illustrate how the system works.

Observe that "carrying" involves the placing of the numeral one in the next two places, rather than in the next one as in positive bases. The reasons are simple to discover upon investigating the system. It is fascinating for a student to

TABLE 2

Base Ten	Base (−2) 1st Carry	Base (−2) 2nd Carry	Base (−2) 3rd Carry	Base (−2) Note*
			1 1	1 1
		1 1	1 1	1 1
	1 1	1 1	1 1	1 1
1→	1→	1→	1→	1
+3→	+1 1 1→	+ 1 1 1→	+ 1 1 1→	1 1 1
4→	0→	0 0→	1 0 0→	0 1 0 0

* Note that the sum of either of the combinations at the right will equal zero. A look into the structure of the system will verify it. This pattern will come in handy later.

$$
\begin{array}{cc}
1\ 1 & 1 \\
+\ \ 1 & +1\ 1 \\
\hline
0 & 0
\end{array}
$$

note here that a number plus its additive inverse will equal zero, although the numerals would seem to indicate differently. It is significant to note that the addition of four ones in one column are equivalent to a single one in the column two places to the left. A look into the structure of the system will quickly verify this.

Subtraction is also a most fascinating

TABLE 3

Base Ten	"Exchange" Base (−2)	"Additive Inverse" Base (−2)	
2	1 1 0→ ~~1 1~~ ¹¹⁰	1 1 0→	1 1 0
− 1	− 1→	− 1→	+ 1 1
1			0 1

operation in base negative two, simply because there are a number of ways of performing it. Examples are found in Tables 3 and 4.

A little study of the examples above will give the reader an insight into the method used in each. It might be well to observe here that the common exchange method ("borrowing") will work only if there is something to "borrow" from. (The

reader might try $4_{ten} - 2_{ten}$ in base negative two to verify it.) The "replacement" method above appears to be unique to a negative base. It would seem that the "additive inverse" and the "equal additions" methods are sounder mathematics than the others.

Multiplication entails only repetitive addition. Once addition has been mastered, multiplication is relatively easy, as indicated in the example below:

$$
\begin{array}{cr}
5 \rightarrow & 1\ 0\ 1 \\
\times\ 2 \rightarrow & \times\ 1\ 1\ 0 \\
\hline
 & 1\ 0\ 1\ 0 \\
 & 1\ 0\ 1 \\
\hline
10 \rightarrow & 1\ 1\ 1\ 1\ 0
\end{array}
$$

The younger student might well find the product of two negative numbers and the product of a positive and a negative of some interest.

A stimulating area of discovery opens up when we attempt division. It will be found that our more sophisticated division algorisms are extremely difficult when working in base negative two, whereas the so-called "modern" method is relatively easy. Using the "modern" method to

TABLE 4

"Replacement" Base (−2)		"Equal Additions" Base (−2)		"Complement" Base (−2)	
1 1 0 →	1 1 0 (with 1 1 carry)	1 1 0 →	1 1 ¹¹⁰	1 1 0 →	1 1 0
− 1 →	− 0	− 1 →	− ₁ ₁ 1	− 1 →	+1 0 0 0 1
	0 1		0 0 1		~~1~~ 0 0 0 1

divide twelve by two, we get:

```
1 1 0 / 1 1 1 0 0
        1 1 0 0 0        1 0 0  →  (+4)
        ─────────
            1 0 0
          1 1 0 0        1 0  →  (−2)
        ─────────
        1 1 0 0 0
        1 1 0 0 0        1 0 0  →  (+4)
        ─────────    ─────────
              0 | 1 1 0 1 0  →  (+6)
```

If we attempt the problem using our more common division algorism, we run into a number of difficulties. Using the problem mentioned above for an example, we get:

```
            1 1
1 1 0 / 1 1 1 0 0
        1 1 0
        ─────
          1 0
        1 1 0
        ─────
        1 0 0
```

At this point we must stop, since the remainder (1 0 0) is larger than the divisor.

```
          1 0 1
1 1 0 / 1 1 1 0 0
        1 1 0
        ─────
          1 0 0
        1 1 0
        ─────
          1 1 0
```

Again a problem, since the remainder is equal to the divisor. Starting at the third position leads nowhere; therefore, we are left with the alternative of trying another. If we start in the second position, we get:

```
            1
1 1 0 / 1 1 1 0 0
        1 1 0
        ─────
        1 1 0 1
```

This time the remainder is a negative number whereas the divisor is positive.

```
        1 1 0 1 0
1 1 0 / 1 1 1 0 0
        1 1 0
        ─────
          1 1 1
          1 1 0
          ─────
            1 1 0
            1 1 0
            ─────
              0 0
```

Even in this step there were some complications that might have been difficult. Rather than continue for a long time, I terminated the problem, since the main idea has been demonstrated sufficiently. This method has been done in a purely mechanical way, but if one stops to think about it, is not this the way most of us do division? A great deal of insight into the system would, of course, enable us to use the more sophisticated algorism above.

Some amazing results are obtained when attempting division of rational numbers. One startling result is the nonuniqueness of expressions of certain rational numbers. Uniqueness is a property of so many mathematical structures that we have a tendency to overlook its importance. In the case of base negative two, the nonuniqueness is, of course, in the representation of certain numbers, and not in the numbers themselves. In base negative two, the rational number $1/111$ ($1/3_{ten}$) can be represented as $0.0101\overline{01}$ or as $1.1010\overline{10}$. A quick check, using the formula for the sum of an infinite geometric sequence, will show that both equal $1/111$. The student investigating base negative two might well note here the distinction between a property of number such as uniqueness and the nonuniqueness noted, which is a property of the system of numeration. It is mystifying to see that $1/111$ ($1/3_{ten}$) is the only "proper" rational number with two ways of expressing it. The proof of this is relatively easy if one observes that the maximum value of any "bicimal" expansion is $.0101\overline{01}$ or $1/111$. The only other way of expressing a "proper" rational is to use "1" along with a negative "bicimal" expansion. The maximum negative bicimal expansion is $.1010\overline{10}$ or $110/110$ ($-2/3_{ten}$), which when combined with "1" is $1.1010\overline{10}$ or $1/111$ ($1/3_{ten}$). The so-called "improper" rationals $100/111$ ($4/3_{ten}$), $11011/111$ ($7/3_{ten}$), $11110/111$ ($10/3_{ten}$), etc., can also be expressed in two ways ($100/111$ is $110.1010\overline{10}$ or $1.0101\overline{01}$). The proof is similar to that above.

It is also possible to express base negative two using scientific notation. For example:

$110000000 = 1.1 \times 10^{11000},$ $[11000 = 8_{ten}]$

$0.000000011 = 1.1 \times 10^{1000},$ $[1000 = -8_{ten}]$

An attempt to construct logarithms with negative two as a base leads to some rather interesting events. We run into discontinuities, nonexistence, and the rather startling result of a real value for the logarithm of a pure imaginary. E.g.,

$\text{Log}_{(-2)} 2i \sqrt{2} = 3/2$ since $(-2)^{3/2} = 2i \sqrt{2}.$

An example of nonexistence is

$$\text{Log}_{(-2)} 8 = ?$$

I am sure that investigations by others will lead to many more discoveries, maybe something of value about base negative two, but if these considerations do nothing more than challenge curiosity, this paper will have been of value. Investigation into prime numbers and repeating decimals with base negative two will lead students to distinguish between a property of number (prime) and a property of the system of numeration, such as terminating and nonterminating decimals (or "bicimals"). Many explorations will yield nothing of value, but the student will gain a more mature insight into the structure of mathematics and—just as important—have some fun in doing so.

2   There are various algorithms that can be employed to do the problem. One algorithm is given below and other algorithms, plus the one presented here, can be found in the references listed.

The algorithm presented is a generalization of a common algorithm that is used to change a numeral in base ten into a numeral in some other base.

Change 125_{ten} into a numeral in base seven.

$$
\begin{array}{rl}
7 \underline{|\ 125} & \quad 6 \\
7 \underline{|\ 17} & \quad 3 \\
7 \underline{|\ 2} & \quad 2 \\
0 &
\end{array}
\tag{1}
$$

Thus $125_{ten} = 236_{seven}.$

Change 243_{seven} into a numeral in base three.

$$
\begin{array}{rl}
3 \underline{|\quad 243_{seven}} & \quad 0 \\
3 \underline{|\quad 61_{seven}} & \quad 1 \\
3 \underline{|\quad 20_{seven}} & \quad 2 \\
3 \underline{|\quad 4_{seven}} & \quad 1 \\
3 \underline{|\ 1_{seven}} & \quad 1
\end{array}
\tag{2}
$$

Thus $243_{seven} = 11210_{three}.$

The procedure in (2) is the same as the procedure in (1) except that all computations in (2) are in base seven.

It might be instructive to look at the following example, which is a little more complicated.

Change 11210_{three} into a numeral in base seven.

Since all computations are to be done in base three, then the first step is to rewrite 7 in base three as 21.

$$
\begin{array}{r|l}
21_{three} & 11210_{three} \\
21 & \overline{200_{three}} \\
21 & \overline{2_{three}} \\
& 0
\end{array}
$$

$$10_{three} = 3_{seven}$$
$$11_{three} = 4_{seven}$$
$$2 \quad = 2_{seven}$$

Thus $11210_{three} = 243_{seven}$.

Thus, if one is changing a numeral in base x into a numeral in base y, then the procedure is to divide y (expressed in base x) into the numeral in base x where all computations are in base x.

Additional algorithms can be found in the references listed below.

(1)   M.J. Barrett, "A method for changing numerals in certain nondecimal bases to numerals in other certain nondecimal bases, directly." *The Arithmetic Teacher*, May 1968, pp. 453–54.

(2)   James Husk, "Changing bases without using base ten." *The Arithmetic Teacher*, May 1968, pp. 461-62.

(3)   John Lee, "Changing bases by direct computation." *The Mathematics Teacher*, December 1972, pp. 752-53.

(4)   Joe Smith, "A method for converting from one nondecimal base to another." *The Arithmetic Teacher*, April 1968, pp. 344-46.

3   For an answer to this question, read the following article by Charles Brumfiel.* Also read:

Boyd Henry, "Zero, the Troublemaker," *The Arithmetic Teacher*, May 1969, p. 365.

Zero is highly overrated

CHARLES BRUMFIEL

University of Michigan, Ann Arbor, Michigan

Mr. Brumfiel is a professor in the mathematics department at the University of Michigan.
He is well known to teachers of mathematics through the Ball State Experimental Project.

It is instructive to consider a place value system without a zero. We modify our base ten system by writing t for ten and agreeing to count

1, 2, 3, 4, 5, 6, 7, 8, 9, t, 11, 12, . . . , 19, 1t, 21, . . . , 9t, t1, . . . , tt, 111, 112, ...

Notice that one hundred is written as 9t (nine tens and ten ones). The symbol tt represents ten tens and ten ones, or one hundred ten. If a "t" does not occur in a number symbol the meaning of the symbol is the familiar one: 342 is still

3 hundreds + 4 tens + 2 ones.

In expanded notation, and using t for ten,

*From *The Arithmetic Teacher*, May 1967, pp. 377-78. Reprinted by permission.

we have

$$342 = 3 \cdot t^2 + 4 \cdot t + 2.$$

Any "old-fashioned" number symbol can be easily replaced by a symbol in this new notation. The reasoning is no more difficult than that used when we "borrow" in subtraction. We are accustomed to think of 200 as

$$100 + 90 + 10$$

and we have

Old Symbol		New Symbol
200	=	19*t*.

The reader should verify several relationships like the following:

Symbol in Base Ten with Zero		Symbol in Base Ten without Zero
40	=	3*t*.
5,000	=	499*t*.
70,302	=	6*t*2*t*2.

Let's take a look at computation in this numeration system. First we should make sure that we really can count—

After 99	comes 9*t*.
After 3*tt*	comes 411.
Before 371	comes 36*t*.
After *tttt*	comes 11,111.
Before 74,111	comes 73*ttt*.

Addition and subtraction techniques in this numeration system require very little modification of our usual habits. We "carry" and "borrow" tens, hundreds, etc., just as before. However, we can now record ten units in any place and we *must* record at least one in each place.

43	87	*t*65	1*ttt*
+ 27	+ 23	+ 844	+ *ttt*
6*t*	*tt*	18*t*9	321*t*

65	511	432.
− 25	− 24*t*	− *tt*
3*t*	261	322

Notice that in the first subtraction problem we had to borrow one of the 6 tens since we can't record the difference 5 − 5.

A subtraction problem like

$$3111$$
$$-\ \ ttt$$

deserves a little special thought. The

reader should enjoy testing his understanding by seeing how quickly he can produce the answer.

As preparation for multiplication we should first practice counting by tens.

$$t, \quad 1t, \quad 2t, \quad \ldots, \quad 14t, \ldots$$
$$1 \cdot t, \quad 2 \cdot t, \quad 3 \cdot t, \ldots, 15 \cdot t, \ldots$$

Notice that 15 · *t* or fifteen tens is fourteen tens and ten ones,

$$15 \cdot t = 14t.$$

The rule for multiplying by ten should be clear: 7652 tens is 7651 tens + 1 ten.

$$7652 \cdot t = 7651t.$$

Multiplying by any number less than *t* is straightforward.

25	36	42*t*
2	5	7
4*t*	17*t*	29*tt*

Now that we can multiply by *t* and by any number less than *t* we can combine these skills and work more complicated multiplication problems. Since $12 = t + 2$ we can work the multiplication problem below as shown.

$$32t$$
$$12$$
$$*65t = 2 \cdot 32t.$$
$$329t = t \cdot 32t.$$
$$395t$$

For a product like 35 · 346 we have

$$35 \cdot 346 = (3 \cdot t + 5) \cdot 346.$$
$$= 3 \cdot t \cdot 346 + 5 \cdot 346.$$

The work is shown below. On the side we calculate 3 · *t* · 346.

346		345*t* = *t* · 346
35		3
172*t* = 5 · 346		
*t*37*t* = 3 · *t* · 346		*t*37*t* = 3 · *t* · 346.
11 *ttt* = (3*t* + 5) · 346.		

For larger multipliers we must multiply repeatedly by *t*.

---

* There are excellent opportunities to "cheat" here. You can think: "32*t* is really 330 and 2 · 330 is 660. I'll write this as 65*t*."

4 t2
326

$$2\,t12 = 6 \cdot 4\,t2$$
$$9\,t3\,t = 2 \cdot t \cdot 4\,t2$$
$$14\,t59\,t = 3 \cdot t^2 \cdot 4\,t2$$

$$163{,}652 = (3\,t^2 + 2\,t + 6) \cdot 4\,t2.$$

The second and third partial products are computed thus:

$4\,t1\,t = t \cdot 4\,t2$	$4\,t1\,t = t \cdot 4\,t2$
2	$4\,t19\,t = t^2 \cdot 4\,t2$
$9\,t3\,t = 2 \cdot t \cdot 4\,t2$	3
	$14\,t59\,t = 3\,t^2 \cdot 4\,t2.$

Multiplication by ten and by powers of ten is so simple we could do the later calculations mentally. We wouldn't think of permitting our students to use such a crutch in multiplying (would we?).

The reader is urged to practice multiplication until he can abandon the crutch. Check the examples below.

```
  34            513
  25            286
  --            --
 16 t          2 t78
 67 t          3 t t3 t
  --           t259 t
 84 t           --
            146,718
```

A division example is worked below by a repeated subtraction process.

$$32\overline{)45\,t8}$$
$$319\,t = t^2 \cdot 32$$
$$\overline{13\,t8}$$
$$127\,t = 4 \cdot t \cdot 32$$
$$\overline{128}$$
$$128 = 4 \cdot 32.$$

The quotient is $1 \cdot t^2 + 4 \cdot t + 4 = 144$.

The reader might find the following an interesting exercise. Construct a base-three system without zero. It is natural to use the symbols 1, 2, 3, and count

1, 2, 3, 11, 12, 13, 21, 22, 23, 31, 32, 33, 111, 112, . . .

but any three distinguishable symbols will do as well. Formulate and work some problems in this notation.

In conclusion, we remark that we had always considered the symbol for zero an essential feature of any place value system. Clearly, this is not the case. Zero is indeed highly overrated. It isn't even needed as a placeholder!

4   It really does not make any difference since the answer would be the same in any case. If the student multiplies 3 × 6 to get 18, adds 2 to get 20 (all in base ten) and then converts to base twelve, the student would get 18 in base twelve. This is the same answer the student would get working strictly in base twelve. In general, whether one works directly in the given base or works in base ten and then converts, the same answer would be obtained in either case.

5   For an answer to this question, read the following article by Norman Woo.* Also read:

   J. Jordan, "Small-Digit Representation of Real Numbers," *The Mathematics Teacher*, January 1968, p. 36.

*From *The Mathematics Teacher*, February 1973, pp. 169-70. Reprinted by permission.

A GENERALIZED BASE FOR INTEGERS

By **NORMAN WOO**

California State University at Fresno
Fresno, California

ONE of the most important notations in mathematics, the positional system of notation of numbers, seems to have been invented in India by the Hindus. It was certainly transmitted to the Western world by the Arabs in about the eighth century A.D. At first the Hindu-Arabic system of notation was of interest only in the marketplace, but eventually it came to be of interest to mathematicians, and it is still the object of considerable study.

It is well known that the set of nonnegative integers can be represented by selecting an integer, $n > 1$, as a base. The digits $0, 1, 2, 3, \ldots, n - 1$ are then used, and with these any nonnegative integer m can be uniquely represented as

$$m = a_t n^t + a_{t-1} n^{t-1} + \cdots + a_1 n^1 + a_0$$

where are a_j's are digits.

Some effort was made a few years ago to study representations of integers when the base was $n < -1$. In particular, negative two was suggested by N. G. De Bruijn (1950) and by Chauncey H. Wells, Jr. (1963), and then negative ten by Richard D. Twaddle (1963). The digits used in the representation for base negative two were 0 and 1; 0, 1, 2, 3, 4, 5, 6, 7, 8, 9 were used in the representation for base negative ten. James Jordan (1968) generalized these concepts of representation to an arbitrary base h (a positive or negative integer) and chose as the digits the integers x where

$$-\frac{|h|}{2} < x \leq \frac{|h|}{2}.$$

However, he did not give the complete details of the representation for any arbitrary integer n. The purpose of this paper is to give some examples to show how one deals with the actual representation.

For example, if we take $h = 16$ as a base, then the digits for representation would be taken from the set

$$A = \{-7, -6, -5, -4, -3, -2, -1,$$
$$0, 1, 2, 3, 4, 5, 6, 7, 8\}.$$

In order to avoid any confusion between the subtraction of an integer n and the negative integer n used in the representation, we adopt the following notation for the set

$$A = \{\bar{7}, \bar{6}, \bar{5}, \bar{4}, \bar{3}, \bar{2}, \bar{1},$$
$$0, 1, 2, 3, 4, 5, 6, 7, 8\}.$$

If we want to express a number 1769 in base 16, we apply the division algorithm:

$$1769 = 110(16) + 9.$$

But 9 is not an element of set A. However, 9 can be expressed in the following form:

$$9 = 1(16) + (\bar{7}).$$

Therefore,

$$1769 = 110(16) + 1(16) + (\bar{7})$$
$$= 111(16) + (\bar{7}).$$

Furthermore,

$$111 = 7(16) + (\bar{1}).$$

Finally, we have

$$1769 = [7(16) + (\bar{1})](16) + (\bar{7})$$
$$= 7(16)^2 + \bar{1}(16) + (\bar{7}).$$

Or,

$$1769 = 7\bar{1}\bar{7} \text{ in base 16.}$$

Let us now express an integer in a negative base. For example, if $h = -7$, the corresponding set of digits would be

$$B = \{\bar{3}, \bar{2}, \bar{1}, 0, 1, 2, 3\}.$$

If we want to express the number 173 in this base, we have

$$173 = (-25)(-7) + (\bar{2})$$
$$-25 = (4)(-7) + (3)$$
$$4 = (-1)(-7) + (\bar{3}).$$

Finally,

$$173 = ([(-1)(-7) + (-3)](-7)$$
$$+ (3))(-7) + (\bar{2})$$
$$= ((\bar{1})(-7)^2 + (\bar{3})(-7)$$
$$+ (3))(-7) + (2)$$
$$= (\bar{1})(-7)^3 + (\bar{3})(-7)^2$$
$$+ (3)(-7) + (\bar{2})$$
$$= \bar{1}3\bar{3}\bar{2} \text{ in base } -7.$$

Note that the base and its digits are very much interrelated with each other. In fact, any integer h, other than $1, 0, -1$, can be used as a base if we select its digits x such that

$$-\frac{|h|}{2} < x \le \frac{|h|}{2}.$$

The purpose of this paper is not to encourage students to adopt "nonten" bases, but rather to promote the understanding of the base ten system. It is hoped that work with bases other than ten will increase understanding as well as improve skills for both secondary school mathematics teachers and students.

REFERENCES

De Bruijn, N. G. "On Bases for the Set of Integers." *Publication Mathematics Debrecen* 1 (1950) : 232–42.

Jordan, James H. "Small-digit Representation of Real Numbers." MATHEMATICS TEACHER 61 (January 1968) : 36–38.

Twaddle, Richard D. "A Look at Base Negative Ten." MATHEMATICS TEACHER 56 (February 1963) : 88–90.

Wells, Chauncey H., Jr. "Using a Negative Base for Number Notation." MATHEMATICS TEACHER 56 (February 1963) : 91–93.

6   The Roman numeration system essentially is an additive system with subtractive and multiplicative features. If symbols decrease in value from left to right, then their values are added. If a symbol has a smaller value than a symbol on the right, then the first symbol is subtracted from the second symbol.

Also, the Romans invented their system with the restriction that no more than two symbols were involved in the subtractive feature and not more than three identical symbols were used in succession. The first feature was used probably to avoid ambiguity in expression. For example, what would IVX represent? In one case, IVX could mean I(VX) = I(V) = 5 − 1 = 4. In another case, IVX could mean (IV)X = 10 − 4 = 6. Since the Romans did not use parenthesis, which answer would be the correct one? The second feature was probably used for economy in order to use fewer symbols.

Thus, in the student's question, using the subtractive features, IXX would represent X − (IX) = 10 − 9 = 1, not 19.

7   Roman fractions were used in base twelve. Special symbols and words were used for

$$\frac{1}{12}, \frac{2}{12}, \dots, \frac{11}{12}, \frac{1}{24}, \frac{1}{36}, \frac{1}{48}, \dots$$

Base twelve was used probably because of the relation of the lunar month to the year. The Roman unit of weight was the "As" which weighed one pound and was divided into 12 uniciae or "ounces." Successive parts were divided into halves and thus fractional units of 12ths, 24ths, etc. were involved. The Romans also used an abacus for computation. The abacus had 2 grooves for fractions. One groove measured units of twelve and the second groove represented fractions of 24ths, 36ths, etc.

8 Johnny is correct in trying to use as few symbols as possible, and he is doing some good thinking. However, he is violating a condition of the Roman numeration system, which states that no more than two symbols are to be involved in the subtractive feature of this numeration system. (See discussion in Answer 6 of this section for further information.)

9 If 148 was written as CIIL, then this notation would violate the condition that no more than two symbols be involved in the subtractive feature of the Roman numeration system. (See discussion in Answer 6 for further information.)

A1.11   *Percent*

1 On the surface it looks like the student has the correct answer but the wrong multiplication. It seems like the student was solving the problem of finding 50% of 28. You would probably want to question him to find out what he was doing. In any case, an unexpected situation has occurred, which an alert teacher might want to explore. In this particular case, it seems as if 28% of 50 is equal to 50% of 28. The question that immediately comes to mind is the following: "Is x% of y equal to y% of x?" A teaching strategy that one might use in this case is to ask each student to make up five different problems on his own and test the above hypothesis. After this exploratory work is completed, you might ask if anyone found a case that does not work. Assuming that each student has multiplied correctly, the answer would be no. Thus it seems as if the above statement is true, and you might ask if anyone can devise a proof of the above hypothesis. Not only do students get meaningful practice using this strategy, but they also get involved in a neat discovery situation.

A proof of the statement that x% of y is equal to y% of x might run along the following lines:

$$x\% \text{ of } y = \frac{x}{100} \cdot y = \frac{x \cdot y}{100} = \frac{y \cdot x}{100} = \frac{y}{100} \cdot x = y\% \text{ of } x.$$

2 In effect one is paying a certain amount of money for the privilege of borrowing money; i.e., one is really *buying* money. Just as the same brand of a product such as a television set has different prices in different stores, so the buying of money from different companies has different prices. There are different procedures that various finance agencies use to figure out how much they will charge for borrowing money such as the time payment plan, revolving charges, unpaid balances, etc. It might be interesting to have the students find out about these various methods and discuss them in class.

3 The *P*th percentile of a group of scores is defined to be the point below which *P* percent of the scores are. Thus if the 100th percentile of a group of scores was calculated, what would this point be and what information would it give? For example, suppose that the following represent scores received by a group of students on a given test:

25 40 70 85 90 92.

What would be the 100th percentile of this group of scores: 93, 92.5, 94, 95, etc.? In fact, any real number greater than 92 would be the 100th percentile. What information does this give someone? All that this really says is that all of the scores are below a certain point, but one could readily get this information by looking at the highest score. Thus no 100th percentile is computed.

4   The student is, of course, using simple interest for one year and must realize that the mortgage stretches over a longer period of time, usually 20 or 30 years. In this case only part of the debt is paid off (a small part) during the first year; thus interest is computed on the amount of money still owed. The usual home mortgage requires that a person make equal monthly payments, part of which is used for paying the interest on the outstanding debt and part of which is applied to reducing the outstanding debt. For figuring out the mortgage payments mathematically, one has to use a geometric series. Whether a teacher should go into a detailed explanation of how a mortgage is actually determined at this level is doubtful. However, if one wanted to delve into such an explanation, the following paper shows how this is done (C. Sloyer, "Fantastiks of Mathematiks").

THAT #%&*? MORTGAGE PAYMENT
Mathematics Used: Algebra, Geometric Series

Suppose that an individual obtains a $30,000 mortgage at an interest rate of 6% for a period of 20 years. (This interest rate is not very realistic in 1976.) Each month, the individual is to make a payment of P dollars (the same each month). We show here how to determine the value of the number P.

At the end of the first month, the individual pays P dollars (the first payment). A part of this, say P_1, is on the principal, while $\frac{.06}{12}(30,000) = .005(30,000) = 150$ is for interest. We thus see that $P > \$150$. We write

$$P = \underbrace{P_1}_{\substack{\text{on} \\ \text{principal}}} + \underbrace{(30,000).005.}_{\substack{\text{on} \\ \text{interest}}} \tag{1}$$

In order to simplify what follows, let $i = .005$, so that (1) becomes

$$P = P_1 + (30,000)i. \tag{2}$$

At the end of the second month, the payment P is P_2 dollars on the principal plus interest on the remaining principal $30,000 - P_1$. Thus,

$$P = P_2 + (30,000 - P_1)i. \tag{3}$$

Continuing, at the end of the third month, we have

$$P = P_3 + (30,000 - P_1 - P_2)i, \tag{4}$$

and at the end of the fourth month

$$P = P_4 + (30,000 - P_1 - P_2 - P_3)i. \tag{5}$$

In general, at the end of month k, we have

$$P = P_k + (30,000 - P_1 - P_2 - \cdots - P_{k-1})i. \tag{6}$$

Now, from (2) and (3), we have

$$P_1 + (30,000)i = P_2 + (30,000 - P_1)i$$

or

$$P_2 = P_1 (1 + i). \tag{7}$$

From (3) and (4), we have

$$P_2 + (30,000 - P_1)i = P_3 + (30,000) - P_1 - P_2)i$$

or

$$P_3 = P_2 (1 + i),$$

which, together with (7), yields

$$P_3 = P_1 (1 + i)^2. \tag{8}$$

From (4) and (5), we have

$$P_4 = P_3 (1 + i),$$

which, together with (8), yields

$$P_4 = P_1 (1 + i)^3. \tag{9}$$

Summarizing, we see

$$\left. \begin{array}{l} P_1 \\ P_2 = P_1 (1 + i) \\ P_3 = P_1 (1 + i)^2 \\ P_4 = P_1 (1 + i)^3 \\ \vdots \end{array} \right\} = P \tag{10}$$

This pattern continues (the student can show this by induction) so that

$$P_k = P_1 (1 \pm i)^{k - 1}.$$

Now, P_1, P_2, P_3, etc. are payments on the principal and so

$$P_1 + P_2 + P_3 + \cdots + P_{240} = 30,000$$

or, using the summary in (10) and the general term, we have

$$P_1 + P_1 (1 + i) + P_1 (1 + i)^2 + \cdots + P_1 (1 + i)^{239} = 30,000.$$

The left hand side of the above equation is a geometric series. Using the formula for the sum of such series, we have

$$\frac{P_1 [(1 + i)^{240} - 1]}{(1 + i) - 1} = 30,000 \qquad \text{or} \qquad P_1 = \frac{(30,000)i}{(1 + i)^{240} - 1}.$$

Using interest tables, logarithms, or a calculator, one obtains

$$P_1 = 64.93 \text{ (to the nearest cent)}.$$

So that (from (1)) we have

$$P = 64.93 + 150 \qquad \text{or} \qquad P = \$214.93.$$

Problem Determine the monthly payments on a $40,000 mortgage at an interest rate of 9% for a period of 25 years.

5   The method that this student is using is a round about but correct way of doing this problem. The student should be commended for devising this unusual method, assuming, of course, that she understands what has been done. You would also want to know why she used this method and then show her the standard way of doing the problem, which involves less work and less chance of error.

6   This is a common error; one way of helping the student is:

$$\frac{1}{10}\% = \frac{1}{10} \text{ of one percent, i.e., } \frac{1}{10} \cdot (1\%).$$

Since $1\% = \frac{1}{100}$, then

$$\frac{1}{10} \cdot (1\%) = \frac{1}{10} \cdot \frac{1}{100} = \frac{1}{1000}.$$

Thus $\frac{1}{10}\%$ of 50 is

$$\frac{1}{1000} \cdot 50 = \frac{50}{1000} = .05.$$

A1.12   Sets

1   The student is correct. Either $A \subseteq B$ or $A \nsubseteq B$. If $A \nsubseteq B$, then A must contain at least one element that is not in B. The student is saying that this is not the case. Therefore, $A \nsubseteq B$ cannot happen, and thus A must be a subset of B.

2   The student is incorrect. Probably the best way to convince the student is to make the analogy that the empty set is similar to an empty paper bag. Thus $\{\emptyset\}$ would be classified as an empty paper bag inside another empty paper bag. Thus the second paper bag contains something inside it — another empty paper bag.

3   For an answer to this question, read:

(1)   I. Feinstein, "Sets: A Pandora's Box?", *School Science and Mathematics*, June 1973, pp. 495-500.

(2)   Geddes and Lipsey, "The Hazards of Sets," *The Mathematics Teacher*, October 1969, p. 454.

4   The student is incorrect, but he does have the correct idea, that A would have to be equal to B. However, the main difficulty that the student has here is with the notation $A \subseteq B$. This notation means A is either a proper subset of B *or* A is equal to B. Since the last alternative is certainly the case in this situation, then the notation $A \subseteq B$ may be used.

5   The student is correct in both the method used and the answer given. The student is intuitively using the well-known formula:

$$n(A \cup B \cup C) = n(A) + n(B) + n(C) - n(A \cap B) - n(A \cap C)$$
$$- n(B \cap C) + n(A \cap B \cap C)$$

where n(S) is the number of elements in set S. Thus,

n(A ∪ B ∪ C) = (28 + 23 + 23) − (12 + 8 + 11) + 5
n(A ∪ B ∪ C) = 74 − 26
n(A ∪ B ∪ C) = 48.

A1.13   *Square Root*

1   For an answer to this question, read:

John G. Frederiksen, "Square Root +," *The Arithmetic Teacher*, November 1969, p. 549-55.

Also consult Answer 7 in Section A2.15.

2   There are two square roots of 25, 5 and −5. The symbol $\sqrt{25}$ is reserved for the positive square root, and $-\sqrt{25}$ is used for the negative square root.

A1.14   *Trigonometry*

1   This problem involves an error on the part of the teacher in drawing the diagram. According to the diagram

$$\sin 20° = \frac{12}{20} = .6.$$

However, since sin 20° is approximately .342, the diagram is incorrect. A correct diagram is shown in Figure 1.14.1.

FIGURE 1.14.1

2 Algebra I

QUESTIONS

Q2.1 Absolute Value

1 A student asks, "Why isn't y = |x| an equation that can be represented as a line, since each term is a monomial of degree one?" How do you reply?

2 A ninth grade student gives the following definition of absolute value:

|x| = x   if x ⩾ 0.
|x| = ⁻x   if x < 0.

Comment on her definition.

3 A student asks, "Why aren't the following equal?"

|x + y| = 5.
|x| + |y| = 5.

How do you respond?

4 How would you answer if a student asks, "What are some other uses for absolute value besides keeping distance positive?"

Q2.2 Cancellation

1 While studying algebraic fractions, a student gets to this point in a simplification problem:

$$\frac{x + 5(a + b)}{a + b}.$$

The student says this is equal to x + 5. How do you deal with this student's reasoning?

2   A student hands in the following work.

$$\frac{x+6}{2} = \frac{x + \overset{3}{\cancel{6}}}{\cancel{2}} = x + 3.$$

When the student asks us why he can't cancel the 2 into the 6, how would you answer him?

3   A tenth grade student hands in the following work.

$$\frac{x^{\cancel{2}} - y^{\cancel{2}}}{x + y} = x - y.$$

The student wants to know why her method is wrong. How would you answer?

4   You ask the students to simplify $\dfrac{x^2 - 9}{x - 3}$. One student does the following:

$$\frac{x^2 - 9}{x - 3} = \frac{x^{\cancel{2}} - 9}{\cancel{x} - 3} = \frac{x - 9}{-3} = \frac{x + 9}{+3} = \frac{x + \overset{3}{\cancel{9}}}{\cancel{3}} = x + 3.$$

Is the student correct? Will his method work all the time?

5   You ask the students to simplify $\dfrac{1}{x} + \dfrac{1}{x}$. A student writes

$$\frac{1}{x} + \frac{1}{x} = 2.$$

What is this student's problem?

6   A student asks you if $\sqrt{a^2 + b^2} = a + b$? How do you respond?

7   A student is evaluating the expression

$$\frac{3^2 + 7^2}{\left(\dfrac{58}{10}\right)^2} ,$$

and the student does the following:

$$\frac{3^{\cancel{2}} + 7^{\cancel{2}}}{\left(\dfrac{58}{10}\right)^{\cancel{2}}} = \frac{10}{\left(\dfrac{58}{10}\right)} = \frac{100}{58}.$$

Which is the correct answer? How would you help this student?

8   A student is asked to simplify the following:

$$\frac{x + \dfrac{1}{x}}{x - \dfrac{1}{x}} .$$

His work is: $\dfrac{\cancel{x} + \dfrac{1}{\cancel{x}}}{\cancel{x} - \dfrac{1}{\cancel{x}}} = \dfrac{1}{-1} = -1.$ How would you help this student?

Q2.3   **Decimals and Percent**

1   A student who was told that .999... = 1 says, "If .999... = 1, then you should be able to change $\frac{9}{9}$ to .999... by dividing the denominator into the numerator. But $9\overline{)9.00}$ = 1.00 not .999..." Can you show the student how $9\overline{)9.00}$ equals .999... and explain why you can do that?

2   A student hands in the following work.

$$n\% = \frac{n}{100} = 0.0n.$$

Is the student correct?

Q2.4   *Equations, Solving Equations, Equivalence*

1   While solving the equation,

$$\frac{x}{x-1} = 1 + \frac{1}{x-1} ,$$

a student gets down to the part where x = x and x ≠ 1. The student says that he doesn't know where to go from here. How would you help this student?

2   A student solves $\frac{3}{8} = \frac{x+2}{16}$ in the following way.

$$\frac{3-2}{8-2} = \frac{x+2-2}{16-2}$$

$$\frac{1}{6} = \frac{x}{14}$$

$$6x = 14$$

$$x = \frac{14}{6} .$$

Is the student's reasoning correct?

3   A student hands in the following solution to this problem. "Solve the following equation by factoring.

$$4x^2 - 23x + 15 = 0."$$

$$4x^2 - 23x + 15 = 0$$

$$\dot{x}^2 - 23\dot{x} + 60 = 0$$

$$(\dot{x} - 20)(\dot{x} - 3) = 0$$

$$\dot{x} = 20 \quad \text{or} \quad \dot{x} = 3.$$

Therefore x = 20/4 = 5 or x = 3/4.   Is this method correct?

4   A student asks you if every equation of a line is a first degree equation in x and y. What is your response?

5   You are asked: "What is the difference between an open phrase and an open equation?" What do you tell this student?

6   You ask your students to solve the equation $x/7 = 3$. One of your students raises his hand and says that it is impossible to do this problem because the domain of the variable has not been specified. What is your response?

7   A student asks you if x/x and $(x - 3)/(x - 3)$ are equivalent expressions. What is your response?

8   The students in your class are asked to solve the following problem. "Find the roots of $x^3 = 2x^2 + 8x$." One student does the following work.

$$x^3 = 2x^2 + 8x$$
$$x^2 - 2x - 8 = 0$$
$$(x - 4)(x + 2) = 0$$
$$x = 4 \quad \text{or} \quad x = -2$$
$$x \in \{4, -2\}.$$

Is the student correct?

Q2.5   *Exponents*

1   In your ninth grade class, a student hands in the following solution. "$(a + b)^2 = a^2 + b^2$ because, except for the operation being different, this problem is just like $(a \cdot b)^2$, which is equal to $a^2 \cdot b^2$. Therefore, it follows that $(a + b)^2 = a^2 + b^2$." How would you help this student?

2   A student asks, "Can you change a positive exponent to a negative one by taking the reciprocal of the base? Does $2^{2/3} = (1/2)^{-2/3}$?" How do you reply?

3   A student asks, "Why isn't $2^5 \cdot 2^{-5} = 4^0 = 1$?" How do you reply?

4   A student asks you if multiples of a number under addition are related to powers of a number under multiplication. How do you respond?

5   You are asked: "How would you evaluate the expression 2^{3^2}? Is it $(8)^2 = 64$ or $2^9 = 512$?" How would you reply?

6   You ask the class whether they would rather have your annual salary of $10,000 or would they like to have the total amount of money they would get in the following way: one cent on the first day, two cents on the second day, four cents on the third day, eight cents on the fourth day, etc. for thirty days. The class chooses your salary, and then you proceed to tell them that from a computer you determined that they would have received $10,737,400 by the other method. However, one student says that the computer is wrong and shows you the following work. "We would have received 2^{30} cents. Now, $2^5 = 32$, and therefore $(2^5)^2 = \$10.24$.

Thus $2^{30} = (10.24)^3$, which is about $1004.86." Who is correct, the computer or the student?

Q2.6   *Factoring and Factors*

1   A student says that $3a - 2a = 1$. How would you help him?

2   A student is trying to factor $y^2 - 2xy + x^2 - w^2$. The student's work is as follows:
$$(y - x)^2 - w^2 = (y - x - w)(y - x + w).$$

However, another student rewrites the problem as $x^2 - 2xy + y^2 - w^2$, and the work is as follows:
$$(x - y)^2 - w^2 = (x - y - w)(x - y + w).$$

Which way is correct?

3   You are teaching factoring of quadratic polynomials. A student asks, "Is there any other way, other than trial and error?" How would you answer this student?

4   You have given your students a quiz on factoring polynomials. After grading the quiz and handing it back to the class, a number of students complain that you should not have marked (c) wrong in the following problem.

Factor the polynomials listed below.

(a) $x^2 - y^2$ (b) $9y^2 - 25x^2$ (c) $3x + 8$

The work in (c) is: $3x + 8 = 3\left(x + \dfrac{8}{3}\right)$. What is your reply.

5   A student asks you if zero is considered a factor of any number. What is your reply?

6   A student hands in the following work for the following problem.

"Solve: $x^2 - 14x + 24 = 3$."
$$(x - 12)(x - 2) = 3$$
$$(x - 12)(x - 2) = 3 \cdot 1$$
$$x - 12 = 3 \quad \text{or} \quad x - 2 = 1$$
$$x = 15 \quad\quad x = 3$$
$$x \in \{3, 15\}.$$

Is the student correct?

7   A student asks, "Is it possible to factor a trinomial (when it can be factored) by an exact method rather than the usual trial and error method?" How would you respond?

8   A student asks, "Why is this procedure called *completing the square*; a square is a geometric shape?" How do you reply?

Q2.7 *Functions and Relations*

1 A student asks you if all linear functions are direct variations. What is your response?

2 A student suddenly smiles and makes the following assertion: "Addition, subtraction, multiplication, and division are all examples of functions, aren't they?" What response do you give?

3 A student says, "The function $f(x) = 3x + 2$ is a linear function." Do you agree?

4 You are asked if equation and function mean the same thing. What is your reply?

5 You ask your class the following question. "What is the relation between A X B and B X A when A and B are arbitrary sets?" One student says that it is an illustration of the symmetric property of equality because if $(a, b) \in A \times B$, then $(b, a) \in B \times A$. Do you agree?

Q2.8 *Graphs*

1 You give your students the following problem. Graph $x = 3$. One student hands in the following work.

Another student hands in the work below.

Which student is correct?

2 You are teaching the distance formula to your class, and a student asks, "Suppose that the coordinate axes are not perpendicular but they form some other angle (i.e., oblique axes), say, 60°. How would you find the distance between points in this system?" How would you respond?

3 While studying a unit on the graphs of straight lines, a student asks you if having the slope zero means the same thing as having no slope. What is your response?

Q2.9   Inequalities

1 You solve $3x + 3 < x + 5$ over the set of integers and come out with $x < 1$. A student asks, "How would you check this problem like you do in an equation?" What is your response?

2 A student asks, "How do I know whether the solution of an inequality such as an absolute value inequality is the union or the intersection of the individual solution sets of each part?" How do you respond?

3 "When we write $a \leqslant b$, we mean that a is less than b *or* a is equal to b, but when we write $a \not\leqslant b$, you say that this means that a is not less than b *and* a is not equal to b. I don't understand why it changes from *or* to *and*?" How do you respond to this student?

4 While studying a unit on inequalities, a student asks you if it is true that if $a > b$ and $c > d$, then $a - c > b - d$. What is your response?

5 A student asks you if it is mathematically correct to use $a \lessgtr b$ to mean a is less than b or a is greater than b. What is your response?

6 A student asks you if it is possible to use the symbolism $6 > -3 < 1$ for the idea that 6 is greater than -3 and -3 is less than 1. How do you reply?

Q2.10   Logic and Proof

1 You class is trying to prove the following theorem. "For all real numbers b and c, $(b + c) + (-c) = b$." The proof is as follows:

Statement	Reasons
(1) b and c are real numbers	Hypothesis
(2) b + c is a real number	Closure for addition axiom
(3) −c is a real number	Axiom of additive inverse
(4) $(b + c) + (-c) = b + [c + (-c)]$	Associative axiom of addition
(5) $c + (-c) = 0$	Axiom of additive inverses
(6) $b + [c + (-c)] = b + 0$	Substitution principle
(7) $b + 0 = b$	Addition axiom of 0
(8) $b + [c + (-c)] = b$	Transitive property of equality

At this time, one student raises his hand and says that he disagrees with the reason given in statement (8). He says that the reason should be the substitution principle. What do you think?

2 A ninth grade student was asked to prove the following theorem. "A positive number multiplied by a negative number equals a negative number. You may assume the following properties under multiplication:

   (1) Commutative   (2) Associative   (3) Inverses   and   (4) Identity."

His proof follows.

Let x = a positive number, and let y = a positive number. I must show that x(−y) = −(xy).

$$x(-y) = (-y) \cdot x \qquad \text{Commutative}$$
$$(-y) \cdot x = [-1 \cdot (y)] \cdot x \qquad (-y) = -1(y)$$
$$[-1(y)] \cdot x = -1[y \cdot x] \qquad \text{Associative}$$
$$-1[y \cdot x] = -[y \cdot x] \qquad -1 \cdot z = -z$$
$$-[y \cdot x] = -[x \cdot y] \qquad \text{Commutative}$$

Is the student correct in this proof?

3   A student asks you what is wrong with the following proof.

Let $c > 1$ and $c = d$.

(1) $c - 1 = d - 1$

(2) $c - 1 = -1(1 - d)$

(3) $(c - 1)^2 = (-1)^2(1 - d)^2$

(4) $(c - 1)^2 = (1 - d)^2$

(5) $(c - 1) = 1 - d$

(6) $c - 1 = 1 - c$

(7) $2c = 2$

(8) $c = 1$

(9) $1 > 1$

How do you reply?

4   A student asks, "What happens when you try to prove the $\sqrt{4}$ to be irrational as was done with $\sqrt{2}$, i.e., using 2 as a factor?" How do you respond?

Q2.11   *Operations on Rational and Irrational Numbers*

1   A student says that −3 is a whole number because it is not split up. What do you think?

2   While studying a unit on subtraction of directed numbers, a student asks you if it is possible to subtract numbers on the number line directly with vectors rather than defining subtraction in terms of addition and then doing the problem on the number line. What is your response?

3   A student asks you if there are more rational numbers than irrational numbers or are they equal in number. What is your reply?

4   A student asks, "How can you make a one-to-one correspondence between the counting numbers and the whole numbers?" What is your response?

5   How do you answer when a student in your class asks, "Since we say that $\pi = 22/7$ and $\sqrt{2} = 1.4$, why aren't these numbers rational?"

6   A student is given the problem $-7 - 2(-5)$. Her solution is: $-9(-5) = 45$. How would you explain the correct way of doing this problem to her?

7   A student is your class hands in the following work. "$12.2x^2 + 13x^2 = 25.22x^2$ because $12.2 + 13 = 25.2$ and $x^2 + x^2 = 2x^2$, so put the 2 after the 25.2, and there's the answer!" How would you react to this work?

8   A student in your class asks, "Is $\dfrac{100\sqrt{a}}{100} = \sqrt{a}$ an example of multiplicative inverse or multiplicative identity?" How do you respond?

9   A student says that he has trouble differentiating between the symmetric property of equality and the commutative property of addition. How could you help him?

10   For solving equalities a textbook states:

Example   If $7x - 13 = 3x - 1$, then $7x - 13 + 13 = 3x - 1 + 13$. To use the addition property you add 13 to each member of the equality.

The student does the following:

$$7x + 13 - 13 + 13 = 3x + 13 - 1 + 13$$
$$7x + 13 = 3x + 25.$$

How would you explain to him that his method is wrong?

11   In your ninth grade algebra class, you are asked, "Does $(A + B)(C + D)$ equal to $AC + BD$?" How would you answer?

12   You tell your class that 4/0 has no meaning. Some students reply that four divided by zero is still four. Since you are not dividing the four by anything, the four does not change. How do you reply?

13   A student asks, "Why doesn't $0 \div 0 = 0$, since $0 \cdot 0 = 0$?" What is your reply?

14   A student is asked to simplify $3 \div 6 + 2 - 2 \times 10$ and hands in the following:

$$3 \div 6 + 2 - 2 \times 10$$
$$\tfrac{1}{2} + 2 - 2 \times 10$$
$$2\tfrac{1}{2} - 2 \times 10$$
$$\tfrac{1}{2} \times 10$$
$$5$$

Is the student correct?

15   A student asks, "What is 0^0?" What is your reply?

Q2.12   *Number Theory and Average*

1   You make the statement that there is no last prime. A student says there is. The student reasons that since the distance between the primes increases as the numbers get larger, then it follows that at some point the space becomes infinitely long, which is the same as not having an end. How would you handle this situation?

2   A student asks you why we only consider positive numbers as primes and do not consider negative numbers. What is your reply?

3   In a discussion on rates a student says, "If I walk 4 mph for one mile, I'll have to run 8 mph the second mile in order to average 6 mph for 2 miles. Right?" How do you reply?

4 "If I know all the prime numbers which precede a certain given prime, is there any way to generate additional primes? Is there any way, other than trial and error, to find the prime number which follows a given prime?" How do you respond?

Q2.13   *Operations, Algorithms, Properties of Operations*

1 A student asks you if addition is distributive over multiplication. What do you say?

2 A student asks you why $(-1)(-1) = 1$. The student says that it doesn't make sense. How would you help this student?

3 A student asks you if $\dfrac{1}{a+b} = \dfrac{1}{a} + \dfrac{1}{b}$. How do you reply?

4 "What is the difference between the additive inverse of a number and the negative of a number?" What do you tell this student?

5 A student hands in the following work.

$$(6t)\sqrt{3} = 6\sqrt{3} \cdot t\sqrt{3}$$

How would you help this student?

6 In discussing combination of like terms, the teacher has used the analogy of adding numbers with like units (i.e., 5 days + 2 days). Students have just been told that they can't add 5 days and 2 hours without changing one of the units. When asked what to do with $2x + 5y$, one student wants to know how he can change x and y so that they can be added. What is your response?

7 A student says that $\frac{1}{2}(18\sqrt{3}) = \frac{1}{2}(18) \cdot \frac{1}{2}\sqrt{3}$. How would you explain to your student that he is incorrect?

8 Students in your class are asked to simplify $(3 + T) - (T - 5)$. A student replies:

$$(3 + T) - (T - 5) = 3 + (T - T) - 5$$
$$= 3 - 5$$
$$= -2.$$

Is the student correct?

Q2.14   *Polynomials and Rational Expressions*

1 While dividing $15x^4 + 9x^3 + 4x^2 + 1$ by $x^2 - 1$, one student writes that the quotient is $15x^2 + 9x + 19$ and the remainder is $\dfrac{9x + 20}{x^2 - 1}$. Is the student correct?

2 A student makes the following statement. "You said that $2x^2 + 2x$ is a polynomial, but $2(x^2 + x)$ is not a polynomial even though it is equivalent to $2x^2 + 2x$. I don't understand." How could you help this student?

3 You make the statement that the polynomial $x^2 - 2$ cannot be factored. One student says, "Yes, it can because $x^2 - 2 = (x - \sqrt{2})(x + \sqrt{2})$." What reply would you make?

4 The following item is on an algebra test:

Which of the following are not rational expressions and why.

(1) x (2) $\dfrac{1}{x}$ (3) $\dfrac{1}{x^2}$ (4) $\dfrac{1}{|x|}$ (5) $\dfrac{1}{x^2 + 2}$

A student in your class circles number (4) $\dfrac{1}{|x|}$ and says that it is not a rational expression because it has two values. How would you handle this situation?

5 A student in your class asks, "Do rational operations performed with irrational numbers always result in irrational numbers?" How would you answer?

Q2.15   *Radicals and Square Roots*

1 While discussing cube roots, you give your class the following problem.

$$\sqrt[3]{16} + \sqrt[3]{-16} = ?$$

A student says that the answer is zero because $16 - 16 = 0$. Is the student right?

2 A student asks, "Is it correct to write $2^{1/16}$ as

$$\sqrt{\sqrt{\sqrt{\sqrt{2}}}}$$

What is your reply?

3 While showing your students how to find a square root using the standard algorithm, one student asks you why it works. What do you tell the student?

4 In response to the question, "How do you define $\sqrt{x^2}$?" a student says that $\sqrt{x^2} = x$. Is this student correct?

5 A student asks, "Why isn't $\sqrt{3} + \sqrt{12} = \sqrt{15}$?" How do you reply?

6 You have worked the following problem on the board. "Simplify $\sqrt{11/3x^2}$ and you get your final answer of $\sqrt{33}/3x$." However, one of your students says that the final answer should be $\sqrt{33}/3|x|$. What is your reply?

7 While studying an algorithm for finding square roots, a student asks you if there is an algorithm for finding the cube of a number. What is your response?

Q2.16   *Sets*

1 In your ninth grade class, you make the statement that the empty set is a subset of every set. A student doesn't believe it. How could you help this student?

2 A student says that a set is finite if it has a largest element. Do you agree?

3 A student asks, "Are any two infinite sets equivalent sets? For example, is the set of whole numbers equivalent to the set of integers?" How would you respond?

4 A student asks, "How can we tell whether a set is finite or infinite?" How would you answer?

Q2.17   *Simultaneous Systems of Equations*

1 A student is trying to solve the set of simultaneous linear equations below.

$$2x + 3y = 6$$
$$\underline{-6x - 9y = -14}$$

He comes up with 0 = 4 but doesn't know what it means. How would you help this student?

2 A student is trying to solve the set of simultaneous linear equations below.

$$2x + 3y = 6$$
$$\underline{-4x - 6y = -12}$$

A student ends up with 0 = 0 and doesn't know what to do from here. How would you help this student?

3 A student hands in the following work.

$$2x + 3y = 4 \qquad\qquad -x - \frac{3}{2}y = -2$$
$$\underline{x - y = 5} \qquad\qquad \underline{x - y = 5}$$
$$-\frac{5}{2}y = 3 \qquad\qquad\quad y = -\frac{6}{5}$$

Is the student's work correct?

4 While studying a unit on systems of open sentences in two variables, a student asks, "What is the difference between equivalent systems of equations and equivalent equations?" What is your response?

Q2.18   *Slope*

1 "Can you determine the slope of a line from its graph if you don't know the equation of the line and vice versa." How would you answer this student?

2 A student asks, "Since slope is such an important concept, why hasn't the slope of a vertical line been defined?" What is your reply?

3 A student asks, "Why is the letter m used to denote the slope of a line?" How do you respond?

Q2.19   *Word Problems*

1   The problem is: "John rows up the river at 6 mph and down the river at 8 mph. What would John's rate be in still water and what is the rate of the current of the river?"   A student says, "To solve this, I add 6 mph and 8 mph and divide by 2. This is John's rate in still water. To find the rate of the current, I subtract 7 from 8 or else subtract 6 from 7. They both give the same answer." Is the student correct?

2   The following problem and solution are done in class. "A person invests half a sum at 3.5% interest rate and half a sum at 4.5% interest rate. At the end of a year the person received $300.00 in interest. How much did the person invest at each sum?"

$$\tfrac{1}{2}(.035)x + \tfrac{1}{2}(.045)x = 300$$
$$.0175x + .0225x = 300$$
$$.04x = 300$$
$$x = \$7,500$$

A student asks, "Why can't you always average the two interest rates and then divide that percent rate into the interest to find the principal?" How do you reply?

3   The following problem is given to your class. "A pump can fill a tank in 3 hours. With the drain open, it will empty in 5 hours. With the pump working and the drain open, how long will it take to fill the tank?" A student handed in the following response.

$$\left(\frac{1}{3} - \frac{1}{5}\right)x = 1$$
$$\left(\frac{5}{15} - \frac{3}{15}\right)x = \frac{15}{15}$$
$$\frac{2}{15}x = \frac{15}{15}$$
$$x = 7\frac{1}{2}$$

Is the method correct? Is the solution correct?

4   The following problem is given to your class. "In an election one candidate received 96 votes more than his opponent. Since there were 804 votes cast, the candidates received____votes and____votes." A student says, "Divide 804 by 2 since there were two candidates. 804/2 = 402. One candidate got 402 + 96 = 498 votes. The other got 804 − 498 = 306 votes." A student asks, "Why doesn't this work?" How do you respond?

5   A ninth grade student is trying to solve the following word problem. "A boat travels downstream 24 miles in two hours and comes back upstream in four hours. Find the rate of the boat in still water." The student reasons that the current going one way cancels it going the other way. Therefore, the boat goes a distance of 48 miles in six hours, and the rate of the boat is 8 mph. Is the student correct?

6   The problem given is: "If 4 pounds of meat must cook for 2.5 hours, how much meat do you have if it must cook for 9 hours?" Student solution follows (see page 77).

$$\begin{array}{r} .625 \\ 4\overline{\smash{\big)}2.500} \\ \underline{2\,4} \\ 10 \\ \underline{8} \\ 20 \\ \underline{20} \end{array}$$

$$\begin{array}{r} .625 \\ \times\ \ 9 \\ \hline 5.595 \end{array}$$

Is this student correct?

7   While studying word problems in Algebra I, a student in your class makes the following comment: "It seems to be the case that every integer can be expressed as a sum of consecutive integers except for those integers that are a power of two. For example:

   $3 = 1 + 2$
   $5 = 2 + 3$
   $6 = 1 + 2 + 3$
   $9 = 4 + 5$ Is it true?"

What response do you make?

8   The following problem was given to your class. "Mike is 30 years older than Jim. Two years from now Mike will be twice as old as Jim. How old is Mike now?" A student solves as follows:

   x = Jim's age
   x + 30 = Mike's age
   2x + 2 = x + 30
   x = 28   (Jim)
   x + 30 = 58   (Mike)

Is the answer correct? Is the method correct?

9   Your class is doing a word problem concerning three consecutive even integers. You ask a student how can these numbers be represented and he replies, "...x, x + 2, x + 4." Is the student correct?

ANSWERS

A2.1   Absolute Value

1   The graph of an equation in the variables x and y is a line if and only if the equation is equivalent to an equation of the form ax + by = c, a, b, c ∈ R with a, b ≠ 0. The graph of an equation, which is not equivalent to the above, is not a line. Since y = |x| is an equation that is not equivalent to ax + by = c, then the graph of this

equation is not a line. If one sketches the graph of y = |x| in the Cartesian plane, one gets Figure 2.1.1, and it is easy to see that this graph is not a straight line.

FIGURE 2.1.1

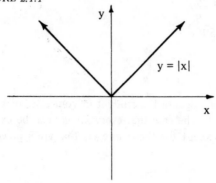

2   If −x means the opposite or additive inverse of x, then her definition is correct. However, if −x means negative x, then you should question what she means by this notation. If x is a negative number, then −x is not usually defined since the minus sign, as used in this context, is usually part of the symbol for a negative number. It is possible that she might be using −x to represent a negative number. Thus there might be a serious defect in her definition depending upon how −x is interpreted.

3 |x + y| = 5 and |x| + |y| = 5 do not have the same solution sets. For example, x = 3 and y = −2 is not a solution of |x + y| = 5, but it is a solution of |x| + |y| = 5. In general, |a + b| ≤ |a| + |b|, with equality only when a, b have the same sign, i.e., either both positive or negative. It might be instructive to graph both of the equations as shown in Figures 2.1.2 and 2.1.3 to give a visual demonstration of the difference.

FIGURE 2.1.2   FIGURE 2.1.3

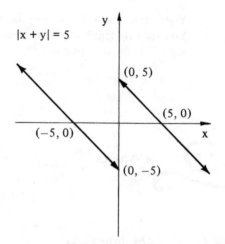

4   Refer to Section A 4.1,   Answer 2.

A2.2   *Cancellation*

1,2   The type of errors made in Questions 1 and 2 occur frequently in an Algebra I class and is one of the reasons why many teachers do not like to use the term *cancel* when teaching this course. One way of handling this situation is to make sure that students realize at the beginning of the course that *cancelling* really involves the identity element for multiplication, i.e., multiplying by 1. Thus many problems of this nature should be worked out in great detail by the teacher and the class. The teacher should also point out the difference between problems such as Questions 1 and 2, where "cancelling" is done incorrectly, with the following problems, which are correctly simplified.

(a) $\dfrac{x \cdot 5(a + b)}{a + b} = 5x \cdot \left(\dfrac{a + b}{a + b}\right) = 5x$

(b) $\dfrac{x \cdot 6}{2} = 3x \cdot \left(\dfrac{2}{2}\right) = 3x$

The teacher might point out that the answer, $x + 5$, is the answer to the problem of simplifying

$$\frac{x(a + b) + 5(a + b)}{a + b} = \frac{(x + 5)(a + b)}{a + b} = x + 5.$$

For Question 2 the teacher might point out that the answer, $x + 3$, is the answer to the problem of simplifying

$$\frac{2x + 6}{2} = \frac{2(x + 3)}{2} = \frac{2}{2} \cdot \frac{x + 3}{1} = x + 3.$$

However, there does not seem to be a sure-fire method which will always guarantee success in this situation. It seems to be the case that at least one student will make at least one of these errors at some point in an algebra course.

3   If the student's method was correct, then she should be able to get the correct answer on all problems of this type. Thus, you might ask her to do the following problem.

$$\frac{x^2 + y^2}{x + y}$$

Using her method the student would get $x + y$, but

$$(x + y)(x + y) \neq x^2 + y^2.$$

For example, take $x = y = 1$, then one might proceed to show the student a correct method; i.e.,

$$\frac{x^2 - y^2}{x + y} = \frac{(x + y)(x - y)}{x + y} = \frac{x + y}{x + y} \cdot (x - y) = x - y,$$

assuming, of course, that $x + y \neq 0$.

4   Even though the student gets the correct answer in this case, the method will not work all the time. Consider the following problem.

Simplify $\dfrac{x^2 + 9}{x + 3}$.

Using the student's method, we get

$$\frac{x^2 + 9}{x + 3} = \frac{x\!\!\!/^2 + 9}{x\!\!\!/ + 3} = \frac{x + 9}{+3} = \frac{x + \overset{3}{\cancel{9}}}{\cancel{3}} = x + 3.$$

But, $(x + 3)(x + 3) \neq x^2 + 9$ unless $x = 0$.

5   It is very difficult to pinpoint exactly what the student's problem is, without talking further to the student, but two possibilities, which seem to be good bets, are given below.

(a)   One possibility is that the student cancelled incorrectly as follows:

$$\frac{1}{\underset{1}{x\!\!\!/}} + \frac{1}{\underset{1}{x\!\!\!/}} = \frac{1}{1} + \frac{1}{1} = 2.$$

If this is the case, then you might try to show the student that the answer is incorrect by substituting values in for x; i.e., if $x = 4$, then

$$\frac{1}{x} + \frac{1}{x} = \frac{1}{4} + \frac{1}{4} = \frac{1}{2}.$$

(b)   Another possibility is that the student thought along the following lines. "If I have one object plus another object, then altogether I have *two* objects." Then the student just wrote *two* for the answer without attaching the label (i.e., $2 \cdot \frac{1}{x}$).

6   No, $\sqrt{a^2 + b^2} \neq a + b$. One way to see this is to consider $a = -5$ and $b = 5$. Then

$$\sqrt{a^2 + b^2} = \sqrt{(-5)^2 + (5)^2} = \sqrt{50} = 2\sqrt{5}.$$

However, $a + b = -5 + 5 = 0$. Since $2\sqrt{5} \neq 0$, then $\sqrt{a^2 + b^2} \neq a + b$.

Another way of looking at this situation is to assume that $\sqrt{a^2 + b^2} = a + b$. Then

$$a^2 + b^2 = (a + b)^2 = a^2 + 2ab + b^2.$$

However, for a and $b \neq 0$, $a^2 + b^2 \neq a^2 + 2ab + b^2$.

7   One way of helping this student is to find a counterexample such as

$$\frac{3^2 + 4^2}{5^2} = \frac{25}{25} = 1.$$

Using the student's method, one gets

$$\frac{3^2 + 4^2}{5^2} = \frac{3\!\!\!/^2 + 4\!\!\!/^2}{5\!\!\!/^2} = \frac{7}{5}.$$

The student's method just happened to work on this particular exercise. An interesting problem would be to find all such problems like the one above for which the student's method gives the correct solution; i.e., what are the conditions on a, b, c, and d such that

$$\frac{a^2 + b^2}{\left(\frac{c}{d}\right)^2} = \frac{a + b}{\frac{c}{d}} ?$$

8   One way of helping this student would be as follows. The student's work indicates
that the expression on the left is the same as the expression on the right for all defined values of x. Suppose we substitute 2 for x in the expression on the left.

$$\frac{x + \frac{1}{x}}{x - \frac{1}{x}} = \frac{2 + \frac{1}{2}}{2 - \frac{1}{2}} = \frac{\frac{5}{2}}{\frac{3}{2}} = \frac{5}{3} .$$

Thus it would seem that something is wrong. The main problem here is that the
student has confused the processes of simplifying the following expressions:

(a) $\dfrac{x + \dfrac{1}{x}}{x - \dfrac{1}{x}}$ and   (b) $\dfrac{x \cdot \dfrac{1}{x}}{x \cdot \dfrac{-1}{x}}$

What the student has done is to use a process which would correctly simplify (b).
Notice that in (b) one has multiplication and the expression involves factors, but in
(a) there is addition and the expression involves addends.

A2.3   *Decimals and Percent*

1   When presenting the algorithm of division, it is usually standard to present the following assertion.

> For given integers a and b with b > 0, there exists unique integers q and r
> such that $a = b \cdot q + r, 0 \leqslant r < b$.

Then, the practice is to show how this assertion is related to our usual algorithm for
division. However, one can modify this assertion if one wishes, although it is not
standard practice, so that the restrictions, *unique integers* and $0 \leqslant r < b$, are omitted. If this is done, then one could answer the student's question by doing the following:

$$\begin{array}{r} .999... \\ 9\overline{)9.000...} \\ \underline{8.1} \\ 90 \\ \underline{81} \\ 90 \end{array}$$

At this level a student probably would not understand the subtleties involved mathematically, but the student could be expected to follow the arithmetic.

2   No, the student is not correct. Consider n $= 12$, then 12% is equal to 12/100, but
$12/100 \neq 0.012$. Note that the student is correct if *n* is a digit.

A2.4   *Equations, Solving Equations, Equivalence*

1   The logic involved in solving open sentences is to use properties of the algebraic system to transform an open sentence into an equivalent open sentence; that is, the open sentences have the same solution set. Thus when the student gets to the part where x = x and x ≠ 1, the student should realize that the solution set of the original open sentence is equivalent to the solution set of this open sentence. By inspection the solution set of x = x and x ≠ 1 is the set of all numbers of the domain except 1. Thus the solution set of $\dfrac{x}{x-1} = 1 + \dfrac{1}{x-1}$ is the set of all numbers of the domain except 1.

2   No, the student's reasoning is not correct. Solving the equation in the standard way, one gets {4} as the solution set. The student is trying to use a procedure that he probably made up (as students often do), which is not mathematically correct. The student is assuming that

$$\frac{a}{b} = \frac{c}{d} \quad \text{implies} \quad \frac{a-k}{b-k} = \frac{c-k}{d-k}$$

where k is a real number. That this is not correct can be shown by taking a = 1, b = 2, c = 3 and d = 6. With k = 1, one obtains the false statement 0 = 2/5.

Problem   Under what conditions will the student's method work?

3   Yes, this method is correct as illustrated here. Let $ax^2 + bx + c = 0$, a ≠ 0 be the expression for the general quadratic equation in the variable x. Using the quadratic formula, one gets the following solutions.

$$x = \frac{-b \pm \sqrt{b^2 - 4ac}}{2a} \tag{1}$$

Using the student's method, let $\dot{x}^2 + b\dot{x} + ac = 0$ be the general expression in the variable $\dot{x}$. Using the quadratic formula, one gets

$$\dot{x} = \frac{-b \pm \sqrt{b^2 - 4ac}}{2}. \tag{2}$$

If one compares (1) and (2), then it can be seen that if (2) is divided by a, then the the result is (1).

4   This question seems to have at least two different interpretations depending on what the student is really asking. In answering this question, the assumption is made that the student is referring to lines in two dimensions.

    If the student is asking if the *only* way to write an equation of a line is as a first degree equation in x and y, then the answer is no since there are different ways to write equations for lines such as parametric and vector equations.

    If the student is asking if every *rectangular* equation of a line is a first degree equation in x and y, then the answer depends on how a first degree equation in x and y is defined. If in (1) below neither a nor b can be zero, then the answer is no because of the special cases y = k and x = f, where k and f are real numbers. If a or b, but not both, can be zero, then the answer is yes.

$$ax + by = c \qquad a, b, c \text{ real numbers} \tag{1}$$

5   An open equation is an open sentence such as $3x + 2 = 4$ or $3x = 1$. An open phrase is an expression such as $3x + 2$ or $3x$. Thus an open phrase is an algebraic expression that contains one or more variables but no equality sign, inequality sign, etc. The situation is similar to the difference between a phrase and a sentence in English. A sentence contains a verb whereas a phrase does not.

6   Technically speaking, the student is correct. The domain of the variable should always be specified. However, usually the convention is made that if the domain is not specified, then one should assume that the domain consists of all those elements of the largest number system we are currently working with for which the expression is defined.

7   By definition two algebraic expressions are equivalent if and only if the values of the expressions are equal for every numerical replacement of the variables. Thus, for every value of the variables, equivalent expressions represent the same number. Thus the expression x/x and $(x - 3)/(x - 3)$ are not equivalent since when $x = 3$, $x/x = 1$, while $(x - 3)/(x - 3)$ is undefined. Likewise when $x = 0$, x/x is undefined while $(x - 3)/(x - 3) = 1$.

      Another, but similar, way to respond is to consider x/x and $(x - 3)/(x - 3)$ as functions. The domain of x/x would be all real numbers except 0 while the domain of $(x - 3)/(x - 3)$ would be all real numbers except 3. Since the domains differ, the functions differ and hence x/x and $(x - 3)/(x - 3)$ are not equivalent expressions.

8   No, the student is not correct. In the second step, the student divided through by x, and this is valid as long as $x \neq 0$. The student must then find out what happens when $x = 0$. Is it a solution or not? In this particular case, 0 is a solution; thus the solution set should be $\{0, -2, 4\}$.

A2.5   *Exponents*

1   Although the student should be commended for looking for patterns in mathematics, one must be wary of extensions and this particular pattern does not extend to addition. Several different ways of explaining this to a student are given below.

(a)   If $(a + b)^2 = a^2 + b^2$, then this equality should hold for all values of a and b. Let $a = 2$ and $b = 3$, then $(a + b)^2 = (2 + 3)^2 = 5^2 = 25$, while $a^2 + b^2 = 2^2 + 3^2 = 13$ and $25 \neq 13$.

(b)   A geometric consideration of $(a + b)^2$ could help students. $(a + b)^2$ is the area of the square shown in Figure 2.5.1. and it is easily seen that

$$(a + b)^2 = a^2 + b \cdot a + a \cdot b + b^2$$
$$\therefore (a + b)^2 = a^2 + 2ab + b^2$$

Thus, in general, $(a + b)^2 \neq a^2 + b^2$.

FIGURE 2.5.1

2   Yes. Let a be a real number not equal to zero, and let r and s be real numbers, $s \neq 0$. Then $(a)^{r/s} = (a^{-1})^{-r/s}$.

3   In this particular case, the student gets the correct answer. However, it seems as if the student is using an incorrect method. For example, if the student is asked to simplify $2^5 \cdot 2^2$, it looks as if the student would get 4^7 instead of 2^7.

4   Yes, they are isomorphic systems. A few of the properties are illustrated as follows. Let $a \neq 0$ be a real number. Then

$$ma \longleftrightarrow a^m$$
$$\textit{addition} \qquad \textit{multiplication}$$

is an isomorphism and every property of multiplies has a corresponding property of powers.

(a)   The multiple of a multiple is a multiple.   The power of a power is a power.

$n(ma) = (n \cdot m)a$ $(a^m)^n = a^{mn}$

(b)   The multiple of a sum is the sum of multiples.   The power of a product is the product of the powers.

$m(a + b) = ma + mb$ $(ab)^m = a^m b^m$

5   It is conventional in mathematics to evaluate the expression 2^{3^2} as $2^{(3^2)}$ or 2^9, i.e., from the top to the bottom. Notice that this example says that the operation of raising to a power is not associative. For an interesting article concerning this problem when there are an infinite number of terms, consult:

M.C. Mitchelmore, "A Matter of Definition," *The Mathematical Monthly*, (Classroom Notes Section), June-July 1974, pp. 643-7;

Problem Find all values of x, y, z such that $(x^y)^z = x^{(y^z)}$.

6   The computer is correct and the student is wrong. The following computer program is given which shows the amount received in each day in the first column and the total sum of money received in the second column. Thus at the end of thirty days, the student would have received $10,737,400.

Problem Why is the student incorrect?

```
LIST
MONEY       03:06 PM          50 S=S+Z
10 S=0                        51 PRINT Z,S
20 FOR I=0 TO 63              60 NEXT I
30 LET Z = 2↑I/100            80 END

        READY

        RUNNH
    1     .01              .01
    2     .02              .03
    3     .04              .07
    4     .08              .15
```

5	.16	.31	
6	.32	.63	
7	.64	1.27	
8	1.28	2.55	
9	2.56	5.11	
10	5.12	10.23	
	10.24	20.47	
	20.48	40.95	
	40.96	81.91	
	81.92	163.83	
	163.84	327.67	
	327.68	655.35	
	655.36	1310.71	
	1310.72	2621.43	
	2621.44	5242.87	
20	5242.88	10485.7	
	10485.8	20971.5	
	20971.5	41943	
	41943	83886.1	
	83886.1	167772	
	167772	335544	
	335544	671089	
	671089	.134218E 7	
	.134218E 7	.268435E 7	
	.268435E 7	.536871E 7	
30	.536871E 7	.107374E 8	
	.107374E 8	.214748E 8	

A2.6   *Factoring and Factors*

1   This error by a student is one that frequently comes up in an algebra course, and there are various ways that one may help the student. One way would be to use an inductive approach as shown in Table 2.6.1.

TABLE 2.6.1

Value of a	Value of $3a - 2a$
1	$3 - 2 = 1$
2	$6 - 4 = 2$
3	$9 - 6 = 3$
4	$12 - 8 = 4$
5	$15 - 10 = 5$
6	$18 - 12 = 6$

The student should now realize that $3a - 2a$ seems to be always equal to a. Then you might ask the student if he can find a value of a for which this would not be true. After the student tries a few more cases, then you might want to show him that $3a - 2a = a$ by using the distributive property of multiplication over subtraction as follows.

$$3a - 2a = (3-2) \cdot a = 1 \cdot a = a$$

2   Both students are correct.

$$(y - x - w)(y - x + w) = (-x + y - w)(-x + y + w)$$
$$= [-(x - y + w)] [-(x - y - w)]$$
$$= (x - y + w)(x - y - w)$$

Therefore, $y^2 - 2xy + x^2 - w^2 = (y - x - w)(y - x + w) = (x - y + w)(x - y - w)$

3   For an answer to this question, read the following article by G.H. Palagi.*

A CONVERSATION ON FACTORING

By **GEORGE   H.   PALAGI**

Lincoln Junior High School
Billings, Montana

STUDENT: When the coefficient of the quadratic term in a trinomial is not 1, I sometimes have a lot of trouble finding the factors.

PROFESSOR: Yes, the number of combinations to be tried on a trial and error basis can be quite large.

STUDENT: I don't suppose there is a "general form," of which you are so fond, that can be applied to factoring trinomials, or is there?

PROFESSOR: Let us see if we are able to find one. Perhaps if we work the problem backwards, so to speak, we will at least find a general approach to the problem.

STUDENT: I should be of help in that case for I quite often get things backwards.

PROFESSOR: Come now, you have a nice feeling for mathematics. Suppose we had worked the problem and this was our answer:

$$(ax + b)(cx + d).$$

Apply the distributive axiom and what do we get?

STUDENT: I suppose we would get

$$(ax + b)cx + (ax + b)d.$$

PROFESSOR: Good. Now apply the "right" distributive axiom twice.

STUDENT: Then we get

$$acx^2 + bcx + adx + bd.$$

PROFESSOR: Now apply the same axiom to the linear terms.

STUDENT: Let's see. We get

$$acx^2 + (bc + ad)x + bd.$$

PROFESSOR: Excellent. Now by studying this result, we shall, perhaps, be able to make some progress towards finding a general solution, if there is one.

STUDENT: This is the part I usually don't see.

PROFESSOR: Let us study a little more and ask ourselves some questions. If we were to multiply the coefficient of the quadratic term by the constant term, we would have

$$abcd.$$

STUDENT: And the coefficient of the linear term, if multiplied instead of added,

---

*From *The Mathematics Teacher*, November 1973, pp. 671-672. Reprinted by permission.

is also

abcd.

PROFESSOR: That should give us a clue. Let us see if we can apply this to a specific problem, for instance,

$$6x^2 + 19x + 15.$$

STUDENT: The product of the quadratic term and the constant is $90x^2$. So we want to replace the coefficient of the linear term, $19x$, with the factors of $90x^2$ that add up to $19x$.

PROFESSOR: Precisely, and in this case it is $9x + 10x$.

STUDENT: Then we have

$$6x^2 + 9x + 10x + 15.$$

PROFESSOR: Apply the "left" distributive axiom to the first two terms and also to the last two terms.

STUDENT: Then we have

$$3x(2x + 3) + 5(2x + 3).$$

PROFESSOR: Now use the "right" distributive property.

STUDENT: Now we have

$$(3x + 5)(2x + 3).$$

PROFESSOR: And so our algorithm works on this problem.

STUDENT: Will it work on this one?

$$15x^2 - 7x - 2.$$

PROFESSOR: Of course. But let us work it out. The product of the quadratic term and the constant term is $-30x^2$; so we want to replace $-7x$ with the factors of $-30x^2$ that add up to $-7x$.

STUDENT: And they are $-10x$ and $+3x$.

PROFESSOR: So now we have

$$15x^2 - 10x + 3x - 2$$

$$5x(3x - 2) + (3x - 2)$$

$$(5x + 1)(3x - 2).$$

STUDENT: Does it matter if we put $3x - 10x$ rather than $-10x +3x$?

PROFESSOR: No, for when we were working in the general form, we could apply the commutative axiom of addition to $(bc + ad)x$ and get $(ad + bc)x$. But let

us work it out anyway.

$$15x^2 + 3x - 10x - 2$$

$$3x(5x + 1) - 2(5x + 1)$$

$$(3x - 2)(5x + 1).$$

PROFESSOR: Once we factor the first two terms, we must be careful to get a common factor when we factor the third and fourth terms.

STUDENT: Suppose the trinomial is prime? What happens then?

PROFESSOR: Do you mean by prime, a polynomial that cannot be factored into polynomials of lower positive degree with integral coefficients and whose greatest common monomial factor is 1?

STUDENT: Yes, that is what I meant.

PROFESSOR: Let us work a specific problem and then see if we can generalize from that.

STUDENT: How about

$$4x^2 + 2x - 1?$$

PROFESSOR: Fine. The product of the quadratic term and the constant term is $-4x^2$. The possible pairs are

$$-4x, x$$
$$-2x, 2x$$
$$-x, 4x$$
$$4x, -x$$
$$2x, -2x$$
$$x, -4x$$

STUDENT: And none of those add up to $+2x$ and so we know it is prime.

PROFESSOR: And now, just to make sure you can use this algorithm, work this problem,

$$10x^2 - 11x - 6.$$

STUDENT: Let's see. The product of the constant and the quadratic term is $-60x^2$. That means we have these possible pairs,

$x, -60x$	$-x, 60x$
$2x, -30x$	$-2x, 30x$
$3x, -20x$	$-3x, 20x$
$4x, -15x$	$-4x, 15x$

$$5x, \; -12x \qquad -5x, \; 12x$$

$$6x, \; -10x \qquad -6x, \; 10x$$

And the pair that adds up to $-11x$ is $4x$ and $-15x$. Then we have

$$10x^2 + 4x - 15x - 6$$

$$2x(5x + 2) - 3(5x + 2)$$

$$(2x - 3)(5x + 2).$$

I think I've got it now. Thank you, Professor, for your help.

PROFESSOR: I'm always glad to help when I can.[1]

———

1. The reader who is interested in a more complete exposition is referred to Drooyan, Hadel, and Fleming, *Elementary Algebra, Structure and Skills* (New York: John Wiley and Sons, 1966, 1969).

4   The assumption here is that the factoring is done over the set of integers. If this was specified beforehand, then the students were wrong. However, if this was not specified beforehand, then the students are correct. They have factored 3x + 8 over the set of rational numbers.

5   We say that *a* is a factor of c over a given set of numbers if and only if a · b = c where a, b, c belong to the given set. Thus 0 is a factor of 0 over a set of numbers because 0 = 0 · r where r could be any number from the set of given numbers. Thus 0 is a factor of only one number, 0, because 0 · b = c would only be true when c is zero.

6   By substituting 3 and then 15 into the given equation, we get

$$3^2 - 14 \cdot 3 + 24 = 3 \qquad \text{and} \qquad 15^2 - 14 \cdot 15 + 24 = 3$$

which simplifies   which simplifies

to   to

$-9 = 3$, $39 = 3$,

a *false* statement   a *false* statement

Therefore, the student is not correct. The student is trying to use the theorem that "if a and b are real numbers and a · b = 0, then a = 0 or b = 0." However, an essential condition is that the product must be equal to zero. One cannot generalize this theorem for the situation where a product is equal to a nonzero number.

Problem   Under what conditions will the student's method work?

7   See Answer 3 of this section.

8   Suppose we use the equation $x^2 + 9x - 36 = 0$ as an example. Now,

$$x^2 + 9x - 36 = 0$$

can be written as $x^2 + 9x = 36$. Geometrically we have the situation shown in Figure 2.6.1.

FIGURE 2.6.1

Let us now divide the second rectangle in half as in Figure 2.6.2.

FIGURE 2.6.2

Then we attach each half to the square of side x as in Figure 2.6.3.

FIGURE 2.6.3

In order to complete the square, we must add a square of side 9/2 as shown in Figure 2.6.4.

FIGURE 2.6.4

Geometrically, we get the situation shown in Figure 2.6.5.

FIGURE 2.6.5

Algebraically we arrive at the following solution.

$$x^2 + 9x = 36$$

$$x^2 + 9x + \left(\frac{9}{2}\right)^2 = 36 + \left(\frac{9}{2}\right)^2$$

$$\left(x + \frac{9}{2}\right)^2 = \frac{225}{4}.$$

Thus this process of solving a quadratic equation gets its name *completing the square* from a geometric process.

A2.7   *Functions and Relations*

1   In most texts, the function defined by the equation $y = ax + b$ is normally considered a linear function, but does not represent a direct variation unless $b = 0$ and $a \neq 0$. However, in one text reviewed by the authors, direct variation was defined as follows. A function defined by an equation of the form $y + b = k(x + a)^n$ when k, a, b and n are constants, $k \neq 0$, $x \neq -a$ and $n > 0$, is called a direct variation. We say that $y + b$ varies directly as $(x + a)^n$ or that $y + b$ is directly proportional to $(x + a)^n$. Thus this definition might be considered to be more general than the one given above. But if one makes the transformation $Y = y + b$ and $X = (x + a)^n$, then one can see that they are equivalent in form, i.e., $Y = k \cdot X$.

2   You might ask the student to explain what she means by that statement. The student's explanation should be somewhat along the following lines. For every ordered pair of numbers where defined, each operation assigns only one number. Thus each operation, over the appropriate domain, is a mapping of $A \times A \to A$ and is therefore a function. The domain in each case is a set of ordered pairs while the range is set A. For example, A is the set of real numbers, then one can regard addition as a function

$$+ : A \times A \to A$$

with $+(2, 6) = 8$; $+(3, 1) = 4$, etc.

3   The problem here is one of long standing and involves precise use of language. Technically speaking the student is incorrect. The expression $f(x)$ refers to an element in the range of the function, not the function itself. Strictly speaking, x refers to an element in the domain of a function, $f(x)$ refers to the element in the range corresponding to the element x in the domain and f refers to the function itself. However, it is often the case, especially in advanced mathematics, where f and $f(x)$ are used interchangeably with the context of the instruction showing which interpretation is intended.

   For more information on this subject, read:

   (1)   R.B. Deal, "Some Remarks on 'A Dilemma in Definition'," *The Mathematical Monthly*, Vol. 74, No. 10, p. 1258.

   (2)   H.A. Thurston, "A Reply to 'A Dilemma in Definition'," *The Mathematical Monthly*, Vol. 74, No. 10, p. 1259.

4   Equations and functions are not the same thing. An equation often, although not always, determines a function. Thus $y = 2x + 1$ is an equation that describes the rule used to determine a function and as such is not a function itself. Again in various situations, such as in advanced mathematics, impreciseness is tolerated in that both terms are used interchangeably. This convention is done in order to simplify the writing chore in mathematics texts.

   Another difficulty is that an equation such as $x^2 + y^2 = 1$ does not give x as a (single-valued) function of y nor y as a function of x.

5   Although the student shows good thinking, he is incorrect. It seems as if he means that if $(a, b) \in A \times B$, then $a = b$. However, it does not follow that the symmetric property of equality is the only relation illustrated in this case; i.e., that $(a, b) \in A \times B$ infers $a = b$ and $(b, a) \in B \times A$ infers $b = a$. One should probably question the student in order to find out exactly what the student means. The correct answer should be that $A \times B$ and $B \times A$ are equivalent sets (i.e., they contain the same number of elements).

A2.8   *Graphs*

1   Since a restriction was not included as to whether the students should graph in one or two-dimensional spaces, both students are correct. Marking one of the students correct and the other one incorrect would be quite unfair.

2   Suppose that $P_1(x_1, y_1)$ and $P_2(x_2, y_2)$ are two points in this coordinate system as shown in Figure 2.8.1.

FIGURE 2.8.1

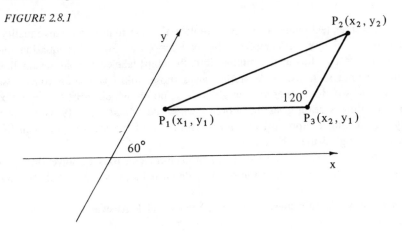

In order to find the distance between P_1 and P_2, we proceed in the usual case for rectangular coordinates by drawing segments parallel to the x and y axes. Let P_3 be the point of intersection of these two segments. The coordinates of P_3 are (x_2, y_1) and angle $P_1P_3P_2$ equals $120°$. Why? Using the law of cosines, we get

$$d(P_1P_2)^2 = d(P_1P_3)^2 + d(P_2P_3)^2 + 2d(P_1P_3) \cdot d(P_2P_3) \cdot \cos 120°$$

i.e., $$d(P_1P_2)^2 = (x_2 - x_1)^2 + (y_2 - y_1)^2 + 2(x_2 - x_1)(y_2 - y_1) \cdot \cos 120°$$

or $$d(P_1P_2) = \sqrt{(x_2 - x_1)^2 + (y_2 - y_1)^2 + 2(x_2 - x_1)(y_2 - y_1) \cdot \cos 120°}$$

Problem 1   Suppose that the axes intersect at an angle of θ degrees. Generalize the above argument for this case.

Problem 2   Show how the usual case of rectangular coordinates, i.e., perpendicular axes, is a special case of the result you found in Problem 1.

3   If a line has a slope of zero, then the line is horizontal, while a line having no slope would be a vertical line. Thus having slope zero does not mean the same thing as having no slope. The question here is one concerning the equality of zero with nothing, which is mathematically incorrect in this case.

A2.9   *Inequalities*

1   Since there is an infinite number of solutions for this problem, there is no corresponding method (substitution) for checking each solution as one would do in an equation. However, there are techniques which can be used to justify the result. For example, one might work backwards and try to show that

$$x < 1 \Rightarrow 3x + 3 < x + 5$$

as follows:

$$x < 1 \Rightarrow 2x < 2$$
$$2x < 2 \Rightarrow 3x < x + 2$$
$$3x < x + 2 \Rightarrow 3x + 3 < x + 5$$

Another technique to use is to replace the less than sign by an equality sign; so that $3x + 3 < x + 5$ is replaced by $3x + 3 = x + 5$. Solve this equation, and the result is $x = 1$. Thus in the number line, the point labeled 1 separates the line into three distinct sections. One section gives those points whose coordinates satisfy $3x + 3 < x + 5$, another section gives those points which satisfy $3x + 3 = x + 5$, and the third section gives those points whose coordinates satisfy $3x + 3 > x + 5$. By substituting an appropriate number from one of the sections, one can find the section that gives the solution set.

Notice that this is exactly the procedure one uses to solve the following problem in the plane. Find the set of ordered pairs (x, y) such that $2x + 3y < 5$.

2   For an answer to this question, refer to Section A4.1, Answer 1.

3   One way of answering this question depends on whether the student has worked with logic and truth tables. If so, then you could show the student that the negattion of the statement p or q is $\sim$p and $\sim$q.

Another way of answering would be the following. When we write $a \not< b$, then this means that it is not true that a is less than b or that a is equal to b; i.e., neither of them are true. Thus another way of saying this is that both $a < b$ and $a = b$ are false; i.e., $a \not< b$ and $a \neq b$. If we use the word *or*, then this leaves the option that one of them might be false but the other one is true.

If De Morgan's law has been taught to the class, then the analogy between sets and statements could be shown. That is, $\overline{A \cup B} = \overline{A} \cap \overline{B}$ corresponds to the negation of A, or B is the negation of A and the negation of B.

4   No, it is not true in general. Consider $a = 5$, $b = 2$, $c = -2$, $d = -8$. Thus $a > b$ and $c > d$, but $a - c = 7$ is not greater than $b - d = 10$.

5   This symbolism is used in some textbooks, and if defined properly, it is obviously mathematically correct. However, this is not a universally accepted conventional notation. Essentially it means that a and b are representations for two different numbers.

6   Yes, it is possible although it is not standard notation. Usually one would write
$-3 < 1 < 6$. It is important for the student to understand that the symbolism
$1 < 3 < 6$, as a similar example, represents *two* inequalities, namely, $1 < 3$ and
$3 < 6$. Thus, $6 > -3 < 1$ represents the two inequalities $6 > -3$ and $-3 < 1$, both
of which are true. Hence one would regard the inequality represented by the given
symbolism as true. Thus, although the student's notation is not standard, it could
certainly be used with the above agreements.

A2.10   *Logic and Proof*

1   Either reason is correct in this case. One can show that, in many instances, the two
properties are equivalent. It is easy to see that whenever the transitive property of
equality can be used as a supporting reason, then the substitution principle can be
used. However, the converse is not generally valid. In order to save time and effort,
textbooks frequently give both properties and allow students the choice of which one
to use. For example, suppose we were given

$$x + 3 = 7 \quad \text{and} \quad x^2 + (x + 3) = 9.$$

We would usually say that, therefore, $x^2 + 7 = 9$ by the substitution principle.
However, with a little work, we could show that the transitive property could be
used as follows:

$$x + 3 = 7 \Rightarrow 7 = x + 3$$
$$x^2 + (x + 3) = 9 \Rightarrow x + 3 = 9 - x^2$$

Therefore, $7 = 9 - x^2$ by the transitive property or, equivalently, $x^2 + 7 = 9$.
In order to save time and effort, textbooks frequently give both properties
and allow students the choice of using the one that seems more appropriate.

2   When the student writes that $(-y) = -1 \cdot (y)$ and $-1[y \cdot x] = -[y \cdot x]$, the student is really using a special case of the theorem that he is trying to prove.

3   The error is made in the fifth step; $(c - 1)^2 = (1 - d)^2$ does not imply that $c - 1 = 1 - d$. The correct way of going from (4) to (5) is:

$$(c - 1)^2 = (1 - d)^2 \Rightarrow \sqrt{(c - 1)^2} = \sqrt{(1 - d)^2}.$$
$$\sqrt{(c - 1)^2} = \sqrt{(1 - d)^2} \Rightarrow |c - 1| = |1 - d|.$$

Thus (5) should be $|c - 1| = |1 - d|$. The problem here is that $c - 1$ is positive
while $1 - d$ is negative.

4   Let $\sqrt{4} = a/b$, $b \neq 0$, where a/b is in lowest terms, i.e., greatest common divisor, is 1.
Then $4 = a^2/b^2$, which implies that

$$4b^2 = a^2. \tag{1}$$

Thus a^2 is even and therefore a is even; i.e., $a = 2 \cdot k$. Substituting in (1) we get

$$4b^2 = 4k^2 \text{ or } b^2 = k^2 \tag{2}$$

However, (2) gives no indication of whether b is even or odd, and thus this is as far
as we can go.

A2.11 *Operations on Rational and Irrational Numbers*

1 For an answer to this question, read the following article by Charles Brumfiel.*

NUMBER DEFINITIONS

By CHARLES BRUMFIEL

University of Michigan
Ann Arbor, Michigan

AFTER reading David Rappaport's article in the March 1970 MATHEMATICS TEACHER, I turned to my dictionary and found the following definitions:

whole number . . . . an integer
integer . . . . a whole number

Under *integer* I was referred to *complex integer*, and this definition was:

complex integer . . . . a number $a + bi$ where a and b are real integers.

But real integers are not defined in my dictionary!

As badly as we handle our definitions, dictionaries do worse. This is some consolation.

I feel somewhat involved in the *whole number–counting number* terminology. University mathematicians have for centuries used *whole number* and *integer* interchangeably. I am sure that most still do so. Hence, when we began to write school texts in 1955 on the Ball State Project, I did not feel free to refer to the set of cardinal numbers, {0, 1, 2, . . .}, as the set of whole numbers. I wish now I had used the simple terminology *cardinal numbers*, but this seemed pretentious and I used *counting numbers* instead. A few years later, SMSG decreed that *whole numbers* should be used. I suggest that the phrase *counting numbers* be gracefully withdrawn from circulation.

It does seem desirable to have a short name for the positive integers, and *natural numbers* is as good as any. We should understand, however, that mathematicians have carried along two definitions for centuries. Some include zero in the set of natural numbers and some do not. This condition will persist. It is best to tell students the truth. One of the worst things you can do in teaching mathematics is to treat definitions as if they were "right" or "wrong."

I think I see the wave of the future. We shall tell children about integers in kindergarten. Having done so, we shall be able to speak of the *positive integers* and the *negative integers* from the beginning. I think this will be ill advised.

A short time ago I visited a junior high school class. A student argued that -3 *is* a whole number because it *is not broken*. The teacher could not satisfy him. I had the morbid desire to tell the student that -3 is still a whole number to most university mathematicians, excluding those who wrote for SMSG or who have been trained in the new mathematics, but I refrained. Actually, I feel that it is healthy to discuss definitions, and all teachers, including elementary teachers, should utilize opportunities that arise in the classroom to do so. The task of mathematics educators is to train teachers so that they can manage such discussions.

Mr. Rappaport devoted most of his energies to fraction and rational-number terminology. I share his regret that this language is so messy. I don't know what

*From *The Mathematics Teacher*, April 1972, pp. 313-314. Reprinted by permission.

to do about it. We should teach as many teachers as possible the standard mathematical set-theoretic definitions of ordinal numbers, cardinal numbers, and rational numbers. Every teacher who understands these definitions will realize that they are not meant for children. We must tell children something else.

One basic difficulty in choosing a school terminology for fractions and rational numbers is that so many writers wish to pretend to give precise definitions. Let's face it. The mathematical definitions are too complicated. Let's concentrate on making teachers and children comfortable without lying to them.

Why not let the terminology flow along with the use of the symbols. When the emphasis is on the use of fractions to describe the real world—and this is surely the major emphasis in the six elementary grades—just let a fraction be a symbol, written by separating two whole-number symbols by a bar and used to compare two "things" in the real world. The fraction ⅔ may compare a set of boys to a set of girls, or a line segment to a unit segment, or a rectangular region to a unit region, and so on. This is the only meaning one needs to ascribe to a fraction in its use to describe the real world.

Late in the elementary school years, and in junior high school, teachers can note that for one physical situation it may be natural to use any one of many fractions to compare two given sets. The concept of *equivalent fractions* is a natural one, and we can agree that a rational number is "associated" with each equivalence class. There is no need to insist that the rational number *is* the equivalence class. This is the standard mathematical class. This is the standard mathematical definition; but when this set-theoretic definition is formulated in a careful mathematical development, it has been presaged by a sequence of meticulous definitions, including the concepts of *ordinal number* and *ordered pair*. There is something phony about pretending to present precise definitions at this level. However, I have no objection if teachers prefer to say that the rational number *is* the equivalence class of fractions, even though the concept of an *equivalence class of symbols* is a bit hazy.

The great number-numeral controversy seems to be running its course. I shall be glad when it has faded away. Through the elementary school years, numbers are to most children simply symbols that describe the real world. This is the way we should talk about numbers. The child unblushingly adds and multiplies symbols. Don't give him a guilt feeling by telling him that he can *write* symbols but he can't *add* them, that he can *add* numbers but he can't *write* them. If you really think carefully about the process by which the game of arithmetic is abstracted from the real world, you may come to the conclusion that there is a stage when addition and multiplication really are things we do with symbols.

I do wish that someone would take his tape recorder into the heartland of America and record the definitions that children and teachers would formulate if they were asked to define whole number, natural number, integer, fraction, rational number, and so on. Mathematics educators might be greatly surprised if they knew what children and teachers really think about these things.

2 Yes, it is. The subtraction problem $3 - 5$ can be represented as in the following diagram.

In general $a - b$ can be represented as a vector from b to a as shown:

3 There are more irrational numbers than rational numbers. The rational numbers form a countable set while the real numbers form an uncountable set. If the set of irrationals formed a countable set, then the set of real numbers would be countable since the reals would then be the union of two countable sets, which is again countable. (Thus the set of irrationals is not countable.)

An intuitive way of showing this to students would be as follows. Let r be any rational number and i be any irrational number. Then $r + i$ will always be an irrational number. Let us fix r and let i run through the set of all irrational numbers. If we repeat this process for each rational number, then we can say that for each rational number, there are an infinite number of irrational numbers. Since there are an infinite number of rational numbers, we would get an infinite number of infinite sets where each set consists of irrational numbers.

4 Consider $n \rightarrow n + 1$. This is a one-to-one correspondence between the counting numbers and the whole numbers.

5 If we say that $\pi = 22/7$ and $\sqrt{2} = 1.4$, then we have made incorrect statements. What we should say is that $22/7$ is a rational approximation of π and that 1.4 is a rational approximation of $\sqrt{2}$. In symbols this is usually denoted by $\pi \approx 22/7$ and $\sqrt{2} \approx 1.4$. π and $\sqrt{2}$ are irrational numbers, but the value of these two numbers can be approximated by rational numbers. This is what is meant by $\pi = 22/7$ and $\sqrt{2} = 1.4$.

6 In problems of this nature, the convention is to do the operations in this order:
(1) Numbers in parentheses first, etc.
(2) Multiplication and division from left to right in that order, etc.
(3) Addition and subtraction from left to right in that order, etc.
Thus, $-7 - 2(5) = -7 - (-10) = -7 + 10 = 3$.

7 Of course, the student is incorrect. One might show the student how the distributive property of multiplication over addition is used in this situation:

$$12.2x^2 + 13x^2 = (12.2 + 13)x^2 = (25.2)x^2 = 25.2x^2.$$

Another approach might be to ask the student to do a simple problem such as $2x + 2x$. Two groups of x plus two groups of x are four groups of x. Thus $2x + 2x = 4x$. Using the student's method:

$$2 + 2 = 4 \quad \text{and} \quad x + x = 2x, \quad \text{so} \quad 2x + 2x = 8x.$$

By substituting values in for x, the teacher can show the student that this answer is incorrect.

8   The answer to this question involves more than one property. Frequently the problem would be stated something like the following. "Solve for $\sqrt{a}$ in the problem below."

$$100\sqrt{a} = y.$$

$100\sqrt{a} = y$	Given
$\dfrac{1}{100}(100\sqrt{a}) = \dfrac{1}{100} \cdot y$	Multiplication property of equality; i.e., if a, b, c, d are real numbers such that a = b and c = d, then ac = bd.
$\left(\dfrac{1}{100} \cdot 100\right)\sqrt{a} = \dfrac{1}{100}y$	Associative property of multiplication
$1 \cdot \sqrt{a} = \dfrac{1}{100}y$	Multiplicative inverse
$\sqrt{a} = \dfrac{1}{100}y$	Multiplicative identity

9   One way of helping this student would be as follows. The commutative property of addition says that the order in which we add two numbers makes no difference since the result will be the same number. For example, 3 + 4 = 4 + 3 = 7. Using the same numbers, the symmetric property of equality says that if 3 + 4 = 4 + 3, then 4 + 3 = 3 + 4. Notice that the commutative property involves switching the order of the addends while the symmetric property involves switching the whole expression.

10   You might rephrase the expression from the book so that it reads, "To use the addition property, you add 13 to each side of the equality." The student is interpreting the word *member* to mean each monomial in the equation.

11   No, $(A + B)(C + D) \neq AC + BD$. If one uses the distributive property twice, one can see that

$$(A + B)(C + D) = (A + B)C + (A + B)D = AC + BC + AD + BD.$$

Another way of showing this is to ask the student to substitute numbers in for A, B, C, D. For example, if A = 1, B = 2, C = 3 and D = 4,

$(A + B)(C + D) = 3 \cdot 7$ or   21,

$AC + BD = 3 + 8 = 11$

Since $11 \neq 21$, then $(A + B)(C + D) \neq AC + BD$.

12   If $\dfrac{4}{0} = 4$, then it should be the case that $4 = 0 \cdot 4$. Since $4 \neq 0$, then it cannot be true that $\dfrac{4}{0} = 4$. Since $\dfrac{4}{0}$ is equivalent to $4 \div 0$ and division can also be interpreted as repeated subtraction, then another way to look at this problem is as follows. How many times can we subtract zero objects from 4 objects until the 4 objects are gone. One could never accomplish this task. Thus $\dfrac{4}{0}$ does not represent any number.

13   It is true that 0 · 0 = 0, but the logic used to infer 0 ÷ 0 = 0 could also be used to infer 0 ÷ 0 = r since 0 · r = 0. Thus, how does one decide which number r should be used. It is this lack of uniqueness that has led mathematicians to say that 0 ÷ 0 is undefined.

14   No, the student is not correct. According to convention, multiplication and division are done first from left to right in whatever order they occur. Then addition and subtraction are done in the same manner. Thus, according to this convention, $3 \div 6 + 2 - 2 \times 10$ should be done as follows.

$$3 \div 6 + 2 - 2 \times 10 = \tfrac{1}{2} + 2 - 20 = 2\tfrac{1}{2} - 20 = -17\tfrac{1}{2}.$$

15   Probably at this level the best answer would be to say that 0^0 is an undefined expression. However, the case is not as clear cut as it might seem, and the two articles cited below give background information on this expression.

Herbert Vaughan, "The Expression '0^0'," *The Mathematics Teacher*, Vol. 63 (1970), pp. 111-2.

Also consult Answer 5 in Section A4.4

A2.12   *Number Theory and Average*

1   This student is making an unwarranted conclusion. The fact that the distance between numbers "gets longer" does not mean that at some point this distance becomes infinitely long. For example, the distance between the numbers 0, 1, 3, 6, 10, 15, 21, 28, ... gets longers as one considers consecutive pairs "further out" in the sequence. However, at no stage does this distance become infinite. The teacher might suggest that the student consider (intuitively) that distance *between* numbers cannot possibly be infinite because, in order to be *between*, the distance must be finite.

2   The study of prime numbers began with the Greeks long before negative integers were invented. Thus, historically, primes were developed with positive integers only, and it has been customary to follow, at least at the elementary level, this historic precedent.

      However, in advanced mathematics, such as abstract or modern algebra, it is the case that a more general approach is taken. In this case, one deals with irreducibles rather than primes, and one studies such notions as unique factorization domains, principal ideal domains, Euclidian domains, algebraic and Gaussian integers, norms, etc. For more information on this approach consult:

Fraleigh, *A First Course in Abstract Algebra*, Addison-Wesley Publishing Co., Reading, Ma., 1969, Section 32, 33 and 34.

3   No, the student is not correct. Average speed is defined as follows.

$$\text{Average speed} = \frac{\text{total distance}}{\text{total time}} \tag{1}$$

Thus substituting your values in (1), we get

$$\text{Average speed} = \frac{2}{(1/4)+(1/8)} = \frac{2}{3/8} = \frac{16}{3} = 5\tfrac{1}{3}.$$

In order to average 6 mph for the two miles, you would have to solve for x as follows. Let x denote the speed for the second mile. Then

$$6 = \frac{2}{(1/4) + (1/x)}$$

$$6 = \frac{8x}{4 + x}$$

$$8x = 24 + 6x$$

$$x = 12.$$

Thus you must run at 12 mph for the second mile.

4   If $n_1, n_2, ..., n_k$, is a list of primes, then the integer

$$n_1 n_2 \cdots n_k + 1$$

is not divisible by any one of the primes $n_1, n_2, ..., n_k$. Thus it is either a prime that is not in the given list, a power of a prime that is not in the given list, or a composite integer divisible by a prime that is not in the given list. For example, given the list of primes 3, 5, 7, then $3 \cdot 5 \cdot 7 + 1 = 106 = 2 \cdot 53$ leads to the new prime 53.

As far as the authors know there is no way to find the *next* prime after a given prime except by trial and error. In order to find out if x is a prime number, one only has to divide by primes less than $\sqrt{x}$, which simplifies the work considerably but still leaves a great deal of work if x happens to be a large number.

For more information on primes consult:

(1)   Stanley Ogilvy, *Tomorrows's Math*, 2nd ed., Oxford University Press, New York, 1972, Chap. 5.

(2)   Hans Rademacher and Otto Toeplitz, *The Enjoyment of Mathematics*, Princeton University Press, Princeton, N.J., 1957, Chap. 1.

A2.13   *Operations, Algorithms, Properties of Operations*

1   If addition was distributive over multiplication, then

$$a + (b \cdot c) = (a + b) \cdot (a + c) \tag{1}$$

However, (1) is not true for all real numbers a, b, c. For example, if $a = 1, b = 2, c = 3$, then (1) becomes

$$1 + (2 \cdot 3) = (1 + 2)(1 + 3),$$

which simplifies to the *false* statement $7 = 12$. However, we might be tempted to try to find out under what conditions (1) would be true.

$$a + (b \cdot c) = (a + b)(a + c) \Rightarrow a + b \cdot c$$
$$= a^2 + ab + ac + bc \Rightarrow a = a^2 + ab + ac.$$

If $a \neq 0$, then $1 = a + b + c$. Thus (1) is true when either $a = 0$ and b and c are any real numbers, or when $a \neq 0$ and $a + b + c = 1$.

Note that it might be pointed out to the student that even though (1) is not generally valid in our algebraic system, it is valid in a mathematical system called

Boolean Algebra. Perhaps at this point some students might want to explore this interesting mathematical system.

2   For an answer to this question, read:

> John C. Peterson, "Fourteen Different Strategies for Multiplication of Integers or Why $(-1)(-1) = +1$," *The Arithmetic Teacher*, May 1972, pp. 396-403.

3   The correct answer is "No." To show this, ask the student to substitute $a = b = 1$, which should lead the student to the *false* statement $\frac{1}{2} = 2$.

Actually, for *any* choice of a and b for which $\frac{1}{a+b}$ and $\frac{1}{a} + \frac{1}{b}$ are defined, the resulting expressions will be different. To show this might require more sophistication than can be expected at this level, but one method is following.

We seek numbers a and b such that $\frac{1}{a+b} = \frac{1}{a} + \frac{1}{b}$. Now by definition,

$$\frac{1}{a} + \frac{1}{b} = \frac{a+b}{ab},$$

Hence one is looking for numbers a and b such that the above equation is true. Or equivalently,

$$(a+b)^2 = ab \quad \text{or} \quad a^2 + 2ab + b^2 = ab, \quad \text{or}$$
$$a^2 + ab + b^2 = 0. \tag{1}$$

Now, pick *any* number b, $b \neq 0$, and substitute into (1). Then one obtains a quadratic in a, which gives

$$a = \frac{-b \pm \sqrt{b^2 - 4b^2}}{2} \quad \text{or} \quad a = \frac{-b \pm \sqrt{-3b^2}}{2}.$$

It is clear now that there is *no* corresponding (real) number a.

4   For an answer to this question, read the following article by Gary Musser.*

ADDITIVE INVERSES and NEGATIVES— TWO DIFFERENT CONCEPTS

By GARY L. MUSSER

Northern Illinois University

De Kalb, Illinois

CERTAINLY one of the best-known statements in arithmetic is the statement "The product of two negatives is positive." This expression is generally associated with the study of the ring of integers, but it also applies in the fields of rational and real numbers. Usually a ring-theoretic proof of the fact $(-a)$

$(-b) = ab$ is provided to prove the statement quoted above; however, the equation $[-(-5)](-3) = (-5)3$ is an instance of $(-a)(-b) = ab$, but certainly the equation $[-(-5)](-3) = (-5)3$ is not described by the sentence "The product of two negatives is positive." Sometimes a and b are restricted to be positive integers; thus $(-a)$ and $(-b)$ are negative integers and all is well. Also, $(-x)$ is sometimes referred to as "the negative of x," and then, in this context, $(-a)$ $(-b) = ab$ is considered to be an in-

From The Mathematics Teacher, April 1972, pp. 301-304. Reprinted by permission.

stance of "The product of two negatives is positive." However, it seems that more needs to be said. It is the purpose of this article to clarify the distinction between the two statements "The product of two negatives is positive" and "The product of the additive inverses of a and b is ab." I begin by establishing the fundamental notions that form the foundation of my discussion.

Rings and Additive Inverses

A set R together with two binary operations addition and multiplication defined on R is called a *ring* if the following familiar properties are satisfied.

R1: $(a + b) + c = a + (b + c)$ for all a, b, $c \in R$.

R2: There exists an element $0 \in R$ such that $a + 0 = a$ for all $a \in R$.

R3: For each $a \in R$ there exists an element $(-a) \in R$ such that $a + (-a) = 0$.

R4: $a + b = b + a$ for all $a, b \in R$.

R5: $(ab)c = a(bc)$ for all $a, b, c \in R$.

R6: $a(b + c) = ab + ac$ and $(b + c)a = ba + ca$ for all $a, b, c \in R$.

The integers, rational numbers, real numbers, and complex numbers, together with their usual additions and multiplications, are rings.

Using the properties of a ring and the (provable) fact that $a \cdot 0 = 0 \cdot a = 0$, the following detailed ring-theoretic proof of the fact $(-a)(-b) = ab$ can be given.

THEOREM. $(-a)(-b) = ab$ *for all $a, b \in R$.*

Proof.

$(-a)(-b)$	Reasons:
$= (-a)(-b) + 0$	R2
$= (-a)(-b) + a \cdot 0$	$a \cdot 0 = 0$ for all a
$= (-a)(-b) + a[(-b) + b]$	R3 and R4
$= (-a)(-b) + [a(-b) + ab]$	R6
$= [(-a)(-b) + a(-b)] + ab$	R1
$= [(-a) + a](-b) + ab$	R6
$= 0 \cdot (-b) + ab$	R4 and R3
$= 0 + ab$	$0 \cdot a = 0$ for all a
$= ab$	R4 and R2

In words, this theorem says that "the product of the additive inverses of a and b is ab." Applied to the ring of integers, it shows that $(-5)(-3) = 5 \cdot 3$ where -5 and -3 are viewed as additive inverses of 5 and 3 respectively. To gain more insight into the statement "The product of two negatives is positive," the

concepts of a partial order and a partially ordered ring will be considered next.

Partially Ordered Rings

A binary relation "$\leq$" on a set R is called a *partial order* if it satisfies the following properties where $a, b, c \in R$:

P1: $a \leq a$ for all $a \in R$.

P2: If $a \leq b$ and $b \leq a$, then $a = b$.

P3: If $a \leq b$ and $b \leq c$, then $a \leq c$.

In the ring of integers, the usual order, $a \leq b$ if $b - a \in \{0, 1, 2, \cdots\}$, is an example of a partial order. Graphically, $a \leq b$ holds if a coincides with b or a is to the left of b on the usual integer number line. Also, in any collection of sets, the relation "is a subset of" satisfies P1, P2, and P3; hence it is a partial order.

A ring R together with a partial order on R is called a *partially ordered ring* if for all $a, b, c \in R$ the following computational properties are satisfied:

PR1: If $a \leq b$, then $a + c \leq b + c$.

PR2: If $a \leq b$ and $0 \leq c$, then $ac \leq bc$ and $ca \leq cb$.

Notice that properties PR1 and PR2 relate the ring operations with the order relation just as distributivity connects addition with mutliplication in R6. The integers, the rational numbers, and the real numbers with their usual orders are partially ordered rings. The elements a such that $0 \leq a$ are called *positive* elements and those satisfying $a \leq 0$ are called *negative* elements. (Note: I follow Fuchs [1963] in considering zero to be both positive and negative. Nonzero positive elements are called strictly positive, denoted by $0 < a$, and nonzero negative elements, denoted by $a < 0$, are called strictly negative.)

The integers, rational numbers, and real numbers as partially ordered rings satisfy an additional property called the *trichotomy property:*

P4: For all $a \in R$, one and only one of the following holds—

$$a < 0 \text{ or } a = 0 \text{ or } 0 < a.$$

A partially ordered ring R that also satisfies the trichotomy property is called a *linearly ordered ring*, since the order among the elements of R can be displayed by the points of a line. Not all partially ordered rings are linearly ordered rings; in other words, there are partially ordered rings that contain nonzero elements that are neither positive nor negative. Later, using examples, an appeal to this fact will be made to clarify the distinction between the terms *negative* and *additive inverse*.

Negatives and Additive Inverses

Let R be a partially ordered ring. If a is a negative element, then $a \leq 0$. By PR1, $a \leq 0$ implies that $a + (-a) \leq 0 + (-a)$, or $0 \leq (-a)$. Thus, if a is negative, its additive inverse is positive. Now let a and b be negative; hence, $(-a)$ and $(-b)$ are positive. Since R is a ring, we have $(-a)(-b) = ab$. Furthermore, it follows from PR2 that the product of two positives is positive; hence, $(-a)(-b)$ is positive. Therefore the product ab of two negative elements a and b is positive. It is apparent from this proof that in a partially ordered ring the fact that the product of two negatives is positive is a *consequence* of the ring-theoretic fact $(-a)(-b) = ab$. Now let us consider examples that illustrate how the notions of additive inverses and negatives differ.

Our first example, though nonstandard, clearly illustrates the necessity for distinguishing between additive inverses and negatives. Define a relation "$\leq\leq$" on the ring of integers by having $a \leq\leq b$ if $b - a \in \{0, 2, 4, \cdots\}$. Then it is easy to show that "$\leq\leq$" is a partial order for the integers; moreover, the integers form a partially ordered ring with respect to "$\leq\leq$." As usual, we say that a is 'positive' if $0 \leq\leq a$ and that a is 'negative' if $a \leq\leq 0$. Therefore, $\{0, 2, 4, \ldots\}$ is the set of all 'positive' integers, and $\{0, -2, -4, \ldots\}$ is the set of all 'negative' integers (see fig. 1). It still follows from the ring-theoretic proof that $(-5)(-3) = 15$; however, $(-5)(-3) = 15$ is *not* an instance of the statement "The product of two 'negatives' is 'positive,'" since neither (-5) nor (-3) is negative (nor is 15 positive) with respect to the partial order "$\leq\leq$."

Neither 'Positive' nor 'Negative' Integers

$$-5 \quad -3 \quad -1 \quad 1 \quad 3 \quad 5$$

$$-6 \quad -4 \quad -2 \quad 0 \quad 2 \quad 4 \quad 6$$

'Negative' Integers   'Positive' Integers

Fig. 1

For a second example, let $C(R)$ denote the set of all continuous functions having the field of real numbers as their domain and range. For $f, g \in C(R)$, if $f + g$ and $f \cdot g$ are defined by $(f + g)(x) = f(x) + g(x)$ and $(f \cdot g)(x) = f(x)g(x)$ respectively, then $C(R)$ together with this addition and multiplication is a ring. Furthermore, if an order on $C(R)$ is defined by $f \leq g$ whenever $f(x) \leq g(x)$ for all real numbers x, then the ring $C(R)$ together with this order relation is a partially ordered ring. Graphically, $f \leq g$ holds if and only if the graph of f is never above the graph of g. Hence, a function f is positive if $0 \leq f(x)$ for all real numbers x and negative if $f(x) \leq 0$ for all real numbers x. Clearly, there are many functions in $C(R)$ that are neither positive nor negative; for example, $f(x) = x$ is such a function. In fact, any function whose graph has points both above and below the x-axis is such a function (fig. 2). Now consider

$f \leq g$ $0 \leq f$

$f \leq 0$ $0 \not\leq f$ and $f \not\leq 0$

Fig. 2

the functions f and g defined by the equations $f(x) = x$ and $g(x) = 5 - x$. Then $(-f)$ and $(-g)$ are defined by $(-f)(x) = -x$ and $(-g)(x) = x - 5$, and $f \cdot g$ is given by $(f \cdot g)(x) = x(5 - x) = 5x - x^2$. Now $(-f)(-g) = f \cdot g$; however, it is easily seen that neither $(-f)$ nor $(-g)$ is negative, nor is $f \cdot g$ positive (fig. 3).

$(-f)(x) = -x \qquad (-g)(x) = x - 5 \qquad (f \cdot g)(x) = 5x - x^2$

Fig. 3

Here again, the statement "The product of two negatives is positive" is not an appropriate description of the equation $(-f) \cdot (-g) = f \cdot g$.

There are many other examples of partially ordered rings which clearly distinguish between negatives and additive inverses. For example, let R be the ring of 2-by-2 matrices over the real numbers and define "$\leq$" by

$$\begin{bmatrix} a & b \\ c & d \end{bmatrix} \leq \begin{bmatrix} e & f \\ g & h \end{bmatrix}$$

if $a \leq e$, $b \leq f$, $c \leq g$, and $d \leq h$. Also, let R be the field of complex numbers, and define "$\leq$" by $a + bi \leq c + di$ if $a \leq c$ and $b \leq d$. Both these examples are partially ordered rings, and as in the preceding examples, they are not linearly ordered rings; so they both contain elements that are neither positive nor negative.

The above discussion indicates the importance of distinguishing between negatives and additive inverses, and, furthermore, it demonstrates the need to use precise language when discussing these two concepts.

Epilogue

To illustrate the necessity for differentiating between statements involving additive inverses and negatives, partially ordered rings have been used. Appealing to partially ordered rings is quite natural because they play such a fundamental role in mathematics. However, the critical reader may have observed that it was necessary to appeal only to an algebraic structure that is "between" a ring and a partially ordered ring.

To elaborate, let R be a ring under addition and multiplication, and let P be a nonempty subset of R that is closed under multiplication. Then call the elements in P positive and their additive inverses negative. Now, as before, we can prove that the product of two negatives is positive. This reasoning is the kind that is sometimes used to justify the statement "The product of two negatives is positive" in the ring of integers. There, the natural numbers are called positive integers and their additive inverses are called negative integers. Although this is a correct approach, a partially ordered ring structure seems to be the appropriate mode of justification because of its importance among the structures of mathematics.

REFERENCES

Birkhoff, G., and S. MacLane. *A Survey of Modern Algebra.* 3d ed. New York: Macmillan Co., 1965.

Fuchs, L. *Partially Ordered Algebraic Systems.* New York: Pergamon Press, 1963.

Halmos, P. *Naive Set Theory.* Princeton: Van Nostrand Co., 1960.

5   The student is assuming that multiplication distributes over multiplication, which is not valid in our algebraic system; i.e., a · (b · c) = (a · b)(a · c). You might try to convince the student of this fact by asking the student if 2 · (3 · 4) = (2 · 3) · (2 · 4). Since 24 ≠ 48, then

   a · (b · c) ≠ (a · b)(a · c).

Another approach might be to show that if $(6t)\sqrt{3} = 6\sqrt{3} \cdot t\sqrt{3}$, then the right hand side should name the same numbers as the left hand side for all values of

t. If t = 1, then $(6t)\sqrt{3} = 6\sqrt{3}$ while $6\sqrt{3} \cdot t\sqrt{3} = 6\sqrt{3}\sqrt{3} = 18$. In general,

$$6\sqrt{3} \cdot t\sqrt{3} = (6t)(\sqrt{3} \cdot \sqrt{3}) = 6t \cdot 3 = 18t$$

and $18t \neq 6t\sqrt{3}$.

6 For adding 5 days and 2 hours, we know that there is a definite relationship between days and hours; i.e., 5 days = 120 hours. Thus 5 days and 2 hours = 120 hours and 2 hours = 122 hours. However, if we are just given x and y, then without additional information we do not know of the relationship between these two quantities. Thus the only thing we can do is to leave them as they are. For more information on this subject, consult:

Hassler Whitney, "The Mathematics of Physical Quantities,"*The Mathematical Monthly*, Vol. 75, No. 2, Part I. (Part II appears in the next issue.)

7 One way of explaining to the student that he is incorrect is to write the problem as follows.

$$\frac{1}{2}(18\sqrt{3}) = \frac{1}{2} \cdot (18 \cdot \sqrt{3}).$$

Since the numbers involved are real numbers, and since multiplication is associative,

$$\frac{1}{2} \cdot (18 \cdot \sqrt{3}) = \left(\frac{1}{2} \cdot 18\right)\sqrt{3} = 9\sqrt{3}.$$

However, by the student's method $\frac{1}{2}(18\sqrt{3}) = (9/2)\sqrt{3}$.

Another way of convincing the student that he is wrong is to write $\frac{1}{2}(18\sqrt{3})$ as $\frac{18\sqrt{3}}{2}$ or $(18\sqrt{3}) \div 2$. Then you might explain to the student that there are 18 square roots of 3 and we want to divide them by 2. Thus, we should get 9 square roots of 3 for the answer.

The basic procedure here is to show the student that multiplication is not distributive over multiplication. Thus, you might ask the student if

$$2 \cdot (3 \cdot 4) = (2 \cdot 3)(2 \cdot 4).$$

Hopefully, the student would see that since $24 \neq 48$, then

$$a \cdot (b \cdot c) \neq (a \cdot b) \cdot (a \cdot c).$$

8 No, the student is not correct.

$$\begin{aligned}
(3 + T) - (T - 5) &= (3 + T) + (-(T - 5)) \\
&= (3 + T) + (5 - T) \\
&= (3 + 5) + (T - T) \\
&= 8
\end{aligned}$$

The student is trying to use a form of the associative property in a problem involving subtraction, but subtraction is not associative.

A2.14   *Polynomials and Rational Expressions*

1   No, the student is not correct. The division algorithm for polynomials states that if A and B are polynomials where B is not the zero polynomial, then there exists unique polynomials, Q and R, such that $A = B \cdot Q + R$, where R is either the zero polynomial or where the degree of R is less than the degree of B. If the above is multiplied by $1/B$, then one obtains the quotient

$$\frac{A}{B} = Q + \frac{R}{B}$$

or, in our problem,

$$\frac{15y^4 + 9y^3 + 4y^2 + 1}{y^2 - 1} = 15y^2 + 9y + 19 + \frac{9y + 20}{y^2 - 1}.$$

2   A polynomial over the set of integers is defined to be a monomial or the algebraic sum of two or more monomials over the set of integers. A monomial over the integers is defined to be either a product of integers or a product of integers and variables with the exponents of the variables being positive and integral. The expression $2(x^2 + x)$ is thus not a polynomial by definition. However, $2(x^2 + x)$ is a polynomial expression where the term polynomial expression is defined to be any polynomial or any expression that can be formed by using two or more polynomials and indicating the operations by addition or multiplication. Thus all polynomials are polynomial expressions, but not all polynomial expressions are polynomials.

3   The problem here is that the teacher made a statement leaving out a necessary restriction. The teacher meant to say that $x^2 - 2$ cannot be factored over the set of rational numbers. The student is correct since $x^2 - 2$ can be factored over the set of real numbers.

4   The student is correct in saying that $1/|x|$ is not a rational expression, but the reason given by the student is incorrect. $1/|x|$ is not a rational expression because $|x|$ is not a polynomial. One should question the student further as to what he means by *two values.*

5   No, not always. Consider the following expression $\sqrt{3} - \sqrt{3}$ which equals the rational number 0. Another example would be $\sqrt{2} \cdot \sqrt{2} = 4$.

A2.15   *Radicals and Square Roots*

1   The student's answer is correct, but the method given is not. Consider the following problem:

$$\sqrt{16} + \sqrt{-16} = ?$$

According to the student's method, the answer should be zero because $16 - 16 = 0$. However, $\sqrt{16} = 4$ while $\sqrt{-16} = 4i$ and $4 + 4i \neq 0$.

   The student will get the correct answer in the case where the root is the same odd number. This is reflected in the example on the following page.

$$\sqrt[n]{k} + \sqrt[n]{-k} = 0 \quad \text{when } n = 2t + 1, \, t \in I \text{ and } k \in I.$$

2   Yes, it is correct as illustrated below.

$$2^{1/16} = \left(2^{1/8}\right)^{1/2} = \sqrt{2^{1/8}}$$
$$2^{1/8} = \left(2^{1/4}\right)^{1/2} = \sqrt{2^{1/4}}$$

Thus $2^{1/16} = \sqrt{\sqrt{2^{1/4}}}$,

$$2^{1/4} = \left(2^{1/2}\right)^{1/2} = \sqrt{\sqrt{2}}.$$

Thus $2^{1/16} = \sqrt{\sqrt{\sqrt{\sqrt{2}}}}$.

3   For an answer to this question, refer to Section A1.13, Answer 1.

4   No, this student is not correct. $\sqrt{x^2}$ means that nonnegative number t such that $x^2 = t^2$. If $x = -5$, then according to the student's definition $\sqrt{(-5)^2} = -5$, but -5 is a negative number. The correct definition should be $\sqrt{x^2} = |x|$.

5   What you are really saying is that $\sqrt{a} + \sqrt{b} = \sqrt{a + b}$ for all a, b. However, this is not correct. Consider $a = 4$ and $b = 4$, then $\sqrt{a} + \sqrt{b} = 4$ while $\sqrt{a + b} = \sqrt{8} = 2\sqrt{2}$, which is less than 4. Thus, in general, $\sqrt{a} + \sqrt{b} \neq \sqrt{a + b}$.

   Problem   Under what conditions will the student's method work?

6   Simplifying the expression $\sqrt{11/3x^2}$ is usually done as illustrated:

$$\sqrt{\frac{11}{3x^2}} = \frac{\sqrt{11}}{\sqrt{3x^2}} \tag{1}$$

$$\frac{\sqrt{11}}{\sqrt{3x^2}} = \frac{\sqrt{11}}{\sqrt{3}\sqrt{x^2}} \tag{2}$$

$$\frac{\sqrt{11}}{\sqrt{3}\sqrt{x^2}} = \frac{\sqrt{33}}{3\sqrt{x^2}} \tag{3}$$

$$\frac{\sqrt{33}}{3\sqrt{x^2}} = \frac{\sqrt{33}}{3|x|} \tag{4}$$

Thus, the student is correct. However, after a set of exercises using the definition of absolute value are assigned to students, textbooks frequently specify that henceforth we shall assume that all variables are positive unless otherwise specified. If this is the situation with the given problem, then the teacher is justified in writing $\sqrt{33}/3x$ in (4) above. However, this restriction should be pointed out to the students in order to avoid confusion.

7   One algorithm for finding cube roots is given below. This algorithm is similar to one of the algorithms for finding square roots and is based on the binomial theorem; i.e.,

$$(a + b)^3 - a^3 = (3a^2 + 3ab + b^2) \cdot b.$$

Thus, to find the cube root of 9685, one proceeds as follows on the next page.

```
        9  685.000   (21.3)
        8
  1200 |1  685
    60 |
     1 |1  261
  1261
 132300 |  424 000
   1890 |
      0 |  402 597
 134199 |   21 403
          etc.
```

One might tell the student that there are other methods for finding cube and higher order roots such as using logarithms, Newton's method and Horner's method which the student will learn in more advanced courses in mathematics. For example, using logarithms:

$$\log \sqrt[3]{9.685} = \frac{1}{3} \log 9.685$$

$$= \frac{1}{3} \cdot (3.9861)$$

$$\log \sqrt[3]{9.685} = 1.3287$$

$$\sqrt[3]{9.685} = 21.3$$

A2.16   Sets

1   One way of helping the student would be to use indirect proof as follows. Let A be an arbitrary set. Either $\phi \subseteq A$ or $\phi \not\subseteq A$. Suppose that $\phi \not\subseteq A$. It would then follow that ϕ must contain at least one element that is not in A. However, if ϕ contains at least one element, then ϕ is not the empty set. Thus ϕ must be a subset of A.

An intuitive way of helping the student follows. Let A be an arbitrary set containing say n elements. Then one way of getting a subset of A could be to take elements out of A one by one. After we take all of the elements out of A, we are left with the empty set, which would also be a subset of A.

2   No. Consider A where $A = \{x | 0 \leqslant x \leqslant 1, x \in \text{real numbers}\}$. This set has a largest element, namely 1, but it certainly is not finite.

This student is also assuming that there is some "natural" order associated with *every set*. It should be made clear to the student that this is *not* the case. For example, consider the set of students in the class. One might order this set according to height or according to weight, but one should be able to consider this set without reference to any such order.

3   Two infinite sets are not necessarily equivalent (i.e., contain the same number of elements). For example, the set of natural numbers is not equivalent to the set of real numbers. The proof below is standard in illustrating the above statement.

Assume that there is a one-to-one correspondence between the real numbers and the natural numbers. Let each real number be represented by a nonterminating decimal in this correspondence. If the following represents the correspondence between the natural numbers and the real numbers, then one can find a real number that is not listed.

TABLE 2.12.1

Natural numbers	Real numbers
1	$0.a_{11}a_{12}a_{13}a_{14} \cdots$
2	$0.a_{21}a_{22}a_{23}a_{24} \cdots$
3	$0.a_{31}a_{32}a_{33}a_{34} \cdots$
4	$0.a_{41}a_{42}a_{43}a_{44} \cdots$
5	$0.a_{51}a_{52}a_{53}a_{54} \cdots$
6	
$\vdots$	

Replace each digit along the diagonal, $a_{11}, a_{22}, a_{33}, a_{44}, \ldots$, by a different one, c_1, $c_2, c_3, c_4, \ldots$, where c_n is not 0 or 9. The number given by the nonterminating decimal $0.c_1 c_2 c_3 \ldots$ is a real number that is not paired with any natural number since it differs from each given number by at least one digit. Thus, our assumption that there was a one-to-one correspondence between the natural numbers and the real numbers is false.

4   A set is finite if we can count the elements in the set and the counting comes to an end. A set is infinite if in trying to count the elements in the set, the counting never ends.

More precisely, a set A is finite if there exists a nonnegative integer k such that the set A contains precisely k elements. That is, there is a one-to-one correspondence between the elements of A and the elements of the set $\{1, 2, 3, \ldots, k\}$ where $k \geqslant 1$. The empty set is considered to be finite since it contains precisely zero elements. A set is infinite if it is not finite. That is, for every positive integer n, one can find n + 1 distinct elements in A.

A2.17   Simultaneous Systems of Equations

1   In solving the simultaneous linear equations.

$$2x + 3y = 6$$
$$-6x - 9y = -14$$

we are looking for the set of all ordered pairs (x, y) that satisfy both equations. Now

(a) $\left. \begin{array}{l} 2x + 3y = 6 \\ -6x - 9y = -14 \end{array} \right\}$ is equivalent to   (b) $\left. \begin{array}{l} 6x + 9y = 18 \\ -6x - 9y = -14 \end{array} \right\}$

which is equivalent to   (c) $\left. \begin{array}{l} 0 \cdot x + 0 \cdot y = 4 \\ -6x - 9y = -14 \end{array} \right\}$ (1)
                                                                                      (2)

Since no ordered pair (x, y) is a solution of (1), then (c) has no solution. Since (a) and (c) are equivalent systems of equations, then (a) also has no solution. If one sketches the graph of (a), then the graph would consist of two parallel lines, which do not intersect and thus have no common solutions for the given equations.

2   In solving the simultaneous linear equations

$$2x + 3y = 6$$
$$-4x - 6y = -12,$$

we are looking for the set of all ordered pairs (x, y) that satisfy each equation. Now

(a) $\left.\begin{array}{l} 2x + 3y = 6 \\ -4x - 6y = -12 \end{array}\right\}$ is equivalent to   (b) $\left.\begin{array}{l} 4x + 6y = 12 \\ -4x - 6y = -12 \end{array}\right\}$

which is equivalent to   (c) $\begin{array}{l} 0 \cdot x + 0 \cdot y = 0 \\ -4x - 6y = -12 \end{array}$ (1)
                                                                (2)

Since any ordered pair (x, y) satisfies (1), then the solution set of (c) consists of all those ordered pairs (x, y) that satisfy (2), which is an infinite number since one simply chooses an x and then finds y. Since (c) is equivalent to (a), then the solution set of (a) is an infinite set and consists of all ordered pairs that satisfy (2). If one sketches the graph of (a), then the graph would turn out to be a straight line. The equations in (a) are equivalent equations and thus each has the same line for its graph.

3   The student is saying that the system of equations

$$\left.\begin{array}{l} 2x + 3y = 4 \\ x - y = 5 \end{array}\right\}$$

is equivalent to $y = -6/5$, which is of course incorrect. The student should complete the problem, getting the equivalent system of equations as follows:

$$y = -6/5$$
$$x = 19/5.$$

Thus $\{19/5, -6/5\}$ is the solution set of the original system of equations.

4   Equivalent equations are equations that have the same solution set; for example,

$$2x + 3 = 5 \text{ is equivalent to } 2x = 2 \text{ or } x = 1.$$

Equivalent systems of equations are *systems* (two or more) of equations that have the same solution set; for example,

$\left.\begin{array}{l} x + 2y = 8 \\ 2x - 3y = 2 \end{array}\right\}$ is equivalent to $\left.\begin{array}{l} x = 4 \\ y = 2 \end{array}\right\}$

Thus the concept of equivalent systems of equations is a generalization of equivalent equations. Notice, however, that even though equivalent systems of equations have the same solution set, the equations forming the equivalent systems need not be equivalent; i.e., $x + 2y = 8$ is not equivalent to $x = 4$, and $2x - 3y = 2$ is not equivalent to $y = 2$.

A2.18   *Slope*

1   Yes, you can. Consider the graph shown in Figure 2.18.1.

FIGURE 2.18.1

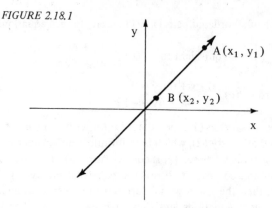

If we can pick convenient points such as A and B whose coordinates can be determined, then $\dfrac{y_1 - y_2}{x_1 - x_2}$ would be the slope of the line.

If the equation of the line is given, then two points can readily be determined by substituting into the equation, and the slope can be found as above.

2   Slope has been defined in a meaningful way as the change of the y coordinates of two distinct points, Δy, divided by the change of x coordinates, Δx, of these two points. When the line is vertical, then we run into the expression $\Delta y / \Delta x$ where $\Delta x = 0$ and $\Delta y \neq 0$. Since this expression does not represent any definite number, then we say that the slope of a vertical line is not defined as a number.

3   As far as we know there does not seem to be a good reason for using the letter m for slope. As Howard W. Eves points out in his book *Mathematical Circles Revisited,** "When lecturing before an analytic geometry class during the early part of the course, one may say: 'We designate the slope of a line by m, because the word slope starts with the letter m; I know no better reason',".

In many situations such as this one, we really do not know why a particular letter or symbol is used, such as θ for angle. However, what usually happens is that after a choice is made, this choice seems to carry over in the writings of other people. In this particular case, it might have been that since slopes were first studied with respect to mountains that the first letter of the word mountain was used to designate slope, but we really do not know.

**Howard W. Eves, *Mathematical Circles Revisited,* Prindle, Weber & Schmidt, Boston, Ma., 1971, p. 141, 267.*

A2.19   *Word Problems*

1   Yes, the student is correct. Solving this problem using a standard method, one gets the following:

> x = rate of boat in still water,
> r = rate of current.

> $x + r = 8$
> $\underline{x - r = 6}$
> $2x = 14$
> $x = 7$

Thus $r = 1$.

2   As the first equation shows, the student is correct only when half the money is invested at each interest rate for the same amount of time.

> If the money is invested for different time periods or if some other combination other than half of the money at each interest rate is given, then the student's method will not work. However, a method might be worked out in the latter cases by using a weighted average.

3   The method is correct, and the solution would be completely correct if the student had put 7½ *hours* for the answer.

4   By adding 96 to 402 and subtracting 96 from 402, the student is saying that one candidate received 192 votes more than his opponent. If the student subtracts 48 (½ of 96) from 402 and then adds 48 to 402, the difference between the number of votes each candidate received would be 96.

5   Although the student shows good intuitive thinking in this problem, the student is incorrect. The main difficulty is that the current going one way does not cancel it going the other way, since the time going each way is not the same. If one solves the problem using the standard method, one gets the following:

> x = rate of boat in still water,
> r = rate of current.

> $24 = (x + r)2$
> $24 = (x - r)4$

Thus $12 = x + r$
> $\underline{6 = x - r}$
> $x = 9$
> $r = 3$.

6   No, the student is not correct. In dividing 2.5 by 4, the answer of .625 represents the time needed to cook one pound of meat. In multiplying .625 by 9, the student is multiplying two numbers that both represent time. A correct way of doing the problem is:

$$\begin{array}{r} 1.6 \\ 2.5\overline{)4.00} \\ \underline{2\,5} \\ 1\,50 \end{array}$$

Thus 1.6 represents the number of pounds of meat cooked in one hour. Then

$$\begin{array}{r} 1.6 \\ 9 \\ \hline 14.4 \end{array}$$

represents the number of pounds of meat cooked in 9 hours.

7 Yes, the student is correct. The student has conjectured this well-known result in a
number theory: The number of different ways of writing n as a sum of consecutive
integers equals d(m) where m is the largest odd number dividing m and d(m) is the
number of positive divisors of m*. For example, 15 has four odd divisors, 1, 3, 5,
15, and thus it can be written in four different ways as a sum of consecutive integers; namely,

$$15 = 7 + 8$$
$$15 = 15$$
$$15 = 4 + 5 + 6$$
$$15 = 1 + 2 + 3 + 4 + 5.$$

The result is one that a teacher, using an inductive discovery teaching method, could use to good advantage in any class. For example, the teacher could give
each student in the class five different numbers and see if each of those numbers
that is not a power of two can be written as a sum of consecutive integers. After
doing this, the teacher could ask the students to find the number of different ways
each of their numbers can be written as a sum of consecutive integers. Perhaps
after doing this, the students could conjecture the result given above. This result
could be very useful in classes called general mathematics or basic skill classes. Notice the number of different addition combinations that a particular student has to
perform while working on this problem.

We suggest that you do not ask your students to prove this result but rather
have them conjecture the general result.

For more information on this problem, read:

Robert W. Prielipp and Norbert J. Kuenzi, "Sums of Consecutive Positive Integers," *The Mathematics Teacher*, Jan. 1975, pp. 18-21.

8 The student's answer is correct. If one compares the student's method with the following "standard" method of solving this problem, one might suspect that the student's method is incorrect and just happened to work in this case.

x = Jim's age now	x + 2 = Jim's age in 2 years
x + 30 = Mike's age now	x + 32 = Mike's age in 2 years

$$\therefore x + 32 = 2(x + 2)$$

$$x + 32 = 2x + 4 \tag{1}$$

However, if one compares (1) with the student's equation at this point, one finds
that they are equivalent. If the problem was changed from "2 years from now" to
"y years from now," it looks as if the student would get the following:

$$2x + y = x + 30 \tag{2}$$

---

*Andrews, George, *Number Theory*, W. B. Saunders and Co., Philadelphia, 1971,
p. 84, Problem 4.

Solving this generalized problem in the standard way, one gets

$$x + 30 + y = 2(x + y),$$
$$x + 30 = 2x + y \tag{3}$$

Thus even in the generalized problem, the student gets the correct equation. Whether the student just happened to stumble across this method by sheer accident and it happens to work in this problem, or whether the student has insight into the problem (or simplified his equation in his head) cannot be determined by what is given.

9 	Yes, the student is correct. Many students and teachers assume that three consecutive even integers must be represented by 2y, 2y + 2, 2y + 4. However, if we let 2y = x, then it is obvious that either representation can be used.

3

Geometry

QUESTIONS

Q3.1   *Angles*

1   A student asks you if a dihedral angle is really an angle. What is your response?

2   One of your students says that the angle shown in (b) is bigger. How do you respond?

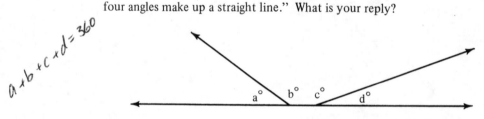

(a)   (b)

3   A student makes the statement, "In the diagram below a + b + c + d = 180 since the four angles make up a straight line." What is your reply?

$a + b + c + d = 360$

4   After showing students how to bisect an angle, how do you answer the student who asks, "Is it possible to divide an angle into three equal parts?"

5   A student says, "I think that the theorem which states that vertical angles are congruent is wrong. Look at the diagrams below. Angle 1 is not congruent to angle 3." How do you respond?   (See page 115 for figure.)

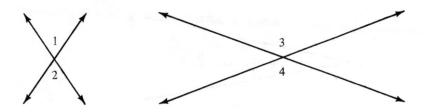

6   You draw the following figure on the blackboard.

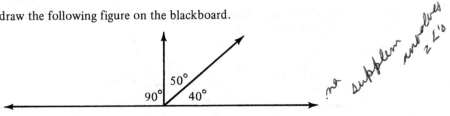

no supplem involves 2 L's

A student said that these angles are supplementary because their sum is 180°. Is the student correct?

7   The problem is: "The measure of each interior angle of an equiangular polygon is five times as large as the measure of an exterior angle of the polygon. How many sides does the polygon have?" Student's solution:

$$5(\cancel{360}) = (n - 2)\cancel{180}$$
$$10 = n - 2$$
$$12 = n$$

Is this method of solving the problem correct?

8   A student asks, "We have defined an angle as the union of two distinct rays that have the same endpoint but do not lie in the same line. However, in the figures below the angles are the same (i.e., same set of points rotate $\overrightarrow{BC}$ about point B) but they look different. I don't understand." How do you respond?

9   A student asks, "We said that a bisector of an angle is the set of all points that are the same distance from both sides of an angle. Yet in the figure below, R is not the same distance as S from the sides of the angle. What is wrong?" How do you respond? (See figure on page 116.)

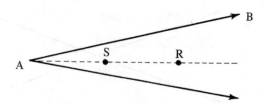

10   A student claims that there are four different angles in this drawing: ∠1, ∠2, ∠3, ∠4. What is your response?

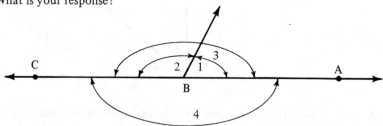

11   "In studying the concept of an angle, we have seen that it is related to an arc of a circle. Is there an analogue of this relationship in three dimensions?" How do you reply to this student?

12   A student asks, "Can two angles have a common side and a common vertex and not be adjacent?" How do you respond?

13   You are going over the following problem. "Represent as a single fraction, the measure of the complement of an angle whose measure is x − 10." One of the students says that he did the problem as follows:

Let x = the measure of the complement of the angle
x − 10 = the measure of the angle

x + (x − 10) = 90
2x − 10 = 90
2x = 100
x = 50,   x − 10 = 40

Is the student correct?

14   A textbook makes the statement that an acute angle is an angle whose measure is less than 90°. A student then asks you if an angle whose measure is zero is an acute angle? How do you respond?

15   You have assigned the following problem to your class. "The measures of the acute angles of a right triangle have the ratio 3:4. Find, to the nearest whole minute, the number of degrees and minutes in the smaller angle." One student hands in the following work. Let 3x equal the measure of the smaller angle and 4x equal the measure of the larger angle. Then

$$7x = 90 \quad \text{or} \quad x = \frac{90}{7}.$$

$$\begin{array}{r} 12.8 \\ 7\,\overline{)89°60'} \\ 7 \\ \hline 19 \\ 14 \\ \hline 56 \end{array}$$

$x = 12.8$

$3x = 38°40'$

Is the student correct?

Q3.2   *Axioms and Definitions*

1   A student questions the statement that a point is an undefined term. The student reasons that a point can be defined as the intersection of two lines, and that a line could then be defined as the intersection of two planes. Thus, the only necessary undefined term in a high school geometry class would be *plane*. What is your response?

2   A student asks, "What is the difference between a postulate and an axiom?" How do you respond?

3   A student makes the following statement. "Explain how the completeness axiom for the real numbers provides the numbers necessary to fill up the number line, not already filled by the rationals." How do you respond?

4   A student comments that we often use function notation in other ways. For example, the notation that we use to name segments, rays, or lines, etc. is actually function notation. What would your reaction to this statement be? Explain what the student meant using the following symbolism.

(a) $\overleftrightarrow{AB}$ (b) $\angle ABC$

Can you show what the function symbol f refers to in each example and what f(x) refers to?

5   A student asks, "In geometry if the definition of the word *point* is undefined, how is it possible to use something that is not really there?" How do you respond?

6   "What is the difference between *necessary* and *sufficient* in the statement and proof of a theorem?" How do you respond to this student?

7   A student asks, "If AB≅CD means AB = CD, why do we need the notation AB≅CD since we have the notation AB = CD already?" How do you respond?

8   A student asks you why axioms are not proved like theorems are. How do you respond?

Q3.3   *Circles and Constructions*

1   A student asks you if a circular region is really a region. How do you respond?

2   While studying circles in your geometry class, a student asks you what is the relationship between a tangent to a circle and the tangent of an angle that he studied in Algebra I. What is your answer?

3   A student asks you why great circles have the name *great*? How do you respond?

4   You ask your students to draw two circles such that they have three common tangents. One student says that it can't be done. Is the student right?

5   A student asks you if all circles are similar. How do you respond?

6   A student asks you if it is always possible to find a great circle through any two points in a given sphere. One student claims that it is impossible to find a great circle through the points P and Q in the diagram below. Is this student correct?

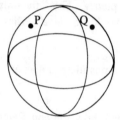

7   A student asks if you can draw a circle by using only straight lines. How do you respond?

8ᶜ   "Can circles only be circumscribed about regular polygons?" How would you reply to this student?

9   A student asks you why the center of an arc is not also the midpoint of the arc? How do you respond?

10   "In the constructions that we have done, we were allowed to use both a compass and a straightedge. How many of these constructions can be done with only a compass?" How would you respond to this student?

Q3.4   Congruence

1   A student asks, "I understand what is meant by two triangles being congruent, but how do we define congruence for sets of figures in general?" How do you respond?

2   A student asks, "In proving that two triangles are congruent, we have seen that it is not necessary to test the congruence of all six pairs of corresponding parts. Three pairs are sufficient, SSS or SAS or ASA. How many pairs would be sufficient for a quadrilateral or, in fact, any polygon?" What is your answer?

Q3.5   *Convexity and Inequalities*

1   While studying convex polygons, a student asks, "Does the theorem concerning the sum of the interior angles of a polygon hold not only when it is convex but also when it is concave?" How would you answer the student? (*Hint* The sum of the interior angles of a convex polygon of n sides is $(n - 2)180°$.)

2   A student asks you if the empty set or a set containing one point are convex sets. The student does not think so because the textbook's definition states that for every two distinct points A and B, $\overline{AB}$ must be in the figure. How would you answer the student?

3   A student asks, "Are there situations in which an inequality is true in both half planes?" How would you answer?

4   "How do I know that the feasible region which arises in a linear programming problem will be a convex set?" How do you respond to this student?

Q3.6   *Logic*

1   You ask your class if the following statement is true or false. "If not a square, then not a rhombus." One student says "if not a square" implies it could be a rectangle and a rectangle is not a rhombus. Therefore the statement is true. Do you agree?

2   You are beginning the proof of the statement that the diagonals of a parallelogram bisect each other. A student asks, "Don't we have to show that the diagonals intersect in the interior of the parallelogram?" Is this student correct?

3   The problem given to the class is as follows.

Prove If 2 lines are intersected by a transversal, such that the two alternate interior angles are congruent, then the lines are parallel.

Given $\overleftrightarrow{DC}$ and $\overrightarrow{EA}$ intersected by transversal $\overleftrightarrow{AC}$ so that $\angle EAC \cong \angle ACR$.

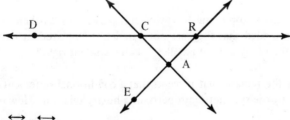

Prove $\overleftrightarrow{DC} \parallel \overleftrightarrow{EA}$.

A student offers the following proof. "Suppose $\overleftrightarrow{DC}$ is not parallel to $\overleftrightarrow{EA}$, then the two lines intersect at some point, say R. A triangle ACR is formed having an exterior angle EAC. According to a previous theorem, the measure of an exterior angle of a triangle is greater than either remote interior angle. Therefore

$$m\angle EAC > m\angle ACR,$$

but this contradicts the given that $\angle EAC \cong \angle ACR$. Therefore assumption that $\overleftrightarrow{DC}$ is not parallel to $\overleftrightarrow{EA}$ is false; therefore two lines are parallel."

This proof could be used to prove any pair of lines are parallel. What is wrong with the theory? The above problem was given to a geometry class by a student teacher. The answer given by the student teacher was the following: "By assuming that willing something is so, if two lines are not parallel, then alternate interior angles could never be formed that were congruent, and the balance of the proof is fallcious." How would you react to this problem and the statement offered by this student teacher?

4   In your tenth grade class, you are now going over the truth table for a conditional statement. The students are having trouble understanding why the last two rows of the conditional are marked true (i.e., antecedent false, consequent true, and antecedent false, consequent false). How would you help them?

5   A student asks, "While studying these truth tables, we have assumed that a statement is either true or false. Is there a mathematical study of truth tables in which statements could be true, false, and possibly true?" How do you respond?

6   A student asks you if there is any connection between the biconditional and the idea of equivalent expressions that he learned in Algebra I. What is your response?

7   During a lesson on indirect proofs, a student says, "Why do we have to assume the opposite of the conclusion? Why can't we assume the opposite of the given and try to contradict the conclusion?" What is your reply?

8   You ask a student to give you the negation of "All men are good." The student says that the negation would be "All men are not good." Is the student right?

9   "If we can always use direct proof, why do we need to know about indirect proofs?" How would you answer the student?

10   A student asks, "How do we know that we are talking about straight lines when there has been no indication that a line must be straight. Couldn't it be curved?" What is your response?

11   You ask your students to put the following statement into "if-then" form. "Two planes intersect provided that they are not parallel." One student writes, "If two planes intersect, then they are not parallel." Is the student right?

12   A student makes the remark that it seems that a conditional statement and its converse are related to the symmetric property of a binary relation. How do you react to this remark?

13   A student makes the following statement. "A sphere is the three-dimensional figure analogous to a circle, a two dimensional figure. Since at a point on a circle there is exactly one line tangent to the circle, there is exactly one line tangent to a sphere at a point on the sphere." Is this student correct?

14   A student asks, "Our book says that the geometry written by Euclid had defects in it, but the book does not say what they were. Could you tell me?" How would you reply?

15   A student says that the number of points on a line segment is finite. How can you convince the student that this is not correct?

16   "Is it ever possible in mathematics to prove a statement or theorem by proving a special case of the statement or theorem?" How do you respond to this student?

17   One of the problems in your textbook is stated as follows: "What is the negation of the statement 'Some men are not wise'." A student replies that the negation would be "Some men are wise." Do you agree?

18   You have asked your class to write a false conditional so that its converse is also false. A student says that it is impossible to find one. How do you respond?

Q3.7   *Midpoints (Segments and Rays)*

1   A student asks you ˙why lines or rays don't have bisectors as segments do. In response, you tell the student that rays or lines do not have midpoints. The student then looks at you puzzled and asks you why rays or lines do not have midpoints? How do you respond?

2   A student is trying to find the midpoint of $\overline{AB}$. The coordinate of A is x, and the coordinate of B is y with $y > x$. The student reasons as follows: "The coordinate of the midpoint m of $\overline{AB}$ should be ½ of the distance between A and B. Therefore the coordinate y of the midpoint m is $\frac{1}{2}(y - x)$." Is the student correct?

Q3.8   *n-Dimensional Space, n ⩾ 3*

1   "We have been talking about simple closed curves in two-dimensional space. What, in three dimensions, would be the analogue of this idea?" How do you respond to this student?

2   In your geometry class, the following question arises. "In mathematics is there a fourth, fifth, and nth dimensional space? If so, is there any use for such spaces?"

3   A student asks, "If a regular polyhedron is made up of regular polygons and there are an infinite number of regular polygons, then why are there only five regular polyhedrons?" How do you respond?

Q3.9   *Non-Euclidean Geometry*

1   A student asks, "In Euclidean geometry, why is a distinction sometimes made between the *real* Euclidean plane and the *complex* Euclidean plane?" How do you reply?

2   A student asks, "Do we live in a Euclidean or non-Euclidean world?" How do you respond?

3   "What distinguished Euclidean geometry from non-Euclidean geometry?" How would you answer this student?

Q3.10   *Parallelism*

1   A student asks you if it is possible for two lines to be parallel and for the lines to be contained in intersecting planes. What is your response?

2   A student asks you if parallel lines meet at infinity. What is your response?

3

Given $l_1 \parallel l_2$, $m\angle 7 = 150°$, $m\angle 5 = 70°$. Find $m\angle 1$.

A student gives the following answer. "$m\angle 1 = 150°$ because it is an angle alternate interior to $\angle 7$." Is the student correct?

4   One student says that segments which have no points in common are either parallel of skew segments. Do you agree?

5   A student asks, "In the construction of a brick school building, a bricklayer uses a plumb bob to be sure the corners are all vertical. Are the corners (edges) then parallel?" How do you respond?

6   "In our text it says to extend line $\overleftrightarrow{AB}$... How can you extend a line when a line is infinite in nature? I don't understand." How would you help this student?

7   A student is working on the following problem. "Name segments that can be deduced to be parallel in the figure if $m\angle 8 = m\angle 4$."

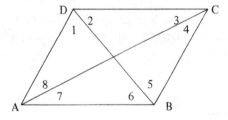

One student says that segments $\overline{AD}$ and $\overline{BC}$ are parallel and segments $\overline{AB}$ and $\overline{CD}$ are parallel. Is the student correct?

Q3.11 *Perpendicularity and the Pythagorean Theorem*

1 A student asks, "If a line, *l*, is perpendicular to a line in the plane, is *l* perpendicular to the plane?" How do you answer?

2 "When studying the Pythagorean Theorem, we learned that the square constructed on the hypotenuse equals the sum of the squares constructed on the other two sides. Do similar relationships hold for other figures such as pentagons or hexagons?" What is your response to this student.

3 While studying non-Euclidean geometry, a student asks, "Since the Pythagorean Theorem is not true in hyperbolic geometry, how do we define area in this geometry?" How do you respond?

4 A student asks, "In the definition of a line perpendicular to a plane, why is it necessary that every line in the plane passing through the point of intersection of the given line and plane be perpendicular to the line? Couldn't the definition be restated with just one line in the plane perpendicular to the given line at the point of intersection, or two lines?" How would you answer this student?

Q3.12 *Polygons*

1 A student asks, "Since an equilateral triangle must also be an equiangular triangle, then is an equilateral hexagon also equiangular?" What is your answer?

2 "If two polygons have their corresponding angles equal, are their sides proportional?" How do you answer this student?

3 A student asks, "What is the relationship between parallelograms, trapezoids, rectangles, squares, and rhombuses." What is your response?

4 A geometry book defines a trapezoid as a quadrilateral with *exactly* two sides parallel. A student asks why it can't be defined as a quadrilateral with at least two sides parallel? What is your response?

5 A student makes the following statement. "It looks like that if you join the midpoints of the sides of a quadrilateral, the resulting inscribed figure is always a parallelogram." Is this a true statement? What is your response?

6 A student asks, "In a triangle, an exterior angle is greater than each of its remote interior angles. Is this statement true if we replace triangle with quadrilateral, pentagon, hexagon, etc.?" How would you respond?

7 "Is the area of a geometric (two-dimensional) figure always smaller than its perimeter? Likewise, is the volume of a solid always smaller than its surface area?" How do you respond to this student?

8   You are discussing the idea of exterior angles of polygons. One student asks you why the following is not an exterior angle of a polygon since it is *outside* of the polygon. How would you answer?

Q3.13   *Similarity*

1   A student asks you if the SSS, SAS and AAA similarity theorems for triangles also hold for other polygons. What is your response?

2   You are comparing sides of similar triangles, and you ask your class to find EC as shown in the following figure.

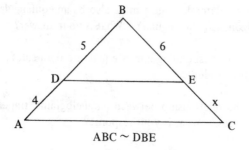

ABC ~ DBE

You show that $\dfrac{5}{9} = \dfrac{6}{6+x}$ or $5x = 24$. A student shows his way:

$$\frac{5}{4} = \frac{6}{x} \text{ or } 5x = 24.$$

How do you handle this situation?

3   While studying a unit on similar triangles, a student asks, "Are there other uses for the projection of a segment on a line?" How do you respond?

4   A student asks you if similar polygons must also be regular polygons. How would you reply?

Q3.14   Skewness

1   A student says that any two lines that are in different planes are skew lines. Is this student correct?

Q3.15   Symmetry

1   A student asks you if it is possible for a figure to be symmetric about a point but not symmetric about any line. What is your response?

Q3.16   Transformations and Functions

1   While you are teaching geometry through a transformational approach, a student asks you if the composition $\alpha \circ \beta$ of two mappings α and β can be one-to-one if neither α nor β are one-to-one mappings. How do you reply?

2   A student asks you if the composition $\alpha \circ \beta$ of two mappings α and β can be an *onto* mapping if neither α nor β are onto mappings. How do you reply?

3   You have just shown that the set of isometrics (distance-preserving transformations) form a group. A student in your class makes the following comment. "A couple of weeks ago we showed that congruence of triangles is an equivalence relation. It seems that what we have just shown is related to that idea by the following:

congruence ⎯⎯⎯⎯⎯→ transformation
reflexive   ⎯⎯⎯⎯⎯→ identity isometry
symmetric ⎯⎯⎯⎯⎯→ inverse isometry
transitive   ⎯⎯⎯⎯⎯→ product of isometries

Am I correct in my thinking?" How do you respond?

4   A student asks, "Since the *composition* of two translations is *always* a translation, why can a translation be *decomposed* into two transformations that are *not* translations?" How do you respond?

5   "If a glide reflection is defined to be the composition of a line reflection and a translation (or glide) in a direction parallel to the axis of reflection, what is the composition when the translation is *not* parallel to the axis of the reflection?" How do you reply to this student?

6   A student asks, "The composition of two rotations about the same point as center is always a rotation about that point. What is the composition of two rotations about different points as centers?" How do you respond?

7   "What are examples of transformations that leave lines or other figures fixed but do not leave all their points fixed?" How do you respond to this student?

8   A student asks, "If 'figure' is defined to be any set of points in the plane, (a) would

mean that a set of *exactly two* points is a figure? (b) If so, what would be the meaning of saying one figure of two points is congruent to another figure of two points?" How do you respond?

9   A student asks, "If a square ABCD is folded on either of its diagonals, it is mapped onto itself. Does this occur for a rhombus which is not square?" What is your answer?

Q3.17   Triangles

1   A student asks you if there is such a thing as equivalent triangles. What is your reply?

2   A student asks, "Is it possible for one triangle to have five parts (angles, sides) congruent to five parts of another triangle and still not have the two triangles congruent?" How do you reply?

3   A student asks you if there are any triangles in which the perimeter equals the area. What is your reply?

4   "If a leg and an acute angle of one right triangle are congruent to a leg and an acute angle of another right triangle, then the triangles are congruent." Do you agree with this student's statement?

5   A student in your class asks the following questions.

(a)   "If $\triangle ABC \cong \triangle DEF$, is $\triangle ABC \cong \triangle EDF$?" How do you reply?

(b)   "If $\triangle ABC \sim \triangle DEF$, is $\triangle ABC \sim \triangle EDF$?" How do you reply?

Why or why not (in each case)?

6   After you have introduced congruent triangles in your geometry class, a student asks, "If we can write $6 + 4 = 10$, then if $\triangle ABC$ is congruent to $\triangle DEF$, why can't we write $\triangle ABC = \triangle DEF$?" How would you answer?

7   A student asks, "Why is the triangle inequality so named?" How do you reply?

8   A student asks, "The two triangles below are congruent and you said that we must write it a certain way, i.e., $\triangle ACB \cong \triangle EGF$. If congruent triangles mean same size and shape, then why can't we write $\triangle ACB \cong \triangle GFE$ since triangle GFE is the same triangle as EGF, i.e., the same set of points?" How do you respond?

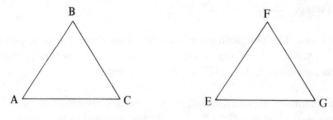

$$\triangle ACB \cong \triangle EGF$$

9   You have asked a student to name the shortest segment in the following figure. The student answers, "$\overline{AC}$ because it's opposite the smallest angle (∠CBA is the smallest angle in the figure)." Is the student correct?

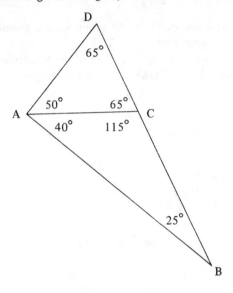

10 A student asks, "Does the segment containing the midpoints of two sides of a triangle have a name?" How would you answer?

11 A student asks you if the bisector of an angle of a triangle also bisects the opposite side. How do you respond?

 ANSWERS

A3.1   Angles

1   A dihedral angle is really the 3-dimensional analogue of a planar angle. Thus a dihedral angle is not a special type of planar angle, but rather it is an "angle" in three dimensions. It is interesting to note that the measure of a dihedral angle is defined to be the measure of the plane angle formed on the faces of the dihedral angle by a plane perpendicular to the edge of the given dihedral angle.

   For additional information, consult the references listed in Answer 11 of this section.

2   A good question to ask the student in this case is: "What do you mean by bigger?" What you should really be getting after is the distinction between a thing and its

representation, in this particular case, an angle and its graphical representation.

One might ask the student which of the following is "bigger"

3   or   *3*

This latter problem involves the difference between a numeral and a number and is the arithmetic counterpart to the given problem.

Essentially you want the student to see that each of the following is a representation for the same angle; i.e., $\angle BAC = \angle DAE = \angle FAG$, etc. (Figure 3.1.1).

FIGURE 3.1.1

3   Suppose that we label the given diagram as shown in Figure 3.1.2.

FIGURE 3.1.2

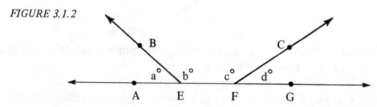

One way of answering this student is as follows. Suppose we separate Figure 3.1.3 as shown.

FIGURE 3.1.3

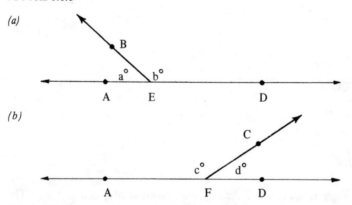

(a)

(b)

Doing this, one can see that $m\angle AEB + m\angle BED = a + b = 180$ and $m\angle AFC + m\angle CFD = c + d = 180$.

Problem   Under what conditions will the student's assertion be correct?

4   For some special angles, it is possible to divide an angle into three congruent parts, that is, to trisect an angle, but for the general case, one cannot trisect an angle using only a straightedge and compass. This involves one of the three famous problems from antiquity each of which cannot be solved by using only a straightedge and compass. The other two problems are constructing a square equal in area to a given

circle and constructing the side of a cube whose volume is twice that of a cube of a given side. For more information on these problems consult:

> Heinrich Tietze, *Famous Problems of Mathematics*, Graylock Press, New York, 1965.

5   The theorem that the student is using is stated as follows.

> If two lines intersect, then the vertical angles formed are congruent.

Thus referrring to the given diagram, $\angle 1 \cong \angle 2$ and $\angle 3 \cong \angle 4$. The student is assuming that the theorem states that all vertical angles are congruent, which certainly is not true.

6   No, the student is not correct because by definition supplementary angles are *two* angles the sum of whose measures equals $180°$.

7   Yes, the method is correct. The problem can be solved by letting n equal the number of sides of the equiangular polygon. Then $(n - 2) \cdot 180)/n$ is the measure of an interior angle of the polygon. Likewise, $360/n$ is the measure of an exterior angle of this polygon. Thus

$$\frac{(n - 2) \cdot 180}{n} = \frac{5(360)}{n} \quad n \neq 0.$$

Therefore $(n - 2) \cdot 180 = 5 \cdot 360$, which is the equation given by the student.

8   In rotating $\overrightarrow{BC}$ about point B, the student does get a different set of points. Thus, the angles would not be the same; that is, they are not the same set of points. For an interesting discussion about the definition of angle, read the following article by Harry Sitomer and Howard F. Fehr.*

HOW SHALL WE DEFINE ANGLE?

By HARRY SITOMER

Teachers College, Columbia University
New York, New York

and HOWARD F. FEHR

Teachers College, Columbia University
New York, New York

IN PUBLICATIONS of the School Mathematics Study Group, an angle is defined as the union of two noncollinear rays having the same origin. This definition is now widely used in the United States, and has found its way into many contemporary textbooks. On the other hand, many Europeans use the word "angle" to describe what SMSG calls an angular region: that is, the set of points in the union of the interior of an SMSG angle with the angle itself. The distinguished Professor Gustave Choquet of Faculty of Science, Institute Henri Poincaré, University of Paris, who has given considerable attention to the teaching of elementary geometry, maintains that the angular region approach to the topic is closer to pupils' intuition and hence is to

*From *The Mathematics Teacher*, January 1967, pp. 18-19. Reprinted by permission.

be preferred pedagogically. He lists the following arguments:

1. Suppose one side of an angle is rotated about the vertex as center to another position. The pupil thinks he has the same set of points, two rays, but a "larger" or "smaller" angle. This can be, and is, terribly confusing.

2. Consider two angles with one common ray. If they are SMSG angles, their union is a set of three rays—a strange geometric animal. On the other hand, the union of the related angular regions is still an angular region.

3. Consider two angles having one ray and at least one interior point in common. Then as SMSG angles their intersection is one ray. The interesection of the related angular regions is still an angular region.

The last two arguments have the same force as "like should beget like."

4. The midray of an SMSG angle does not belong to the angle; however, it *is* a ray of the angular region if we accept the proposition that every interior point of the midray is in the angular region. There is no mathematical reason why a midray of an angle must be a ray of the angle; but when we consider the analogous situation for segments, we find its midpoint to be a point of the segment. This disturbs the students.

This suggests a closer examination of the analogy between angular regions and line segments. They do resemble each other in a number of ways. Below is a list of parallel statements in which we have the following correspondences:

Line segment	Angular region
Endpoint	Endray
Midpoint	Midray
Line measure	Angular measure

1. The midpoint of a line segment belongs to the segment.

1'. The midray of an angular region belongs to the region.

2. The union of two collinear line segments having exactly one endpoint in common is a line segment.

2'. The union of two coplanar angular regions having one endray in common is an angular region.

3. The intersection of two coplanar line segments having one endpoint and one interior point in common is a line segment.

3'. The intersection of two coplanar angular regions having one endray and one interior ray in common is an angular region.

4. The measure of a line segment is accomplished by taking a piece of segment, called a unit, and covering the segment with nonoverlapping (only one point in common) units. The number of covering units is the measure.

4'. The measure of an angular region is accomplished by taking a piece of angular region, called a unit, and covering the region with nonoverlapping (only one ray in common) units. The number of covering units is the measure.

Of course this analogy, like most analogies, cannot be pressed far without running into serious difficulty. The point of the matter is that we cannot even *begin* to make such analogies between line segments and the SMSG angles. A more fruitful analogy could be made between a segment, defined as a pair of points, and the SMSG angle. But for most students, the intuitive (natural) line segment is the convex set of two points and all the points between them—not a pair of points. Similarly, the angle should be the convex set formed by a pair of rays with common vertex and all rays (with the same vertex) lying between them—not a pair of rays.

There is also the relationship between circular arcs and angles that arises when we study angular measures and arc measures. When the vertex of the angle is the center of a circle, then the related arc is the intersection of the circle and the angular region; the related sector is the intersection of the circular region and the angular region. In neither case do we take or use the intersection with the SMSG angle.

In view of these cogent arguments, we in the United States should reconsider the definition we give to *angle*, especially at the elementary and secondary school level.

9   The student has misinterpreted the given statement. This reasoning error is common and is one that should always be anticipated. Essentially what you must do is interpret for the student what the statement means, i.e., that the perpendicular distance from S to $\overrightarrow{AB}$ equals the distance from S to $\overrightarrow{AC}$, and the distance from R to $\overrightarrow{AB}$ equals the distance from R to $\overrightarrow{AC}$. The statement does not mean that the distance from S to $\overrightarrow{AB}$ must be the same as the distance from R to $\overrightarrow{AB}$. In general, the point P is on the bisector $\overrightarrow{SR}$ iff the distance between P and $\overrightarrow{AB}$ equals the distance between P and $\overrightarrow{AC}$.

    Problem   Prove the statement above that the point P is on the bisector $\overrightarrow{SR}$ iff the distance between P and $\overrightarrow{AB}$ equals the distance between P and $\overrightarrow{AC}$. Use the definition of an angle bisector: $\overrightarrow{SR}$ is the bisector of ∠ABC if m∠RAB = m∠RAC.

10   The student is not correct. There are at least two different angles, ∠1 and ∠2. If a straight angle is defined as an angle in the student's text (some books do not define straight angle), then there are three different angles, ∠1, ∠2 and either ∠3 or ∠4. Angle 3 and angle 4 are the same angle; i.e., they are the same set of points.

11   For an answer to this question consult:

    Howard Fehr, "On Teaching Dihedral Angle and Steradian" (Article 51), and "On Teaching Trihedral Angle and Solid Angle" (Article 52). *Mathematics in the Secondary Classroom: Selected Readings*, eds. Gerald Rising and Richard Wisen, Thomas Y. Crowell Co., New York, 1972. (These articles also be found in the April 1958 and May 1958 issues of *The Mathematics Teacher*.)

12   Consider Figure 3.1.4. ∠BAC and ∠BAD are not adjacent even though they have a common side and a common vertex since adjacent angles do not have interior points in common.

FIGURE 3.1.4

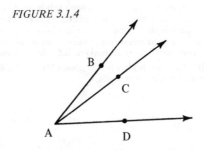

13   No, the student is not correct. Although this problem is easy for you to analyze, convincing some students that the method given is incorrect turns out be be quite difficult. Ley y equal the measure of the complement of an angle whose measure is x − 10. Then

    y + (x − 10) = 90.

Thus y = 90 − (x − 10) = 100 − x.

The student has made the false assumption that if x − 10 is the measure of an angle then x is the measure of its complement.

14 An angle in plane geometry is usually defined as the union of two noncollinear rays with the same endpoint. If an angle has a measure of zero, then these two rays coincide, and thus they are usually considered as one ray. Some definitions of angle exclude an angle of measure zero because of the above. However, in some texts and especially in trigonometry courses, an angle is defined differently (perhaps by including a rotation as part of the definition), and it is convenient to include an angle of measure zero.

15 No, the student is not correct. The correct answer is x = 90°/7 = 12°52′ and thus 3x = 38°36′.

Problem Why is the student's method of dividing (7 $\overline{\smash{\big)}\,89°60′}$) not correct?

A3.2   *Axioms and Definitions*

1 For an answer to this question, read the following two letters, which appeared in *The Mathematics Teacher.**

DEAR EDITOR:

In a recent discussion in a high school geometry class, one of my students questioned my statement that a point is an undefined term. His reasoning was that a point can be defined as the intersection of two lines. And then I carried his reasoning a little further and said that a line could then be defined as the intersection of two planes. Thus, the only necessary undefined term in a high school geometry class would be "plane."

Would you tell me if there is an error in our reasoning that we have overlooked? Or is this a good way to teach high school geometry—with only one undefined term, rather than three?

Sincerely yours,
JO-ANN SCHIFFBAUER
Lake High School
Hartville, Ohio

DEAR MRS. SCHIFFBAUER:

Your students should be commended for their interest and curiosity concerning the structure of their geometry. The possibility of reducing the number of undefined terms is a most intriguing one. If, however, we attempt to define line and point as your class suggests, we might find ourselves in logical difficulties.

Suppose we define a point as the intersection of two lines. Since we are speaking of a set theoretic intersection, we would be implying that we already knew something about points, i.e., lines are sets of points. A similar difficulty would arise concerning the proposed definition of line.

A more reasonable approach might be to leave plane and point as undefined. Then state an axiom which indicates that a plane is a set of points and proceed from there. This would mean a complete re-examination of the axiomatic structure of high school geometry—a task of considerable magnitude.

---

*From *The Mathematics Teacher*, May 1970, p. 396. Reprinted by permission.

2   In older texts, such as Euclid's, there was a difference between these terms. A postulate was an assumption applicable only to a particular branch of mathematics. For instance, in geometry, there is the postulate that states: two points determine one and only one line.   An axiom was an assumption applicable to all branches of mathematics; e.g., equals added to equals give equals.   In modern texts, the distinction is not given, and the two terms are synonymous.

3   For an answer to this question, read the well-written section "The Completeness of the Real Number System" beginning on page 31 of:

> William G. Chinn and N.E. Steenrod, *First Concepts of Topology*, Random House, New York, 1966.

4   The student should certainly be commended for good thinking.

(a)   The notation $\overleftrightarrow{AB}$ can be related to function notation as follows:

Domain   Pairs of points.

Range   The geometric figure consisting of the points on line $\overleftrightarrow{AB}$; i.e., $f(A, B)$ is the set of points on line $\overleftrightarrow{AB}$. The function symbol f refers to $\leftrightarrow$ and the rule is to associate the points on the line $\overleftrightarrow{AB}$ with the pair of points A and B.

(b)   The notation $\angle ABC$ can be related to function notation as follows:

Domain   Triples of points.

Range   The geometric figure consisting of the points on the angle $\angle ABC$, $f(A, B, C)$, is the set of points on $\angle ABC$.

The function symbol f refers to the angle and the rule is to associate the points on $\angle ABC$ with ABC.

Problem 1   If a student uses the notation $\triangle ABC$, what does he mean?

Problem 2   Find three other examples in mathematics of the notion involved in Question 4.

5   The word *undefined* is not synonymous with *non-existence*. This idea might be conveyed to the student by asking her for a definition of set. A student will usually come up with something like "A set is a group of objects." However, what is a group?   After several exchanges of this nature, you can convince the student that set is also usually left as an undefined term. Does this mean that sets do not exist? It might also be pointed out to the student that many of the concepts that we study are not physical objects but are abstract ideas that exist only in our minds.

6   The terms *necessary* and *sufficient* are usually associated with theorems that are written in the form of a conditional or biconditional. For example in the statement, "If a triangle is equilateral, then it is isosceles," the statement, "A triangle is equilateral," is a condition that is sufficient or guarantees that a triangle is isosceles. The statements "the fact that a triangle is isosceles is necessary for a triangle to be equilateral" or "before a triangle can be equilateral, it must be isosceles," can be stated in another way: "If a triangle is not isosceles, then there is no way for it to be equilateral."

Perhaps an illustration that might be useful in conveying the difference between the terms necessary and sufficient would be the following. Consider a bug that is traveling in a straight path such as on the number line below. Assume that the bug starts at point A and always travels in a straight path on the number line.

Suppose that our attention is directed away from the bug for a moment. If upon looking at the bug again, we observe that the bug is at point C, then under the conditions of the problem, we know that the bug must have passed through point B. That is, seeing the bug at C is sufficient for us to conclude that the bug must have passed point B. However, if we observe the bug at point B, then this informaion is not sufficient for us to say that the bug passed through C. However, we might say that before the bug can get to C, the bug has to pass at least once through B; i.e., it is necessary for the bug to pass through B before it can get to C.

7   The notation AB = CD means that the distance between points A and B is equal to the distance between the points C and D. The notation $\overline{AB} \cong \overline{CD}$ means that the segments $\overline{AB}$ and $\overline{CD}$ have the same size and shape. Thus, in the first case we are talking about the *distance* between points while in the second case we are talking about *a set of points* (the set of points contained in segments $\overline{AB}$ and $\overline{CD}$). It is not absolutely essential that the two different notations be used. In fact, at least one textbook series has used the notation $\overline{AB} = \overline{CD}$ to include both interpretations discussed above with the context of the problem determining which interpretation was meant. However, in some cases, there might involve ambiguity of meaning, and thus it is now standard practice to use both notations.

8   In proving statements such as theorems in mathematics, one would have to use other statements or theorems or definitions as reasons in the proof. These statements used as reasons would likewise depend on other statements, theorems and definitions. This process would continue until one gets back to the very beginning or foundation of the subject. Eventually one has to stop in this process and the question comes up as to how these beginning statements are proved. In other words, there are no other theorems that one can use as reasons for proving these beginning statements and thus these beginning statements must be assumed to be true. These are the axioms of the system under consideration. Indeed mathematics is defined as the study of axiomatic systems. The process is one that is very similar to the idea of undefined terms in mathematics.

A3.3   Circles and Constructions

1   It depends on the definition of region that is used. One definition is as follows:

A region is a set of points in a plane for which each of the following holds:

(a) Any two points of the set are the endpoints of a polygonal path, which is contained entirely in the set.

(b) Each point of the set is on at least two noncollinear line segments, which are contained in the set.

If this definition is used, then a circular region is a region.

In some texts a region is identified with a polygonal region and is usually defined as:

A polygonal region is the union of a finite number of coplanar triangular regions, such that if any two of these intersect, the intersection is either a segment or a point.

If this definition is used, then one can say that a circular region is not a polygonal region. If polygonal region is synonymous with region, then clearly a circular region is not a region.

However, it should be pointed out that according to the definitions above the terms *polygonal region* and *region* are not synonymous. If a geometric figure is a polygonal region, then it is a region, but the converse is not valid. For example, a plane is a region, but it is not a polygonal region. It is usually the case, however, that one would want a circular region to be a region.

2 Consider Figure 3.3.1 where 0 is the unit circle, $x = 1$ is a line tangent to the circle and $\overrightarrow{OT}$ intersects the dashed line $x = 1$ at A. Now ray $\overrightarrow{OT}$ has slope $(\sin \phi)/(\cos \phi)$ or $\tan \phi$ and thus ray $\overrightarrow{OT}$ is contained in the line $y = (\tan \phi)x$. Thus the ray $\overrightarrow{OT}$ intersects the line $x = 1$ at the point $A(1, \tan \phi)$.

FIGURE 3.3.1

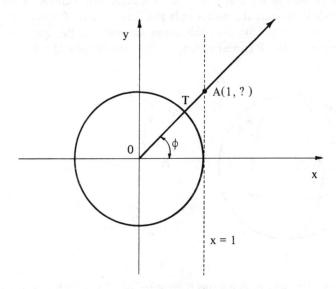

3 The term *great circle* probably originated because of its use in navigation; i.e., the shortest distance from one point on the earth to another point is along the path of a great circle. The adjective *great* was probably used because these circles have the largest circumference of any circles on a sphere.

4   No, the student is not correct. In Figure 3.3.2, l_1 is a common internal tangent while l_2 and l_3 are common external tangents.

FIGURE 3.3.2

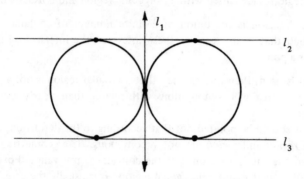

5   For an answer to this question, read:

Paul Johnson, "Are Circles Similar?", *The Mathematics Teacher*, January 1966, pp. 9-13.

6   Suppose one considers a sphere, as shown in Figure 3.3.3, with N representing the north pole and S, the south pole. If R is a point on the sphere, then it should be easy for the student to see that there is a great circle thru N and R. Simply rotate the great circle C, holding the points at N and S fixed, until C meets R. One can now apply the same technique to the sphere illustrated in this question. Simply rotate the sphere so that P corresponds to N, and then consider Q = R.

FIGURE 3.3.3

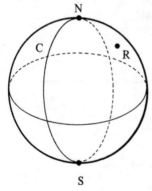

7   Yes, you can. One way of doing this is given below. Cut a circle out of wax paper. Any circle of radius r would be adequate, but the larger it is, the better. Locate the center of the circle and call it C. Lay the circle on a flat surface, and bring a point on its circumference up to meet point C; then crease. Repeat this process about thirty times, using different points on the circumference. (About thirty repetitions should indicate the process to the student.) The creases will then enclose a circle.

Problem 1 How would you modify the above procedure in order to get an ellipse, a hyperbola, a parabola?

Problem 2 How would you convince the student that the process indicated and the processes you would use for Problem 1 do lead to the desired configurations?

Problem 3 If you have studied differential equations can you provide more insight into the above construction? That is, what idea is relevant to this question?

8 No. Consider the circle given and the quadrilateral ABCD shown in Figure 3.3.4. Obviously, quadrilaterial ABCD is not regular. However, for quadrilaterals, there is a condition involving angles that must be met in order for a circle to circumscribe it. Can you find out what it is?

FIGURE 3.3.4

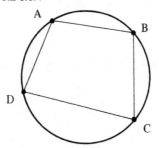

Problem 1 In Question 8, we found out that the answer is no because of the cases involving quadrilaterals. If polygons of n sides, n ⩾ 5, are the only polygons considered, is the answer to the student's question still no? Explain.

Problem 2 Can a circle be circumscribed about any triangle? Explain.

9 Many geometry textbooks used at the secondary school level do not even mention the idea of the center of an arc. Those that do mention it define the center of an arc of a circle P to be the center of circle P. The reason for this is probably due to the fact that an arc is described with respect to a given circle and the circle already has a center. If the midpoint of an arc was defined as the center of the arc, then possible confusion might result over which center was intended, the center of the arc or of the circle. Also, we have a name for the "centerpoint" of an arc, namely, the midpoint.

10 For an answer to this question, read:

J.H. Hlavaty, "Mascheroni Constructions," *The Mathematics Teacher*, November 1957, pp. 482-87.

A3.4   *Congruence*

1 The following statement or some such variant is often given as a general definition of congruence. Two sets of points X and Y are congruent if and only if there exists a one-to-one correspondence between their points such that if r ∈ Y corresponds to a ∈ X and s ∈ Y corresponds to b ∈ X, then $\overline{ab} \cong \overline{rs}$. Such a correspondence is called an isometry.

2   It can be shown that for convex quadrilaterals, one need only have five corresponding pairs in order to insure congruence of the quadrilaterals. One of these corresponding pairs is four sides and one angle.

Problem 1   Find all other corresponding pairs that would insure congruence
of convex quadrilaterals.

Problem 2   Find all other corresponding pairs that would insure congruence
of pentagons and hexagons.

Problem 3   Generalize your answer to Problem 2, for a geometric figure of
n sides.

A3.5   *Convexity and Inequalities*

1   For an answer to this question, read the following article by R. Berman and M.
Berman.*

Concave polygons

ROSLYN M. BERMAN, *Cranston High School East,*
Cranston, Rhode Island.
MARTIN BERMAN, *Physics Department, Brown University,*
Providence, Rhode Island.

Finding the sum of the interior and exterior angles of a concave polygon

ALL PLANE GEOMETRY books examined by
the present writers contain a discussion of
convex polygons. Many texts define a
polygon, convex polygon, and concave
polygon, in that order. It is then explicitly
stated that throughout the remainder of
these texts the term "polygon" will sig-
nify a *convex polygon*.

Why do geometry books neglect to discuss concave polygons? Perhaps their
authors are not aware that convex and
concave polygons have many common
properties, or they do not wish to confuse
students with two different types.

Some high school geometry students
asked one of the present writers whether
the theorem concerning the sum of the

interior angles of a polygon holds not only
when the figure is convex, but also when
it is concave. Consideration of this problem led to the following.

THE SUM OF THE INTERIOR ANGLES
OF A CONVEX POLYGON

First we will present proofs of how to
determine the sum of the interior angles of
a convex polygon. It will then be shown
that these demonstrations cannot always
be extended to a concave polygon.

Method 1. Euclid's *Elements*[1] is one of
many subsequent texts which employed

[1] Thomas L. Heath (trans.), *The Thirteen Books of
Euclid's Elements* (Vol. 1. 3 vois.; second edition; New
York: Dover Publications, Inc., 1956), p. 322.

*From *The Mathematics Teacher*, October 1963, pp. 403-406. Reprinted by
permission.

the means described in this paragraph. Figure 1 illustrates the convex polygon *ABCDEFG*. Pick any arbitrary vertex, such as *A*, and draw diagonals from *A* to all the other vertices. It is seen that if there

Figure 3

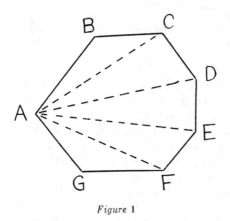

Figure 1

are *n* sides to the polygon, $(n-2)$ triangles will be formed. The sum of the angles of the triangles will be equal to the sum of the interior angles of the polygon. The sum of the interior angles of a convex polygon of *n* sides is therefore $(n-2)180°$.

Method 2. Any interior point *O* of the polygon is chosen as the common vertex; lines are drawn from all the vertices of the polygon to point *O* (Fig. 2). If the original

polygon has *n* sides, *n* triangles will be formed. Accordingly, the sum of the interior angles of an *n*-sided convex polygon is equal to the sum of the angles of the *n* triangles minus the sum of the angles around point *O*. The sum of the angles around point *O* is, of course, 360°. This again yields the correct answer.

Method 3. Diagonals are drawn so as to fill the inside of the polygon with separate adjacent triangles (Fig. 3). To accomplish this, none of the internal lines may cross one another. It can easily be seen that $(n-2)$ triangles will thereby be formed if the polygon has *n* sides, once more indicating the proper conclusion.

To determine if the proofs given above hold for concave polygons, examine Figure 4. Polygon *ABCDEFGH* possesses no vertex, as in Method 1, nor interior point,

Figure 2

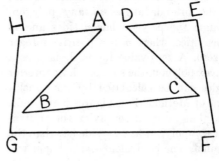

Figure 4

At the same time

$$\angle 6 = \angle 5 + 180° = \angle 2 + \angle 3 + 180°.$$

The sum, S, of the interior angles of the original polygon is

$$S = \angle A + \angle E + \angle 1 + \angle 4 + \angle 6$$
$$= \angle A + \angle E + \angle 1 + \angle 4 + \angle 2 + \angle 3$$
$$+ 180°.$$

Let S' designate the sum of the interior angles of the new polygon $ABDE$. Thus, the following is true:

$$S' = \angle A + \angle E + \angle 1 + \angle 2 + \angle 3 + \angle 4.$$

This gives the desired result, that

$$S' = S - 180°.$$

The new polygon is equivalent to the original polygon (with respect to the sum of its interior angles), except that the convex figure $ABDE$ contains 180° less. Since it is equivalent minus 1 times 180°, the present writers call it an equivalent-1 polygon to the original.

Suppose the concave polygon has more than one concavity, as in Figure 7. Then the construction described above is performed for each concavity. Polygon $ABCEFGI$ is equivalent-2 to polygon $ABCDEFGHI$, which means that it has the same total number of degrees in its interior angles minus 2 times 180°. If the polygon has m concavities, the construction would be repeated m times, resulting in an equivalent $-m$ convex polygon.

THE SUM OF THE INTERIOR ANGLES OF ANY POLYGON

It is now possible to investigate the sum of the interior angles of any polygon. Assume the polygon has n sides and m concavities, where m is a positive integer or zero. A zero-value for m designates a convex polygon, the sum of whose interior angles can be calculated by the conclusions of Methods 1–3. Figures 6 or 7 indicate that for each concavity the equivalent$-m$ polygon has one side less than the original. The equivalent$-m$ polygon will have $(n-m)$ sides and will be convex.

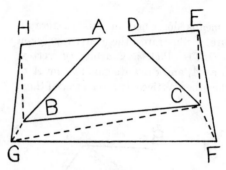

Figure 5

as in Method 2, from which triangles can be drawn whose sides will not cross the sides of the original polygon; many complications will ensue if such crossing does occur. As shown in Figure 5, Method 3 may be applied without difficulty. Method 3 is thus seen to be more general than either Methods 1 or 2. Although it seems intuitively obvious that Method 3 would hold for any polygon, the proof is difficult for intricate figures and, for this reason, was not attempted. Instead, the present writers have developed a simple means of proving that the sum of the interior angles of any n-sided polygon, be it convex or concave, is $(n-2)180°$.

EQUIVALENT$-m$ POLYGONS

Consider a concave polygon which has only one concavity or re-entrant angle (an interior angle greater than 180°). In Figure 6, $\angle 6$ is the re-entrant angle. Construct line BD, thus forming $\triangle BCD$. $\angle 5$ is an exterior angle of $\triangle BCD$, so that

$$\angle 5 = \angle 2 + \angle 3.$$

Figure 6

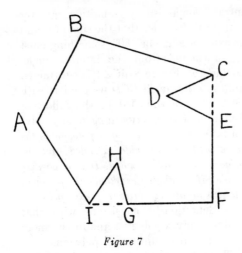

Figure 7

From the previous sections we know the following:

$$S = S' + 180°m$$

and

$$S' = [(n-m)-2]180°.$$

Combining the above gives

$$S = [(n-m)-2]180° + 180°m$$

$$= (n-2)180°.$$

THE SUM OF THE EXTERIOR ANGLES OF A CONCAVE POLYGON

A topic usually considered with regard to the convex polygon, aside from the sum of its interior angles, is the total measure of its exterior angles. It is questioned: Can the concept of exterior angles, as defined for triangles and convex polygons, be extended to concave polygons? If so, it would be pedagogically desirable to demonstrate the same angle-sum theorems for both types of polygons.

The teacher could then discuss only convex polygons for simplicity and tell the students that the results are the same for concave polygons; otherwise he could prove the results for both types if class ability and time allow it; finally he could designate the material on concave polygons as exercises for brighter students.

An exterior angle is usually defined as the angle between any side of a polygon extended and the adjacent side not extended. This is the definition used for triangles and convex polygons.

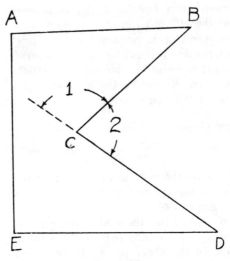

Figure 8

Consider the exterior angle of a re-entrant angle of concave polygon *ABCDE* (see Fig. 8). Which is the exterior angle of interior angle *BCD*? Is it ∠1 which would fit the definition but is inside the figure (which seems strange for an exterior angle) or is it ∠2, which is exterior to the figure but does not seem to fit the definition? To decide this question, it will be necessary to calculate the sum of the exterior angles and see which definition will give results consistent with the definition of convex polygons.

To calculate the sum of the exterior angles of a convex polygon, look at Figure 9. ∠1 is the interior angle and ∠2 is its

Figure 9

corresponding exterior angle. It is seen that the sum of an interior angle and its corresponding exterior angle is 180°. Thus, for a convex polygon of n sides, the sum of the exterior and interior angles is $180n°$. However, the sum of the interior angles is $(n-2)180°$ and we have:

(sum of exterior angles)

$$+(n-2)180° = 180n°.$$

This gives the well known result that the sum of the exterior angles of a convex polygon is 360°.

We would like the sum of the exterior angles of a concave polygon also to be 360°. In the above proof, the reasoning depended upon the supplementary angle relation between each interior angle and its corresponding exterior angle. A re-entrant angle is, by definition, greater than 180°. In order that the sum of it and its exterior angle be 180°, something must be subtracted from the interior angle. Looking at Figure 8, if $\angle 1$ is subtracted from interior angle BCD we are left with 180°. We are thus led to the following definition of an exterior angle of any polygon: *An exterior angle of a polygon is the angle between any side extended and the adjacent side not extended. It is a positive number if the angle lies outside the polygon, and it is negative if it lies inside the polygon.* This definition is consistent with that used for convex polygons and furthermore gives the same sum for all polygons.

This article has shown that the sum of the interior as well as of the exterior angles of any polygon does not depend upon whether it is concave or convex.

2   The empty set or a set containing exactly one point are convex since there does not exist two distinct points X and Y such that $\overline{XY}$ is not in the set. That is, in these cases, the definition is vacuously satisfied.

3   If the student means any inequality, then the answer is yes. Consider the following:

$$\{(x, y) | x^2 + 1 > x^2\}.$$

This inequality is satisfied by all points in the plane. If the student is referring to *linear inequalities* such as

$$\{(x, y) | ax + by > c \text{ or } ax + by < c\}$$

where either a or b is not zero, then the answer is no.

Problem   Find two more inequalities that are satisfied by all points in the plane.

4   Each constraint in a linear programming problem yields a convex set. The feasible region is the intersection of these convex sets and hence is convex.

Problem   Prove that the intersection of convex sets is again convex.

A3.6   *Logic*

1 No, the statement is not true. Perhaps, the best way of showing this fact is to look at the contrapositive of the given statement. Thus, suppose we look at the statement, "If a rhombus, then a square." This statement is certainly not true. Since this statement is equivalent to the given statement, then we can conclude that the given statement is not true.

   Problem Where is the student having difficulty in this question?

2 Logically speaking, the student is correct. Usually, however, in a high school course in geometry, we assume that the diagonals do intersect in the interior of the paralellogram.

3 The proof is valid and the student teacher is incorrect. In fact, the argument given by the student teacher, i.e., if two lines were not parallel, then alternate interior angles could never be formed that were congruent, is the basis for arriving at the contradiction in this indirect proof.

4 One might make up an example which would help students see why it is reasonable that the last two rows of a conditional are marked true. Two examples are given below which have been found to be effective in accomplishing this aim.

   Example 1 Suppose a teacher in a certain algebra course makes the following statement. "If a student in this course gets A's on all four exams, then that student will get an A in the course."

   > *Case 3* Suppose a student in this course does not get A's on all four exams but still the student gets an A in the course. Has the teacher broken his promise to the students in this course? No, the teacher has not; he has still kept his word.

   > *Case 4* Suppose a student in this course does not get A's on all four exams and does not get an A in the course. The teacher still has not broken his promise; i.e., the original statement is still true.

   Example 2 Suppose that a man who lives in Maryland makes the following statement. If I live in Delaware, then I live in the United States. The hypothesis is false and the conclusion is true but still his statement is true. Suppose that a woman who lives in France makes the same statement as above. In this case, both the hypothesis and the conclusion are false, but the statement is still true.

5 Yes, there is. Kramer gives the following account. In 1921 two research papers appeared, one by the Polish mathematician Jan Lukasiewicz on three-valued logic, and one by the American Emil Post on general n-valued systems. Table 3.6.1 is an example of a three-valued truth table.* (See page 144 for Table 3.6.1.)

---

*Kramer, Edna. *The Nature and Growth of Modern Mathematics*. Hawthorn Books, Inc. New York, 1970, pp. 132-33.

TABLE 3.6.1

p	q	$p \to q$
T	T	T
T	M	M
T	F	F
M	T	T
M	M	M
M	F	M
F	T	T
F	M	T
F	F	T

T True
F False
M Possible (not known to be true or false)

6 Yes, the ideas are related, and they are really isomorphic systems.

Let p be a statement, and let P be an arbitrary set. Then under the correspondence shown below, set theory and logical analysis have essentially the same underlying structure.

(1) $p \to P$
(2) $\wedge \to \cap$
(3) $\vee \to \cup$
(4) $\sim \to$ Complement $(\bar{\ })$

Thus, properties such as De Morgan's laws in set theory have a corresponding property in logical analysis.

(a) $\overline{A \cap B} = \overline{A} \cup \overline{B}$ $\sim(p \wedge q) \leftrightarrow \sim p \vee \sim q$
(b) $\overline{A \cup B} = \overline{A} \cap \overline{B}$ $\sim(p \vee q) \leftrightarrow \sim p \wedge \sim q$

One can go further in this respect as shown in Tables 3.6.2 and 3.6.3.

TABLE 3.6.2

p	q	$p \wedge q$
T	T	T
T	F	F
F	T	F
F	F	F

TABLE 3.6.3

$x \in P$	$x \in Q$	$x \in P \cap Q$
T	T	T
T	F	F
F	T	F
F	F	F

If p and q are closed statements, then p is equivalent to q $(p \to q)$ whenever p and q have the same truth value. That is, when p is true, then q is true; when p is false, q is false. If P_x and Q_x are open statements, then P_x is equivalent to Q_x $(P_x \leftrightarrow Q_x)$ Both open statements have the same solution set. That is, when P_x is true then Q_x is true; when P_x is false, Q_x is false.

7 One form of an indirect proof is to prove the contrapositive of a given conditional. Thus if one is trying to prove the conditional $p \to q$, then one might prove the contrapositive $\sim q \to \sim p$. Since a conditional and its contrapositive are logically equivalent, then the original conditional is valid. The student seems to be saying that one should also be able to prove a conditional $p \to q$, by proving the statement $\sim p \to \sim q$ to be true. However, the problem here is that these two statements are not logically equivalent. Thus proving the statement $\sim p \to \sim q$ to be a valid statement does not determine the validity of the statement $p \to q$.

In a more general sense, the idea of an indirect proof is as follows. One assumes that the given (p) is true and that the negation of q is true. The idea is then to try to show that these two statements lead to a false statement; i.e., $(p \wedge \sim q) \rightarrow s$ where s is a statement that is known to be false. Frequently s takes the form $r \wedge \sim r$, which is definitely a false statement. Since the reasoning was correct (the conditional is true), then by looking at a truth table for a conditional one finds that this is the case only if $p \wedge \sim q$ is false. But p is assumed to be true and thus $\sim q$ must be false, which in turn implies that q is true. Since p is assumed true and q is true, then $p \rightarrow q$ must be true.

What happens if we try to prove a conditional, $p \rightarrow q$ using the student's method. In this case, we would try to show that $\sim p \wedge q \rightarrow t$ where t is a false statement. As in the previous case, $\sim p \wedge q$ must be false; since we know that p is true, therefore $\sim p$ is false. However, this is as far as we can go because in this case q could be either true or false; i.e., we cannot deduce absolutely that q is true. Thus the method suggested by the student will not allow us to prove a conditional, $p \rightarrow q$ indirectly.

8   This is a tricky question to answer because we really do not know what the student meant. The best advice that we can offer is to try to find out exactly what meaning the student is attaching to his statement. If you find out that the student is really saying that not all men are good, then the student is correct. However, if the student meant *all* (or every single) men are not good, then the student is incorrect. Thus, your evaluation of the student's response depends upon what the student emphasized in the response. You should certainly try to lead the student to a better interpretation, which has no ambiguous meaning attached to it such as "There is at least one man who is not good."

9   Although one might always be able to use the method of direct proof, there are some theorems that are extremely difficult to prove using this method, whereas an indirect proof could be quite simple.

10   No, the lines could not be curved. The postulates and theorems rule out the possibility of curved lines. For example, it is usually given as a postulate that through any two different points there is exactly one line. It is usually proved as a theorem that if two lines intersect, they intersect in exactly one point, These two statements, along with others, obviously rule out the possibility that "lines" are curved.

11   No, the student is incorrect. The correct form is: if two planes are not parallel, then they intersect.

12   The student is correct in seeing an analogy in this case, but caution should be exercised. The symmetric property of a binary relation is stated as follows:

If R is a binary relation, then R is symmetric if $a R b \Rightarrow b R a$; i.e., if *a* is in the relation R to *b*, then *b* is in the relation R to *a*.

However, it does not have to be the case that *if p, then q* is true that the converse, *if q, then p*, is true. Thus although the two situations are similar, they are not totally related.

13   No, the student is incorrect. There are an infinite number of lines tangent to a sphere at a point on the sphere. A correct statement can be made which shows the analogy. That is, at a point on a sphere there is exactly one plane tangent to the sphere.

14 (1) Euclid did not recognize the need for undefined terms. Instead of beginning with a few undefined terms whose meaning comes from the axioms, he tried to define every term. Thus he defined line as follows: "A line is breadthless length." But what does breadthless mean?

(2) Euclid did not include axioms of incidence, order and congruence. Euclid assumed and used many properties that were not included in his list of axioms and could not be derived from them. For example, Euclid says nothing about the relation of betweenness and thus we do not know what the following statement means: point y is between points x and z. Also Euclid did not spell out incidence axioms, which express basic relationships of points, lines and planes. For example:

(a) All lines and planes are sets of points.

(b) If two distinct planes intersect, then their intersection is a line.

Euclid made the concept of congruence depend on the concept of superposition, i.e., that a triangle can be picked up and put down in another place with all the properties remaining invariant. But no statement of this was made.

(3) Euclid's axioms say nothing about continuity yet he assumed that a line segment intersected a triangle in a point as shown in Figure 3.6.1. However, this idea depends upon continuity.

FIGURE 3.6.1

Euclid also assumed that a line is infinite in extent, but no axiom states this. He does state that "A finite straight line can be produced continuously in a straight line," but this does not imply that the line is infinite in extent. It implies only that it is boundless.

(4) Euclid assumed that if a straight line enters a triangle at a vertex, it must intersect the opposite side. An axiom stating this needed to be given.

15   One way of doing this is as follows. Suppose that segment $\overline{AB}$ contains a finite number of points. Without loss of generality, we can consider a coordinate system set up on line $\overleftrightarrow{AB}$ such that the coordinate of A is zero and the coordinate of B is one. It is a well-known fact that there exists a one-to-one correspondence between the set of real numbers and the set of points on $\overleftrightarrow{AB}$. In particular, there is a one-to-one correspondence between the points of $\overline{AB}$ and the set of all real numbers between 0 and 1. Thus if $\overline{AB}$ contains only a finite number of points, then this would imply that there is only a finite number of real numbers between 0 and 1. However, this last statement contradicts the well-known fact that there are an infinite number of real numbers between 0 and 1. Thus, the number of points on a line segment is infinite.

16   Generally, the answer is no. In fact, at this level, proving a special case and then

assuming that the general case has been proved is one of the common mistakes made by students, e.g., using coordinates that depict a square when proving a theorem on rectangles. However, in some cases, when one can show that a general statement is equivalent to a special case, then one can prove the special case and thus assert that the general case is valid. Polya makes this point in his book, *Mathematics and Plausible Reasoning*, Vol. 1. He shows that the equation $a^2 = b^2 + c^2$ is equivalent to the equation $\lambda a^2 = \lambda b^2 + \lambda c^2$. He states, "The general theorem is equivalent not only to the special case ($a^2 = b^2 + c^2$), but to any other special case. Therefore, if any such special case should turn out to be obvious, the general case would be demonstrated." He goes on to say, "It shows also the fact, so usual in mathematics and still so surprising to the beginner...that the general case can be logically equivalent to a special case."*

17 No. The statement made by the student, "Some men are wise," implies the possibility that there are some men who are not wise, i.e., at least one man who is not wise, which is not the negation of the given statement. A correct negation would be "Every man is wise."

18 One way of looking at the question is to look at the truth table for a conditional as given in Table 3.6.4.

TABLE 3.6.4

p	q	$p \to q$
T	T	T
T	F	F
F	T	T
F	F	T

If a conditional is false, then we are looking at the second row in the truth table; i.e., if $p \to q$ is false, then p is true and q is false. Therefore, the converse would be $q \to p$ where q is false and p is true. But in this case, $q \to p$ is a true statement. Thus the student is correct.

A3.7   Midpoints (Segments and Rays)

1 A midpoint of a segment $\overline{AB}$ is defined to be that point X such that AX = BX. The question then is whether this idea can be extended to include rays and lines. However, one can probably see that if such a point X existed for either a ray or a line, then there exist infinitely many points that could be classified as midpoints. Since a unique answer is not available, it is customary to say that rays and lines do not have midpoints.

2 No, the student is not correct. The coordinate z of the midpoint m is

$$x + \tfrac{1}{2}(y - x) = x + \tfrac{1}{2}y - \tfrac{1}{2}x = \tfrac{1}{2}x + \tfrac{1}{2}y = \tfrac{1}{2}(x + y)$$

*Gyorgy Polya, *Mathematics and Plausible Reasoning*, Vol. 1, Princeton University Press, Princeton, N.J., 1954, p. 17.

A3.8   *n-Dimensional Space, n ⩾ 3*

1   In three dimensions the analogue would be any closed surface which does not cross itself. The ideas are connected by Jordan's theorem. In two dimensions the theorem states that "any closed curve in the plane, which does not cross itself, divides the plane into an inside and an outside." In three dimensions, the theorem states that "any closed surface, which does not cross itself, divides space into an inside and an outside." For more information on this idea consult:

> Edward Kasner and James Newman, *Mathematics and the Imagination,* Simon and Schuster, New York, 1963, pp. 265-98.

2   Mathematically, there are spaces of dimension n where n is any positive integer. This is a major concern in the study of vector spaces. Indeed, mathematicians now study infinite dimensional spaces. Such studies have, for example, led to a greater knowledge of polynomial approximations of rather complicated functions.

Einstein suggested that in order to study the universe in which we live one must regard space as four dimensional. In addition to three position coordinates, one should also add a fourth dimension of time. In many engineering applications of mathematics, one deals with several variables, say position in space (three variables), time, temperature, velocity, etc., so that one is frequently working in a space of dimension greater than three.

3   The reason that there are only five regular polyhedra is based upon the fact that the sum of the measures of the angles at each vertex os a geometric solid must be less than $360°$. (Why?) Remember that a regular polyhedron of a geometric solid, all of whose faces are congruent regular polygons in which the same number of polygons meet at each vertex. Now, at least three faces must meet at each vertex of a polyhedron. (Why?) Thus since each angle of a regular hexagon has a measure of $120°$ there is no regular polyhedron whose faces are regular hexagons. Since each angle of a regular pentagon has a measure of $108°$, then there are no regular polyhedron in which four pentagons meet at each vertex. Table 3.7.1. gives each regular polyhedron with its corresponding number of regular polygons at each vertex.

TABLE 3.7.1

Polyhedron	Number of Regular Polygons at Each Vertex	Reason
Tetrahedron	3 equilateral triangles	$3 \cdot 60° < 360°$
Cube	3 squares	$3 \cdot 90° < 360°$
Octahedron	4 equilateral triangles	$4 \cdot 60° < 360°$
Dodecahedron	3 pentagons	$3 \cdot 108° < 360°$
Icosahedron	5 equilateral triangles	$5 \cdot 60° < 360°$

A3.9   *Non-Euclidean Geometry*

1   The *complex* Euclidean Plane, though not studied at the secondary school level, is defined to be the set of all points (z_1, z_2) where z_1 and z_2 are complex numbers. Thus the *complex* Euclidean Plane is an extension of the *real* Euclidean Plane,

which is defined to be the set of all points (x, y) where x and y are real numbers.

This extension to complex values makes it possible to consider theorems in a more general setting and avoid many of the constraints that are imposed by a restriction to real values. For more information consult:

(1)   Felix Klein, *Elementary Mathematics From An Advanced Standpoint — Geometry*, Dover Publications, New York, 1939, pp. 117-29.

(2)   Rafael Artzy, *Linear Geometry*, Addison-Wesley Publishing Co., Reading, Ma., 1965.

2   If we assume that something is uniformly distributed over a surface, we can determine whether the surface is Euclidean (flat) or non-Euclidean (curved) by measuring numbers of a given thing at varying distances from a given point on the surface. This is one of the methods that astronomers have used to try to determine whether space is Euclidean or non-Euclidean.

Radio astronomers at Ohio State University have discovered that the farther out in space one looks, the more the number of observed radio sources falls short of what one would expect if space were Euclidean. If one assumes that radio sources are uniformly distributed in space, an implication that can be drawn is that space is non-Euclidean, specifically, Riemannean as Einstein has formulated.*

However, over relatively small regions, Euclidean and non-Euclidean methods give essentially the same results. Whether space is Euclidean or non-Euclidean is usually not the domain of mathematicians but is best for physicists and astronomers to ponder.

3   The main point that distinguishes these two is the parallel postulate. In Euclidean geometry, it is assumed that through a point P not on line $\overleftrightarrow{AB}$, there is only one line through P parallel to $\overleftrightarrow{AB}$. In non-Euclidean geometry modifications of this postulate plus other modifications are made. Thus in elliptic or Riemannean geometry, it is assumed that two straight lines always intersect each other; i.e., through a point P not on $\overleftrightarrow{AB}$, there are no lines parallel to $\overleftrightarrow{AB}$. In hyperbolic geometry, it is assumed that through a point P not on $\overleftrightarrow{AB}$ there exists more than one line that does not intersect $\overleftrightarrow{AB}$. For more details on this question the following references are recommended:

(1)   E.T. Bell, *Men of Mathematics*, Simon and Schuster, New York, 1937.

(2)   Courant and Robbins, *What is Mathematics?* Oxford University Press, New York, 1941.

(3)   Howard Eves, *A Survey of Geometry*, Vol. 1, Allyn and Bacon, Boston, 1963.

(4)   Edwin Moise, *Elementary Geometry from an Advanced Standpoint*, Addison Wesley Publishing Co., Reading, Ma., 1963.

(5)   Harold E. Wolfe, *Non-Euclidean Geometry*,   Holt, Rinehart and Winston, New York, 1945.

(6)   *Topics for Mathematics Clubs*, N.C.T.M., Reston, Va., 1973, Chap. 8.

*Adapted from Harold Jacobs, *A Teacher's Guide to Geometry*, W.H. Freeman and Co., San Francisco, 1974, p. 96.

A3.10   Parallelism

1   Yes, it is possible. Let l_1 and l_2 be two parallel lines contained in plane P_1. Let P_2 be a plane that intersects P_1 where the line of intersection is l_1. Then P_1 and P_2 are intersecting planes; l_1 is contained in P_2; and l_2 is contained in P_1.

   Problem   Construct an example of the above different from the one given.

2   In ordinary Euclidean geometry parallel lines are not considered as "meeting at infinity." However, there are many different kinds of geometry and there is a geometry, projective geometry, in which it was found desirable to consider parallel lines as having a common point called an ideal point. Likewise, parallel planes can be considered as meeting at a distinct line, called an ideal line. Thus in projective geometry, any two lines have a point in common and in three-dimensional projective geometry any two planes have a line in common. For more information on projective geometry consult the following references.

   (1)   *Topics for Mathematics Clubs*, N.C.T.M., Reston, Va., Chap. 2, 1973.

   (2)   Morris Kline, "Projective Geometry," *Mathematics in the Modern World, Readings from Scientific American*, W.H. Freeman and Co., San Francisco, 1968.

   (3)   David Gans, *Transformations and Geometries*, Appleton-Century-Crofts, New York, 1968.

3   No, the student is not correct. If we break the diagram apart and show the two transversals separately, one can see that ∠1 is an alternate interior angle to ∠5. Thus m∠1 = 70°. Angle 1 is not an alternate interior angle to angle 7.

4   No. Consider Figure 3.10.1. $\overline{RS}$ is neither parallel to, nor skew to, $\overline{XY}$.

   FIGURE 3.10.1

   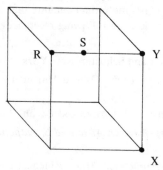

5   For the practical purposes of the bricklayer, the answer is *yes*. However, from a theoretical point of view, the answer is *no*. For suppose Figure 3.10.2 represents a "side view" of the earth. The plumb bob, if properly affixed, points to the center of the earth, and on a large scale, one would obtain the nonparallel results indicated. (See Figure 3.10.2 on page 151.)

FIGURE 3.10.2

FIGURE 3.10.2

6   The statement made by the text has to be read in context. The main difficulty here is one between a geometric entity (a line) and its representation. What the statement in the book means is to extend our representation for a line (the figure). The student is correct in saying that we cannot extend a line. It is the representation, not the line itself, that is extended.

7   No, the student is not correct. Only segments $\overline{AD}$ and $\overline{BC}$ can be deduced to be parallel. In order to say that $\overline{AB}$ and $\overline{CD}$ are parallel, one would have to know that $m\angle 7 = m\angle 3$. But one cannot make this assertion without additional information.

A3.11   *Perpendicularity and the Pythagorean Theorem*

1   No, it is not. Consider a line l that is vertical and perpendicular to a line m at point r in plane P. If l is now rotated about m through point r, then each of the infinite positions thus generated will still have l perpendicular to m at r, but l would not be perpendicular to P. Thus there are an infinite number of lines perpendicular to a given line in a plane but only one of these lines is perpendicular to the plane.

2   Yes, it does. Consider three similar figures constructed on the sides of a right triangle as shown in Figure 3.11.1.

FIGURE 3.11.1

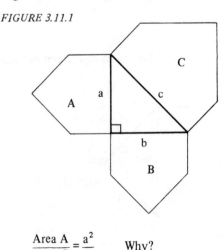

$$\frac{\text{Area A}}{\text{Area C}} = \frac{a^2}{c^2} \qquad \text{Why?}$$

$$\frac{\text{Area B}}{\text{Area C}} = \frac{b^2}{c^2} \qquad \text{Why?}$$

$$\frac{\text{Area A}}{\text{Area C}} + \frac{\text{Area B}}{\text{Area C}} = \frac{a^2}{c^2} + \frac{b^2}{c^2} = \frac{a^2 + b^2}{c^2} \ .$$

But $c^2 = a^2 + b^2$, thus

$$\frac{\text{Area A} + \text{Area B}}{\text{Area C}} = \frac{c^2}{c^2} = 1;$$

i.e., Area A + Area B = Area C.

3   Any definition of area should satisfy the following properties.

(1)   To each region there is assigned a unique real number called the area of the region.

(2)   Regions that are congruent must have the same area.

(3)   If a region is split into a finite number of nonoverlapping parts, then the area of the region is the sum of the areas of these parts.

Any function that assigns to each geometric figure a number that satisfies the above three properties is called an area function.

In Hyperbolic Geometry, an area function is defined as the amount by which the sum of the angles of a triangle differs from 180°. This area function is usually called the defect of the triangle.

4   For the case of one line refer back to Answer 1 in this section. In the case of two lines, the story is quite different. In fact in some texts, the following statement is given as a theorem.

If a line is perpendicular to each of two intersecting lines at their point of intersection, then it is perpendicular to the plane that contains them.

Problem Prove the statement given above.

A3.12   *Polygons*

1   Not necessarily; consider Figure 3.12.1. The figure is an equilateral hexagon, but it is not equiangular.

FIGURE 3.12.1

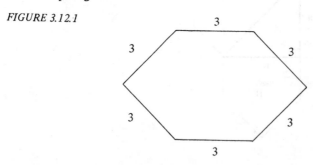

2   Not necessarily; consider Figure 3.12.2. These polygons have corresponding angles congruent, but their sides are not proportional. (See page 153 for Figure 3.12.2.)

FIGURE 3.12.2

Problem 1 Construct two other examples using figures other than rectangles.

Problem 2 If the lengths of the corresponding sides of two polygons are proportional, are the polygons similar?

3   If a trapezoid is defined as a quadrilateral with exactly two sides parallel, then the relationship is as shown in Figure 3.12.3 where a name under another name means that the second type of named figure is a special case of the first figure named.

FIGURE 3.12.3

Problem How would Figure 3.12.3 be changed if a trapezoid is defined to be a quadrilateral with two sides parallel?

4   In some geometry texts, a trapezoid is defined either as a quadrilateral with at least two sides parallel or as a quadrilateral with exactly two sides parallel. According to the first definition a parallelogram is then a special type of trapezoid. Which definition is used, (exactly two sides parallel or at least two sides parallel), seems to be arbitrary and is usually left up to the discretion of the authors of a particular geometry text.

For more information on this question consult the following articles.

(1)   David Dye, "What is a Trapezoid," *The Mathematics Teacher*, November 1967, pp. 727-28.

(2)   Don Ryoti, "What is an Isosceles Trapezoid," *The Mathematics Teacher*, November 1967, pp. 729-30.

5   Yes, the statement is true and is known as Varignon's Theorem:

If the midpoints of consecutive sides of a quadrilateral ABCD are connected, the result is a parallelogram.

Problem 1 Prove the above theorem.

Problem 2 Does the above theorem hold for concave quadrilaterals?

Problem 3 What is the resulting figure if the quadrilateral is: (a) a rectangle, (b) a rhombus, (c) a square, (d) a trapezoid?

6   Consider the square shown in Figure 3.12.4 and the exterior angles at A. The measure of each exterior angle at A is equal to, not greater than, the measure of each of the remote interior angles of square ABCD.

FIGURE 3.12.4

Problem 1 Construct two examples different from the one shown above.

Problem 2 Is the answer the same for all polygons of n sides where n ⩾ 5?

7   No. Consider a square whose side has length x. The area of this square is x^2 while its perimeter is 4x. If the area of this figure is smaller than its perimeter, then

$$x^2 < 4x,$$

whose solution set is $\{x|x < 4\}$. That is, when x ⩾ 4, then the area of a square is greater than its perimeter.

Problem 1 Give two other examples different from the one above that you might use to answer this question.

Problem 2 Answer the second part of the student's question.

8   If the angle referred to in this question is defined to be an exterior angle, then the measure of this angle is greater than 180. However, in plane geometry, it is shown that the measure of an angle (with the usual definition of angle) is between 0 and 180.

Problem What is the usual definition of an exterior angle in plane geometry?

A3.13   *Similarity*

1   If the polygons considered are quadrilaterals, then Figures 3.13.1 and 3.13.2 show that quadrilterals must have both congruent angles and proportional sides to have similarity. In Figure 3.13.1, the corresponding rectangles have congruent angles, but the rectangles are not similar. (See Figure 3.13.1 on page 155.)

FIGURE 3.13.1

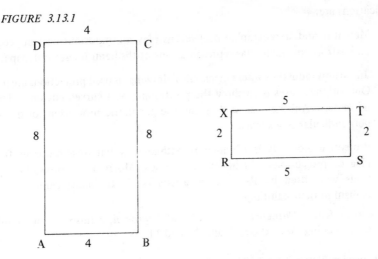

In Figure 3.13.2, the corresponding sides are proportional, but the figures are not similar.

FIGURE 3.13.2

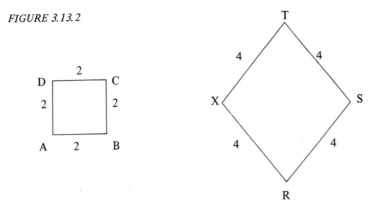

Problem Does the answer given above for quadrilaterals also remain valid for other polygons of n sides where n ⩾ 5?

2   How you handle this situation depends on several factors, but ultimately comes down to what you are trying to accomplish in your teaching through this problem. It seems as if the teacher is trying to show how similar triangles can be used to solve a given problem. The student's method is correct but it is based on the following assertion.

> If a line is parallel to one side of a triangle and intersects the other two sides, it divides them proportionally.

If this assertion has been previously discussed, then the student is correct in using it. However, if this assertion has not been previously discussed, then there are several options open to you. Perhaps the best option is to ask the student to justify the way that the student solved the problem since this method would lead to the discovery and proof of the assertion stated above.

3   The idea of projections has many applications in the physical world. Some of these

applications are:

(1)   Mercator and stereographic projections play an important part in geography and astronomy as in atlas representations of the hemispheres and map making.

(2)   In various industries where mechanical drawing is used projections are involved. One of these uses is to show the positioning of a curved cut on a flat sheet of metal. Another use is to show the geometric projections of dropping a perpendicular to a surface.

(3)   Projective geometry is a branch of mathematics that arose primarily from the idea of projections. In his excellent book, Morris Kline shows how projections were used by Renaissance artists (such as Albert Durer) to achieve realism in their paintings.

   Morris Kline, *Mathematics: A Cultural Approach*, Addison-Wesley Publishing Co., Reading, Ma., 1962, Chaps. 10 and 11.

4   No. Consider Figure 3.13.3. These figures are similar, but not regular.

FIGURE 3.13.3

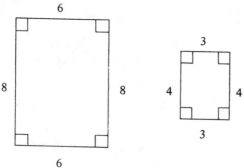

Problem Construct two more examples different from the above. (Do not use rectangles.)

A3.14   *Skewness*

1   No, the student is not correct. Consider a plane such as represented by the floor of a room and a plane such as represented by the ceiling of the same room. Let a third plane, represented by the front wall of the room, intersect the given parallel planes. Each intersection will be a line, and even though these two lines are in different planes, they are not skew lines.

   Problem Modify the student's statement so that it is correct.

A3.15   *Symmetry*

1   Yes. Consider the parallelogram shown in Figure 3.15.1. This figure is symmetric about a point but not symmetric about any line. (See page 157 for Figure 3.15.1.)

FIGURE 3.15.1

Problem 1   Figure 3.15.1 is symmetric about a point. What point is that?

Problem 2   Draw two other figures that are symmetric about a point but not symmetric about any line.

Problem 3   Is it possible for a figure to be symmetric about a line but not symmetric about any point?

Problem 4   Give a precise definition of each of the following: (a) symmetry with respect to a point, (b) symmetry with respect to a line.

A3.16   *Transformations and Functions*

1   This depends upon the definition of the composition of two functions that is being used. Two common definitions are given below.

(1)   If α and β are mappings, then $\alpha \circ \beta$ is the mapping given by $[\alpha \circ \beta](x) = \alpha(\beta(x))$ for all $x \in$ domain of β for which $\beta(x) \in$ domain α.

(2)   If β is a mapping with domain X and range Y and if α is a mapping with domain containing Y and range Z, then the composition of α and β, denoted by $\alpha \circ \beta$, is defined on the domain X and $[\alpha \circ \beta](x) = \alpha(\beta(x))$.

If Definition 1 is used, then the answer to the student's question is yes. Consider

$$\alpha(x) = \frac{x^2}{x^2 - 1} \qquad \text{for x a real number, } x \neq 1, -1,$$

and

$$\beta(x) = 1 \qquad \text{for all } x \neq 2$$
$$ 0 \qquad \text{for } x = 2.$$

Then according to Definition 1, $\alpha \circ \beta$ is the mapping that has domain consisting of $\{2\}$ and range consisting of $\{0\}$; i.e., it is one-to-one.

If Definition 2 is used, then the answer to the student's question is no. The domain of β is the same as the domain of $\alpha \circ \beta$. Thus if $\beta(x_1) = \beta(x_2)$, $x_1 \neq x_2$, then $[\alpha \circ \beta](x_1) = (\alpha \circ \beta)(x_2)$.

Problem 1   Suppose that α is not one-to-one, but β is one-to-one. Can $\alpha \circ \beta$ be one-to-one? Consider both definitions.

Problem 2   Suppose that α is one-to-one, but β is not one-to-one. Can $\alpha \circ \beta$ be one-to-one? Consider both definitions.

2   Whether definition 1 or 2 is used (see Answer 1 of this section), the answer is no. Since β is not "onto," then $\alpha \circ \beta$ cannot be onto.

Problem Suppose that α is not "onto," but β is onto. Can α ∘ β be onto?

3   Yes, the student is correct. The identity isometry (every figure is mapped onto itself) makes congruence reflexive. Since every isometry has an inverse, then congruence is symmetric and the transitive property of congruence depends on the idea that the product of two isometries is an isometry. Thus one can define two figures X and Y as congruent if there exists an isometry that maps X onto Y.

4   The student is assuming that a conditional is equivalent to its inverse; i.e., $p \to q$ and $\sim p \to \sim q$ are equivalent. Thus in this case, the student is really saying that if (1) below is valid then (2) is also valid.

(1)   If r and t are translations, then r ∘ t is a translation.

(2)   If r or t are not translations, then r ∘ t is not a translation.

Logically, however, a conditional and its inverse are not related in this manner. Thus even though (1) is true, (2) may or may not be true. In fact, in this particular case, it can be shown that if r and s are reflections over lines m and n where m ∥ n, then r ∘ s is a translation.

5   The composition, in either order, of a reflection and a translation when the translation is not parallel to the axis of the reflection is a reflection.

Problem Prove the statement given above.

6   The composition of two rotations about different points as centers is either a rotation or a translation.

Problem 1 Find two rotations about different points that again form a rotation.

Problem 2 Find two rotations about different points that form a translation.

Problem 3 Prove the statement made in Answer 6.

7   There are numerous examples that could be given; a few are cited:

(a)   Any reflection of the Euclidean plane across a line will leave the line fixed.

(b)   One can prove that any isometry that leaves each of two points fixed must leave every point of their line fixed. Thus all one must do is locate two points that are fixed by an isometry, and the line determined by these two points is a fixed line under that isometry.

(c)   Any rotation or reflection will leave a circle in the plane fixed.

(d)   In the plane, a reflection over a line *l* followed by a translation parallel to the line *l* leaves the line *l* fixed. This transformation is called a glide reflection, and the fixed line is called the axis of the glide-reflection.

(e)   Any reflection over a line g of a figure symmetric with g will leave the figure fixed.

Problem 1 Find two more examples not given above.

Problem 2 In (d), if the translation is performed first, and then the reflection, will *l* still be a fixed line?

8   According to the definition given, a set of two points would be a figure (albeit a

trivial one). A figure F of two points is congruent to another figure G of two points if and only if one can be mapped onto the other by an isometry; i.e., there is a one-to-one correspondence between the points of F and G such that the distance between the two points of F equals the distance between their images in G.

9 Yes. One can show that a rhombus is reflection symmetric to the lines containing its diagonals. A geometric figure in the plane is reflection symmetric if and only if there is a reflecting line r such that the figure and its image over r coincide. The line r is called a line of symmetry of the figure.

A3.17   *Triangles*

1 Equivalent triangles are frequently defined to be triangles that have the same area. Thus if △ABC has an area of 10 square units and △DEF has an area of 10 square units, then △ABC is equivalent to △DEF.

   Problem Is the relation "is equivalent to" an equivalence relation on the set of triangles in a plane?

2 For an answer to this question, read:

   R. Pawley, "5-Con Triangles," *The Mathematics Teacher*, May 1967, pp. 438-442.

3 For an answer to this question, read the following article by L.W. Smith.* Also consult the references given in Section A1.6(B), Answer 4.

Conditions governing numerical equality of perimeter, area, and volume

LEANDER W. SMITH, *The University of Oklahoma, Norman, Oklahoma.*

Development of theorems leading to pattern generalization

UNDER WHAT CONDITIONS will the area and the perimeter of a triangle be numerically equal? Since the right triangle affords us some computational simplicity, let us consider the class of right triangles first.

Given right triangle *ABC*, with sides *a* and *b* and hypotenuse *c*, having area and perimeter numerically equal, we may write:

$$a^2+b^2=c^2, \tag{1}$$

*From *The Mathematics Teacher*, April 1965, pp. 303-307. Reprinted by permission.

$$a+b+c=\text{perimeter}, \qquad (2)$$

$$\tfrac{1}{2}ab=\text{area}. \qquad (3)$$

By equating (2) and (3), we obtain

$$a+b+c=\tfrac{1}{2}ab \qquad (4)$$

and since

$$c=\sqrt{a^2+b^2},$$

we can rewrite (4) in two variables as

$$a+b+\sqrt{a^2+b^2}=\tfrac{1}{2}ab \text{ for some } a \text{ and } b. \quad (5)$$

Then,

$$\sqrt{a^2+b^2}=\tfrac{1}{2}ab-(a+b)$$

$$4(a^2+b^2)=(ab-2[a+b])^2$$

$$4a^2+4b^2=a^2b^2-4ab(a+b)+4a^2$$
$$+8ab+4b^2$$

$$0=a^2b^2-4ab(a+b)+8ab$$

$$0=ab-4a-4b+8$$

$$0=a(b-4)-4(b-2)$$

so

$$a=\frac{4(b-2)}{b-4}, \qquad b\neq4. \qquad (6')$$

We also know that $a>0$, $b>0$, and that $a+b>c$ by the assumption of triangularity. By inspection we can see that $a>0$ for values of $b>4$, and that $a<0$ for $2<b<4$. It would appear that for $0<b<2$, $a>0$. However, knowing that $2c>0$ and from (5) that $2c=ab-2(a+b)$ we find

$$ab>2a+2b$$

$$ab-2a>2b$$

so

$$a>\frac{2b}{b-2}, \qquad b\neq2. \qquad (5')$$

From the above conclusion, we see that $0<b<2$ would permit $a<0$, which is a contradiction. Combining the results of (5') and (6'), we can now write

$$a=\frac{4(b-2)}{b-4} \text{ for all } b>4. \qquad (6)$$

By examining the graphic solution of (6) we shall find a clue to motivate a more general solution to the problem of having

area and perimeter numerically equal. Consider the X, Y plane and allow $x \in X$ and $y \in Y$ such that a function G maps X onto Y by the following rule:

$$G: x \to \frac{4(x-2)}{x-4} \text{ for all } x>4.$$

By projecting each point (x, y) of G to the axes and joining the intercepts, we generate the set of right triangles from which we obtained (6). (See Fig. 1.)

$$Y=\frac{4(X-2)}{X-4}$$

Figure 1

It should be noted that an isosceles right triangle is formed when $x=y=4+2\sqrt{2}$, the projection of the vertex of the curve. It can be seen that as x increases without bound, y approaches 4; moreover, the interval $(4, 4+2\sqrt{2}]$ is the set of all points whose coordinates represent the possible lengths of the short sides of right triangles, for which area and perimeter are numerically equal. Since 4 is not in the domain of y, there are exactly four integral solutions of G, namely, $(5, 12)$, $(6, 8)$, $(8, 6)$, and $(12, 5)$; thus, there are exactly two right triangles having sides of integral measure and having area and perimeter numerically equal. These are the 6-8-10 and 5-12-13 triangles.

Now, then, let us turn our attention to the set of hypotenuses in Figure 1. Looking at the drawing, it appears that the set of hypotenuses form a set of tangents to a circle of radius 2. This leads us to the solution for the general triangle.

Let us draw a scalene triangle ABC with its incircle (center at O). Note that we may now join the incenter O to each vertex, thus partitioning triangle ABC into three triangles AOB, BOC, and COA. (See Fig. 2.) Each of these triangles has as its altitude the radius of the incircle. Then, assuming triangle ABC has its area

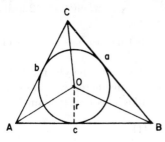

Figure 2

and perimeter numerically equal, we may write:

$$\tfrac{1}{2}ra + \tfrac{1}{2}rb + \tfrac{1}{2}rc = a + b + c \qquad (7)$$

or

$$\tfrac{1}{2}r(a + b + c) = a + b + c$$

hence,

$$r = 2.$$

Theorem I′

If the area and the perimeter of a triangle are numerically equal, the radius of the incircle is two.

Since the proof of the converse of Theorem I′ is trivial, we may use the more powerful theorem below.

Theorem I

The area and the perimeter of a triangle are numerically equal *if and only if* the radius of the incircle is two.

Many mathematicians will argue that the result is trivial, since, by proper choice of the unit of measure, the inradius can be made to be two units. But to the high school student, the problem has interesting motivational properties and even more useful practice in applying the algebraic properties of the field. Students can also see the production of extraneous roots from (5) to (6) and are forced to think about the order properties on inequalities in the handling of (5′) and (6). What follows should afford even greater motivation and student level research.

If any polygon has an incircle of radius two, the area and the perimeter of the polygon are numerically equal. Is this immediately obvious? If not, draw an irregular polygon about a circle O. Then join O to each vertex and note that the radius of the incircle is the altitude of each triangle formed. (Teachers of geometry will recognize that for regular polygons, the area is often given as one half the product of the perimeter and the apothem.)

Hence, we need not limit our discussion to triangles only. We can increase the number of sides of the polygon without bound, making sure that each side is tangent to the incircle. What happens? As the number of sides increases, the polygon approaches the incircle and its area approaches that of the circle. This seems like a good time to provide an intuitive notion of limit for, sure enough, as the number of sides increases without bound, a limit is being approached.

$$\pi r^2 = 2\pi r \text{ when } r = 2.$$

What is the area of a square having an incircle of radius two?

Some polygons do not have incircles and yet have area and perimeter numerically equal. For example, rectangles with length (l) and width (w) where $l = \dfrac{2w}{w - 2}$ and $w > 2$ satisfy this condition. How many rectangles having sides of integral length are there? More generally, the set of all parallelograms for which the area and the perimeter are numerically equal may be given by

$$a = \frac{2b}{b \sin \alpha - 2}$$

where a and b are the sides of the parallelogram and α is the included angle.

For those whose background includes an introduction to the calculus, a bit of generalization follows. Let a square have sides of measure x. Its area is then given by the formula $A = x^2$ and its perimeter by $p = 4x$. Using the calculus produces some interesting results:

If $A = x^2$, then $\dfrac{dA}{dx} = 2x$. Since $p = 4x$,

we may write $p = 2\dfrac{dA}{dx}$. But when the area

and the perimeter of a square are numerically equal, the length of a side, x, is four units and we could rewrite the expression for p as

$$p = \frac{x}{2} \cdot \frac{dA}{dx} . \qquad (8a)$$

Examine another case, that of the equilateral triangle having area and perimeter numerically equal. This occurs when the length of a side is $4\sqrt{3}$ units. If the area is

given by the formula $A = \dfrac{s^2\sqrt{3}}{4}$ when the

perimeter is given by $p = 3s$, $\dfrac{dA}{ds} = \dfrac{s\sqrt{3}}{2}$.

So, if $p = 3s$, we may write

$$p = 4\sqrt{3}\,\frac{dA}{ds}$$

or, more compactly,

$$p = \frac{s}{2} \cdot \frac{dA}{ds} . \qquad (8b)$$

Do you see a pattern emerging from (8a) and (8b)? Try examining a circle in the same way. Sure enough, the result generalizes:

Theorem II

If the area (A) and the perimeter (p) of a polygon are numerically equal, then

$$p = \frac{x}{2}\,\frac{dA}{dx}$$

where x is a linear measure on A and p.

Let us turn our attention to a similar problem in three-space: Under what conditions are the volume (V) and the surface area (S) of a polyhedron numerically equal? An examination of discrete cases will help lead to our conclusion.

Begin with a cube in which $V = S$. Then since $s^3 = 6s^2$, $s = 6$ units, where s is the length of the edge of the cube. What is the radius of the inscribed sphere?

Next, examine the sphere for which $V = S$. Since $\frac{4}{3}\pi r^3 = 4\pi r^2$, $r = 3$ units.

Finally, the regular tetrahedron for which $V = S$ has this relationship stated

by $\dfrac{s^3\sqrt{3}}{12} = s^2\sqrt{3}$, whence $s = 12$ units. The

insphere in this case has a radius of three units.

Since there are polyhedra for which there is no insphere, we state a weak theorem, like Theorem I', namely:

Theorem III

If a polyhedral n-gon has an insphere of radius three, the volume (V) and the surface area (S) are numerically equal.

A proof of Theorem III may be based on the fact that for any pyramid, the volume is one-third of the product of the base area (B) and altitude (h) of the pyramid. Hence, when the altitude is three units, the volume and surface area are numerically equal. (Bear in mind that the polyhedron we are describing may be thought of as a set of planes tangent to an insphere.)

Resorting to the calculus again, we discover an interesting relationship. In the case of the cube, with edge e, if $V = e^3$ then

$\dfrac{dV}{de} = 3e^2$; since we are concerned with the

case when $V = S$, we find that $e = 6$, so

$$S = \frac{e}{3}\,\frac{dV}{de} . \qquad (9a)$$

In the case of the tetrahedron, if $V = \dfrac{e^3\sqrt{3}}{12}$

then $\dfrac{dV}{de} = \dfrac{e^2\sqrt{3}}{4}$, and when $V = S$,

$$S = \frac{e}{3}\,\frac{dV}{de} . \qquad (9b)$$

The sphere itself (as a limiting case) is also of interest. If $V = \frac{4}{3}\pi r^3$ and $S = 4\pi r^2$ then

$\dfrac{dV}{dr} = 4\pi r^2$, and when $V = S$, $r = 3$ and

$$S = \frac{r}{3}\,\frac{dV}{dr} . \qquad (9c)$$

Again we are about to generalize from (9a), (9b), and (9c).

Theorem IV

If the volume (V) and the surface area (S) are numerically equal, then

$$S = \frac{x}{3} \frac{dV}{dx}$$

where x is a linear measure on V and S. "Aha," you say, "in two-space

$$p = \frac{x}{2} \frac{dA}{dx}$$ and in three-space $$S = \frac{x}{3} \frac{dV}{dx}!"$$

One of the beauties of mathematics is the persistence of pattern generalization. What happens if we extend this problem to n-space and talk about the volume (V) and surface area (S)? Let's see.

If $V = c_1 x^n$ and $S = c_2 x^{n-1}$, then we see

that if $V = S$, $x = \dfrac{c_2}{c_1}$. Using the calculus,

$$\frac{dV}{dx} = nc_1 x^{n-1}$$ and we can express S in

terms of $\dfrac{dV}{dx}$ as follows:

$$S = \frac{c_2(nc_1 x^{n-1})}{c_1 n}.$$

The parentheses enclose what we recog-

nize to be $\dfrac{dV}{dx}$ and $\dfrac{c_2}{c_1} = x$ when $V = S$; so

our equation becomes $S = \dfrac{x}{n} \dfrac{dV}{dx}$. Hence,

we have a general theorem which summarizes the results of Theorem II and Theorem IV, which follows.

Theorem V

In n-space, if the volume and the surface area are numerically equal, i.e., $V = c_1 x^n$ and $S = c_2 x^{n-1}$, then

$$S = \frac{x}{n} \frac{dV}{dx}$$

where x is a linear measure on V and S.

Further extensions remain to be explored. Meanwhile, the spontaneous generation of theorems resulting from conjectures in this paper provide a model of student-teacher directed classroom inquiry.

REFERENCES

COURT, NATHAN A. *College Geometry*. New York: Barnes & Noble, 1952 (2nd ed.).
COXETER, H. S. M. *Regular Polytopes*. New York: The Macmillan Company, 1963 (2nd ed.).
SMITH, LEANDER W. "A dialogue on Two Triangles," THE MATHEMATICS TEACHER, LVII (April, 1964), 233–34.

4   No. Consider Figure 3.17.1. $\angle A \cong \angle F$ and $\overline{BC} \cong \overline{EF}$, but $\triangle ABC$ is not congruent to $\triangle DEF$. A correct statement would be:

If a leg and an acute angle of one right triangle are congruent to the corresponding parts of another right triangle, then the triangles are congruent.

FIGURE 3.17.1

5   Part (a) is answered here, but (b) is left for the reader.

  (1)   Not necessarily. Since △ABC ≅ △DEF, then by the convention adopted by
        many texts we know the following:

        $\overline{AB} \cong \overline{DE}$ ∠A ≅ ∠D
        $\overline{BC} \cong \overline{EF}$ ∠B ≅ ∠E
        $\overline{AC} \cong \overline{DF}$ ∠C ≅ ∠F

  (2)   If △ABC is congruent to △EDF, then similarly it would follow that:

        $\overline{AB} \cong \overline{ED}$ ∠A ≅ ∠E
        $\overline{BC} \cong \overline{DF}$ ∠B ≅ ∠D
        $\overline{AC} \cong \overline{EF}$ ∠C ≅ ∠F

However, these latter congruences do not necessarily follow from the former congruences.

> *Problem 1*   Under what conditions will the student's statement be true in (1).

> *Problem 2*   Under what conditions will the student's statement be true in (2).

6   This problem presents a difficulty as to what the student is really asking. That is,
    what does 6 + 4 = 10 have to do with the rest of the question. However, this ques-
    tion is worded exactly as it occurred in a high school classroom. It seems as if the
    student is asking that since one can have two different names for the number ten
    under equality, then why can't we have two different names for triangles under
    equality.

    The notation △ABC = △DEF is usually reserved to mean that these two tri-
    angles are the same set of points. The notation △ABC ≅ △DEF means, intuitively,
    that two triangles have the same size and shape. Thus two triangles that are con-
    gruent (≅) do not necessarily have to have the same set of points.

7   If three points A, B and C are situated so that AB + BC = AC, then the point B is
    between A and C, and all three points lie on one line. If AB + BC > AC, and B is
    not on the same line as A and C, then the points A, B and C determine a triangle.
    A familiar theorem from geometry states that the sum of the lengths of any two
    sides of a triangle exceeds the length of the third side.

8   The notation that is usually used for congruent triangles, △ACB ≅ △EGF, was se-
    lected so that one could tell easily which parts in one triangle correspond to which
    parts in another triangle. Suppose we are given the situation shown in Figure
    3.17.2. Then we know that ∠A ≅ ∠E, ∠B ≅ ∠F and ∠C ≅ ∠G. Also $\overline{AB} \cong \overline{EF}$,
    $\overline{BC} \cong \overline{FG}$ and $\overline{AC} \cong \overline{EG}$. All of this information is given to us by using the sug-
    gested notation, i.e. △ACB ≅ △EGF.

FIGURE 3.17.2

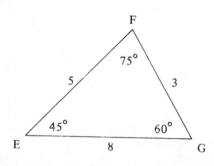

If we were to also write that $\triangle ACB \cong \triangle GFE$, then with the notational convention cited above, this would imply that, for example, $\overline{AC} \cong \overline{GF}$ and $\angle A \cong \angle G$, etc., which is certainly not true.

A congruence between triangles is often defined as follows.

If a correspondence between the vertices of two triangles is such that each side and each angle of one triangle is congruent to the corresponding part of the other triangle, then the correspondence is called a congruence between the triangles.

Thus in the above, the correspondence $\triangle ACB \leftrightarrow \triangle GFE$ is not a congruence.

Thus even though $\triangle EGF$ and $\triangle GFE$ are the same triangle, i.e., the same set of points, in order to show that two triangles are congruent, one must be careful to show which parts of one triangle correspond to which parts of the other triangle.

9   No, the student is not correct. The shortest segment in the figure is $\overline{DC}$.

Problem 1 Write out a detailed explanation showing that the above statement is true.

Problem 2 State and prove the main theorem that you used to justify your assertions in Problem 1.

10   In some texts, this segment is given the name *midline* while in other texts no name is given.

11   The following statement is usually proved as a theorem or given as an exercise in many geometry texts.

If a ray bisects an angle of a triangle, it divides the opposite side into segments whose lengths are proportional to the lengths of the other two sides.

Problem 1 Accepting the above theorem, what example(s) would you give to show the student that his statement is not necessarily true? Under what circumstances would the student's statement be true?

Problem 2 Prove the theorem given in the answer above. (*Hint* Use parallel lines and a transversal.)

4

Algebra II

QUESTIONS

Q4.1   Absolute Value

1   "If we solve $|x + 2| \geqslant 7$, we get $x \geqslant 5$ *or* $-9 \geqslant x$; if we solve $|x + 2| \leqslant 7$, we get $x \leqslant 5$ *and* $-9 \leqslant x$. How do we account for the use of *and* and *or*?" How would you answer this student?

2   A student asks, "What good is the absolute value function?" How do you reply?

3   A student asks, "If you use the definition of absolute value using a line graph and labeling regions, why is the right (of 2) negative territory and the left (of 2) positive territory in equations like $|2 - x| = 5$." What is your response?

4   A student solves the problem $|x - 5| \geqslant 6$ in the following way.

$$|x - 5| \geqslant 6$$
$$x - 5 \geqslant 6 \qquad -x + 5 \geqslant 6$$
$$x \geqslant 11 \qquad -1 \geqslant x$$

Therefore, $-1 \geqslant x \geqslant 11$. Is this student correct? If not, why not?

Q4.2   Binomial Coefficients

1   A student asks you if binomial coefficients are defined for fractions and negative numbers and if so, what are the definitions? How do you reply?

2   You ask your students to do the following problem. "Find the sum of the coefficients of $(x - 2y)^{18}$."

    One of the student gives the following explanation. "In finding the sum of the coefficients, all one need do is look at the coefficient of x and y in the above problem and compute the following expression: $(1 - 2)^{18} = (-1)^{18} = 1$. Therefore the sum of the coefficients $(x - 2y)^{18}$ is 1." Is this method correct? Is the solution correct?

3 You have just shown your class Pascal's Triangle. A student then asks, "Do the diagonals of the Pascal Triangle have any geometric interpretations?" How do you respond?

4 While studying Pascal's Triangle, a student asks you if there is a corresponding configuration for figuring out the coefficients of a trinomial? How do you reply?

Q4.3 *Discriminants and Equations*

1 After studying a unit on imaginary numbers, a student is given the quadratic equation $x^2 - 14x + 53 = 0$ and is asked whether the roots of the equation are real or complex, equal or unequal, and rational or irrational. The student is to use the discriminant to arrive at the answers to these questions. He arrives at the value of -16 for the discriminant. He reasons that a quadratic equation with rational coefficients has rational roots if its discriminant is the square of a rational number. The student says that the roots of this equation are rational since the first requirement is met and we now know how to take the square root of a negative number. The student has also found the roots to be real and unequal. Is his answer to whether the roots are rational or irrational a reasonable answer?

2 A student asks, "What is the difference between a quadratic function and a quadratic equation?" How would you answer?

3 "We can use the quadratic formula to find the roots of any quadratic equation. Is there a similar formula for cubic equations?" How do you answer this student?

4 You ask your class to solve the following for x:

$$3^{2x + 1} + 3^2 = 3^{x + 3} + 3^x.$$

A student hands in the following work. "Since we are adding numbers of the same base, we multiply the exponents

$(2x + 1)2 = (x + 3)x$
$x^2 - x - 2 = 0$
$(x - 2)(x + 1) = 0$

Therefore, $x = 2$ or $x = -1$. Is the student correct?

5 While working with irrational equations, a student does the following:

$\sqrt{2m + 1} = \sqrt{m} + 3$
$2m + 1 = m + 9$
$m = 8$

Is the method correct?

6 A student solves $y^2 + iy + 2 = 0$ and finds that the roots are i and $-2i$. He then says

that this example contradicts the theorem, which says that if $b^2 - 4ac < 0$, then the equation $ax^2 + bx + c = 0$ has two complex conjugate roots. Do you agree?

7   A student asks, "What is the difference between the equations

$$\{(x, y) | y = x^2 - x - 6\} \quad \text{and} \quad \{(x, y) | x^2 - x - 6 = 0\} ?$$

They look the same to me." How would you reply?

Q4.4   *Exponents*

1   A student makes the following observation.

$$(-8)^{1/3} = \sqrt[3]{-8} = -2, \quad \text{but} \quad (-8)^{2/6} = \sqrt[6]{(-8)^2} = 2.$$

This student then reasons that $(-8)^{1/3} \neq (-8)^{2/6}$ even though $1/3 = 2/6$. Why? How would you help this student?

2   A student shows you the following work and asks if it is correct.

$$\sqrt{(-3)^2} = [(-3)^2]^{1/2}$$
$$= (-3)^{2 \cdot 1/2}$$
$$= -3$$
$$\sqrt{9} = -3.$$

How would you respond?

3   A student hands in the following: $(x^{-1} + y^{-1})^{-1} = x + y$. Do you agree?

4   A student asks you if $(\sqrt[n]{b})^n = \sqrt[n]{b^n}$ when $b \geq 0$. How do you reply?

5   A student says, "0^0 should be equal to one because:

$$a^n \cdot a^0 = a^{n + 0} = a^n.$$

Thus $a^0 = 1$.

Therefore $0^0 = 1$.

How do you react to this statement?

6   A student reasons, "Since $(a^{1/2})^2 = a$ means a number $(a^{1/2})$ whose square is a, then $3^{1/2} = -\sqrt{3}$ or $\sqrt{3}$ (since $(-\sqrt{3})^2 = 3$ and $(\sqrt{3})^2 = 3$)." Do you agree?

7   A student solves the following exponential expression this way.

$$\frac{2\sqrt{27}}{8\sqrt{3}} = \frac{1\sqrt{27}}{4\sqrt{3}} = \frac{1}{4\sqrt{3}}$$

Is this student correct?

Q4.5   *Functions*

1   A student asks you if it is possible for a relation that is not a function to have an inverse that is a function. What is your answer?

2   A student asks you if there is a function that is equal to its inverse. What is your answer?

3   A student asks you if the empty set is a function. What answer do you give?

4   The students conjecture, "The abcissa of the point of inflection of a general cubic function is the average (mean) of the three zeros of the function." How would you show that this conjecture is true?

5   A student asks, "How can you show that $f(x) > 0$ and $(f(x))^2 > 0$ are not equivalent?" What is your reply?

6   "How do you tell if a function is into or onto? Is there a difference or are they the same?" How would you answer this student?

7   "Why is the concept of function important to the teaching of algebra?" What is your reply?

8   A student asks, "What is the difference between the notions of single valued and one-to-one correspondence?" What is your reply?

9   A student asks: "What is the difference, if any, between range and codomain?" How would you respond to this student?

10   An eleventh grade student makes the following remark in class. "The idea of a function is really a basic idea in mathematics and occurs at all grade levels. For example, percent can be thought of in a functional way, as well as finding combinations of objects in probability and areas of figures in geometry." Do you agree?

11   The following question is asked in your class. "Does a function have an inverse if the inverse of the function is the function itself?" How do you respond?

Q4.6   *Graphs: Conic Sections*

1   One student asks you what the graph of $x^2 + y^2 = -9$ would look like. What do you tell this student?

2   A student asks, "Isn't a circle just a special case of an ellipse?" How do you reply?

3   A student asks you if the graph of $y = (x^2)^2 = x^4$ is a parabola. How do you respond?

4   A student asks, "Is there any equation where the graph crosses its own asymptote before it approaches the asymptote?" How do you reply?

5   A student asks, "If a curve is asymptotic to an oblique line, how could you find the equation of the asymptote?" How do you reply?

6   "In the definition of the hyperbola, we took the set of all points (in one plane) whose distances from the foci differ by the same constant. What kind of a figure would you get if we took all points in space whose distances from the foci differ by the same constant?" How do you reply to this student?

7   A student asks, "Is it possible to define the ellipse and the hyperbola in terms of a focus and directrix as one does with a parabola?" How do you respond?

8   One of your students comments, "A hyperbola is really just two parabolas put together." How do you reply?

9   If $d(PM) = \frac{1}{3} d(PQ)$, what are the coordinates of M in the figure?

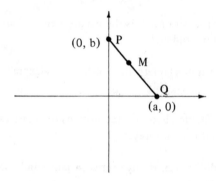

A student says that since $d(PM) = \frac{1}{3} d(PQ)$ the x coordinate of M is $\frac{1}{3} a$. Is this true for any M, P, and Q? How do you reply?

10   A student asks, "In this figure, how can the x-axis be tangent to x^3 since it intersects it?" How would you answer this student?

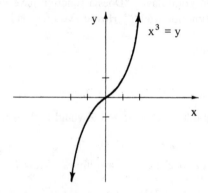

11   A student asks, "If a tangent means touching a curve at one point, how can a line, be tangent to a straight line?" How would you respond?

12 "A parabola is defined to be the set of points equidistant from a fixed point and a given straight line, right? What kind of a figure would we get if the straight line was replaced by a circle, an ellipse, another parabola, or a hyperbola?" How would you answer this student?

13 A student asks you for some application of the conic sections. How would you respond?

Q4.7   *Irrational Numbers*

1 A student asks, "Are there fewer irrational numbers than rational numbers?" How do you respond?

2 A student asks, "How do you know for sure that some irrational number does not have a repeating decimal eventually?" What reply would you give?

3 "If we deny the existence of rational numbers, can we define an irrational number? After all the only way I have heard it defined was that it is any real number that is not *rational*." How would you answer this student?

4 A student asks, "How can one prove that π or e, or any of the transcendental irrational real numbers have nonrepeating decimal representations?" How would you respond?

5 A student asks, "Are all nonterminating decimals irrational numbers?" What reply would you give?

Q4.8   *Logarithms*

1 You tell your class that a logarithm is really just an exponent. One of your students then asks, "If a logarithm is just an exponent, then why do we call it a logarithm rather than an exponent?" How do you reply?

2 A student is trying to solve the following problem using logarithms. " Compute $\frac{.843}{2}$." She hands in the following work.

$\log .843 - \log 2$
$-1.9258 - .3010$
-1.9258
$- \ \ .3010$
$\overline{-2.2268}$
.0167 approximately

Is this student correct?

3 A student asks you why logarithms in base e are called natural logarithms and why

are they so important? How would you respond?

4   A problem on a test is stated as follows. "Find antilog −9.0386." The student says that it is impossible to log a negative number. Therefore, it is impossible to antilog a negative number. How do you help this student?

5   A student asks, "I have worked this problem four times, but I don't get the answer that is in the book.

$$\frac{\log_{10} 4}{\log_{10} 2} = \log_{10} 4 - \log_{10} 2 = .6021 - .3010$$

$$= .3011$$

The answer in the book is 2. Is the book wrong?" How do you reply?

6   A student hands in the following work.

$$\frac{\log_{10} 4}{\log_{10} 2} = \frac{\log_{10} 4}{\log_{10} 2} = \frac{4}{2} = 2.$$

Is this method correct?

7   A student asks you why can't one find the log of a negative number like $\log_{10} (-5)$. How would you answer this student?

Q4.9   *Logic and Proof*

1   An algebra student was asked to prove the following theorem. "If a and b are real numbers such that $a \cdot b = 0$, then $a = 0$ or $b = 0$."
    The student said, "I will restate the conclusion of the theorem. What I shall prove is that if $a \neq 0$, then $b = 0$. This is the same thing as proving that $a = 0$ or $b = 0$." Classmates were not convinced. Some said that one should also prove that if $b \neq 0$, then $a = 0$. What is your opinion?

Q4.10   *Mean*

1   You ask a student to explain why zero is the geometric mean of zero and any real number. One student says that zero cannot be the geometric mean because if you said it was then you would get $0/0 = 0/r$, where r is any real number and $0/0$ is undefined. Do you agree?

2   A student asks you if there are any other means besides the arithmetic, geometric and harmonic and if they are of any importance. How would you reply?

3   While studying a unit on sequences, a student asks you why $\sqrt{ab}$ is called the geometric mean of a and b. What do you reply?

Q4.11   *Rational and Complex Numbers*

1   A seventh grade student asks, "What is the difference between 3 and +3?" How do you respond?

2   A student comments, "C = πD where C is the circumference of a circle and D is the diameter of the circle. Therefore π = C/D; thus π is a rational number since C and D are rational numbers." How do you reply?

3   A student says, "3 + 4i = 4 + 3i because numbers are commutative." What do you tell this student?

4   A student asks, "We can represent the sum of two complex numbers graphically as a vertex of a parallelogram. Is it possible for the product of two complex numbers to have a similar geometric meaning?" What is your reply?

5   "Are there numbers other than those in the complex number system?" How do you respond to this student?

6   A student asks you if imaginary numbers are only numbers in our imagination. What do you say?

7   A student asks you why they call such numbers *complex* numbers? What is your response?

8   You put the following problem on the board for your students to do. "Simplify $\sqrt{-4} \cdot \sqrt{-9}$." One student does the following work.

$$\sqrt{-4} \cdot \sqrt{-9} = \sqrt{36} = 6.$$

Another disagrees and says that

$$\sqrt{-4} \cdot \sqrt{-9} = 2i \cdot 3i = 6i^2 = -6.$$

What do you do?

9   A student asks, "If $\sqrt{-1}$ = i, what is $\sqrt{i}$?" How do you reply?

10 A student makes the statement that since $-3 > -5$, then $\sqrt{-3} > \sqrt{-5}$. How do you react to this statement?

11 A student asks, "Does the set of real numbers have the same number of elements as the set of rational numbers?" How would you answer?

12 A student asks you for some applications of complex numbers. How would you respond?

13 The problem is: "Find all pairs of complex numbers (x, y) for which 3x + 5yi = 9 + 35i." A student hands in the following work.

$$3x + 5yi = 9 + 35i \leftrightarrow 3x = 9 \text{ and } 5y = 35.$$

Therefore,

$$x = 3 \text{ and } y = 7.   \text{Is the student correct?}$$

14   A student asks, "Is $\sqrt{-4}$ equal to $i\sqrt{2}$ or $-i\sqrt{2}$?"

15   A student hands in the following work.

(a) $\dfrac{\sqrt{-4}}{\sqrt{-9}} = \sqrt{\dfrac{4}{9}} = \dfrac{2}{3}$

(b) $\dfrac{\sqrt{-4}}{\sqrt{9}} = \sqrt{\dfrac{-4}{9}} = i\sqrt{\dfrac{4}{9}} = \dfrac{2}{3}i$

Is the student correct?

16   Two students hand in the following work.

(a) $\dfrac{\sqrt{4}}{\sqrt{-9}} = \sqrt{\dfrac{-4}{9}} = i\sqrt{\dfrac{4}{9}} = \dfrac{2}{3}i$

(b) $\sqrt{\dfrac{4}{-9}} = \dfrac{2}{3i} = \dfrac{2}{3} \cdot \dfrac{1}{i} = -\dfrac{2}{3}i$

Which student (if either) is correct?

Q4.12   *Operations, Properties and Systems*

1   A student asks, "Does a mathematical system that is commutative also have to be associative?" How do you respond?

2   In multiplying 5½ by 5½, a student writes:

$5\tfrac{1}{2} \cdot 5\tfrac{1}{2} = 5 \cdot 6 + \tfrac{1}{4} = 30.25.$

Is this student correct?

3   While studying a unit on matrices and determinants, a student asks you if the multiplication of matrices is related to the inner product of two vectors. How do you respond?

4   You have asked your class to find the number of different elements on one side of the diagonal of a square matrix. A student hands in the following work. "$n^2/2$ gives 1/2 of the number of elements. $(n^2/2) - (n/1)$ gives 1/2 of the numbers of elements minus the number of elements in the diagonal. Therefore, $(n^2/2) - (n/1)$ is the number of different elements on one side of the diagonal of a square matrix." Is the student correct?

5   An advanced algebra student solves the following matrix to find the value of its determinant. The student uses the diagonal line method:

$$\begin{bmatrix} 2 & 4 & 1 \\ 2 & 4 & 1 \\ 0 & 2 & 1 \end{bmatrix} \longrightarrow$$

The first thing that you notice is that the student has used the method backwards. You tell the student to work it the other way. He returns and makes the comment that it does not matter what method is used or which way the problem is done, that one will arrive at the same answer. Is this student correct?

6   A student asks you if there is a field between the rational numbers and the real numbers. What is your reply?

7   A student asks, "How can the set of real number be closed under division if division by 0 gives no answer?" How do you reply?

8   A student says, "You know, there are really many distributive properties. For example, raising to a power distributes over multiplication; conjugation of complex numbers distributes over addition; multiplication and division and cross product of sets distributes over union of sets." Is the student right?

9   A student asks you if the matrix (5) is the same as the real number 5. How do you respond to this question?

10   A student asks you the following question. "What is the difference between a vector and a ray? They look the same to me." To further complicate things, the student says, "But you said that a matrix is a ray (an array!) and you also said that the reals are called scalars and matrices are called vectors. Then why isn't a ray the same as a vector?" How do you respond?

11   "Of what value is the well-ordering property?" How do you respond to this student?

12   A student asks, "I remember that last year in geometry we learned that two statements are equivalent if and only if they have the same truth table. This year we learned that two open sentences are equivalent if and only if they have the same solution set. Are these two ideas related?" How would you respond?

Q4.13   *Polynomials and Rational Expressions*

1   A student asks you why the constant polynomial zero does not have a degree assigned to it. How do you respond?

2   A student asks, "When we divide $4x^2 - 5x + 9$ by $x - 1$, is the quotient $4x - 1$ or is it $4x - 1 + \dfrac{8}{x - 1}$?" What is your reply?

3   "What is the difference between the terms polynomial, polynomial equation and polynomial function?" How do you answer this student?

4   One student asks you the rationale behind synthetic division. What do you tell this student?

5   While studying the sums and differences of rational algebraic expressions in Algebra II, a student was asked to simplify the expression, $\dfrac{C^{-4} - D^{-4}}{C^{-2} - D^{-2}}$. The student wrote:

$$\frac{C^2 D^2}{C^4 - D^4} = \frac{1}{C^2 - D^2} \qquad \text{Is this student correct?}$$

Q4.14   Radicals

1   A student says that

$$\sqrt[3]{-8^2} = \sqrt[3]{-8}\sqrt[3]{-8} = (-2) \cdot (-2) = 4.$$

Is this student correct?

2   The following problem is an enrichment problem given to a group of superior juniors and seniors..

interpretation

$$x^{x^{x^{x^{\cdot^{\cdot^{\cdot}}}}}} = 2,$$

One student reasons as follows. "Suppose $x = \sqrt{2}$, then $x = 2^{1/2}$, so

$$(2^{1/2})^{2^{1/2^{\cdot^{\cdot^{\cdot}}}}} = 2,$$

Now since exponents multiply, rewrite the problem as:

$$2^{1/2 \, 2^{1/2} \, 2^{1/2^{\cdot^{\cdot^{\cdot}}}}} = 2.$$

It can now be seen that if the circled numbers are multiplied together one has

$$2^{1^{1^{1^{\cdot^{\cdot^{\cdot}}}}}} = 2,$$

which is true. Therefore $x = \sqrt{2}$." Is this student correct?

3   You ask your class to simplify $\dfrac{1 + (1/\sqrt{3})}{1 - (1/\sqrt{3})}$. One student says that all you have to do is invert each part of the fraction, i.e.,

$$\frac{1 + (1/\sqrt{3})}{1 - (1/\sqrt{3})} = \frac{1 + (1/(1/\sqrt{3}))}{1 - (1/(1/\sqrt{3}))} = \frac{1 + \sqrt{3}}{1 - \sqrt{3}}.$$

Is this student correct?

4   A student asks, "Why should we rationalize the denominator? Isn't $1/\sqrt{2}$ just as good as $\sqrt{2}/2$?" How would you answer?

5   A student asks if $\sqrt[n]{a^m} = {}^{m}\!\sqrt[n]{a}$. How would you respond?

6   If a student asks, "Is there such a thing as $\sqrt[\frac{1}{2}]{x}$?" how would you answer this question?"

Q4.15   Roots

1   The problem given is: "Find the real roots of $x + \sqrt{x - 2} = 4$." Using standard methods this student finds that 3 and 6 are possible solutions, but that only 3 is a solution. He asks you why it is that 6 is not a solution (i.e., does not work). How would you respond?

2   A student asks, "You said that 3 was a zero of $x^2 - 4x + 3 = 0$ but 3 is not zero. I don't understand." How would you help this student?

3   A teacher solves $2 - y = 2\sqrt{y + 1}$ as follows.

$$(2 - y)^2 = (2\sqrt{y + 1})^2$$
$$4 - 4y + y^2 = 4y + 4.$$

Thus,

$$y^2 - 8y = 0;$$

hence,

$$y(y - 8) = 0.$$

Therefore, $y = 0$ and $y = 8$, where 8 is an extraneous root.

A student then asks why $(2\sqrt{y + 1})^2$ wasn't written as $4|y + 1|$ because squaring makes a number positive, but $4y + 4$ could be negative. How would you respond?

Q4.16   Sequences and Series

1   A student says that the expressions

(a) $\sum\limits_{n = 1}^{3} (n + 1)$ (b) $\sum\limits_{j = 2}^{4} j$

are not equivalent because the first one equals $2 + 3 + 4$ while the second one equals $2 + 3 + 4 + 5$. What error in understanding does this student have and how would you help?

2   A student says that he understands what $\sum\limits_{j = 1}^{3} j$ means but he does not know what $\sum\limits_{n = 2}^{6} 1$ means because 1 is not a variable. How would you help this student?

Q4.17   Simultaneous Systems of Equations

1   A student asks, "We have said that the systems

$$\begin{cases} 3x + 4y = 18 \\ 2x - y = 1 \end{cases} \qquad \begin{cases} x = 2 \\ y = 3 \end{cases}$$

are equivalent. However, $x = 2$ is not equivalent to either $3x + 4y = 18$ or $2x - y = 1$. Why?" How would you respond?

Q4.18   *Slide Rule*

1   While teaching your class how to use the slide rule, a student asks, "What is the rationale behind the use of the slide rule. Why does it work?" What do you tell this student?

Q4.19   *Variables*

1   A student asks you if there is any difference between the idea of variable and the idea of indeterminate. What is your response?

2   "What is the difference between a variable and a parameter?" What do you tell this student?

Q4.20   *Direct and Indirect Variation*

1   While studying the form y = mx in a unit on direct variation, you tell your students that the origin is a solution for any direct variation of this form. A student comes across the problem: "If 2x + 3 varies directly as 7y + 2, what is x when y = 3?" The student says, "It can't be a direct variation, because (0, 0) doesn't belong to the solution set." What is your response?

 ANSWERS

A4.1   *Absolute Value*

1   One way of illustrating the solution to absolute value inequalities is illustrated below. In the answer to the problem we will use the symbols V for *or* and ∧ for *and* as is used in some secondary materials.

(a)   Solve |x + 2| ≥ 7.

$$(x + 2 \geqslant 0 \wedge x + 2 \geqslant 7) \vee (x + 2 < 0 \wedge -(x + 2) \geqslant 7)$$
$$(x \geqslant -2 \wedge x \geqslant 5) \vee (x < -2 \wedge x + 2 \leqslant -7)$$
$$(x \geqslant -2 \wedge x \geqslant 5) \vee (x < -2 \wedge x \leqslant -9)$$
$$x \geqslant 5 \vee x \leqslant -9$$

i.e., $x \geqslant 5$ or $x \leqslant -9$

(b)   Solve $|x + 2| \leqslant 7$.

$$(x + 2 \geqslant 0 \wedge x + 2 \leqslant 7) \vee (x + 2 < 0 \wedge -(x + 2) \leqslant 7)$$
$$(x \geqslant -2 \wedge x \leqslant 5) \vee (x < -2 \wedge x + 2 \geqslant -7)$$
$$(x \geqslant -2 \wedge x \leqslant 5) \vee (x < -2 \wedge x \geqslant -9)$$
$$(-2 \leqslant x \leqslant 5) \vee (-9 \leqslant x < -2)$$

i.e., $-9 \leqslant x \leqslant 5$

$x \leqslant 5$ and $-9 \leqslant x$

Another way of looking at this question is given in the following article.

> Thomas Green, "The Graphing of Absolute Value Inequalities," *The Mathematics Teacher*, December 1967, pp. 837-38.

2   The absolute value function is important in many ways. On a number line, the standard definition of distance involves the absolute value function. The definition of limit, which is basic to the study of the calculus, involves the absolute value function. For an interesting "real-world" application of absolute value, see:

> Baxter and Sloyer, *Calculus with Probability*, Addison-Wesley Publishing Co., Reading, Ma., pp. 145-50.

3   It should first be pointed out to the student that one obtains regions of the graph only for expressions such as $|2 - x| \geqslant 5$ or $|2 - x| < 5$. In the case where $|2 - x| = 5$ one gets only two points.

However, in the expression $|2 - x|$ when $x > 2$, then $2 - x < 0$; i.e., the expression inside the absolute value is negative. Thus the region to the right of $x = 2$ consists of those values which when substituted in the expression, $2 - x$, give negative values. Likewise, the region to the left of $x = 2$ consists of those values which when substituted in the expression, $2 - x$, give positive values.

4   The student is not correct. See the discussion in Answer 1 of this section. The student should have written $x \geqslant 11$ or $x \leqslant -1$.

A4.2   *Binomial Coefficients*

1   See Answer 1 of Section 5.2(C).

2   Yes, this method and solution are correct. The general case can be illustrated as follows. If a, b, x, y are integers, n, r are counting numbers, $(ax)(by) \neq 0$ and $n \geqslant r$, then

$$(ax + by)^n = \sum_{r=0}^{n} \binom{n}{r}(ax)^{n-r}(by)^r \tag{1}$$

If we let x and y each have the value of one, then in the right side of (1) we have

$$\sum_{r=0}^{n} \binom{n}{r}(a)^{n-r}(b)^r,$$

which is the sum of the coefficients of $(ax + by)^n$. However, from (1) the left-hand side gives us $(a + b)^n$, which also must be the sum of the coefficients.

3   For an answer to this question consult the following article by Lars Jansson.*

SPACES, FUNCTIONS, POLYGONS, and PASCAL'S TRIANGLE

By LARS C. JANSSON

The Pennsylvania State University
University Park, Pennsylvania

TWO recent trends in the teaching of mathematics can often go hand in hand. These two are the spiral approach to content development and the discovery-teaching/learning method. This paper will present some topics that illustrate how these approaches to content and method may complement each other. Space will not permit the full explication as it might occur in·a classroom, but it is hoped that both the discovery approach to mathematical conjecture as well as the spiral nature of the topics will be evident. The specific topics discussed here range from those for the upper elementary school pupil to those for the high school senior—the exact placement depends not only on the topic itself, but on the language and notation as well.

In geometry classes we often discuss the number of lines determined by a given number of points in the plane and the number of divisions of the plane determined by those lines. Polya presents an excellent illustration of reasoning by analogy based on this problem (Polya 1954, pp. 43–52). First, the subdivisions of the plane by lines is discussed and then the subdivision of space by planes. Beginning with simple examples, tables of numbers are kept until a conjecture can be made about the relationships between (1) the number of points on a line, n, and the subdivisions of the line, $n + 1$; and (2) the number of portions into which a plane is divided by n straight lines in general position: $1 + n + n(n - 1)/2$.

Some Initial Conjectures

Rereading Polya's discussion recently, the author was reminded of a geometry lesson observed in a tenth-grade class several years ago. The Pascal triangle as it appears in figure 1 (without the arrows) was on the board.

Fig. 1. The Pascal triangle. The arrows indicate "diagonals."

*From The Mathematics Teacher, January 1973, pp. 71-77. Reprinted by permission.

The students had been discussing such questions as those noted by Polya when someone observed that the second "diagonal" (indicated by the second arrow from the top in fig. 1) gives the number of lines determined by n points, where n is given by the first diagonal. Thus three points determine three lines, whereas four points determine six lines (reading across row 4 to the second diagonal). Of course it was agreed that no three points could be collinear. It was then seen that the same rule works for $n = 5$ as shown in figure 2, namely, that we have ten distinct lines. On further observation and consideration, it appears that this conjecture is a reasonable one, since this diagonal of the triangle is $\binom{n}{2}$. That is, since two points determine a line, the points are taken two at a time and $\binom{n}{2}$ gives us this count, the order of the points being immaterial. Thus four points taken two at a time give $\binom{4}{2} = 6$ distinct lines. The class omitted this formal discussion and soon wanted to know whether the other diagonals of the Pascal triangle had similar geometric interpretations.

Fig. 2. Five points (not necessarily coplanar) determine ten distinct lines, provided no three points are collinear.

Several approaches to this question will be examined here, first the one closest to that suggested by the students' original observations. (It will become evident, however, that this is not the simplest approach.)

The Leap into Space

The analogy that permitted the leap from points to lines was made by the class. By a similar analogy, the next step is clearly from lines to planes or points to planes. The choice will be shown by the development to be arbitrary—the only difference is in the simplicity of the language. Given the triangle and its rows named by n, where n represents the number of given points, the latter relationship based on points will be used. How many points determine a plane? Three. Given three points, it is immediately obvious in the triangle that the third diagonal contains a 1. Given four points (now with a noncoplanar rather than noncollinear condition) taken three at a time, it becomes evident that four distinct planes are determined (see fig. 3). This all seems very reasonable when we realize that the third diagonal is the sequence $\left\{ \binom{n}{3} \right\}$, $n = 3, 4, 5, \cdots$

The next jump requires more imagination, but it is not yet totally abstract. Looking at the triangle, it is clear that we must have at least four points if the fourth diagonal is to have any meaning similar to the preceding ones. The simplest analogous figure beyond the plane (triangle) is the tetrahedron. Just as the plane required three points, the tetrahedron is determined by four, as shown in figure 3. If the tetrahedron is given by the four points A_0, A_1, A_2, and A_3, we can define the *3-space* $A_0A_1A_2A_3$ as the set of all points collinear with pairs of points in one or two faces of the tetrahedron $A_0A_1A_2A_3$. The actuality of this definition is more easily realized by considering the analogous definition for a plane: "If A, B, C are three noncollinear points, the *plane ABC* is the set of all points collinear with pairs of points on one or two sides of the triangle *ABC*" (Coxeter 1969, pp. 183–86). A three-dimensional model of a tetrahedron and a drawing of a triangle, respectively, will aid in visualizing these situations.

Each time we have increased the dimension, it has been necessary to postulate the existence of a point in a space of the next higher dimension. Thus in going from a line to a plane, a noncollinear third point was required. Similarly, in moving from the plane to a 3-space, it was necessary to have a fourth point not in the plane. In order to continue our analogy, we postulate the existence of a fifth point not in our 3-space.

Thus three points determine a 2-space (plane) and four points determine a 3-space. In general, n points determine an $(n-1)$-space. Returning then to Pascal's triangle, five given points determine ten lines, ten planes, five tetrahedra, and, now, one 4-space. Such a set of points, say $A_0A_1A_2A_3A_4$, is a *simplex*. Note that this simplex contains five vertices A_i; ten edges A_iA_j, $i < j$; ten faces $A_iA_jA_k$, $i < j < k$; and five cells, $A_iA_jA_kA_l$, which are tetrahedral regions. This is precisely row 5 of the Pascal triangle. The 4-space thus determined is the set of points collinear with pairs of points in

one or two cells of the simplex. At this point in our development we have become completely abstract!

Clearly the above discussion can be extended to n dimensions (using mathematical induction). The number of vertices (points), edges (lines), faces (planes), and simplexes determined by n points (satisfying a modified noncollinearity condition) is given by the corresponding row and diagonal of the Pascal triangle. The general statement is as follows:

GENERALIZATION 1: *Given n points in real (n − 1)-space, row n and diagonal m of the Pascal triangle gives the number of (m − 1)-spaces determined by the n points taken m at a time.*

This information is summarized in figure 4. Note, for example, that six points determine fifteen straight lines and six 4-spaces.

As the preceding discussion progressed and became more abstract, it became increasingly necessary to introduce some new terminology. The conventional words have been employed here, but students can invent their own terms. If this is all too abstract, a different tack can be taken by restricting the extensions to two dimensions. Two such directions will be suggested here, the more general first.

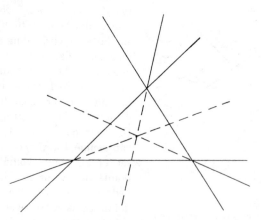

Fig. 3. Four points determine a tetrahedron or a 3-space, provided they are not coplanar.

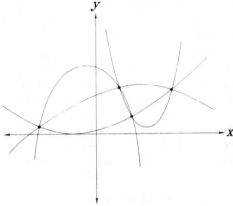

Fig. 4. The Pascal triangle. Summary of the extension of dimensions approach.

Polynomial Functions

We return again to figure 1 and the second diagonal of the triangle. Remember that this was interpreted as giving the number of lines or linear functions determined by taking pairs of points from among a set of n points such that no three were collinear. In this new approach, all points will be restricted to the plane, which will be considered as $R \times R$, the Cartesian plane. Note, however, that given three points, we can determine not only three lines, but also a parabola or quadratic function in one variable. Such a quadratic polynomial function is of the form $ax^2 + bx + c$. A particular polynomial is determined by the values of the coefficients of each power of the variable and the constant term. Thus, since the quadratic has three such values, three points or ordered pairs are required in order to obtain three simultaneous linear equations in a, b, and c of the form $ax^2 + bx + c = y$.

Since each quadratic requires three points for its determination, how many quadratics are given by four points? Reasoning by analogy, is it true that four points determine four quadratic functions? And five points, ten quadratic functions? It takes three points to determine such a function, and since we already know that the diagonal is the sequence $\left\{ \binom{n}{3} \right\}$, $n = 3, 4, 5, \cdots$, it becomes obvious that this diagonal gives the number of quadratics given by n points. Figure 5 shows four quadratics given by four points.

Fig. 5. In the Cartesian plane, four quadratics are determined by four points, no three of which are collinear.

We know that two points determine a line and that three points determine a quadratic. Similarly, four points determine a cubic, and so on. Thus five points determine ten linear functions, ten quadratic functions, five cubics, and one quartic. We may now write as follows:

GENERALIZATION 2: *Given n points in the real plane, row n and diagonal m of the Pascal triangle gives the number of algebraic polynomial functions in one variable of degree $m - 1$ determined by the n points taken m at a time.*

In order that none of these $\binom{n}{m}$ poly-

Fig. 6. The Pascal triangle. Summary of the polynomial function approach.

nomials be degenerate (i.e., with $a_n = 0$, where a_n is the coefficient of the $m - 1$ degree term), no m of the n given points may satisfy a polynomial of degree less than or equal to $m - 2$. This corresponds to the earlier noncollinearity condition. A simple example will illustrate this: Given four (n) points in the plane, three (m) of them will determine a nondegenerate quadratic (degree $m - 1$) polynomial as long as they do not all also lie on the graph of a linear (degree $m - 2$) function. This approach is summarized in figure 6.

Convex Polygons

The third approach to geometric inter-

pretations of the diagonals of the Pascal triangle is perhaps the simplest, although in some senses the least general. In this case we are again in two-dimensional space; the only further restriction is that the n given points be vertices of a convex polygon. These polygons (see fig. 7) need not be regular. The counting problem in this instance is the number of segments, triangles, quadrilaterals, and so on formed by the diagonals and vertices of the polygon. Again we are looking at two, three, four, . . . points taken at a time from n given points. Consider the pentagon (fig. 7(c), which contains the following figures:

Figure		Number of Figures
points	A_1, A_2, A_3, A_4, A_5	5
segments	$A_1A_3, A_1A_4, A_1A_5, A_1A_2,$ $A_2A_3, A_2A_4, A_2A_5, A_3A_4,$ A_3A_5, A_4A_5	10
triangles	$A_1A_2A_3, A_1A_2A_4, A_1A_2A_5,$ $A_1A_3A_4, A_1A_3A_5, A_1A_4A_5,$ $A_2A_3A_4, A_2A_3A_5, A_2A_4A_5,$ $A_3A_4A_5$	10
quadrilaterals	$A_1A_2A_3A_4, A_1A_2A_3A_5, A_2A_3A_4A_5,$ $A_1A_3A_4A_5, A_1A_2A_4A_5$	5
pentagons	$A_1A_2A_3A_4A_5$	1

See figure 8 for the summarized Pascal triangle for *n*-gons. The general case may now be stated:

GENERALIZATION 3: *Given n points in the plane forming the vertices of a convex polygon, row n and diagonal m of the Pascal triangle gives the number of m-gons determined by those points (and the segments joining them).*[1]

---

1. The symmetry of language breaks down at this point. It takes *m* points to determine an $(m - 1)$-dimensional space, an $(m - 1)$-degree polynomial, and an *m*-gon. Thus, as long as we are clear what it is we are counting, there is no difficulty.

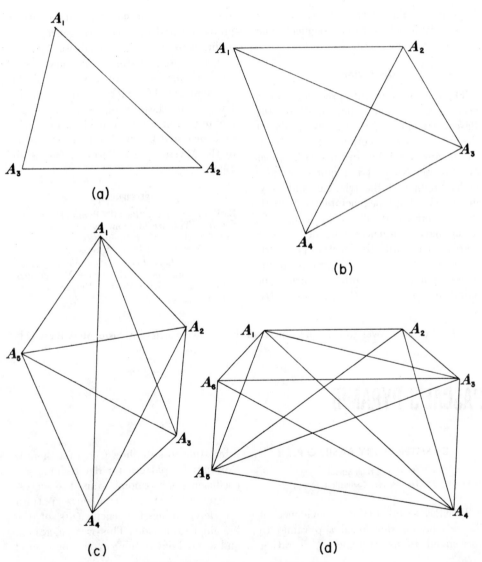

Fig. 7. Convex polygons with diagonals.

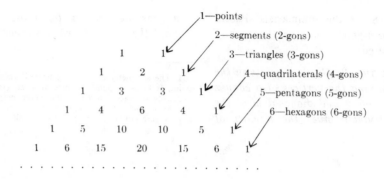

Fig. 8. The Pascal triangle. Summary of the convex-polygon approach.

Thus in the Pascal triangle we see that for six given points, fifteen segments and six pentagons are formed.

Discussion

Three geometric interpretations have been given to the "diagonals" of the Pascal triangle. With the exception of the more abstract notions, this material can be discovered by students with proper questioning. None of it requires previous understanding of the triangle, and may, in fact, be developed before the triangle itself is presented. The triangle may be a summary-and-generalizing device or a starting point, with the levels of geometric abstraction varied according to the group. These approaches (or others) suggest the spiral features for both the Pascal tri-angle (as a representative of counting problems) and the geometric concepts, in addition to encouraging conjecturing.

These examples from elementary geometry are just a few of those that could be examined. The interested reader might try to relate these examples through analogy to the three-dimensional Pascal pyramid suggested by Basil in an earlier issue of the MATHEMATICS TEACHER (see Basil 1968).

REFERENCES

Basil, Sister Mary. "Pascal's Pyramid." MATHE-MATICS TEACHER 61 (January 1968): 19-21.
Coxeter, H. S. M. *Introduction to Geometry.* New York: John Wiley & Sons, 1969.
Polya, G. *Mathematics and Plausible Reasoning:* Vol. 1, *Induction and Analogy in Mathematics.* Princeton, N.J.: Princeton University Press, 1954.

4   For an answer to this question, read the following article by Sister Mary Basil, O.P.*

PASCAL'S PYRAMID

By **SISTER MARY BASIL, O.P.**

St. Mary's High School
New Haven, Connecticut

THERE seems to be no evidence of Pascal's having developed a pyramid to correspond to his triangle. It is rather interesting to note, however, that there is a pyramidal pattern for determining the coefficients of a trinomial raised to successive powers, just as his triangle is a pattern for determining the coefficients of the binomial expansion. This was suggested, and worked out to some extent, by a pupil

*From *The Mathematics Teacher*, January 1968, pp. 19-21. Reprinted by permission.

of a colleague who showed me her paper several years ago.

```
                        1
                     1     1
                  1     2     1
               1     3     3     1
            1     4     6     4     1
         1     5    10    10     5     1
      1     6    15    20    15     6     1
   1     7    21    35    35    21     7     1
```

FIGURE 1

A few lines of Pascal's triangle are reproduced in Figure 1 to help the reader recall the pattern and to refer to throughout the article. Beginning with the second line, there are the coefficients of $(a + b)^1 = a + b$. The third line determines the coefficients for $(a + b)^2 = a^2 + 2ab + b^2$, the fourth for $(a + b)^3 = a^3 + 3a^2b + 3ab^2 + b^3$, and so on.

Inverted Triangular Pyramid

To determine the coefficients of a trinomial raised to successive powers we need an inverted triangular pyramid. Since this is rather difficult to show in a two-space display, the reader can imagine that he is building a pyramid balanced on its vertex instead of standing on its base.

The first layer is 1. This is the value of $(a + b + c)^0$, just as in the triangle $(a + b)^0 = 1$. The next layer is

```
        1
     1     1
```

These are the coefficients of $(a + b + c)^1 = a + b + c$. The third layer appears as follows:

```
        1
     2     2
  1     2     1
```

and $(a + b + c)^2 = a^2 + 2ab + 2ac + b^2 + 2bc + c^2$. The fourth and fifth layers are:

```
        1
     3     3
  3     6     3
1    3     3     1
```

and

```
            1
         4     4
      6    12     6
   4    12    12     4
1     4     6     4     1
```

corresponding to the coefficients of

$$(a + b + c)^3 = a^3 + 3a^2b + 3a^2c + 3ab^2 + 6abc$$
$$+ 3ac^2 + b^3 + 3b^2c + 3bc^2 + c^3,$$

and

$$(a + b + c)^4 = a^4 + 4a^3b + 4a^3c + 6a^2b^2 + 12a^2bc$$
$$+ 6a^2c^2 + 4ab^3 + 12ab^2c + 12abc^2$$
$$+ 4ac^3 + b^4 + 4b^3c + 6b^2c^2 + 4bc^3$$
$$+ c^4.$$

A brief explanation may be necessary to reveal the pattern. The numbers on the outer edge of each layer are determined by adding the two numbers they rest on in building the pyramid. Numbers in the interior of each layer are found by adding the three numbers on which they rest. The outer edges of the sixth layer, then, contain 1, 5, 10, 10, 5, 1, and the interior numbers are $4 + 4 + 12 = 20$, $6 + 12 + 12 = 30$, and so on. See Figure 2. The exponents of the variables can be determined by assigning the highest power of a to the first row. The product of the second highest power of a times the first power of each of the other variables is assigned to the second row. In the next rows, we continue to decrease the power of a and arrange the powers of the other variables so that the sum of the powers equals the power to which the trinomial is being raised. For each row the power of a will remain the same, the power of b will decrease, and the power of c will increase. In the case of the sixth layer, which gives the coefficients for

```
                1
             5     5
          10    20    10
       10    30    30    10
    5    20    30    20     5
 1     5    10    10     5     1
```

FIGURE 2

the expansion of $(a + b + c)^5$, the numbers and variables are arranged as shown in Figures 2 and 3.

$$a^5$$
$$a^4b \qquad a^4c$$
$$a^3b^2 \qquad a^3bc \qquad a^3c^2$$
$$a^2b^3 \qquad a^2b^2c \qquad a^2bc^2 \qquad a^2c^3$$
$$ab^4 \qquad ab^3c \qquad ab^2c^2 \qquad abc^3 \qquad ac^4$$
$$b^5 \qquad b^4c \qquad b^3c^2 \qquad b^2c^3 \qquad bc^4 \qquad c^5$$

FIGURE 3

No doubt the reader has already noticed the outer edge of each successive layer of the pyramid repeats a corresponding row of the triangle. The other numbers of each row of the layers of the pyramid can also be determined from the triangle, independently of the layer of the pyramid immediately below. First, write the left edge of the seventh layer as follows:

$$1$$
$$6$$
$$15$$
$$20$$
$$15$$
$$6$$
$$1$$

Now take the numbers in each row of the triangle and multiply by the number in the corresponding position on the left edge to fill in the rest of the row in the layer of the pyramid, as in Figure 4.

Evidently one needs four-space to determine an array for the coefficients of the expansion of $a + b + c + d$. However, following the multiplication device above and using a row of the triangle on the left times the numbers in each layer of the pyramid, these coefficients can be determined. The array, however, will not be symmetrical. (Maybe it is in four-space!) The procedure for determining the variables is the same as in the pyramid.

The array of $(a + b + c + d)^2$ is formed as follows:

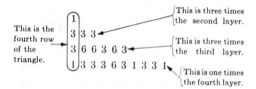

$$(a + b + c + d)^2 = a^2 + 2ab + 2ac + 2ad + b^2$$
$$+ 2bc + 2bd + c^2 + 2cd + d^2.$$

The array for $(a + b + c + d)^3$ is formed in a similar way:

This is the fourth row of the triangle.
$$\begin{cases} 1 \\ 3 \ | \ 3 \ 3 \\ 3 \ | \ 6 \ 6 \ 3 \ 6 \ 3 \\ 1 \ | \ 3 \ 3 \ 3 \ 6 \ 3 \ 1 \ 3 \ 3 \ 1 \end{cases}$$
This is three times the second layer.
This is three times the third layer.
This is one times the fourth layer.

$$(a + b + c + d)^3 = a^3 + 3a^2b + 3a^2c + 3a^2d$$
$$+ 3ab^2 + 6abc + 6abd + 3ac^2 + 6acd + 3ad^2$$
$$+ b^3 + 3b^2c + 3b^2d + 3bc^2 + 6bcd + 3bd^2$$
$$+ c^3 + 3c^2d + 3cd^2 + d^3.$$

The process continues to apply to raising the sum of five numbers to successive powers.

$$1$$
$$6 \cdot 1 \qquad\qquad 6 \cdot 1$$
$$6 \qquad\qquad\quad 6$$

$$15 \cdot 1 \qquad 15 \cdot 2 \qquad 15 \cdot 1$$
$$15 \qquad\quad 30 \qquad\quad 15$$

$$20 \cdot 1 \qquad 20 \cdot 3 \qquad 20 \cdot 3 \qquad 20 \cdot 1$$
$$20 \qquad\quad 60 \qquad\quad 60 \qquad\quad 20$$

$$15 \cdot 1 \qquad 15 \cdot 4 \qquad 15 \cdot 6 \qquad 15 \cdot 4 \qquad 15 \cdot 1$$
$$15 \qquad\quad 60 \qquad\quad 90 \qquad\quad 60 \qquad\quad 15$$

$$6 \cdot 1 \qquad 6 \cdot 5 \qquad 6 \cdot 10 \qquad 6 \cdot 10 \qquad 6 \cdot 5 \qquad 6 \cdot 1$$
$$6 \qquad\quad 30 \qquad\quad 60 \qquad\quad 60 \qquad\quad 30 \qquad\quad 6$$

$$1 \cdot 1 \qquad 1 \cdot 6 \qquad 1 \cdot 15 \qquad 1 \cdot 20 \qquad 1 \cdot 15 \qquad 1 \cdot 6 \qquad 1 \cdot 1$$
$$1 \qquad\quad 6 \qquad\quad 15 \qquad\quad 20 \qquad\quad 15 \qquad\quad 6 \qquad\quad 1$$

FIGURE 4

A4.3   *Discriminants and Equations*

1   No, the student is incorrect. -16 is not the square of a rational number; it is the square of a complex number. For this particular quadratic equation, the roots are $7 + 2i$, $7 - 2i$, i.e., complex conjugates that are complex numbers and not rational numbers.

2   A quadratic function over the set R of real numbers is a function whose domain is R and whose values are given by

$$y = f(x) = ax^2 + bx + c$$

where $a, b, c \in R$ and $a \neq 0$. A quadratic equation is given by

$$ax^2 + bx + c = 0$$

where $a, b, c \in R$ and $a \neq 0$. Thus a quadratic function consists of all ordered pairs, (x, y) where

$$y = ax^2 + bx + c.$$

In a quadratic equation, one is usually interested in finding those values for x that are solutions of the equation; i.e., the solution set of the quadratic equation

$$ax^2 + bx + c = 0$$

consists of those numbers x which satisfy the equation. It turns out that these numbers are precisely the same values as the zeroes of the associated quadratic function. Thus one could say that the solution set of the quadratic equation $ax^2 + bx + c = 0$ is the same set of numbers as the set of zeroes of the related quadratic function.

3   For an answer to this question read:

(1)   Joseph Mandelbaum, "$x = \dfrac{-b \pm \sqrt{b^2 - 3ac}}{3a}$," *The Mathematics Teacher*, December 1972, pp. 707-9.

(2)   William C. Smith, "A Discriminant for the Cubic and its Use in Graphing," *The Mathematics Teacher*, March 1972, pp. 249-53.

4   The student does get the correct answer in this particular case, but the student's method will not work in all situations. Consider the following:

$$3^{2x} + 3^2 = 3^4 + 3^x.$$

The solution set for this problem is $\{2\}$. By the student's method, $(2x)2 = 4x$ or $4x = 4x$, which is satisfied by any integer.

> *Problem 1*   What familiar property has the student applied incorrectly?

> *Problem 2*   Under what conditions will the student's (incorrect) method give the correct answer?

> *Problem 3*   How would you show this student a correct method?

5   No, the method is not correct. One way of solving this equation is as follows on the next page. (See page 190.)

$$\sqrt{2m+1} = \sqrt{m} + 3 \leftrightarrow 2m + 1 = m + 6\sqrt{m} + 9$$
$$\leftrightarrow m - 8 = 6\sqrt{m} \leftrightarrow (m - 8)^2 = 36m$$
$$\leftrightarrow m^2 - 16m + 64 = 36m \leftrightarrow m^2 - 52m + 64 = 0$$
$$\leftrightarrow m = \frac{52 \pm \sqrt{2448}}{2}.$$

6   No. The theorem that the student is using is stated as follows:

If a, b, c are real numbers with a $\neq$ 0, then the quadratic equation $ax^2 + bx + c = 0$ has:

(1)   Two different real roots if $b^2 - 4ac > 0$,

(2)   One double real root if $b^2 - 4ac = 0$,

(3)   Two complex conjugate roots if $b^2 - 4ac < 0$.

This theorem is applicable to quadratic equations with *real* coefficients. This condition is violated in the present case.

7   The graph of $\{(x, y)|y = x^2 - x - 6\}$ is given in Figure 4.3.1 while the graph of $\{(x, y)|x^2 - x - 6 = 0\}$ is given in Figure 4.3.2. The equation $x^2 - x - 6 = 0$ yields only two values of x, namely, -2 and 3, which can be used in forming ordered pairs (x, y) for Figure 4.3.2. The equation $y = x^2 - x - 6$ allows the use of *any* x in forming ordered pairs (x, y) for Figure 4.3.1. The difference between the given sets is now easy to see.

FIGURE 4.3.1

FIGURE 4.3.2

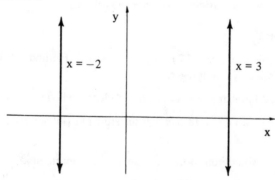

A4.4   *Exponents*

1   There are several definitions that use rational numbers as exponents, but no matter which definition is used, certain difficulties are encountered. In addition, when teaching this topic and related topics on radicals, one must be sure that students recognize the conditions that must be satisfied in a particular definition; i.e., what students will be allowed to do depends on the particular definition used in their text.

One way of defining numbers with rational exponents is as follows:

If $\sqrt[r]{a}$, $\sqrt[r]{a^s}$ are real numbers, where r is a counting number and s is an integer, then

$$a^{s/r} = \sqrt[r]{a^s}. \tag{1}$$

Thus $(-8)^{1/3} = \sqrt[3]{-8} = -2$ is a true statement because $\sqrt[3]{-8}$ is a real number. However, $(-8)^{2/6}$ is not defined because $\sqrt[6]{-8}$ is not a real number.

Another way of defining numbers with rational exponents is to restrict the base in the expression $b^{r/s}$ to be a positive number. However, either definition presents certain difficulties. For example, in (1), the property $(a \cdot b)^m = a^m b^m$ is not generally true. For example, consider $a = b = -2$ and $m = \frac{1}{2}$. Then, one obtains

$$(-2 \cdot -2)^{\frac{1}{2}} = (-2)^{\frac{1}{2}} \cdot (-2)^{\frac{1}{2}}.$$

The left-hand member represents 2, while the right-hand member does not exist in the set of real numbers. If the base is restricted to positive numbers as in the second definition above, then $(-8)^{1/3}$ is not even defined. The problem is that extending the idea of exponents to rational numbers cannot be accomplished without losing some of the properties of exponents that are valid in the set of integers.

2   No, it is not correct. The expression $[(-3)^2]^{\frac{1}{2}}$ is not defined because $(-3)^{\frac{1}{2}}$ is not a real number (see Answer 1 of this section). One could get a correct statement by the following:

$$\sqrt{(-3)^2} = (9)^{\frac{1}{2}} = (3^2)^{\frac{1}{2}} = 3.$$

The main problem is that if $a > 0$, then

$$[(-a)^n]^{1/n} \neq (-a)^{n/n}$$

when n is even.

Problem 1   Under what conditions will $[(-a)^n]^{1/n} = (-a)^{n/n}$?

Problem 2   Under what conditions is $[(-a)^n]^{1/n} = [(-a)^{1/n}]^n$?

3   No. Raising to a power does not distribute over addition. For example,

$$\left[\left(\frac{1}{2}\right)^{-1} + \left(\frac{1}{3}\right)^{-1}\right]^{-1} = \frac{1}{5} \quad \text{while} \quad \frac{1}{2} + \frac{1}{3} = \frac{5}{6}.$$

The given problem can be simplified as follows:

$$(x^{-1} + y^{-1})^{-1} = \frac{1}{x^{-1} + y^{-1}} = \frac{1}{\dfrac{1}{x} + \dfrac{1}{y}} = \frac{xy}{x + y}.$$

4   By definition, $(\sqrt[n]{b})^n = b$. If n is an odd positive integer, $\sqrt[n]{b^n} = b$; i.e., $\sqrt[3]{2^3} = 2$. If n is an even positive integer, $\sqrt[n]{b^n} = |b|$, because $\sqrt[n]{b^n}$ denotes the principal *n*th root, which is nonnegative. Thus if $b \geqslant 0$, then $\sqrt[n]{b^n} = |b| = b$, and the two expressions are identical. However, if $b < 0$ and n is even, then this situation changes since $(\sqrt[n]{b})^n$ is not defined in the set of real numbers while $\sqrt[n]{b^n} = |b|$.

5   In *The Mathematics Teacher*, Herbert Vaughan demonstrated several cogent arguments for assigning the value of 1 to the expression 0^0.

Herbert Vaughan, "The Expression '0^0'," *The Mathematics Teacher*, February 1970, pp. 111-12.

In addition, he pointed out the difficulties encountered with the law of exponents.

The authors of this text would like to suggest a reason for supporting the contention $0^0 = 1$ as follows. In elementary calculus texts, one encounters the following situation. Let g be the function defined by $g(x) = x^n$ for all real numbers where n is a positive integer. Then $g'(x) = n \cdot x^{n-1}$ and, in particular, $g'(0) = n \cdot 0^{n-1}$. If $n = 1$, then $g'(0) = 1 \cdot 0^0$. Now let f be the function defined by $f(x) = x$ for all real numbers. Then $f'(x) = 1$ and, in particular, $f'(0) = 1$. However, when $n = 1$, the function g is precisely the same as the function f. Since $f'(0) = 1$, then $g'(0) = 1$ and in order to be consistent, we must assign the value of 1 to the expression 0^0.

Another reason supporting the contention of $0^0 = 1$ is the following. In elementary calculus texts, one frequently encounters

$$\cos x = \sum_{k=0}^{\infty} \frac{(-1)^k x^{2k}}{(2k)!}, \quad -\infty < x < \infty \tag{1}$$

If $x = 0$, we have

$$\cos 0 = \frac{(-1)^0 0^0}{0!} + \frac{(-1)0^2}{2!} + \frac{(-1)^2 0^4}{4!} + \cdots . \tag{2}$$

But (2) makes no sense unless we agree that $0^0 = 1$. Indeed, expressions such as (2) are offered to support the definition $0! = 1$.

More generally, one could encounter

$$f(x) = \sum_{k=0}^{\infty} \frac{f^k(a)}{k!}(x - a)^k$$

in the student of Taylor's Series, where $f^k(a)$ is the *k*th derivative evaluated at a, $k \geqslant 1$, and $f^0(a) = f(a)$. If $x = a$, we have

$$f(a) = \frac{f^0(a)}{0!} 0^0 + \frac{f^1(a)}{1!} 0^1 + \frac{f^2(a)}{2!} 0^2 + \cdots \tag{3}$$

Again (3) makes no sense unless we agree that $0^0 = 1$.

The example $\sum_{n=1}^{\infty} \frac{x^{n-1}}{(n-1)!} = e^x$, for all x given in (1), is a special case of this.

If one agrees that $0^0 = 1$, however, one has to realize that 0^0 must remain as an indeterminant form in the study of limits. That this is the case is shown by the following very simple examples.

$$\lim_{x \to 0} x^0 = 1 \quad \text{while} \quad \lim_{x \to 0} 0^x = 0.$$

More complicated examples are offered by

$$\lim_{x \to 0^+} x^x = 1 \quad \text{and} \quad \lim_{x \to 0^+} x^{(1/\ln x)} = e.$$

These examples also offer interesting possibilities relative to the use of calculators and computers in the classroom.

6   If a is positive, then the equation $x^2 = a$ has two solutions, one negative and one positive. The symbol $\sqrt{a}$ is reserved, by convention, for the positive solution and the symbol $-\sqrt{a}$ is reserved for the negative solution. In older books the expression $a^{\frac{1}{2}}$ sometimes referred to both of these, but in most of the texts now used the expression $a^{\frac{1}{2}}$ refers to $\sqrt{a}$, while $-(a^{\frac{1}{2}})$ refers to $-\sqrt{a}$.

7   No, the student is not correct. One way of simplifying this expression is:

$$\frac{2\sqrt{27}}{8\sqrt{3}} = \frac{2^{3\sqrt{3}}}{(2^3)\sqrt{3}} = \frac{2^{3\sqrt{3}}}{2^{3\sqrt{3}}} = 1.$$

An interesting problem to explore in this case is to find all of those expressions for which the student's method would give the correct answer.

A4.5   Functions

1   Yes, it is possible. For example, the relation on the set $\{1, 2, 3, 4\}$ given below, which is not a function, has an inverse that is a function:

$$R = \{(1, 1), (1, 2), (1, 3), (1, 4)\}$$

while

$$R^{-1} = \{(1, 1), (2, 1), (3, 1), (4, 1)\}.$$

Problem 1 Find two other relations that are not functions which have inverses that are functions.

Problem 2 Consider the relation on the reals given by $\{(x, y)|y = \pm\sqrt{x}, x \geqslant 0\}$. Is this relation a function? Is the inverse a function?

2   Yes, there is. One such function is the identity function defined by $f(x) = x$. Another example is the function defined by

$$f(x) = \frac{x}{x - 1}, \quad x \neq 1.$$

In fact, any function whose graph is symmetric to the line $y = x$ is a function that is equal to its inverse.

Problem Find two functions, other than the above, that are equal to their own inverses.

3   A function can be defined as a set of ordered pairs. That is, a function f is a set of ordered pairs such that no two ordered pairs have the same first component. Since the empty set vacuously satisfies this condition, then the empty set could be considered a function although an extremely trivial one. However, one should carefully examine the text used since some authors insist that neither the domain nor the range can be the empty set.

4   For an answer to this question, read:

> Mona Fabricant, "A Classroom Discovery in High School Calculus," *The Mathematics Teacher*, December 1972, pp. 744-45.

5   Perhaps the best way to show this would be to take a specific example. Suppose that $f(x) = x$ with domain being the set of real numbers. Then $[f(x)]^2 = x^2$. Thus $f(x) > 0$ or $x > 0$ has as its solution set the set of positive real numbers while $[f(x)]^2 > 0$ or $x^2 > 0$ has as its solution set the set of nonzero real numbers. Since the solution sets are not equal, then the above expressions are not equivalent.

6   Every function is an "into" function. Suppose f is a function from a set A into a set B. Then f is an "onto" function if and only if every element $b \in B$ is such that there is an $a \in A$ with $f(a) = b$. For example, if one regards $f(x) = x^2$ as a function from R (the set of reals) into R, then f is *not* an "onto" function since, for example there is no $a \in R$ such that $f(a) = -1$. However, $f(x) = x^3$, from R into R is an "onto" function since, for any $b \in R$, there is an $a \in R$ (namely $\sqrt[3]{b}$) such that $f(a) = b$.

Geometrically, one can identify a function from R into R as being an "onto" function provided every horizontal line intersects the graph of the function as shown in Figure 4.5.1. The graph in Figure 4.5.2 does not represent an "onto" function.

FIGURE 4.5.1

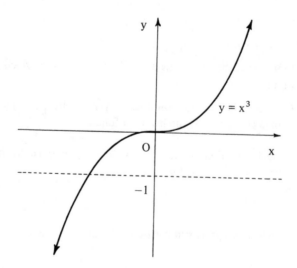

$y = x^3$

FIGURE 4.5.2

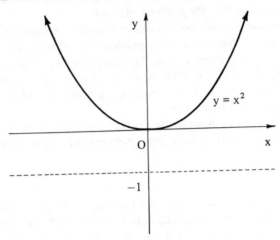

7   The concept of function is extremely important in all branches of mathematics, not only in algebra. The following references delve deeper into the overall importance of functions than can be stated in the space provided.

(1)   Creighton Buck, "Functions," *Mathematics Education* (The Sixty-Ninth Yearbook of the National Society for the Study of Education), Pt. 1, ed. Edward Begle, University of Chicago Press, Chicago, 1970, pp. 236-60.

(2)   *The Growth of Mathematical Ideas from Grades K-12* (Twenty-Fourth Yearbook), N.C.T.M., Reston, Va.,1959, pp. 65-111.

Two reasons why functions are important in algebra are:

(1)   Many of the concepts developed in algebra are really examples of functions, for example: logarithms, circular functions, permutations, combinations, addition, subtraction, multiplication, etc.

(2)   In many cases, a function can be defined by means of an algebraic expression, which in turn can be manipulated according to the properties developed in algebra. That is, algebra helps to transform expressions from one form to another form, which may be more useful in solving the particular problem at hand. For example, if one is trying to graph the expression $y = x^2 + 4x + 3$, it is easier to complete the square in the right-hand side first and then graph the resulting equation.

8   The notion of *single valued* is normally associated with the concept of a function. The standard definition of a *function f* insists that for each x in the domain there is precisely one value of $f(x)$. At times (especially in older texts), one will encounter a discussion of a *multiple-valued function f* where for each value of x in the domain there may be more than one value of $f(x)$. For example,

$$f(x) = x^2, \quad x \in R$$

is a single-valued function while

$$f(x) = \pm\sqrt{x}, \quad x \geqslant 0$$

is a multiple-valued function. For the most part, discussions of multiple-valued functions have been replaced by the study of relations.

The notion of *one-to-one correspondence* is normally found in set theory: two sets A and B are in a one-to-one correspondence if and only if an association can be set up where, for any element of A, there corresponds precisely one element of B, and, for every element of B, there is associated precisely one element of A. For example, there is a one-to-one correspondence between the set of integers and the set of even integers given by $n \leftrightarrow 2n$.

The notion of function, however, is not divorced from set theory, and hence there is a connection. The association given above could be represented by a function defined by

$$f(n) = 2n,$$

where the domain is the set of integers and the range is the set of even integers. Such a function is called a *one-to-one and onto function*. In the manner of this example, every one-to-one correspondence can be represented by a one-to-one and onto function. However, it is not the case that every function represents a one-to-one correspondence as the example $f(x) = x^2$ illustrates.

9   There are at least three terms, namely, range codomain, and image set, that are used interchangeably in many cases. Suppose that f and g are the mappings shown in Figure 4.5.3; i.e., f is a mapping of A into B while g is a mapping of A onto B. In elementary mathematics, it is customary to say that B is the range or codomain of the mapping f while B is the image set of A under g. However, authors are free to use any definition they wish and in some materials the words range or codomain have the same meaning as image set. Thus the best advice in this situation is to look carefully at the definitions employed by the authors of the text that is currently being used. The term codomain is not usually found in elementary texts but is frequently used in college texts.

FIGURE 4.5.3

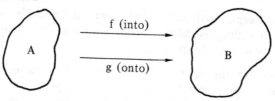

10   Yes, you should agree. Each of these ideas can be considered to be functions as illustrated.

(1)   Areas of geometric figures in geometry.

Domain Geometric figures (squares, circles, etc.) for which the notion of area is meaningful.

Range Set of real numbers.

Each geometric figure has only one number which is the measure of its area.

(2)   Combinations of objects in probability.

Domain Set of ordered pairs (n, k), usually represented by $\binom{n}{k}$ or $_nC_k$.

Range Set of integers; the element in the range is given by the rule $\binom{n}{k} =$ $\dfrac{n!}{k!(n-k)!}$.

(3) Percent.

Domain Set of nonnegative real numbers.

Range Set of nonnegative real numbers.

For example, 30% of 60 can be thought of in a functional way as $(30/100) \cdot (60)$. The element in the domain is 60, the element in the range is $\dfrac{30}{100} \cdot \dfrac{60}{1} = 18$. Notice the similarity here when 30/100 or 30% is replaced by conventional notation; i.e., let 30% be represented by f. Then, $(30/100) \cdot (60) = f(60)$.

Problem Find three other situations similar to the above where the function idea is used.

11 Yes, it does. There is no restriction on the definition of an inverse function that would preclude the inverse function of a function from being equal to the function itself. Some examples of functions which behave in this manner are:

(1) $f: x \to x$ (the identity function).

(2) $g: x \to \dfrac{x}{x-1}$, $x \ne 1$.

In fact, any function that is symmetric with respect to the line $y = x$ has an inverse function that is the function itself.

Problem Find three other functions whose inverse functions are the functions themselves.

A4.6   Graphs: Conic Sections

1 Usually when this question is brought up in an Algebra II class, the domain of definition is the set of real numbers. In this case the graph would be the empty set since the square of a real number is never negative. However, one might wish to pursue this question further by considering what would happen if the domain of definition was extended to the set of complex numbers. One way of attacking this problem is given here.

Suppose we include in addition to the real plane an *argand plane* for complex values drawn perpendicular to the real plane as shown in Figure 4.6.1. Consider now what the graph of $\{(x, y) | x^2 + y^2 = -9$, x, a complex number, and y, a real number$\}$ would look like in the system used in Figure 4.6.1. Letting x be complex and y be real is, in a sense, arbitrary since we could also have x be real and y, complex (see Problem 1 for this answer). (See page 198 for Figure 4.6.1.)

Letting $x = a + bi$ and substituting in $x^2 + y^2 = -9$, we obtain

$$(a + bi)^2 + y^2 = -9$$
$$y^2 = -9 - a^2 + b^2 - 2abi.$$

Since y is to be real, then the coefficient of i is zero and hence $a = 0$ or $b = 0$. If $b = 0$, $y^2 = -9 - a^2$; since y must be real, then the graph is the empty set. If $a = 0$,

FIGURE 4.6.1

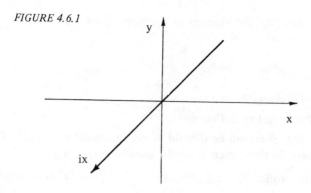

$y^2 = -9 + b^2$ or $b^2 - y^2 = 9$, a hyperbola. Figure 4.6.2 shows the graph of the "complex circle" $x^2 + y^2 = -9$.

FIGURE 4.6.2

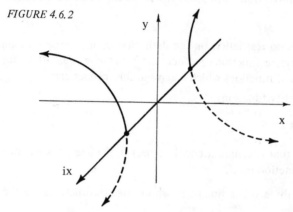

Problem 1 What sort of graph of $x^2 + y^2 = -9$ results if x is real and y is complex?

Problem 2 Graph the following using the system (i) of real numbers and (ii) of complex numbers.

(a) $y = x^2$ (b) $x^2 + y^2 = -4$

(c) $x^2 + y^2 = 9$ (d) $\dfrac{x^2}{5^2} + \dfrac{y^2}{3^2} = 1$

(e) $\dfrac{x^2}{5^2} - \dfrac{y^2}{3^2} = 1$ (f) $|x| + |y| = -1$

Problem 3 Suppose that in $x^2 + y^2 = -9$, both x and y can assume complex number values. Can you modify the above system and graph $x^2 + y^2 = -9$ in your system? (*Hint* First consider if it is possible to construct the graph in three dimensions.) For more information on this topic consult:

(1) Howard Fehr, *Secondary Mathematics: A Functional Approach for Teachers*, D.C. Heath and Co., Lexington, Ma., 1951, pp. 285-92.

(2) Howard Fehr, "Graphical Representation of Complex Roots" *Multi-Sensory Aids in the Teaching of Mathematics*, (Eighteenth Yearbook), N.C.T.M., Reston, Va., 1945, pp. 130-38.

2   Depending upon the definition given in the particular text used by the student, the

student could be correct. The ellipse, which has its center at the origin and foci at the points (c, 0) and (−c, 0), is the graph of the relation

$$\left\{(x, y) \middle| \frac{x^2}{a^2} + \frac{y^2}{b^2} = 1\right\} \qquad \text{where } b^2 = a^2 - c^2. \tag{1}$$

If the foci get closer and closer together, the ellipse approaches a circle. If, in the above, c is given as greater than or equal to zero, then c is allowed to take on the value of zero. When c = 0, the foci coincide at the origin, and one gets a circle with center at the origin and radius a. Since $b^2 = a^2 - c^2$ and c = 0, then $b^2 = a^2$. Thus in this case, one gets by (1)

$$\left\{(x, y) \middle| \frac{x^2}{a^2} + \frac{y^2}{a^2} = 1\right\} \quad \text{or} \quad \left\{(x, y) \middle| x^2 + y^2 = a^2\right\}.$$

However, if c is restricted in the definition to be only c > 0, then the circle is not a special case of the ellipse, although it may be considered in this instance to be a limiting case.

Problem Generalize the above argument for the general case, i.e., foci not on the x or y axis and the center not at the origin.

3   The graph of $y = (x^2)^2 = x^4$ is not a parabola. This can be shown by methods similar to those used in Answer 8 of this section.

Problem Using methods similar to those given in Answer 8, prove that the graph of $y = (x^2)^2 = x^4$ is not a parabola.

4   See Answer 2 of Section A5.2(A).

Problem 1 Find two other equations where the graph crosses an asymptote before approaching the asymptote.

Problem 2 Consider $f(x) = \dfrac{8x^2 + 4x - 7}{4x^2 - 4x}$. Does this curve cross an asymptote?

5   There is no set of rules that one can offer that will *always* lead to an existing oblique asymptote. The following example illustrates a teachnique that can be used in solving certain problems. Suppose one wants to find the asymptotes of

$$y = \sqrt{9x^2 - 1}, \qquad x \geqslant 1/3.$$

It should be clear that there are no vertical or horizontal asymptotes. Now, a line y = mx + b will be an asymptote provided

$$\lim_{x \to \infty} [\sqrt{9x^2 - 1} - (mx + b)] = 0.$$

Using some simple algebra, we have

$$\sqrt{9x^2 - 1} - (mx + b)$$
$$= \frac{[\sqrt{9x^2 - 1} - (mx + b)] [\sqrt{9x^2 - 1} + (mx + b)]}{\sqrt{9x^2 - 1} + (mx + b)}$$
$$= \frac{9x^2 - 1 - m^2 x^2 - 2mbx - b^2}{\sqrt{9x^2 - 1} + (mx + b)} \tag{1}$$

It is now clear that if one selects m = 3 and b = 0 that

$$\lim_{x \to \infty} [\sqrt{9x^2 - 1} - (mx + b)]$$

becomes, (substituting into (1)),

$$\lim_{x \to \infty} \frac{-1}{\sqrt{9x^2 - 1} + 3x} = 0.$$

Hence y = 3x is an oblique asymptote.

Problem   Find all asymptotes of $y = \sqrt{6x^2 - 4} + 1$.

6   Suppose the foci are placed at the points $(-c, 0, 0)$ and $(c, 0, 0)$ in three-dimensional space. One is thus looking for the locus of all points $P(x, y, z)$ such that

$$\sqrt{(x + c)^2 + y^2 + z^2} - \sqrt{(x - c)^2 + y^2 + z^2} = \pm 2k \qquad (1)$$

where $k < c$. Standard algebraic techniques reduce (1) to

$$\frac{x^2}{k^2} - \frac{y^2}{c^2 - k^2} - \frac{z^2}{c^2 - k^2} = 1. \qquad (2)$$

The graph of this equation in three-dimensional space is known as a *hyperboloid of two sheets*. For a discussion and diagram of such a surface see:

> George B. Thomas, *Calculus and Analytic Geometry*, alt. ed., Addison-Wesley Publishing Co., Reading, Ma., 1972, pp. 664-65.

Problem   Show the algebra necessary to reduce (1) to (2).

7   Yes, it is possible. Let l be a line, called the directrix, and F be a point, not on l, called the focus. Let e be a given positive number, called the eccentricity. Let C be the set of all points P such that the ratio of the distance from P to the focus F to the distance from P to the directrix l is e. The set of points C is an ellipse if $e < 1$, a parabola if $e = 1$, and a hyperbola if $e > 1$.

8   One would like to provide an answer which is as intuitive as possible. However, it is very difficult to provide an intuitive answer that is also a *convincing* one. For example, one might suggest that a teacher explain to students that such figures are sections of a cone as illustrated in Figure 4.6.3. Even if a student is convinced that the parabola resulting from Figure 4.6.3(a) is different than either "piece" of the figure in (b), this student may still question whether or not one "piece" of the figure in (b) could not be obtained by taking a different "size" cone in (a).

We now proceed along more formal lines. If one is given a hyperbola in a coordinate plane, it should be easy to see that via appropriate rotations and translations, the hyperbola can be put into a "standard" position as in Figure 4.6.4. Students should be familiar with the fact that the equation of such a hyperbola is given by

$$\frac{y^2}{a^2} - \frac{x^2}{b^2} = 1 \qquad (1)$$

where a, b > 0 are constants.

FIGURE 4.6.3

(a)   (b)

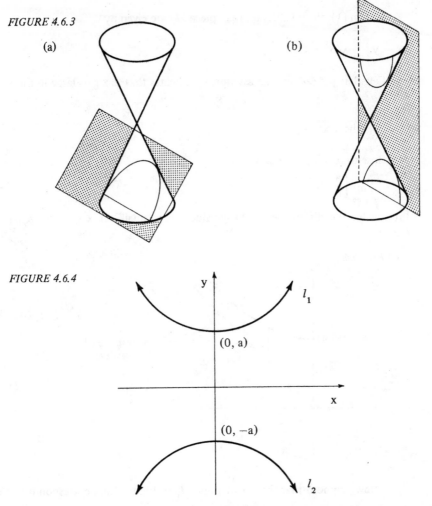

FIGURE 4.6.4

There are standard processes that are normally employed to show that the hyperbola given by (1) has the lines $y = (a/b)x$ and $y = -(a/b)x$ as asymptotes. This is illustrated in Figure 4.6.5.

FIGURE 4.6.5

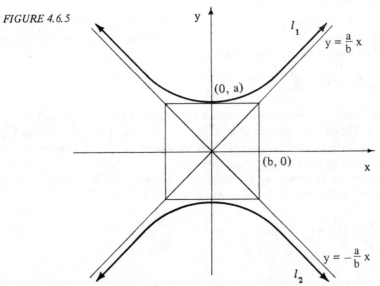

From (1), the y-values on the "piece" l_1 are given by

$$y = \frac{a}{b} \sqrt{b^2 + x^2}.$$

The fact that $y = (a/b)x$ is an asymptote indicates that as x gets large in the positive sense,

$$\frac{a}{b} \sqrt{b^2 + x^2} - \frac{a}{b} x$$

gets close to 0. More formally,

$$\lim_{x \to \infty} \left[\frac{a}{b} \sqrt{b^2 + x^2} - \frac{a}{b} x \right] = 0.$$

Intuitively, the difference of the y-values gets "small" as x gets "large" (Figure 4.6.6).

FIGURE 4.6.6

Now, suppose that the set of points l_1 of Figure 4.6.4 corresponds to the set of points on a parabola. It should be easy to see that the equation of such a parabola must be given by an equation of the form

$$y = cx^2 + a \tag{2}$$

where $c > 0$ is a constant. The set of points satisfying (2) will intersect the line $y = (a/b)x$ in two distinct points, one point, or at no point, depending on whether $(a^2/b^2) - 4ac$ is positive, zero, or negative respectively. *In any case*,

$$\lim_{x \to \infty} \left[c \left(x - \frac{a}{2bc} \right)^2 + a - \frac{a^2}{4b^2 c} \right] = +\infty$$

Geometrically, the behavior of $y = cx^2 + a$ relative to the line $y = (a/b)x$ is as illustrated in Figure 4.6.7 (for the case $(a^2/b^2) - 4ac < 0$). (See page 203 for Figure.)

One is now able to conclude that the "piece" l_1 of the hyperbola of Figure 4.6.4 cannot be represented by *any* parabola.

Another approach to the original question is the following. Suppose the "piece" l_1 of the hyperbola in Figure 4.6.4, given by

$$\frac{y^2}{a^2} - \frac{x^2}{b^2} = 1, \quad y \geqslant a \tag{3}$$

FIGURE 4.6.7

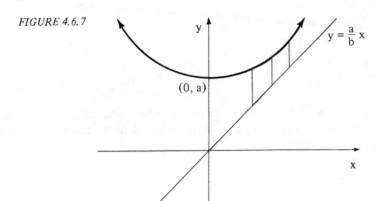

coincides with a parabola. We have already noted that such a parabola must have an equation of the form

$$y = cx^2 + a, \quad c > 0.$$ (4)

From (4) we have

$$x^2 = \frac{y - a}{c}.$$

Substituting into (3), we have

$$\frac{y^2}{a^2} - \frac{(y - a)/c}{b^2} = 1 \quad \text{or} \quad \left(\frac{1}{a^2}\right)y^2 - \left(\frac{1}{b^2 c}\right)y + \left(\frac{a}{b^2 c} - 1\right) = 0.$$ (5)

Given a hyperbola as in (3), we are seeking to determine a value of c such that (5) is satisfied for *all* y, y ⩾ a. However, no matter what value of c is used, the equation (5) is a quadratic equation and hence can be satisfied by *at most* two distinct values of y. Thus one can again conclude that the "piece" l_1 of the hyperbola in Figure 4.6.4 does not correspond to *any* parabola.

There is a somewhat simpler approach which one might use in a calculus class. Suppose, as in the first approach given, that the "piece" l_1 of Figure 4.6.4 corresponds to the set of points on a parabola given by $y = cx^2 + a$. Then, for each x, the slopes of the curves must agree. That is,

$$\frac{y^2}{a^2} - \frac{x^2}{b^2} = 1, \quad y > 0$$ (6)

and $y = cx^2 + a$ (7)

must have the same value of dy/dx for each x.

After solving for y, (6) yields

$$\frac{dy}{dx} = ab \cdot \frac{x}{\sqrt{b^2 + x^2}}$$

while (7) yields

$$\frac{dy}{dx} = 2cx.$$

Thus, for each x, we must have

$$2cx = \frac{a}{b} \cdot \frac{x}{\sqrt{b^2 + x^2}}$$

or $c = \dfrac{a}{2b} \dfrac{1}{\sqrt{b^2 + x^2}}$, $x \neq 0$,   or $\sqrt{b^2 + x^2} = \dfrac{a}{2bc}$.

That is, $\sqrt{b^2 + x^2}$ must be the same number no matter what value of x, $x \neq 0$, is used. This is clearly impossible, and we are again led to the conclusion that the "piece" l_1 of the hyperbola

$$\frac{y^2}{a^2} - \frac{x^2}{b^2} = 1$$

cannot coincide with *any* parabola.

The original question concerning hyperbolas and parabolas can also be answered in terms of eccentricity, directricies etc., but such answers tend to be more formal and obscure than those introduced. For example, one piece of a hyperbola can be described as the locus of all points whose distances from a fixed point are equal to a constant (> 1) times their distances from a fixed line. A parabola, of course, is normally defined as the locus of all points whose distances from a fixed point are equal to their distances to a fixed line. Although these definitions appear to be different, the problem still remains of convincing the questioning student that by varying the fixed point and the fixed line from one definition to the other, the resulting figures cannot be made to coincide. In order to answer such a question, a teacher is forced to return, at least partially, to one of the approaches already given.

It is easy to generalize the question considered. For example, is there a parabola that coincides with a catenary? Is there a parabola that coincides with part of an ellipse?

9   This is true for any M, P, and Q as depicted in the figure given in the question. This fact can be shown by using similar triangles. Construct $\overline{MR}$ parallel to $\overline{OQ}$. Then $\triangle PMR$ is similar to $\triangle PQO$. Thus $PM/PQ = RM/OQ$. Substituting $PM = (1/3)PQ$ and $OQ = a$, one obtains

$$\frac{(1/3)PQ}{PQ} = \frac{RM}{a}$$

Thus $RM = (1/3)a$ as asserted by the student.

Problem   Would the student be correct if the figure given were Figure 4.6.8.

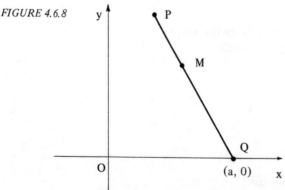

FIGURE 4.6.8

10   The student has the notion that a tangent to a curve only touches the curve at one point. The student is correct for *very special curves* such as the circle, parabola or ellipse. Perhaps one way to convince the student of this is to have him construct tangents to the curve starting at x = 1 and proceeding by increments, for example, 1/4, until one gets to x = 0 as shown in Figure 4.6.9.

FIGURE 4.6.9

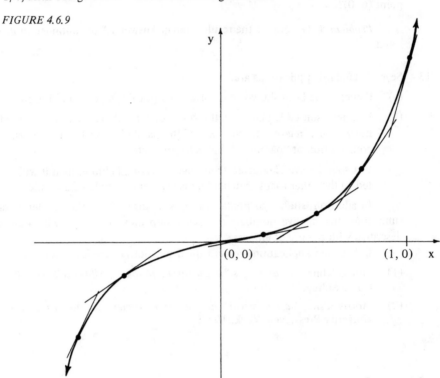

11   Only in very special curves will a tangent touch only one point (see Answer 10 of this section). A tangent to a curve at a point (h, k) is defined to be a straight line that has the same slope as the curve at point (h, k). In the case of a straight line, the slope is constant and thus a tangent to a straight line is the straight line itself and intersects the given curve (the straight line) in infinitely many points.

12   Questions such as this are difficult to answer in front of a regular class but present interesting problems for superior students or honors classes. Probably the best way to begin is with a specific case. For example, suppose one wishes to find the locus of all points P(x, y) that are equidistant from the circle $x^2 + y^2 = 1$ and the point (2, 0). One might start with the equation:

$$\sqrt{x^2 + y^2} - 1 = \sqrt{(x - 2)^2 + y^2}.$$

Simple algebra then leads to the hyperbola

$$\frac{(x - 1)^2}{\frac{1}{4}} - \frac{y^2}{\frac{3}{4}} = 1. \tag{1}$$

Problem 1 Do *all* points on the hyperbola in (1) satisfy the given condition? (What is meant by the distance from a point to a circle?)

Problem 2 What result is obtained if one wishes to find the locus of all points $P(x, y)$ that are equidistant from the ellipse $(x^2/4) + (y^2/9) = 1$ and the point $(6, 0)$?

Problem 3 Generalize the result given in Answer 12 and obtained in Problems 1 and 2.

13   Several standard applications are:

(a)   Planets have been shown to revolve in elliptical orbits around the sun.

(b)   If a light source is placed at the focus of a parabola, then it will be reflected horizontally relative to the axis of the parabola. Such a fact is used in the construction of "parabolic" bulbs for projectors.

(c)   If a sound wave is emitted from one focus of an ellipse, then it will be reflected to the other focus. Such a fact is used in the study of acoustics.

In addition, studies of predator-prey systems indicate that, under certain assumptions, the relative numbers of each group move in cycles, which are closely described with the use of ellipses.

For further applications consult the discussions of conic sections in:

(1)   Morris Kline, *Mathematics: A Cultural Approach*, Addison Wesley Publishing Co., Reading, Ma., 1962.

(2)   Morris Kline, *Mathematical Thought from Ancient to Modern Times*, Oxford Univerity Press, New York, 1972.

A4.7   *Irrational Numbers*

1   No. Actually, there are more irrational numbers than rational numbers. It can be shown, for example, that a rational number plus an irrational number is always an irrational number. Thus for *each* rational number, one can theoretically generate an infinite number of irrational numbers by the above process.

2   Suppose N is the number in question and suppose that N has a decimal expansion, which eventually repeats, say

$$N = b.b_1 b_2 \ldots b_k \overline{a_1 a_2 \ldots a_n}, \quad n > 0$$

Then

$$10^{n+k}N = bb_1 b_2 \ldots b_k a_1 a_2 \ldots a_n . \overline{a_1 a_2 \ldots a_n} \tag{1}$$

and

$$10^k N = bb_1 b_2 \ldots b_k . \overline{a_1 a_2 \ldots a_n}. \tag{2}$$

Subtracting (2) from (1), we have

$$(10^{n+k} - 10^k)N = bb_1 b_2 \ldots b_k a_1 a_2 \ldots a_n - bb_1 b_2 \ldots b_k$$

or

$$N = \frac{bb_1 b_2 \ldots b_k a_1 a_2 \ldots a_n - bb_1 b_2 \ldots b_k}{10^{n+k} - 10^k} \tag{3}$$

But the right side of (3) is the quotient of two integers, and hence N would be a rational number, which contradicts the assumption made in this question.

3   If one denies the existence of the rational numbers, then one, in reality, is also denying the existence of the integers. For, given the integers, the notion of rational number (in terms of ordered pairs, etc.) is immediately present.

    An appropriate way to get this question is the following. Consider a line in a plane. In the usual way, one assigns rational numbers to points on this line. There are "holes" that represent the irrational numbers. It is impossible to talk about such gaps if one denies the existence of the rational numbers.

    One might try and consider the expressions of the form

$$b.a_1 a_2 a_3 \ldots$$

where b and the a_i's are integers and where there is no repetition of groups of integers. This idea does not *directly* involve the notion of a rational number. However, the integers are used, and as previously stated, the notion of rational number is immediately present.

4   It is almost impossible at this level to prove that π, e or any of the transcendental irrational real numbers have nonrepeating decimal representations. With advanced students or students in an honors program, one might be able to use:

(1)   L. L. Pennisi, "Elementary Proof that e is Irrational," *Selected Papers on Calculus*, ed. Tom A. Apostol, Dickenson Publishing Co., Belmont, Ca., 1969.

(2)   Robert Breusch, "A Proof of the Irrationality of π," *Selected Papers on Calculus*, ed. Tom A. Apostol, Dickenson Publishing Co., Belmont, Ca., 1969.

5   If a decimal expression is terminating or repeating, then the decimal expression represents a rational number. All other decimal expressions represent irrational numbers. Thus, it is not the case that all nonterminating decimals represent irrational numbers; e.g., .323232... is not terminating but represents the rational number 32/99 in fractional form.

A4.8   *Logarithms*

1   Although the concept of *logarithm* is often associated today with that of *exponent*, the original discovery by Napier did not use this idea. In fact, logarithms were discovered before exponents were in use and a suitable notation for expressing exponents was not even fully developed at this time. It was not until about seventy years after the discovery of logarithms that John Wallis and Johann Bernoulli devised the possibility of defining logarithms as exponents.

    The word logarithm means *ratio number*, and Napier arrived at his logarithms using this idea. Napier represented numbers and logarithms of these numbers by segments of lines cut off by two moving points. Thus consider (1) and (2) on p. 208.

(1)

(2)

(1) is a segment of fixed length and (2) is infinite in extent. Consider a point P that moves on $\overline{XY}$ with a velocity numerically equal to the distance PY and a point P′ to move on $\overleftrightarrow{ST}$ with a constant velocity equal to the initial velocity of P. Let $P_1′, P_2′, P_3′...$ correspond to $P_1, P_2, P_3,....$ Napier defined the logarithm of PY to be the length of SP′; i.e., the logarithm of $P_1Y = SP_1′$, and the logarithm of $P_2Y = SP_2′$, etc.

2 This is a common error made by students when working with logarithms and the difficulty stems from the notation involved.

$$\log_{10} .843 = -1.9258$$

does not mean that the entire quantity is negative. In this case what is meant is $-1 + .9258$; i.e., the mantissa is positive. One should notice the inconsistency that is involved in some areas of notation used in mathematics. Thus, when working with fractions, $-2\frac{1}{2}$ usually means $-(2 + \frac{1}{2})$, which is not the same meaning as that attached to the above number.

With the above interpretation, the problem is then solved as follows:

$$\begin{array}{r} -1 + .9258 \\ - \quad .3010 \\ \hline -1 + .6248 \end{array} \quad \text{i.e.,} -1.6248.$$

Thus $\dfrac{.843}{2} = $ antilog $-1.6248 = .4215.$

3 For an answer to this question read:

Meyer Jerison, "Natural Bases of Logarithms," *The Mathematics Teacher*, April 1963, pp. 228-33.

4 One way of helping this student is as follows. The student seems to lack the prerequisite concept of inverse function, which is needed in order to understand this problem. Thus one might proceed by reviewing the idea of inverse function with the student using a simple example. Then it should be a relatively simple matter to show the student that antilog of a number is the inverse function of the logarithm function. Thus if $\log_{10} 2 = .3010$, then antilog $.3010 = 2$. Likewise, $\log_{10} \frac{1}{2} = -.3010$, thus antilog $-.3010 = \frac{1}{2}$.

5 This is a common mistake made by students when working with logarithms. The student is inappropriately trying to use the following property of logarithms.

If a and b are positive real numbers, then $\log_{10} \dfrac{a}{b} = \log_{10} a - \log_{10} b.$

The student must be made to realize that $\dfrac{\log_{10} a}{\log_{10} b}$ is not the same expression as

$\log_{10} \dfrac{a}{b}$. In the first instance, one is dealing with two numbers, namely, $\log_{10} a$ and

$\log_{10} b$. In the second instance, one is working with a functional value; i.e.,

$\log_{10} \dfrac{a}{b}$, which is that element in the range of $\log_{10}$ function that is associated with

the element $\dfrac{a}{b}$ in the domain.

The answer in the book is correct as shown:

$$\frac{\log_{10} 4}{\log_{10} 2} = \frac{\log_{10} 2^2}{\log_{10} 2} = \frac{2 \cdot \log_{10} 2}{\log_{10} 2} = 2 \cdot \frac{\log_{10} 2}{\log_{10} 2} = 2.$$

6   No, the method is not correct as the following counterexample illustrates.

$$\frac{\log_{10} 1}{\log_{10} 10} = \frac{0}{1} \quad 0.$$

However, by the student's method,

$$\frac{\log_{10} 1}{\log_{10} 10} = \frac{\log_{10} 1}{\log_{10} 10} = \frac{1}{10}.$$

An interesting question that the teacher could ask the class to explore in this

case is: "Under what conditions will $\dfrac{\log_{10} a}{\log_{10} b} = \dfrac{a}{b}$?" or, in general, "Under what

conditions will $\dfrac{\log_r a}{\log_r b} = \dfrac{a}{b}$?"

7   Suppose that $\log_{10} -5 = x$, then $-5 = 10^x$. However, when x is a real number, 10^x is always positive. Thus, there is no real number x that would satisfy $\log_{10} -5 = x$. In the general case, $\log_B A$ where $A < 0$, $b > 0$ has no real number as its value because if $\log_B A = x$, then $B^x = A$. But if $B > 0$ and if x is a real number, then B^x must be positive. Under these restrictions, a negative number has no logarithm. This causes no hardship in computation for we proceed as if all factors are positive. If the number of negative factors in odd, we mark the final result as negative.

However, one might drop the restriction that x in the expression B^x be real and consider what happens when x can assume complex number values. In this case, one can show that the logarithm of any number, whether positive or negative, has a countably infinite set of values.

Suppose that $x + iy$ is a complex number where x and y are real numbers. Using polar coordinates, one can show that

$$x + iy = r \cos(\theta + 2\pi j) + i \sin (\theta + 2\pi j).$$

Since $e^{i\theta} = \cos \theta + i \sin \theta$, then

$$x + iy = r \cdot e^{i(\theta + 2\pi j)}$$

where $r = x^2 + y^2$ and $\theta = \arctan(y/x)$. Since $x + iy = r \cdot e^{i(\theta + 2\pi j)}$, then

$$\ln(x + iy) = \ln[r \cdot e^{i(\theta + 2\pi j)}] = \ln r + i(\theta + 2\pi j).$$

Substituting in the last expression, one gets

$$\ln(x + iy) = \ln\sqrt{x^2 + y^2} + i(\arctan\frac{y}{x} + 2\pi j).$$

Thus one can see that the number of logarithms of $x + iy$ is countably infinite since j can take on a countably infinite number of integral values.

To find the logarithm of a negative number, say -1, one proceeds as follows:

$$\ln -1 = \ln\sqrt{(-1)^2 + (0)^2} + i(\pi + 2\pi j)$$
$$\ln -1 = 0 + i(\pi + 2\pi j)$$
$$\ln -1 = i\pi, 3i\pi, 5i\pi, \text{etc.}$$

Thus every number has an infinite set of logarithms, the principal value being the value one gets above when $j = 0$. All of these logarithms are complex numbers except when the number is positive.

Problem 1   Find $\ln i$.

Problem 2   The above development was done for the natural logarithms for simplicity purposes. Find the logarithms of a complex number for the general case.

A4.9   *Logic and Proof*

1   The first thing that should be looked at is what the student means by proving that "If $a \neq 0$, then $b = 0$." In this regard, the following article is worth consulting:

> Stanley Smith, "What Does a Proof Really Prove," *The Mathematics Teacher*, May 1968, pp. 483-84.

Smith makes the assertion that what is really proved in a conditional of the form $p \rightarrow q$ is just that: $p \rightarrow q$. We do not prove q. Thus what the student really means in this question is that he will prove that if a, b are real numbers such that $a \cdot b = 0$ then $a \neq 0$ implies $b = 0$.

The student is correct. The statement "If $a \neq 0$, then $b = 0$" is equivalent to the statement "$a = 0$ or $b = 0$" as Tables 4.9.1 and 4.9.2 illustrate. The statement "If $b \neq 0$, then $a = 0$" is the contrapositive of the statement "If $a \neq 0$, then $b = 0$." Since the conditional and its contrapositive are always equivalent, it is not necessary "to prove" the statement "If $b \neq 0$, then $a = 0$."

TABLE 4.9.1

| [p $\vee$ q] | | |
$a = 0$	*or*	$b = 0$
T	T	T
T	F	T
F	T	T
F	F	F

TABLE 4.9.2

| [$\sim p \rightarrow q$] | | |
If a $\neq$ 0,	*then*	*b = 0*
F	T	T
F	F	T
T	T	T
T	F	F

A4.10   *Mean*

1   There are at least two ways of approaching the notion of *geometric mean*. In one, *b* is said to be the geometric mean of *a* and *c* if *a*, *b* and *c* form a geometric sequence. That is, b = ra and c = rb. If neither *a* nor *b* is zero, this leads to

$$\frac{b}{a} = \frac{c}{b}.$$ (1)

If, however, *a* is zero, then *b* and *c* must both be zero and *r* is arbitrary.

In a second approach, the geometric mean of two numbers *a* and *c* is simply defined to be $\sqrt{ac}$. In such a definition, it is customary to require a $\geqslant$ 0 and c $\geqslant$ 0. Thus, if a = 0 and *c* is any positive real number, then the geometric mean of *a* and *c* is zero.

Observe that if *a* and *c* are positive in (1), then b^2 = ac or b = $\sqrt{ac}$.

The geometric mean of 0 and a positive real number is 0, but the student is using (1) in the form

$$\frac{a}{b} = \frac{b}{c},$$

which is not applicable when *a* and *b* are zero.

2   There are a great many different kinds of means besides the arithmetic, geometric and harmonic, which are important in various applications of statistics. One could cite means such as the mode and the median as other examples of measures of central tendency, but there are numerous others.

A general formula for developing many kinds of means is given below:

$$\text{Mean}_x = f^{-1}\left(\frac{\sum\limits_{i=1}^{n} f(x_i)}{n}\right)$$ (1)

Using (1) and substituting in the appropriate functions, one can get various means as shown'

(a)   *Harmonic Mean*   If f(x) = 1/x, then by (1)

$$\sum_{i=1}^{n} \frac{f(x_i)}{n} = \frac{\dfrac{1}{x_1} + \dfrac{1}{x_2} + \dfrac{1}{x_3} + \cdots + \dfrac{1}{x_n}}{n}$$

and thus the harmonic mean is

$$f^{-1}\left(\frac{\sum\limits_{i=1}^{n} f(x_i)}{n}\right) = \frac{1}{\dfrac{1}{x_1} + \dfrac{1}{x_2} + \dfrac{1}{x_3} + \cdots + \dfrac{1}{x_n}} = \frac{n}{\sum\limits_{i=1}^{n} \dfrac{1}{x_i}}$$

(b)   *Geometric Mean*   If f(x) = $\log_{10}$ x, then by (1)

$$\sum_{i=1}^{n} \frac{f(x_i)}{n} = \frac{\log_{10} x_1 + \log_{10} x_2 + \cdots + \log_{10} x_n}{n}$$

$$= \log_{10} \frac{(x_1 \cdot x_2 \cdots x_n)}{n}$$

and thus the geometric mean is

$$f^{-1}\left(\sum_{i=1}^{n} \frac{f(x_i)}{n}\right) = \sqrt[n]{x_1 \cdot x_2 \cdots x_n} \ .$$

(c)   *Quadratic Mean*   If $f(x) = x^2$, $x \geqslant 0$, then by (1)

$$\sum_{i=1}^{n} \frac{f(x_i)}{n} = \frac{x_1^2 + x_2^2 + \cdots + x_n^2}{n}$$

and thus the quadratic mean is

$$f^{-1}\left(\sum_{i=1}^{n} \frac{f(x_i)}{n}\right) = \sqrt{\frac{x_1^2 + x_2^2 + \cdots + x_n^2}{n}} \ .$$

One can find many different kinds of means by repeating this process for any function f that has an inverse function, f^{-1}.

Problem   Using the general formula, (1), find an expression for the arithmetic mean.

3   Suppose that *a* and *b* are two terms in a geometric sequence. The terms between two given terms of a geometric sequence are called the *geometric means* between the given terms. A single (unique) geometric mean between two terms of a geometric sequence is called *the* geometric mean of the two terms. Thus if x is the geometric mean between *a* and *b*, then

$$\frac{x}{a} = \frac{b}{x}$$

where it is assumed that neither *a* nor *x* is zero. That is, $x^2 = ab$. If a and b are positive, then $x = \sqrt{ab}$. If a and b are negative, then $x = -\sqrt{ab}$.

Thus the name *geometric mean* is related to the term *geometric sequence*.

A4.11   *Rational and Complex Numbers*

1   One approach to the construction of the set of integers from the set of whole numbers uses the idea of equivalence classes of ordered pairs of whole numbers. For details, consult:

Birkhoff and MacLane, *A Survey of Modern Algebra*, MacMillan, New York, 1965.

Thus, for instance, +3 is the name of the equivalence class represented by the following set of ordered pairs:

$$\left\{(3, 0), (4, 1), (5, 2), (6, 3), ..., (x, y) \text{ where } x - y = 3\right\} \ .$$

Likewise −3 would be the name of the equivalence class represented by the following set of ordered pairs:

$$\left\{(0, 3), (1, 4), (2, 5), (3, 6), ..., (x, y) \text{ such that } y - x = 3\right\} \ ;$$

i.e., two ordered pairs (a_1, b_1) and (a_2, b_2) are equivalent, $(a_1, b_1) \equiv (a_2, b_2)$, if and only if $a_1 + b_2 = a_2 + b_1$. This relation can be shown to be an equivalence relation. Addition is defined by the following: ·

$$(a_1, b_1) \oplus (a_2, b_2) = (a_1 + a_2, b_1 + b_2)$$

The mapping f: $a \rightarrow \{(a + 1, 1)\}$ = +a can be shown to be an isomorphism of the set of natural numbers onto a subset of the set of integers. Thus, the system of ordered pairs so constructed, in a sense, contains the set of natural numbers; i.e., the set of natural numbers is isomorphic to a subset of the set of integers.

Therefore, +3 is called a positive integer and 3 is usually called a natural or counting number. Thus, strictly speaking the two concepts are not identical, but they are isomorphic. Observe that the integer +3 behaves exactly like the natural number 3. It is customary to omit the plus sign, except when needed for clarity or emphasis, and refer to 3 either as the name of the natural number 3 or as the name of the positive integer 3.

Problem Two statements were made in Answer 1 that certain things could be "shown to be true." Prove each of these statements.

2   The student makes the unjustified claim that C and D are both rational numbers. In effect, D could be either rational or irrational. Since C = πD, then C depends on the value of πD. The assumption is made in this question that one acts as if it is not known whether π is rational or irrational, otherwise, there would be no question. Since D can be either rational or irrational and since π can be either rational or irrational, then it follows that C could be either rational or irrational. This being the case, then no conclusion such as given by the student can be formed for π = C/D.

3   If this student was correct, then it should follow that a + bi = b + ai for all real numbers a, b. Suppose that a = 0 and b = 1; then it follows that 0 + 1i = 1 + 0 · i; i.e., i = 1, which is certainly not correct. A correct statement in this case would be 3 + 4i = 4i + 3. When working with complex numbers of the form a + bi, the "bi" part of the symbol is considered to be together and cannot be separated.

One should carefully define, at the beginning of a discussion on complex numbers, exactly what it means for two complex numbers to be equal. That is, a + bi = c + di if and only if a = c and b = d.

4   Consider z_1 = (a, b) and z_2 = (c, d) = (c, 0) + (0, d), then

$$z_1 z_2 = (a, b)[(c, 0) + (0, d)]$$
$$= (a, b)(c, 0) + (a, b)(0, d)$$
$$= c(a, b) + d(i(a, b))$$
$$= c(a, b) + d(-b, a).$$

Thus the product $z_1 z_2$ corresponds to the sum of two orthogonal vectors. One of these vectors is the product of z_1 and the real part of z_2, while the other vector is the product of z_1 rotated counterclockwise and the imaginary part of z_2.

Problem What kind of figure would you use in your classroom to demonstrate the above to students?

5   There are many extensions of the idea of *number* including quaternions, algebraic

numbers, etc. For a detailed discussion, consult:

(1) *Historical Topics for the Mathematics Classroom* (Thirty-First Yearbook), N.C.T.M., Reston, Va., 1969, Chaps. 2 and 5.

(2) E. T. Bell, *Development of Mathematics*, 2nd ed., McGraw-Hill Book Co., New York, 1945, Chaps. 8, 9 and 10.

(3) *Enrichment of High School Mathematics* (Twenty-Eighth Yearbook), N.C.T.M., Reston, Va., 1963, Chap. 27.

6   Since numbers are ideas, then all numbers exist only in our minds. However, the unfortunate term *imaginary* given to us by Rene Descartes (c. 1637) for numbers that can be written in the form *ai*, where *a* is a real number, conveyed the impression to the mathematicians of his time that numbers of this form were useless and not practical; thus they did not exist. Many of these mathematicians rejected the idea that the square root of a negative number had a meaning since a negative number is not a square. However, numbers of the form *ai*, where *a* is a real number, do exist as a mathematical creation and are very useful at more advanced levels.

For more information, consult:

Historical Topics for the Mathematics Classroom (Thirty-First Yearbook), N.C.T.M., Reston, Va, 1969, pp. 290-94 (Capsule 76).

7   Finding the exact reason why the term *complex* was introduced is a difficult task. In the sources consulted by the authors, we could only find that Gauss introduced the term in 1832. Perhaps the term *complex* was used because of the stormy history of these numbers. *Imaginary* and in turn *complex* numbers had a difficult time gaining acceptance in the mathematical community (see references below) and were thought to be ficticious quantities. Trying to explain the meaning of these numbers in concrete terms was quite a difficult and "complex" matter (as it still is to high school students); this perhaps is the origin of the term *complex*.

(1) *Historical Topics for the Mathematics Classroom* (Thirty-First Yearbook), N.C.T.M., Reston, Va., 1969.

(2) E. T. Bell, *The Development of Mathematics*, 2nd ed., McGraw-Hill Book Co., New York, 1945.

(3) Morris Kline, *Mathematics: A Cultural Approach*, Addison-Wesley Publishing Co., Reading, Ma., 1962.

8   The correct answer is -6. The student who wrote $\sqrt{-4} \cdot \sqrt{-9} = \sqrt{36} = 6$ is incorrect because the student has applied a property proved only for radicals involving real numbers.

Problem   Under what conditions on a and b is $\sqrt{a} \cdot \sqrt{b} = \sqrt{a \cdot b}$ where a and b are integers?

9   One can find the square roots of i by using polar coordinates as given below. Expressing i in polar coordinates, one gets $r = 1$, $\cos \theta = 0$, $\sin \theta = 1$. Thus,

$i = 1(\cos 90° + i \sin 90°).$

If ω is a square root of i, then

$$\omega = 1\left(\cos\frac{90° + k \cdot 360}{2} + i\sin\frac{90° + k \cdot 360}{2}\right)$$

for k = 0, 1, 2, ... When k = 0,

$$\omega = 1(\cos 45° + i\sin 45°) = \frac{\sqrt{2}}{2} + i\frac{\sqrt{2}}{2}\,.$$

When k = 1,

$$\omega = 1(\cos 225° + i\sin 225°) = -\frac{\sqrt{2}}{2} - i\frac{\sqrt{2}}{2}\,.$$

It is customary to let $\sqrt{a}$ represent the principal square root, which, in this case, is

$$\frac{\sqrt{2}}{2} + i\frac{\sqrt{2}}{2}\,, \qquad \text{where } k = 0.$$

10   Although the statement from the student seems plausible, it does not make sense mathematically. If the student's result was generally acceptable, then this fact would imply that the complex numbers could be ordered. However, it is a well-known fact that the complex numbers do not form an ordered field.

       Problem Suppose that you are teaching an honors section of Algebra II and you have studied ordered fields. How would you show the students that the complex numbers do not form an ordered field?

11   No, the set of real numbers does not have the same cardinality as the set of rational numbers; i.e., there is no one-to-one correspondence between the elements of these two sets. The set of rational numbers is equivalent (can be put in one-to-one correspondence) to the set of natural numbers and is said to be denumerably or countably infinite. The set of real numbers has cardinality c (for continuum) and is said to be nondenumerable. A proof that the set of rational numbers is not equivalent to the set of real numbers can be found in more advanced texts.

12   Applications of complex numbers for this level are difficult to find. Indeed, it is precisely this type of problem that, historically, has led to questions concerning the "reasonableness" of such numbers. For example, in 1545, Cardan asked, "Divide 10 into two parts whose product is 40." A solution of x(10 − x) = 40 yields

$$5 + \sqrt{-15} \quad \text{and} \quad 5 - \sqrt{-15}.$$

This led to his statement: "So progresses arithmetic subtlety, the end of which, as is said, is as refined as it is useless." Both Bernoulli and Leibniz used complex numbers in the study of calculus (c. 1700). In 1749, Euler called complex numbers "impossible numbers" and said they were of no use. It was not until 1799 that Gauss showed some use of complex numbers in proving the Fundamental Theorem of Algebra. In 1831, the famous logician De Morgan stated that the symbol "$\sqrt{-a}$ is void of any meaning."

       The above remarks give some indication of the (relatively recent) history of complex numbers. Since 1850, however, such numbers have found extensive use (at higher levels) in the study of fluid dynamics, electrical engineering, and in modern approaches to geometry. One can become aware of such uses by consulting:

       Aleksandov, Kolmogorov, Lavent'er, eds., *Mathematics: Its Contents, Methods, and Meaning*, 2nd ed. (in 3 Vols.), The M.I.T. Press, Cambridge, Ma., Chap. 9, Vol. II, 1963.

13   No, the student is not correct. The student has solved the following problem. "Find all pairs of real numbers (x, y) for which $3x + 5yi = 9 + 35i$."

The solution to the given problem is as follows. Let $x = a + bi$ and $y = c + di$ where a, b, c and d are real numbers. Substituting in $3x + 5yi = 9 + 35i$, we obtain

$$3(a + bi) + 5(c + di)i = 9 + 35i$$

or

$$(3a - 5d) + (3b + 5c)i = 9 + 35i.$$

Thus

$$3a - 5d = 9 \quad \text{and} \quad 3b + 5c = 35$$

or

$$d = \frac{3a - 9}{5} \quad \text{and} \quad c = \frac{35 - 3b}{5}.$$

Thus, we are now free to assign real values for a and b. Therefore, the set of all ordered pairs (x, y) that satisfy the given equation are given by

$$x = a + bi \quad \text{and} \quad y = \frac{35 - 3b}{5} + \frac{3a - 9i}{5}.$$

14   Neither is correct. For $\sqrt{-4}$ is equal to $2i$. One gets the expression $-2i$ if one wants the negative of $\sqrt{-4}$; that is, $-\sqrt{-4} = -2i$.

15   One must be careful in applying properties proved only for radicals involving real numbers to other situations. The student in this particular case is trying to apply the following property:

$$\frac{\sqrt{a}}{\sqrt{b}} = \sqrt{\frac{a}{b}}.$$

In (a) the student does get the correct answer because

$$\frac{\sqrt{-4}}{\sqrt{-9}} = \frac{2i}{3i} = \frac{2}{3}.$$

Thus the property is valid in this case.

In (b) the student also gets the correct answer because

$$\frac{\sqrt{-4}}{\sqrt{9}} = \frac{2i}{3} = \frac{2}{3}i.$$

Thus, the property is also valid in this case.

The fact that the property $\sqrt{a}/\sqrt{b} = \sqrt{a/b}$ is not always valid should be pointed out to the student; see Question 16.

16   The student in (b) is correct.

   Problem   Under what conditions will $\sqrt{a}/\sqrt{b} = \sqrt{a/b}$? Can you prove your claim?

A4.12   *Operations, Properties and Systems*

1   No, it does not. Consider the mathematical system defined as follows.

Let a, b and c be real numbers, and let us define the "operation *" by the following:

$$a * b = \frac{a + b}{2}.$$

Then the operation * is commutative but not associative as the following illustrates.

$$(a * b) * c = \frac{a + b}{2} * c = \frac{\frac{a + b}{2} + c}{2} \qquad (1)$$

and

$$a * (b * c) = a * \frac{(b + c)}{2} = \frac{a + \frac{b + c}{2}}{2} \qquad (2)$$

Simplifying (1), one gets

$$(a * b) * c = \frac{a + b + 2c}{4}, \qquad (3)$$

while simplifying (2) leads to

$$a * (b * c) = \frac{2a + b + c}{4}. \qquad (4)$$

Since (3) does not equal (4) for all values a, b, c, it follows that * is not associative.

Problem 1   For what values of a, b and c will * be associative?

Problem 2   Give a geometric interpretation of * and try to convince yourself geometrically why it is not associative.

Problem 3   Suppose * was defined over the set of real numbers as follows: a * b = |a + b|. Is * commutative? Is * associative?

For more examples, consult:

Joseph Scandura, "Concrete Example of Commutative Nonassociative Systems," *The Mathematics Teacher*, December 1966, pp. 734-36.

2   Yes, the student is correct as shown:

$$5\tfrac{1}{2} \cdot 5\tfrac{1}{2} = (5 + \tfrac{1}{2})(5 + \tfrac{1}{2})$$
$$(5 + \tfrac{1}{2})(5 + \tfrac{1}{2}) = 5(5 + \tfrac{1}{2}) + \tfrac{1}{2}(5 + \tfrac{1}{2})$$
$$5(5 + \tfrac{1}{2}) + \tfrac{1}{2}(5 + \tfrac{1}{2}) = 5 \cdot 5 + 5 \cdot \tfrac{1}{2} + \tfrac{1}{2} \cdot 5 + \tfrac{1}{2} \cdot \tfrac{1}{2}$$
$$5 \cdot 5 + 5 \cdot \tfrac{1}{2} + \tfrac{1}{2} \cdot 5 + \tfrac{1}{2} \cdot \tfrac{1}{2} = 5(5 + \tfrac{1}{2} + \tfrac{1}{2}) + \tfrac{1}{2} \cdot \tfrac{1}{2}$$
$$5(5 + \tfrac{1}{2} + \tfrac{1}{2}) + \tfrac{1}{2} \cdot \tfrac{1}{2} = 5 \cdot 6 + \tfrac{1}{2} \cdot \tfrac{1}{2}$$

Problem   Is 35 · 35 = 30 · 40 + 5 · 5? Can you generalize the answer given above?

3   Yes, they are related. A vector is really a special case of a matrix and the inner product of two vectors is just a special case of matrix multiplication. This fact can be seen as follows.

Let

$$v_1 = (x_1, x_2, ..., x_n) \quad \text{and} \quad v_2 = (y_1, y_2, ..., y_n)$$

be vectors in n-dimensional space. Then

$$v_1 \cdot v_2 = x_1 y_1 + x_2 y_2 + \cdots + x_n y_n$$
(dot product or inner product).

If we now regard v_1 as a row matrix (1 × n) and v_2 as a column matrix (n × 1), then using matrix multiplication,

$$v_1 \cdot v_2 = (x_1, x_2, ..., x_n) \begin{bmatrix} y_1 \\ y_2 \\ \vdots \\ y_n \end{bmatrix} = x_1 y_1 + x_2 y_2 + \cdots + x_n y_n.$$

4   No, the student is not correct. One way of seeing this is as follows. The expression $n^2/2$ does give 1/2 of the elements in the square matrix, which includes the number of elements on one side of the diagonal of the square matrix plus 1/2 of the elements on the diagonal. Thus, one must subtract 1/2 of the number of elements on the diagonal from $n^2/2$, i.e., $(n^2/2) - (n/2)$ in order to get the desired result. The student made the mistake of subtracting all of the elements on the diagonal from $n^2/2$.

Another way of arriving at the correct answer is to compute the sum of the elements on one side of the diagonal. Thus in an n × n square matrix, one would get

$$1 + 2 + 3 + \cdots + (n - 1) = \frac{(n-1)n}{2} = \frac{n^2 - n}{2}.$$

5   For this particular problem, the student is correct. Since the value of the determinant is zero, then either way of computing the result would give the student zero. In general, however, the methods are not equivalent and, in fact, the answer computed would be additive inverses of each other.

Problem   Make up an example that will show the student that his method will not always work.

6   Yes, there are fields between Q and R. For an interesting discussion of this question and several approaches to an answer, read:

James Fey, "What's Between Q and R?" *The Mathematics Teacher*, April 1967, pp. 308-14.

7   The student is correct. The set of real numbers is not closed under division because of the case cited by the student. However, the set of nonzero real numbers is closed under division; i.e., zero must be excluded in order to have closure.

8   Yes, the student is correct. There are numerous distributive properties occurring

throughout mathematics, and they form some of the most useful and unifying ideas in mathematics.

   Problem Find other examples of distributive properties in secondary materials.

9   Formally, the objects are not identical, but they are isomorphic under addition and multiplication as given by the mapping

$$a_{ij} \leftrightarrow [a_{ij}]$$

where a_{ij} is a real number and $[a_{ij}]$ represents a 1×1 matrix.

10   A ray can be defined as follows.

   A ray, $\overrightarrow{AB}$, is the set of points that is the union of the segment $\overline{AB}$ and the set of all points X for which it is true that B is between A and X.

In some books, the endpoint, A, is not included. In either case, a ray, $\overrightarrow{AB}$, has direction and an "infinite" magnitude. A vector, on the other hand is usually defined to be an equivalence class of directed line segments. Any one of these directed line segments can be used as a representative of a vector. However, these geometric entities (directed line segments) have direction but are finite in magnitude. For more information about vectors see Section A5.2(M), Answer 5. Also consult:

   D. E. Mansfield and M. Bruckheimer, "Vectors: A Special Case?", *The Mathematics Gazette*, May 1966, pp. 100-104.

11   Well-ordered sets are related to mathematical induction, which is of great importance throughout mathematics. In fact, these two properties are equivalent. That is, the property of mathematical induction can be derived from the well-ordering principle and vice versa. For more information on this topic and how it relates to Zermelo's Axiom of choice, consult:

   Edna Kramer, *The Nature and Growth of Modern Mathematics*, Hawthorn Books, New York, 1970, pp. 592-97.

12   Yes, the ideas are related, and they are really isomorphic systems. Let p be a statement and P be an arbitrary set. Then under the correspondence below, set theory and logical analysis have essentially the same underlying structure.

(1) $p \rightarrow P$ (2) $\wedge \rightarrow \cap$
(3) $\vee \rightarrow \cup$ (4) $\sim \rightarrow$ Complement $(-)$

Thus, properties such as De Morgan's Laws in set theory have a corresponding property in logical analysis:

(a) $\overline{A \cap B} = \overline{A} \cup \overline{B}$ $\sim(p \wedge q) \leftrightarrow \sim p \vee \sim q$
(b) $\overline{A \cup B} = \overline{A} \cap \overline{B}$ $\sim(p \vee q) \leftrightarrow \sim p \wedge \sim q$

One can go further in this respect as shown in Tables 4.12.1 and 4.12.2.

TABLE 4.12.1

p	q	$p \wedge q$
T	T	T
T	F	F
F	T	F
F	F	F

TABLE 4.12.2

$X \in P$	$X \in Q$	$X \in P \cap Q$
T	T	T
T	F	F
F	T	F
F	F	F

If p and q are statements (closed), then p is equivalent to $q(p \rightarrow q)$ whenever p and q have the same truth value (i.e., when p is true, then q is true, and when p is false, q is false). If P_x and Q_x are open statements, then P_x is equivalent to Q_x $(P_x \leftrightarrow Q_x)$ if both open statements have the same solution set (i.e., when P_x is true, then Q_x is true, and when P_x is false, Q_x is false).

A4.13   Polynomials and Rational Expressions

1   No, degree is given to the zero polynomial in order to make general statements about the degree of products of polynomials. The degree of the product of an nth degree polynomial and a pth degree polynomial is $n + p$. If the zero polynomial was assigned the degree zero, then this general statement would not always be valid; e.g., $0 \cdot (3x^2 + 2x + 5) = 0$ and the above statement would then yield $0 + 2 = 2$ as the degree of zero polynomial. In order to avoid contradictions such as this, one simply does not define a degree for the zero polynomial.

2   In general, if f(x) and g(x) are polynomials with $g(x) \neq 0$, then there exist unique polynomials q(x) and r(x) such that

$$f(x) = q(x)g(x) + r(x)$$

where $r(x) = 0$ or the degree of r(x) is less than that of q(x). It is customary to call q(x) and r(x) the *quotient* and *remainder*, respectively, in the division of f(x) by g(x).

Thus when one divides $4x^2 - 5x + 9$ by $x - 1$, the quotient is $4x - 1$ and the remainder is 8.

3   A polynomial in the variable x with coefficients in some set F, frequently a field, is an expression of the form

$$a_0 + a_1 x + a_2 x^2 + \cdots + a_n x^n.$$

A polynomial equation is an equation having zero as one member and a polynomial as the other member; e.g.,

$$3x^4 + 2x^2 + 3x + 4 = 0.$$

A polynomial function is a function whose values are given by a polynomial; e.g.

$$x \rightarrow 3x^4 + 2x^2 + 3x + 4$$

or, as frequently written,

$$f(x) = 3x^4 + 2x^2 + 3x + 4.$$

4   Several different explanation could be given for this process. One explanation different from the usual one found in an Algebra II book is given below.

Suppose we consider the example given below as a means of explanation. Consider the usual long division method:

$$
\begin{array}{r}
3x^2 + 7x\ + 22 \\
x - 3\ \overline{\smash{\big)}\ 3x^3 - 2x^2 + x + 2} \\
\underline{3x^3 - 9x^2} \\
7x^2 + x \\
\underline{7x^2 - 21x} \\
22x +\ 2 \\
\underline{22x - 66} \\
68
\end{array}
$$

Suppose that we consider simplifying the process by rewriting it, using only the coefficients. We agree to write polynomials in order of descending powers of x, inserting zeros when any terms are missing. Thus the example appears as follows:

$$
\begin{array}{llrrrr}
(1) & & 3 & 7 & 22 & \\
(2) & 1 - 3\ \overline{\smash{\big)}} & 3 - 2 & & 1 & 2 \\
(3) & & 3 - 9 & & & \\
(4) & & & 7 & 1 & \\
(5) & & & 7 - 21 & & \\
(6) & & & & 22 & 2 \\
(7) & & & & 22 - 66 & \\
(8) & & & & 68 &
\end{array}
$$

The first numbers in (3), (5) and (7) merely duplicate the numbers above and thus these numbers can be omitted. The numbers in (1), the quotient, are repeated in (2), (4) and (6) and thus (1) is not really needed. Our example now looks like this:

$$
\begin{array}{rrrr}
1 - 3\ \overline{\smash{\big)}\ 3 - 2} & 1 & 2 \\
\underline{+\ 9} & & \\
7 & 1 & \\
\underline{-21} & & \\
22 & 2 \\
\underline{-66} \\
68
\end{array}
$$

Since our divisor is always of the form x + b then the first "1" is not needed. Since addition is generally easier than subtraction, we now change the sign of the −3 in the divisor. Thus the following:

$$
\begin{array}{rrrr}
3\ \overline{\smash{\big)}\ 3 - 2} & 1 & 2 \\
\underline{+\ 9} & & \\
7 & 1 & \\
\underline{+21} & & \\
22 & 2 \\
\underline{+66} \\
68
\end{array}
$$

Since the last number in (4) and in (6) duplicate numbers in the dividend, they can be omitted. Thus,

$$
\begin{array}{r}
3\,\overline{)3-2\quad 1\quad 2} \\
9 \\
\hline
7 \\
21 \\
\hline
22 \\
66 \\
\hline
68
\end{array}
$$

Now we take the final step and simplify the above so that our example takes just 3 lines as given below:

(1) $3\,\overline{)3-2\quad 1\quad 2}$
(2) $9\quad 21\quad 66$
(3) $3\quad 7\quad 22\quad 68$

The first 3 numbers in (3) are the coefficients of the quotients and the last number is the remainder.

5   No, the student is not correct. One way of simplifying this expression is:

$$
\frac{C^{-4}-D^{-4}}{C^{-2}+D^{-2}} = \frac{\dfrac{D^4-C^4}{C^4D^4}}{\dfrac{D^2+C^2}{C^2D^2}} = \frac{D^4-C^4}{C^4D^4}\cdot\frac{C^2D^2}{D^2+C^2} = \frac{D^2-C^2}{C^2D^2}
$$

Problem 1 What method did the student use to simplify this expression?

Problem 2 Can you find any or all expressions for which the student's method would give the correct answer?

A4.14   Radicals

1   The given problem is ambiguous. If $\sqrt[3]{-8^2}$ means $\sqrt[3]{(-8)^2}$, then the student is correct. However if $\sqrt[3]{-8^2}$ means $\sqrt[3]{-(8^2)}$, then the student is not correct since

$$\sqrt[3]{-(8^2)} = \sqrt[3]{-64} = -4.$$

2   The real problem here is whether or not the student has a definition concerning the value of an "infinite tower" of x's, or is simply using an intuitive approach. For an interesting discussion of this problem including several approaches to a solution, the reader should consult:

M. C. Mitchelmore, "A Matter of Definition," *Mathematical Monthly* (Classroom Notes Section), June-July 1974, pp. 643-47.

3   No, the student is not correct. One way of simplifying the problem is shown on the following page.

$$\frac{1 + (1/\sqrt{3})}{1 - (1/\sqrt{3})} = \frac{((\sqrt{3}+1)/\sqrt{3})}{((\sqrt{3}-1)/\sqrt{3})} = \frac{\sqrt{3}+1}{\sqrt{3}-1}.$$

An interesting problem to explore in this situation is to find those expressions for which the student's method would work.

4   The student is correct in asserting that $1/\sqrt{2}$ is just as good as $\sqrt{2}/2$ as far as an answer is concerned. However, the main reason that "rationalizing the denominator of fractions" is emphasized is for practical purposes. If one wants an approximation of the above number, it is usually easier to find an approximation using the expression $\sqrt{2}/2$ than it is using the expression $1/\sqrt{2}$.

5   The notation $\sqrt[m/n]{a}$ is not standard notation encountered in a mathematics course. However, if one wanted to use this notation, it would be interesting to figure out what the notation would mean. Since, with suitable restrictions,

$$\sqrt[n]{a} = a^{1/n},$$

then it should follow that

$$\sqrt[m/n]{a} = a^{1/(m/n)} = a^{n/m}.$$

Since with suitable restrictions, $\sqrt[n]{a^m} = a^{m/n}$, then $\sqrt[n]{a^m} \neq \sqrt[m/n]{a}$.

6   The notation $\sqrt[1/2]{x}$ is not standard notation encountered in a mathematics course. One might conjecture what $\sqrt[1/2]{x}$ would mean. Since $\sqrt[n]{a}$ means $a^{1/n}$, $a \geqslant 0$, it would follow that $\sqrt[1/2]{x}$ would mean $x^{1/(1/2)} = x^2$ where $x \geqslant 0$. Since this would be the case, then the symbol $\sqrt[1/2]{x}$ simply would not be needed.

A4.15   *Roots*

1   The usual method of solving this problem is:

$$x + \sqrt{x - 2} = 4$$

(1) $\Rightarrow \sqrt{x - 2} = 4 - x$
(2) $\Rightarrow x - 2 = (4 - x)^2$
(3) $\Rightarrow x - 2 = 16 - 8x + x^2$
(4) $\Rightarrow 0 = x^2 - 9x + 18$
(5) $\Rightarrow (x - 3)(x - 6) = 0$
(6) $\Rightarrow x - 3 = 0 \text{ or } x - 6 = 0$
(7) $x = 3 \text{ or } x = 6$.

When solving an open sentence, the main idea is to use properties, definitions, operations, etc. to transform an open sentence into simpler equivalent (having the same solution set) open sentences. For some operations, however, what happens is that the solution set of the original open sentence is contained in, but not equal to, the solution set of the transformed open sentence. This is exactly what happened in Step 2 above. The squaring process produced an open sentence that contained the solution set of the original open sentence, but the open sentences are not equivalent. The logic involved in this process is that if r is a solution of $x + \sqrt{x - 2} = 4$, then r is a solution of $x - 2 = (4 - x)^2$ but the converse need not be true.

2   The main difficulty here is one of terminology. The phrase "zero of an equation" is used in some texts and means the same thing as root or solution of the equation. Thus if

$$ax^3 + bx^2 + cx + d$$

is a polynomial expression, then a zero or a root or a solution is a value r such that

$$ar^3 + br^2 + cr + d = 0$$

is a true statement. Note that the value r might be any number and does not necessarily have to be the number zero. Thus in the equation $3x - 1 = 0$, the number 1/3 is a solution or a zero of the equation.

3   The assumption is made that one is to solve the equation $2 - y = 2\sqrt{y + 1}$ over the set of real numbers. Since this is the case, then the equation $2 - y = 2\sqrt{y + 1}$ is only defined for those values of y such that $y \geqslant -1$ since $y + 1$ must be greater than or equal to zero. Thus the expression $4y + 4$ must be greater than or equal to zero under this restriction. Hence, this expression could not be negative in this particular case.

A4.16   *Sequences and Series*

1   The student is using the upper numeral on the summation symbol to indicate the number of terms in the series; i.e., in (a) 3 terms and in (b) 4 terms. One way of helping this student is to go back to the definition and interpretation of the summation symbol; i.e., in (b) we substitute 2 for j, then 3, and then 4. The process is over when the upper numeral is substituted for the variable indicated.

2   One way of helping this student is to have the student replace 1 by n^0. Then

$$\sum_{n = 2}^{6} n^0 = 2^0 + 3^0 + 4^0 + 5^0 + 6^0 = 5.$$

A4.17   *Simultaneous Systems of Equations*

1   The basic problem in the question is what is meant by equivalent systems of equations. One system of equations is equivalent to another system of equations when the systems have precisely the same solution set. Thus, in the present problem, we are saying that

(a) $\begin{aligned} 3x + 4y &= 18 \\ 2x - y &= 1 \end{aligned}$ and   (b) $\begin{aligned} x &= 2 \\ y &= 3 \end{aligned}$

have the same solution set, which is, in this case, the ordered pair (2, 3).
   A geometric illustration of what is happening may help the student see what

is going on. When solving a system of equations what one is really doing is finding a system of equations equivalent to the original system but simpler in form. Geometrically, there are an infinite number of lines that contain the point (2, 3) as an intersection. Choosing any two of these lines will give us the point (2, 3) as an intersection. Note that none of these lines are equivalent to each other. Of course, one tries to find the pair of lines that have the simplest form; i.e., the lines in Figure 4.17.1(b).

FIGURE 4.17.1

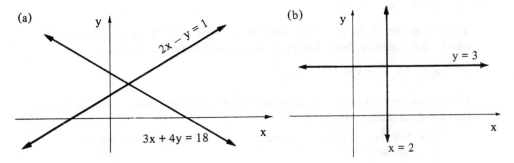

(a)

(b)

A4.18   Slide Rule

1   The rationale behind the use of the slide rule is based on the idea of logarithms. The standard slide rule consists essentially of two rods, C and D, on each of which is constructed a logarithmic scale. This scale is a line of numbers where the distances are proportional to the logarithms of the numbers indicated. Thus, if one wants to multiply 2 by 3 on the slide rule, one would get the situation depicted in Figure 4.18.1.

FIGURE 4.18.1

In order to multiply using the slide rule, one uses the following property of logarithms.

$$\log_{10} a + \log_{10} b = \log_{10} (ab) \tag{1}$$

In the particular example given above, one is essentially adding

$$\log_{10} 2 = 0.301 \quad \text{and} \quad \log_{10} 3 = 0.477$$

and obtains the distance 0.788 which, by (1), is the logarithm of 6.

Problem   Explain how to find $9 \div 3$ on the slide rule, and explain the rationale used as done above.

A4.19   *Variables*

1   The notion of *variable* normally occurs in the study of functions. For example, with $f(x) = x^2$, the symbol x is called a *variable* and represents an arbitrary element in the domain of f.

The notion of *indeterminate* appears in several ways. First, in the study of limits, it is customary to say, for example, that

$$\lim_{x \to 2} \frac{x^2 - 5x + 6}{x^2 - 6x + 8}$$

is *indeterminate* of the form 0/0. Also in the more modern approaches to algebra where a polynomial is defined formally as an *expression* of the form,

$$a_0 x^0 + a_1 x^1 + a_2 x^2 + \cdots + a_n x^n$$

it is customary to refer to x as an indeterminate. For a discussion of the latter, see the section on indeterminates in:

W.W. Sawyer, *A Concrete Approach to Abstract Algebra*, W.H. Freeman & Co., San Francisco, 1956.

2   Variables appear often in mathematics and sometimes they are given special names. The term *parameter* is one of these names. It is used to name a variable for which, in general, one does not want to solve, or which plays some auxiliary role. The term *parameter* is used to distinguish this variable from the variable or variables on which our attention is mainly focused. For example, in the open sentece $2x + 3y = c$, c is a parameter. Clearly one cannot graph $2x + 3y = c$ until a value is substituted for c. By putting in values for c, one gets a family of lines.

Problem   Look at some secondary materials and see how the word *parameter* is used.

A4.20   *Direct and Indirect Variation*

1   It is standard to say that "y varies directly as x" if and only if $y = kx$ where k is the constant of proportionality ($k \neq 0$). When this is the case, $x = 0$ and $y = 0$ is always a solution. However, in some texts one will find variation defined in terms of an equation of the form

$$y + a = k(x + b)^n.$$

That is, $y + a$ varies (in the former sense) directly as $(x + b)^n$. In this case, as in the question asked, $x = 0$ and $y = 0$ is not necessarily in the solution set.

5

Advanced Topics in Secondary Mathematics

QUESTIONS

Q5.1 Calculus

(A) DERIVATIVES AND DIFFERENTIALS

1 A student asks you if the derivative and the integral of a function are both functions. What is your reply?

2 A student gives you the following argument. "The derivative of any function is defined at a value of x. Therefore, the function is constant at the value of x. Therefore, the derivative is zero because the derivative of a constant is zero." Is the student correct? How would you answer this student?

3 A student asks you if the derivative of a function is the rate of change of y or is it the rate of change of y with respect to x. How do you respond?

4 In your twelfth grade class, one student asks you the following question. "What is the difference between a derivative and a differential?" What is your response?

5 A student asks, "Why can't we differentiate $y = x^x$ as $x \cdot x^{x-1} = x^x$?" What is your answer?

6 A student hands in the following work.

$$\frac{d(\sqrt{x^2})}{dx} = \frac{1}{2}(x^2)^{-1/2}(2x)$$

$$= \frac{x}{\sqrt{x^2}} = \frac{x}{x} = 1.$$

Is this answer correct?

7 A student has just been told that the absolute value function does not have a deriva-

tive at zero. He wants to know if the following function has a derivative at zero.

$$f(x) = \begin{cases} |x|, & x < 0 \\ x^2, & x \geq 0 \end{cases}$$

How do you respond?

8   The class is asked to find dy/dx where $4/y = (x - 8)/x$. One student writes $4y - 1 = 1 - 8x^{-1}$ and obtains $dy/dx = -2y^2/x^2$. Another student writes $4x = yx - 8y$ and obtains $dy/dx = (4 - y)/(x - 8)$. Which student has made an error?

9   While studying a unit on differentiation, a student raises the following question. "If $f(x) = x$, then $f'(x) = 1$ and thus $f'(0) = 1$. However, suppose that $g(x) = x^n$, then $g'(x) = n \cdot x^{n-1}$, and in the special case where $n = 1$, then $g(x) = f(x) = x$. Thus $f(x) = x$ and $f'(x) = 1 \cdot x^{1-1} = 1 \cdot x^0$. Thus $f'(0) = 1 \cdot 0^0$, which is undefined." What is wrong? How would you reply?

(B)   FUNCTIONS

1   A student asks, "If a function is continuous on a closed interval, then it is bounded on that interval. Is the converse true?" How do you reply?

2   A student asks you if the hyperbolic functions are related to the hyperbola as the circular functions are related to the circle. How would you answer this student?

3   *Given* f and g are inverses if $f(g(x)) = g(f(x)) = x$.

Question Show that $f(x) = \dfrac{x - 1}{x + 1}$ and $g(x) = \dfrac{1 + x}{1 - x}$ are inverses.

Don's solution

$$f(g(x)) = f\left(\frac{1+x}{1-x}\right) = \frac{\dfrac{1+x}{1-x} - 1}{\dfrac{1+x}{1-x} + 1} = \frac{(1+x) - (1-x)}{(1+x) + (1-x)} = \frac{2x}{2} = x.$$

Therefore, f and g are inverses of each other. Is Don correct?

(C)   INTEGRALS AND THE NOTION OF INFINITY

1   A student asks, "If $\int \tan \theta \, d\theta = -\ln |\cos \theta| + c$, why isn't

$\int \tan^6 \theta \, d\theta = [-\ln |\cos \theta| + c]^6$."

How do you reply?

2   "What is the meaning of ∞?" How would you answer this student?

3   A student asks, "Why is $0 \cdot \infty$ an indeterminate form since zero times anything equals zero?" How would you reply?

(D)   *LIMITS*

1   A student asks, "When can one evaluate

$$\lim_{x \to a} f(x)$$

simply by computing f(a)?" How would you respond?

2   "In showing that $\lim_{x \to 2} x^2 = 4$ using the $\epsilon - \delta$ definition of limit, one frequently sees $\delta = \min\{1, \epsilon/5\}$. This really puts two conditions on δ. Is it necessary to use two conditions?" What is your reply?

3   A student asks, "If f(a) is defined, must $\lim_{x \to a} f(x)$ exist?" How do you respond?

4   "Why isn't the limit of the general term of an infinite series equal to zero sufficient for convergence?" How would you answer this student?

5   "In order to find the limit on some problems such as the variable $\to \infty$, why do you divide through by the highest power in the denominator?" What is your reply?

6   A student asks, "Why is the cancellation of common factors justified when evaluating a limit. For example, $\lim_{x \to 4} \dfrac{(x-4)}{(x-4)(x+3)}$ becomes $\lim_{x \to 4} \dfrac{1}{x+3} = \dfrac{1}{7}$?" What is your response?

7   In a conversation between student and teacher, the student states, "The text talks a lot about limits. What is a limit really?" How would you answer the student?

8   "What happens if ϵ and δ are reversed in the definition of limit; i.e., you are given δ and asked to find an ϵ?" How would you answer this student?

9   A student asks, "What graphical meaning does a limit have if f(x) is undefined at x?" What is your reply?

10   "How does one decide what value to choose for ϵ; i.e., in practice, what are some values of ϵ that would be chosen by engineers, etc?" What is your response?

11   A student asks, "In the definition of the limit of a function, is the $\epsilon - \delta$ method or the neighborhood method more meaningful?" What is your reply?

12   "How can you prove a function does not have a limit. Just because you have no manipulative device at your command to help you guess the limit of a function, how can you be certain the function has no limit if that is the case?" How would you answer this student?

13   A student asks, "What property does a function have or fail to have if it has a limit such as $x \to a$ but is not defined at $x = a$?" What is your reply?

14   A student asks, "Since I have to guess the limit of a function as x (an element in the domain of the function) approaches a given number before I can attempt to prove

it is correct, where does the proof break down should I happen to guess the wrong limit?" What answer would you give?

15   "May one talk of limits in the complex number system?" What answer would you give this student?

16   A student asks, "In finding an appropriate δ, how can you substitute a different x value in both the numerator and the denominator?" What is your reply?

17   "What is an example of a function in which the limit from the right is not the same as the limit from the left?" What is your response?

18   A student asks, "Why does one consider the limit of the function $\left[\lim\limits_{x \to a} f(x)\right]$ only as x approaches a, but not at x = a?" What answer would you give?

19   "Why is the study of limits important to calculus? Is there another development in which the theory of limits is not used?" What reply would you give to this student?

20   A student asks, "How can the $\lim\limits_{x \to 3} \dfrac{x^2 - 5x + 6}{x^2 - 2x - 3} = \dfrac{1}{4}$? If we simply plug in 3, we get 0/0, which is meaningless because 0/0 could be any number. If this is the case, why don't we say that the limit doesn't exist, instead of saying it is 1/4?" What answer would you give?

21   A student shows this graph.

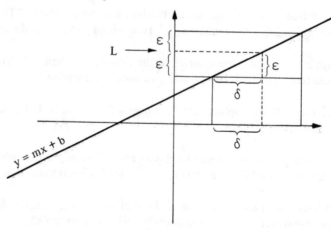

He then asks, "When working with linear functions, why can't I find δ in the following way.

$$\frac{\varepsilon}{\delta} = m$$

$$\delta = \frac{\varepsilon}{m} \text{ ."}$$

How would you respond?

22   A student asks, "Since one must first find the $\lim\limits_{x \to a} f(x)$ before its validity can be

established, what would break down if the statement $\lim_{x \to 2} 3x = \frac{1}{2}$ were made?" What response would you make?

23 "Can you apply limits to a real life situation familiar to us. How will we use them in the future?" What answer would you give?

24 A student asks, "What does it mean if $\lim_{x \to a} f(x) \neq L$?" What response would you give?

25 "Does $\lim_{x \to 0} (1/x) = \infty$ or does this limit not exist?" What answer would you give to this student?

26 A student asks, "What do you mean when you say that a limit does not exist?" What is your reply?

27 A student asks, "In the example $\lim_{x \to 1/3} (1/x) = 3$, you stated that the reasons why you chose $\delta \leqslant 1/6$ instead of the usual $\delta \leqslant 1$. Wasn't the choice of $1/6$ and $\delta \leqslant 1/6$ arbitrary?" How would you help this student?

28 "In a form such as $\lim_{x \to 2} (x^2 - 4x)$, why are you justified in finding the limit by substituting $x = 2$ in $f(x)$ when you have said time and time again that x only approaches but never equals 2?" What response would you give to this student?

29 You ask your twelfth grade students to do the following problem. "Find

$$\lim_{n \to \infty} \frac{(n-1)!}{n!} \text{.''}$$

One student hands in the following work.

$$\frac{(n-1)!}{n!} \cdot \frac{1/n}{1/n} = \frac{(1 - 1/n)!}{1!}$$

$$\lim_{n \to \infty} \frac{(1 - 1/n)!}{1!} = \frac{(\lim_{n \to \infty} 1 - \lim_{n \to \infty} 1/n)!}{(\lim_{n \to \infty} 1)!} = 1.$$

Is this student correct?

(E)   MAXIMUM AND MINIMUM: APPLICATIONS

1 A student asks, "Why use different x's in finding an upper bound for expressions like $\frac{3x^2 + 2x - 5}{7x - 2}$ on the interval $(1, 3)$?" What is your reply?

2 "In finding a maximum for $3x^2 - 2x + 5$ in the interval $(2, 7)$, why do you then use absolute values and what justification do you have for doing it?" What answer would you give to this student?

3   "If we look at the function defined by $y = x^3$ and take its first derivative, we get $f'(x) = 3x^2$. To find the relative maximum or minimum, we set $3x^2 = 0$ and get $x = 0$. But when $x = 0$, $f(0)$ is neither a relative maximum or minimum. Why not?" What is your reply?

4   A student asks you if calculus is really useful? How do you respond?

5   The following problem is presented to a calculus class. "A man 6 feet tall walks at the rate of 5 ft/sec toward a street lamp that is 16 feet above the ground. At what rate is the tip of his shadow moving? At what rate is the length of his shadow changing when he is 10 feet from the base of the light?" The solution to the problem does not use the fact that the man is 10 feet from the base of the light. A student asks why these rates are not dependent on the man's distance from the light? (Why do you get the correct answer without using this piece of information?) What response do you give?

Q5.2   *Elementary Functions and Analysis*

(A)   *ASYMPTOTE AND ABSOLUTE VALUE*

1   A student makes the following statement. "If $.\overline{9} = 1.0$, then it should follow that eventually a hyperbola should meet its asymptote." How do you react to this statement?

2   A student asks, "The graph of $y = f(x)$ has $y = 2$ as an asymptote. Is it possible that $f(x) = 2$ for some x; i.e., can the graph of a function cross an asymptote?" How would you respond?

3   A student asks, "I know how an asymptote behaves, but what is a rigorous definition?" How would you reply?

4   Suppose one wishes to find a number M such that:

$$\left|\frac{x + 3}{x + 1}\right| < M \quad \text{for} \quad 0 < x < 2.$$

A standard technique is to write

$|x + 3| < 5$ (using $x = 2$)   and
$|x + 1| > 1$ (using $x = 0$).

Is it mathematically correct to use one value of x for the numerator and a different value of x for the denominator?

(B)   *AXIOMS AND STRUCTURE*

1   A text defines a field as follows.

(1)   A set of elements closed with respect to two binary operations called addition and multiplication.

(2) The elements form a commutative group with respect to addition.

(3) The nonzero elements also form a commutative group with respect to multiplication.

(4) Multiplication is distributive with respect to addition.

A student then points out that the set consisting of zero is a field. Is this student correct?

(C) BINOMIAL THEOREM

1 A student asks you if the binomial theorem is defined for fractional exponents. What is your reply?

(D) DETERMINANTS

1 A student comments, "A determinant is really a function." Do you agree?

2 You have just given a homework assignment to your twelfth grade class on the evaluation of determinants. There are a few examples of 3×3 and 4×4 determinants whose rows (or columns) form an arithmetic sequence, and a student says that such a determinant always has a value of zero. Do you agree?

(E) EQUIVALENCE RELATIONS

1 A student says that the reflexive property can be derived from the symmetric and transitive properties as follows. "If a ℛ b, then bℛ a, symmetric property. Since the transitive property holds, then a ℛ a." Is the student correct?

2 While introducing the idea of an equivalence relation to your precalculus students, you state the definition of a reflexive relation as stated in your text: "If a ℛ b, then a ℛ a and b ℛ b." A student says that it is not a good statement of the reflexive property. Is the student correct?

3 You put the following example of a relation R on the blackboard where

$$A = \{1, 3, 5, 7\}$$
$$R = \{(1, 1), (3, 3), (5, 5), (7, 7), (1, 3)\}.$$

You tell the class that this relation is reflexive and transitive, but not symmetric. However, many students protest, saying that it is not transitive because, for example, the ordered pair $(3, 3)$ does not have another ordered pair with 3 as the first coordinate to go with it as stated in the definition of the transitive property. How would you respond?

(F) EXPONENTS

1 A student asks, "Since $1/3 = 2/6$, is it true that $x^{1/3} = x^{2/6}$ by the substitution property?" How would you respond?

2   A student asks, "Is $\sqrt[3]{7}$ defined in mathematics?" What is your reply?

(G)   FUNCTIONS

1   A student asks, "Aren't the functions $F(x) = \dfrac{x^2 - 9}{x - 3}$ and $F(x) = x + 3$ really the same function? If not, could they be made identical by adding $F(x) = 6$, when $x = 3$?" What is your reply?

2   "If f has an inverse function, does that mean that f is either strictly increasing or strictly decreasing?" How would you reply to this student?

3   "Given the two functions $f(x)$ and $g(x)$, when can one talk about $(f + g)(x)$ and $f\{g(x)\}$? How does one determine the domain of these latter functions?" How would you answer this student?

4   A student asks, "If one has an equation giving y in terms of x, so that y is a function of x, does one still have a function if one solves for x in terms of y?" How would you answer?

5   A student asks, "In our precalculus book, it says that there are several equivalent definitions of functions and that each definition has its own advantages. What are these definitions and their advantages?" What is your response?

6   "How can $\{(x, f(x)|f(x) = x^2\}$ and $\{(t, f(t)|f(t) = t^2\}$ be the same function if different letters are used?" How would you answer this student?

7   A student asks, "Is there a conventional notation for the function that is defined as the smallest integer greater than or equal to a number?" How would you answer?

8   A twelfth grade student asks you the following question. "What is the difference between a function, a mapping, and a transformation?" What is your reply?

9   A student asks, If the domain of f is the set of real numbers and f is not the zero function, is it always true that $f(1/f) = 1$ (the constant function whose value is 1). What is your response?

10   "What is the difference between $f = 0$ and $f(x) = 0$?" How do you answer this student?

11   A student asks, "If f and g are periodic functions, is $f + g$ also periodic?" What is your reply?

12   You have given the definition of a function in terms of a set of ordered pairs of elements. A few lessons later you are discussing the idea of increasing and decreasing functions. One of your students makes the assertion that you can't talk about increasing or decreasing because sets do not increase or decrease. Is this student right? If so, how are you going to get around the difficulty presented? If not, what explanation do you give for the answer?

13   A student asks, "If F is a periodic function, is it a sum of simple harmonic functions?" What is your reply?

14   A student asks, "If two functions, f and g, have the exact same ranges and domains, are the two functions identical?" What answer do you give?

15   "Explain again the difference between the operations of multiplication and composition on functions f ∘ g and fg. How do you determine the domain of each?" How would you answer this student?

16   A student asks, "Why is an inverse function a reflection about the line y = x?" What is your reply?

17   A student asks, "if y = f(x) is a function, how do I know whether x = f(y) is also a function or not?" What answer do you give?

18   "Is there a function that is equal to its inverse?" How do you answer this student?

19   A student asks, "Can you tell if a given expression is a function or an inverse function?" What response do you give?

20   A student asks, "Why do we call f(x) = sin x a transcendental function? In general, how do I tell whether or not a function is transcendental?" What is your reply?

21   A student asks, "Why is it important to be able to determine zeroes of a function?" How do you respond?

22   A student asks, "Given f(x) and g(x), is there a geometrical interpretation of f(g(x)) and g(f(x))?" How would you reply?

23   A student in your class asks, "For y = log$_b$ x to be a function of x, there is usually the restriction stated so that b > 0. If b < 0, is y = log$_b$ x a function? Why or why not? If *yes*, what is the domain?" How do you respond?

24   A student asks, "If a function is defined as a set of ordered pairs, then what is the difference between a function and the graph of a function?" How would you handle this situation?

25   While studying a unit on the composition of functions, a student asks you the following questions.
      (a)   If f ∘ g is one-to-one, do f and g each have to be one-to-one?
      (b)   If f ∘ g is onto, do f and g each have to be onto?
      How do you reply?

(H)   GRAPHS, CURVES AND TANGENTS

1   A student asks you if conjugate hyperbolas have the same asymptotes. How do you answer?

2   A student asks, "In graphing an inequality of the form $ax + by < c$, why is it sufficient to test only one point, not on $ax + by = c$, to find which region to shade? How would you answer?

3   "If $y = ax^2$ is the equation for the family of parabolas in standard position, is the equation $y = 0 \cdot x^2$ (or $y = 0$) considered a parabola?" How do you respond to this student's question?

4   A student asks, "I have been working on this problem: 'Find the coordinates of the points of intersection of the polar graphs of the equations $r = 2 + 4 \sin \theta$ and $r = 2$.' When I solve the equations simultaneously I get $A(2, 0)$ and $B(2, \pi)$, where the angles are measured in radians, as points of intersection. However, when I graph these equations it seems as if the point C is a point of intersection. Why didn't I get this point by solving the equations? How would you reply?

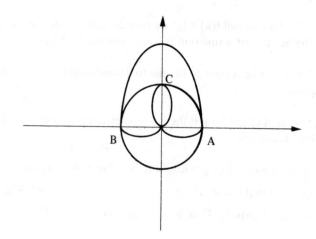

5   In your analysis class, a student gives the following definition of a tangent to a curve. "It is a line that intersects the curve in only one point." Is the student correct?

6   A student asks, "I have noticed that the graphs of $y = x^2$, $y = x^4$, $y = x^6$, etc. get steeper and steeper. Is there some value n for the exponent such that x^n becomes the y-axis?" How do you reply?

(I)   **MATHEMATICAL INDUCTION**

1   A student asks, "Can mathematical induction be used with negative integers?" What is your reply?

2   A student asks, "Is there mathematical induction for the entire set of real numbers?" What is your response?

(J)   **SYSTEMS OF NUMBERS**

1   You are discussing how to solve the following problem. "Find the sum of the first n positive integers." You decide upon the following strategy in solving this problem.

    Suppose we make a table showing the relationship between the number of terms we add and the resulting sum."

Number of y terms	Sum	First Difference	Second Difference
1	1	2	1
2	3	3	1
3	6	4	1
4	10	5	1
5	15	6	1
6	21	7	1
7	28		

You tell the class to form the differences betweeen succeeding terms in the sum (getting the first difference column) and to repeat that again using the second difference column. Then you tell the class that since the second differences are the same constant, the formula representing the sum must be of the second degree; i.e.,

$$S = ax^2 + bx + c.$$

One student asks you why must the formula be of the second degree. What do you tell this student?

2   A student asks you how does one prove there is no largest integer. How do you answer?

3   A student asks, "Are there more rational numbers than integers?" What is your answer?

4   "Why do we use the expression *real numbers*?" What is your reply?

5   A student asks, "How do we know that π, e and other *transcendental* numbers are irrational?" What is your reply?

6   "What is *e*? How does it arise in mathematics? Why does such a complicated number become so important in mathematics?" What is your reply to this student's question?

7   In your twelfth grade precalculus class, you make the statement that every polynomial equation with complex number coefficients of degree n has exactly n complex roots. One of your students says that it isn't true because in some equations you have to use the same root several times. How would you answer this student?

8   You have just shown your class that the set of complex numbers is not an ordered field. One of your students says that it is ordered because the set of real numbers is a subset of the complex numbers and the real numbers are ordered. How do you respond?

(K)   SERIES, SEQUENCES AND PROGRESSIONS

1   You ask your twelfth grade class whether the sequence

$$1, -1/2, 1/3, -1/4, ..., (-1)^{n+1}(1/n)$$

is a convergent or divergent sequence. One student says that it is divergent since by the axiom of completeness every bounded, nondecreasing or nonincreasing sequence of real numbers converges, and its limit is a real number. The sequence is bounded by 1, but it is neither nonincreasing or nondecreasing; therefore, it must diverge. Do you agree?

2   *Definition* An infinite series converges if the sum of the first n terms has a limit as $n \to \infty$, and this limit is called the sum of the series. (That is, to say that a series $\sum\limits_{n=1}^{\infty} u_n$ converges means that the sequence of partial sums $\{S_n\}$ converges.)

The following series diverge but the sequence has a limit. How do the following examples relate to the given definition.

$$\sum_{n=1}^{\infty} \frac{5n}{3n+2} \qquad \sum_{n=1}^{\infty} \frac{2n^2}{n+3} \qquad \sum_{n=1}^{\infty} \frac{4n-3}{2n+1}$$

3   A student asks you if it is possible for a series to converge and yet the associated sequence is a divergent sequence. What is your reply?

4   A student asks you why the definition of a limit of a series is defined in terms of partial sums rather than in terms of members of the series? What is your reply?

5   A student asks, "When we use the symbol 'Σ' as in $\sum\limits_{i=1}^{5} 2i$, are we referring to the series or the sum of the series?" What is your answer?

6   A student asks you if a sequence can diverge even though it is bounded. What is your response?

7   "Are diverging and ∞ synonymous?" How do you answer this student?

(L)   *SYNTHETIC DIVISION*

1   A student asks, "Why in synthetic division when you divide by $2x - 3$, do you not only have to divide the entire problem by 2 but then multiply the remainder by 2 in the answer?" How do you respond?

2   A student asks, "How would you use synthetic division when dividing by a linear polynomial of the form $ax - b$?" What is your response?

3   "Can you use synthetic division when dividing by a quadratic or a cubic?" How would you respond to this question?

(M)   *VECTORS*

1   A student asks you why the vector product of two vectors is defined only for vectors in three-dimensional space.

2   A student asks you if there is a definition of multiplication of vectors that results in a vector, and if so, what is it used for? How do you respond?

3   "If u, v, and w are nonzero vectors and if $u \cdot v = w \cdot v$, is it true that $u = w$?" How do you answer this student?

4   A student asks, "The linear equation of a line $ax + by = c$ seems to be connected with the idea of inner product; is it?" How would you answer?

5   A twelfth grade student makes the following statement. "We have been working with vectors in this course and you keep telling us that the arrows we see in the book are not vectors. I don't quite understand. Could you explain the difference between a vector and an arrow; i.e., what is a vector?" How do you reply?

Q5.3   *Probability*

1   A twelfth grade student asks, "What is the difference between permutations and combinations?" How would you reply?

2   In your twelfth grade class, a student asks you what the difference is between independent and mutually exclusive events. What do you tell this student?

3   You ask your twelfth grade students the following question. "What is the probability that in three throws with a fair die, different numbers appear on all three throws? A student hands in the following work.

$$\frac{\binom{15}{3}}{\binom{18}{3}} = \frac{{}_{15}C_3}{{}_{18}C_3} = .55. \quad \text{Is this student correct?}$$

4   You ask your twelfth grade students to find the probability of both children being boys in a two-child family. One student says the probability is 1/3; another says its 1/4. Is either of the students correct?

5   A student asks, "I have heard from friends of mine that there is a famous problem called the birthday problem. Do you know what it is and how to solve it?"

6   A student makes the following remark. "It looks like you can solve many probability problems using either permutation or combination ideas in the same problem." Do you agree?

7   A student asks you why 0! is defined to be one. How do you answer?

8   You have just finished discussing the so called birthday problem. When you begin a study of the birthmate problem, a student makes the claim that this is really the same problem. How would you handle this situation?

9   A student asks, "How can it be true that the *permutation* of n objects, r alike of one kind and n − r alike of another kind, are equal to the *combination* of n different objects taken r at a time." How would you respond?

Q5.4   *Trigonometry*

1   A student asks, "What is the difference between deriving an identity and verifying an identity?" What is your response?

2   A student hands in a proof to show that:

$$\frac{1}{\cos \theta} - \cos \theta = \tan \theta \cdot \sin \theta \text{ if } \theta \neq \frac{\pi}{2} + k\pi$$

The proof follows:

$$\frac{1}{\cos \theta} - \cos \theta = \tan \theta \cdot \sin \theta \Rightarrow 1 - \cos^2 \theta$$

$$= \cos \theta \cdot \tan \theta \cdot \sin \theta$$

$$\because 1 - \cos^2 \theta = \cos \theta \cdot \frac{\sin \theta}{\cos \theta} \cdot \sin \theta$$

$$= \sin^2 \theta ,$$

which is a known identity. What is your response?

3   The following problem was given for homework. "Verify that

$$\cos^2 (x) = 1 - \sin^2 (x)."$$

A student hands in the following work. "If we add $\sin^2(x)$ to each side of the above, we get $\cos^2 (x) + \sin^2 (x) = 1$, which is a known identity. Therefore,

$$\cos^2 (x) = 1 - \sin^2 (x)."$$

Is his work correct?

4   A student asks, "After establishing a trigonometric identity, e.g.,

$$\sin x \cdot \tan x = \frac{\sec x}{\csc^2 x},$$

One can conclude that the replacement set for the identity is R, where R is the set of all real numbers?" How do you answer?

5   Your eleventh grade students are trying to prove the following identity.

$$\tan x + \cot x = \sec x \cdot \csc x.$$

A student hands in the following work.

$$\frac{\sin x}{\cos x} + \frac{\cos x}{\sin x} = \frac{1}{\cos x} \cdot \frac{1}{\sin x}$$

$$\frac{\sin^2 x + \cos^2 x}{\cos x \sin x} = \frac{1}{\cos x} \cdot \frac{1}{\sin x}$$

$$\frac{1}{\cos x \sin x} = \frac{1}{\cos x \sin x}$$

$$\therefore \tan x + \cot x = \sec x \csc x.$$

What is your response?

6   You ask your trigonometry students to do the following problem. "Show that $\tan^2 x + 1 = \sec^2 x$." A student hands in the following work.

$$\tan^2 x + 1 = \sec^2 x$$

$$\frac{\sin^2 x}{\cos^2 x} + 1 = \frac{1}{\cos^2 x}$$

$$\sin^2 x + \cos^2 x = 1$$

The student says, "Since the above statement is a true identity, then the first identity is true." What is your response?

7   A student writes the following statement.

$$\cos (x_2 - x_1) = \cos x_2 - \cos x_1.$$

When you tell him that he is incorrect, he replies that he is using the distributive property of multiplication over subtraction; i.e., $x(y - z) = x \cdot y - x \cdot z$, and he doesn't understand why it is incorrect. How would you help him?

8   A student asks, "Is there any relationship between the *secant line* and the *secant trigonometric function*?" How would you respond?

9   The area formula for a triangle is $K = \frac{1}{2}(a \cdot b) \sin C$ where K is the area and a, b, c are given in the figure.

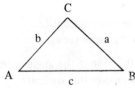

In using the formula, and working with logs, why does the following equation give an incorrect answer?

$$\log K = \tfrac{1}{2}(\log A + \log B + \log \sin C)$$

10   In an explanation of inverse functions, F^{-1} does not equal $1/F$, but $x^{-1} = 1/x$. However, one student said that F^{-1} does equal $1/F$ by showing the following problem.

$$y = \sin^{-1} x$$
$$y = \frac{1}{\sin} x$$
$$\sin y = x$$

What is wrong with the student's reasoning?

11   What is wrong with the solution to the following trigonometric equation.

$$\tan x \cos x = 1$$
$$\frac{\sin x}{\cos x} \cdot \cos x = 1$$
$$\sin x = 1$$

Hence $x = 90°$.

12   A student asks, "In Algebra I, we learned that $a^{-1} = 1/a$. How come $\sin^{-1}(x)$ is not equal to $\frac{1}{\sin(x)}$?" What do you tell him?

13   A student asks, "Is there any way to represent tangent, cotangent, secant, and cosecant functions with respect to the unit circle?" What is your reply?

14   A student asks you if it is possible to write any equation of the form

$$y = A \cos(bx + c_1) + B \sin(bx + c_2)$$

in terms of either a cosine function or a sine function of some kind? What is your response?

15   A student comments, "It seems that we are not precise in our language here. We say that $\sin 30° = 1/2$ for the trigonometic function sine, but the trigonometric functions have angles, not angle measures, for their domain." Do you agree?

16   An eleventh grade student writes the following on a test on trigonometric functions:

$$\sec 38° = \cos \frac{1}{38°}.$$

Is this correct?

17   "We know that

$$\cos a = \frac{\text{length of the side adjacent to } a}{\text{length of the hypotenuse}}$$

What do you do with this rule if the angle is 90°? Which side is adjacent to the angle?" How would you answer this student?

18 A student asks, "Why is rotation in the clockwise direction called negative instead of positive?" How would you respond?

19 A student asks you if it is possible to use other figures besides the circle in discussing the wrapping function; i.e., is it possible to use a square or a rectangle. If so, are the functions of any importance in mathematics? What is your reply?

20 While studying circular functions, a student asks, "When graphing

$$y = \sin(x + (\pi/3)),$$

you said to shift the sine curve $\pi/3$ to the left, but that is in the negative direction. Why don't we shift it to the right $\pi/3$, which is in the positive direction, and $\pi/3$ is positive?" What is your answer?

21 A student asks, "Why are the inverse cotangent, secant, and cosecant functions defined as they are; i.e.,

$$\text{Arccot} = \left[(x, y) | y = \frac{\pi}{2} - \text{Arctan } x\right]$$

$$\text{Arcsec} = \left[(x, y) | y = \text{Arccos } \frac{1}{x}\right]$$

$$\text{Arccsc} = \left[(x, y) | y = \text{Arcsin } \frac{1}{x}\right]$$

How would you reply?

22 If a student asks, "What is the relationship between ordinary trigonometric functions and circular functions; can there be trigonometric functions other than circular?", how do you answer?

23 After a discussion of the domain restrictions necessary for inverse trigonometric functions, a student says, "If you define modulo arithmetic for π to be analogous to modulo arithmetic for integers, for example,

$$\frac{5}{2} \pi \bmod \pi = \frac{\pi}{2},$$

then you could define inverse trigonometric functions for all

$$x \in R \text{ by } \text{Cos}^{-1}(\cos x) = x \bmod \pi?"$$

Is this student correct?

24 A student comments, "sin x and arcsin x are inverse functions. Therefore

$$\text{arcsin } (\sin x) = x."$$

Is this student correct?

25 The following problem is given to a class. "Given

$$\tan \theta = \sqrt{5}/6, \quad \pi < \theta < 3\pi/2,$$

find $\sin \theta$ and $\cos \theta$." The teacher offers the following explanation as a solution.

$$(\sin \theta / \cos \theta) = \sqrt{5}/6$$
$$\sin \theta = (\sqrt{5}/6) \cos \theta$$
$$\cos^2 \theta + \sin^2 \theta = 1, \quad \cos^2 \theta + (5/36) \cos^2 \theta = 1$$
$$\cos^2 \theta = 36/41$$
$$\cos \theta = \pm 6/\sqrt{41}$$
$$\sin \theta = (\sqrt{5}/6)(-6/\sqrt{41}) = -\sqrt{5}/\sqrt{41}.$$

A student asks, "Will the following method work? In order to find $\sin \theta$ and $\cos \theta$, simply take $\sqrt{(\sqrt{5})^2 + 6^2}$ (numerator and denominator of $\tan \theta$) = $\sqrt{41}$. Then

$$\sin \theta = -\sqrt{5}/\sqrt{41} \quad \text{and} \quad \cos \theta = -6/\sqrt{41}."$$

(The signs are negative because one is working in the third quadrant.) The student is reasoning that

$$\frac{\sin \theta}{\cos \theta} = \frac{\sqrt{5}}{6} = \frac{\sqrt{5}/x}{6/x}.$$

What is your response?

26   Given that an angle has a measure of one radian, is there a simple intuitive comparison possible that will help your students get some feeling for the size of such an angle?

ANSWERS

A5.1   *Calculus*

(A)   *DERIVATIVES AND DIFFERENTIALS*

1   The derivative of a function is a function, which indeed, is called the *derivative function*. The domain of the derivative function is the set of all points at which the original function is differentiable. There are two types of integrals. The *definite* integral of a function, assuming the integral exists, is a number. One might interpret such a result as a constant function, but this is not *natural* or *standard* at the elementary level. For example,

$$\int_0^1 x^2 \, dx = \frac{1}{3}.$$

The *indefinite* integral of a function, assuming the integral exists, is not a function, but is a *set* of functions. For example,

$$\int x^2 \, dx = \frac{x^3}{3} + C$$

where C is a constant. For a given value of C, $\frac{x^3}{3} + C$ represents a function. Since C

can be chosen to be any real number, $\frac{x^3}{3} + C$ represents a set of functions.

2   In basic calculus courses, in order for a function to have a derivative at a point x, the domain of the function must include an interval about x. The student is confusing "constant at x" with "constant function over this interval."

3   One should always specify the derivative of one variable with respect to another. For example, suppose y is the price of a certain commodity. The price y could change with time t, demand d or production cost c. Thus, to talk about the derivative of y would be meaningless unless one knew "with respect to what."

4   There are a number of differences. Two are given here. If y = f(x) is a differentiable function, then dy/dx = f'(x) is a function of the one variable x while the differential dy given by dy = f'(x) dx is a function of two variables, namely x and dx.

   A second difference is given by a geometric interpretation. The derivative dy/dx = f'(x), at x = a, gives the slope of the tangent line at x = a as shown in Figure 5.1.1.

FIGURE 5.1.1

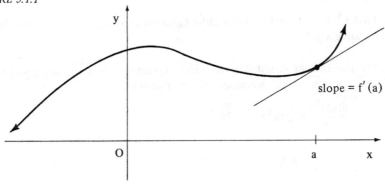

The differential dy = f'(x) dx, when x = a and dx is given, represents the number of y-units needed to return to the tangent line if one moves from (a, f(a)) to (a + dx, f(a)) as in Figure 5.1.2.

FIGURE 5.1.2

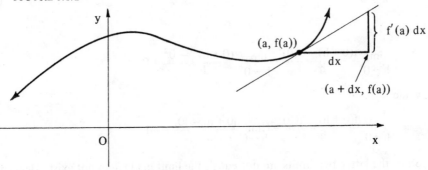

5   This is the type of question that points out the importance of a reasonable amount of theory. When one proves that if

$$y = x^r, \quad r, \text{ a real number,}$$

then $\dfrac{dy}{dx} = rx^{r-1},$

the assumption is made that r is a constant. Moreover, the proof breaks down (no matter what proof is used) if this is not the case. When one reaches the stage where logarithmic differentiation is introduced, then one can do the following:

$$y = x^x, \quad x > 0$$
$$\ln y = x \ln x$$
$$\frac{1}{y}\frac{dy}{dx} = x \cdot \frac{1}{x} + \ln x$$
$$\frac{dy}{dx} = y + y \ln x$$

or finally,

$$\frac{dy}{dx} = x^x + x^x \ln x.$$

That $x^x + x^x \ln x$ is not the same function as x^x can easily be seen, for example, by using $x = 2$.

6   No, the student is not correct. The expression $x/\sqrt{x^2}$ is not equal to x/x; i.e., $\sqrt{x^2} \neq x$, $\sqrt{x^2} = |x|$. A correct solution follows.

$$\frac{d(\sqrt{x^2})}{dx} = \frac{1}{2}(x^2)^{-1/2}(2x)$$
$$= \frac{x}{\sqrt{x^2}}$$
$$= \frac{x}{|x|}, \quad x \neq 0.$$

7   The answer is *no*. One needs to evaluate

$$\lim_{h \to 0} \frac{f(0+h) - f(0)}{h}. \tag{1}$$

Now

$$\lim_{h \to 0^+} \frac{f(0+h) - f(0)}{h} = \lim_{h \to 0^+} \frac{(0+h)^2 - 0^2}{h} = 0$$

while

$$\lim_{h \to 0^-} \frac{f(0+h) - f(0)}{h} = \lim_{h \to 0^-} \frac{|0+h| - |0|}{h} = -1.$$

Since the latter two limits are not equal, the limit in (1) does not exist. Hence the given function does not have a derivative at 0.

8 From $4y^{-1} = 1 - 8x^{-1}$, one obtains

$$-4y^{-2}\frac{dy}{dx} = 8x^{-2}$$

or $\qquad \dfrac{dy}{dx} = \dfrac{-2y^2}{x^2}$ $\hfill$ (1)

From $4x = yx - 8y$, one obtains

$$4 = y + \frac{dy}{dx}x - 8\frac{dy}{dx}$$

or $\qquad \dfrac{dy}{dx} = \dfrac{4 - y}{x - 8}$ $\hfill$ (2)

At any point on the curve $4/y = (x - 8)/x$, the value of the derivative dy/dx represents the slope of the tangent line. The expressions given by (1) and (2) are *formally different*. However, at any point on the curve $4/y = (x - 8)/x$, we have $y = 4x/(x - 8)$. Hence

$$\frac{4 - y}{x - 8} = \frac{4 - (4x/(x - 8))}{x - 8} = \frac{-32}{(x - 8)^2}$$

and $\quad \dfrac{-2y^2}{x^2} = \dfrac{-2(4x/(x - 8))^2}{x^2} = \dfrac{-32}{(x - 8)^2}.$

Thus both students are correct. One should stress, however, that (1) and (2) can only be used at points on the curve. For example, one could use $x = 8$ in (1), but there is *no* point on the curve with $x = 8$. Similarly one could use $x = 0$ in (2), but there is *no* point on the curve with $x = 0$.

9 For an answer to this question, see Section A4.4, Answer 5.

(B)   **FUNCTIONS**

1 No. For example, the function

$$f(x) = \begin{cases} x^2, & 0 \leqslant x < 1 \\ 0, & x = 1 \end{cases}$$

is bounded on the closed interval $[0, 1]$, but it is not continuous on this interval.

2 Yes, they are. Let $x^2 - y^2 = 1$ be the "unit hyperbola" and $\sinh u = \frac{1}{2}(e^u - e^{-u})$, $\cosh u = \frac{1}{2}(e^u + e^{-u})$ be the hyperbolic sine and cosine functions, respectively. Substituting the latter into the former, where $x = \cosh u$ and $y = \sinh u$,

$$\begin{aligned} x^2 - y^2 &= 1 \\ &= \tfrac{1}{4}(e^{2u} + 2 + e^{-2u}) - \tfrac{1}{4}(e^{2u} - 2 + e^{-2u}) \\ &= \tfrac{1}{4}e^{2u} - \tfrac{1}{4}e^{2u} + \tfrac{1}{2} + \tfrac{1}{2} + \tfrac{1}{4}e^{-2u} - \tfrac{1}{4}e^{-2u} \\ &= 1. \end{aligned}$$

Thus, the point (x, y) with $x = \cosh u$ and $y = \sinh u$ lies on the unit hyperbola since $\cosh^2 u - \sinh^2 u = 1$. That is, the hyperbolic functions offer a parametric version of a hyperbola as the circular functions offer a parametric version of a circle.

Problem 1 Is there a one-to-one correspondence between the points on the "unit hyperbola" and the point (x, y) where $x = \cosh u$ and $y = \sinh u$? Explain.

Problem 2 There seems to be an analogy between the ordinary circular functions and the hyperbolic functions. Investigate this analogy; i.e., find additional points of analogy or differences between these two functions.

Problem 3 We have looked at circular and hyperbolic functions. Is it possible to extend what has been done to parabolic and elliptic functions? That is, are there functions that are related to the parabola and the ellipse as the circular functions are related to the circle and the hyperbolic functions are related to the hyperbola?

3   Don has only shown that $f(g(x)) = x$ for every x in the domain of g. It is not sufficient merely to show that $f(g(x)) = x$. One must also show that $g(f(x)) = x$. For example, if $f(x) = x^2$ and $g(x) = \sqrt{x}$, then, for each x in the domain of g,

$$f(g(x)) = f(\sqrt{x}) = x.$$

However,

$$g(f(x)) = g(x^2) = |x|,$$

which is not equal to x for each x in the domain of f.

Problem For the given question, is it true that $g(f(x)) = x$ for every x in the domain of f.

INTEGRALS AND THE NOTION OF INFINITY

1   The student is assuming that if $\int f(x)\, dx = F(x) + c$, then

$$\int [f(x)]^n\, dx = [F(x) + c]^n$$

where n is a positive integer.
   Some simple examples should convince the student that this is not the case.

(1) $\int 1\, dx = x + c$ while $\int 1^3\, dx = \int 1\, dx = x + c$, not $(x + c)^3$.

(2) $\int x\, dx = \dfrac{x^2}{2} + c$ while $\int x^2\, dx = \dfrac{x^3}{3} + c$, not $\left(\dfrac{x^2}{2} + c\right)^2$.

2   The symbol "∞" is used in several ways in the calculus. It should be emphasized that ∞ is only a symbol and not a real number. For example, one uses the symbol ∞ in

$$\lim_{x \to 0^+} \frac{1}{x} = \infty$$

to mean that as x gets closer and closer to zero, $x > 0$, $1/x$ increases without bound. That is, given any number M, one can find an x, $x > 0$, such that $1/x > M$. One also encounters the symbol ∞ in

$$\lim_{x \to \infty} \frac{1}{x} = 0$$

where $x \to \infty$ means that x increases without bound. What one means here is that given $\epsilon > 0$ (no matter how small), there is a number M such that $1/M < \epsilon$, or further, that $1/x < \epsilon$ whenever $x \geq M$.

3 Consider the limit

$$\lim_{x \to \infty} \frac{1}{x} \cdot x.$$

Now, $\lim_{x \to \infty} \frac{1}{x} = 0$ while $\lim_{x \to \infty} x = \infty$. Thus, simple substitution would yield

$$\lim_{x \to \infty} \frac{1}{x} \cdot x = 0 \cdot \infty.$$

However, for any x, $\frac{1}{x} \cdot x = 1$. Hence

$$\lim_{x \to \infty} \frac{1}{x} \cdot x = 1.$$

Similarly, substitution into $\lim_{x \to \infty} \frac{2}{x} \cdot x$ yields $0 \cdot \infty$ while it should be obvious that

$$\lim_{x \to \infty} \frac{2}{x} \cdot x = 2.$$

It should be pointed out to the student that zero times any *real number* equals zero, but ∞ is *not* a real number.

(D)   *LIMITS*

1 We have $\lim_{x \to a} f(x) = f(a)$ whenever f is continuous at *a*. For example, $f(x) = x^2 + 3x + 1$ is continuous at 4 so that

$$\lim_{x \to 4} f(x) = f(4) = 29.$$

The function

$$f(x) = \frac{x^2 - 1}{x - 1}$$

is not *defined* at $x = 1$ and, hence, not continuous at $x = 1$. But,

$$\lim_{x \to 1} f(x) = \lim_{x \to 1} \frac{x^2 - 1}{x - 1} = \lim_{x \to 1} (x + 1) = 2.$$

Observe that there is *no* value of *a* such that $f(a) = 2$. As another example, consider the function

$$f(x) = \begin{cases} x, & x < 1 \\ x^2 + 1, & x \geq 1 \end{cases}$$

In this case $\lim_{x \to 1} f(x)$ does not exist although $f(1) = 2$. That is, $\lim_{x \to 1} f(x) \neq f(1)$.

Observe that f is not continuous at x = 1.

2   For certain functions, such as linear functions, one condition is sufficient. It is impossible, however, to prove that one condition is *always* sufficient. Some sort of bound (for example, $\delta \leqslant 1$), is always implied directly or indirectly.

The fact that two conditions are used is really a bit of mathematical sophistication, which should not go unnoticed by the student. This is part of "mathematical maturity." The fact that if a particular value of δ "works" then any smaller positive value of δ will "work" is a very important bit of knowledge in the understanding of limits.

3   No. Consider the function f defined by

$$f(x) = \begin{cases} 1, & x > 0 \\ 0, & x = 0 \\ -1, & x < 0 \end{cases}$$

Then f(0) exists, but clearly $\lim\limits_{x \to 0} f(x)$ does not exist.

4   One is considering the truth or falsity of the statement:

If $\lim\limits_{n \to \infty} a_n = 0$, then $\sum\limits_{n=1}^{\infty} a_n$ converges.

In order to show that such a statement is false, one need produce only *one* counterexample. That is, one need produce only one example where

$$\lim\limits_{n \to \infty} a_n = 0$$

but

$$\sum\limits_{n=1}^{\infty} a_n$$

does not converge. The familiar

$$\sum\limits_{n=1}^{\infty} \frac{1}{n} = 1 + \frac{1}{2} + \frac{1}{3} + \frac{1}{4} + \cdots$$

is precisely such an example.

5   Let us consider a typical example.

$$\lim\limits_{n \to \infty} \frac{2x^2 + 3x - 1}{7x^2 - 2x + 3} = \lim\limits_{x \to \infty} \frac{2 + \dfrac{3}{x} - \dfrac{1}{x^2}}{7 - \dfrac{2}{x} + \dfrac{3}{x^2}} = \frac{2}{7}$$

In this case, we divided the numerator and denominator by x^2. The reason for doing this is that before taking up such problems, one has normally shown that

$$\lim\limits_{x \to \infty} \frac{a}{x} = 0 \quad \text{and} \quad \lim\limits_{x \to \infty} \frac{a}{x^2} = 0$$

where *a* is a constant. In addition, one knows that

$$\lim_{x \to \infty} a = a$$

and $\lim\limits_{x \to \infty} (f(x) + g(x) + h(x)) = \lim\limits_{x \to \infty} f(x) + \lim\limits_{x \to \infty} g(x) + \lim\limits_{x \to \infty} h(x),$

assuming these limits exist. One should also know that

$$\lim_{x \to \infty} \frac{f(x)}{g(x)} = \frac{\lim\limits_{x \to \infty} f(x)}{\lim\limits_{x \to \infty} g(x)},$$

assuming these limits exist and $\lim\limits_{x \to \infty} g(x) \neq 0.$

By dividing numerator and denominator by x^2 in the above example, one is able to make use of this prior knowledge to calculate the given limit.

6   When one considers $\lim\limits_{x \to 4} \dfrac{x - 4}{(x - 4)(x + 3)}$, one is considering the values of

$$\frac{x - 4}{(x - 4)(x + 3)}$$

for values of x that are "close" to 4 but *not* equal to 4. For any such value of x,

$$\frac{x - 4}{(x - 4)(x + 3)} = \frac{1}{x + 3},$$

and the constraint on x insures that one is not dividing by zero. Hence

$$\lim_{x \to 4} \frac{x - 4}{(x - 4)(x + 3)} = \lim_{x \to 4} \frac{1}{x + 3} = \frac{1}{7}.$$

7   The equation $\lim\limits_{x \to a} f(x) = L$ means that one can get f(x) "as close as one wishes" to L by taking x "sufficiently close" to *a* (but not equal to *a*).

It is usually instructive to offer examples as shown in Table 5.1.1.

TABLE 5.1.1

x	x^2
1.9	3.61
1.99	3.96
1.999	3.996001000
1.9999	3.99960010
1.99999	3.9999600001
2.00001	4.0000400001
2.0001	4.000400010
2.001	4.004001000
2.01	4.0401
2.1	4.410

It should be *intuitively* clear that one can get x^2 as close as one wishes to 4 by taking x sufficiently close to 2. One pupose of mathematics is to make such ideas rigorous, and this is precisely the purpose of the formal ε-δ definition.

8   This is simply a change of notation and *nothing more*. Indeed, some texts use let-

ters such as h and k instead of the classical ε, δ. One should be willing to accept *any* notational variation. For example, the following is a perfectly legitimate definition of limit:

$\lim\limits_{x \to a}$ f(x) = L means that given a real number $\square$, there exists a real number $\triangle$ such that $|L - f(x)| < \square$ whenever $0 < |x - a| < \triangle$.

9   For an answer to this question, see Answer 13 (including Figure 5.1.3) of this section.

10   An answer to this question is, of necessity, vague. The question asked is getting at the problem of approximations and errors. Such problems are of extreme importance in the evaluation of safety factors used by engineers. But safety factors vary widely. For example, the safety factors involved in the construction of a bridge differ from the safety factor involved in the construction of a jet airliner.

   Problem   Which do you think is greater: the safety factor in the construction of a bridge or the safety factor in the construction of a jet airliner?

11   Neither is more meaningful than the other. The neighborhood approach involves the ε- δ technique.

12   This is not an easy question to answer. Indeed, a student will frequently say that a certain function does not have a limit simply because the student cannot find a manipulation device to come up with *some* number. A proof would consist of showing that no matter what number L is chosen

$\lim\limits_{x \to a}$ f(x) $\neq$ L

in the sense of the answer to Question 24 of this section.

13   If $\lim\limits_{x \to a}$ f(x) exists but f(a) is not defined, then f is not continuous at x = a. For example,

$$f(x) = \frac{x - 1}{x^2 - 1}.$$

The domain of f is the set of all real numbers with the exception of x = ±1. Here

$$\lim\limits_{x \to 1} f(x) = \lim\limits_{x \to 1} \frac{x - 1}{x^2 - 1} = \lim\limits_{x \to 1} \frac{1}{x + 1} = \frac{1}{2}.$$

That is, $\lim\limits_{x \to 1}$ f(x) exists, but f(1) does not exist. In this case, f is not continuous at x = 1. A graph of f is shown in Figure 5.1.3.

FIGURE 5.1.3

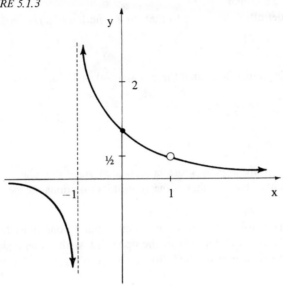

14   There is no proof to break down if one guesses the wrong limit. One will simply be unable to make the necessary computations in order to build a proof.

For example, suppose one tries to show that

$$\lim_{x \to 2} x^2 = 17.$$

That is, given $\varepsilon > 0$, one tries to find a $\delta > 0$ such that

$$|x^2 - 17| < \varepsilon$$

whenever

$$0 < |x - 2| < \delta.$$

However, if $\varepsilon < 1$ and $\delta > 1$, then the interval $2 - \delta < x < 2 + \delta$ will contain the value $x = 3$ and $|3^2 - 17| \not< \varepsilon$. If $\delta < 1$, then the interval $2 - \delta < x < 2 + \delta$ will contain the value $x = 2 + (\delta/2)$ and

$$\left| \left(2 + \frac{\delta}{2} \right)^2 - 17 \right| = \left| 13 - \left(2\delta + \frac{\delta^2}{4} \right) \right|$$

(Why?) But $0 < \delta < 1$ implies

$$0 < 2\delta + \frac{\delta^2}{4} < 2\frac{1}{4}$$

(Why?) Hence

$$\left| 13 - \left(2\delta + \frac{\delta^2}{4} \right) \right| > \varepsilon.$$

15   Yes. Just as one speaks of $\lim_{x \to 2} x^2 = 4$ so one can talk about

$$\lim_{z \to 2 + i} z^2 = 3 + 4i \qquad (1)$$

where z = x + iy is a complex variable.

The formal definition is similar to that for a function of a real variable.

$$\lim_{z \to a} f(z) = L$$

means that if one is given $\varepsilon > 0$, then there is a $\delta > 0$ such that

$$|f(z) - L| < \varepsilon$$

whenever

$$0 < |z - a| < \delta.$$

Geometrically, things are slightly more complicated since one plane is needed to plot a complex number and another plane to plot its functional image. The idea is as follows.

Given the open disk with center at L and radius ε, one must find a $\delta > 0$ such that if z is any complex number in the open disk with center *a* and radius δ, then f(z) is in the previously mentioned disk (see Figures 5.1.4 and 5.1.5).

FIGURE 5.1.4

FIGURE 5.1.5

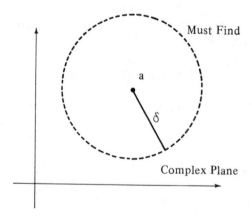

17   Consider the function f defined by

$$f(x) = \begin{cases} 1, & x \geq 0 \\ -1, & x < 0 \end{cases}$$

Then $\lim_{x \to 0^+} f(x) = 1$ while $\lim_{x \to 0^-} f(x) = -1$.

18   This question points out a real weakness of much of mathematics education in that definitions are *given* rather than developed. For example, a similar question might be "Why are logarithms defined the way they are and not some other way?" There was a good deal of mathematical development that led to the need for a definition of logarithms as presently studied. That development, however, is usually omitted in the classroom. Similarly, the mathematics developed by Newton and Leibniz which led to the calculus, indicated a *need* for a definition of limit such as presently studied.

19   Calculus is the study of limiting processes. Therefore, there is no development in which the notion of *limit* does not appear. For ideas about calculus, see:

(1)   W. W. Sawyer, *What Is Calculus About?*, Random House, New York, 1961.

(2)   Morris Kline, *Mathematics: A Cultural Approach*, Addison-Wesley Publishing Co., Reading, Ma., Chaps. 18 and 19, 1962.

(3)   Morris Kline, *Mathematical Thought from Ancient to Modern Times*, Oxford University Press, New York, 1972.

20   The student should be reminded that

$$\lim_{x \to a} f(x) = f(a)$$

only when f is continuous at *a*. That is, one must check for continuity before simple substitution can be used. In this case, the function

$$f(x) = \frac{x^2 - 5x + 6}{x^2 - 2x - 3}$$

is not continuous at $x = 3$ and at $x = -1$. Thus, one cannot use substitution in finding $\lim_{x \to 3} f(x)$ or $\lim_{x \to -1} f(x)$.

    Consider $\lim_{x \to 3} f(x)$. We have said that simple substitution cannot be used, and hence one is forced to use some other means to find out what is happening to $f(x)$ when x is "close" to 3. In this case, for x close to 3 but $x \neq 3$,

$$\frac{x^2 - 5x + 6}{x^2 - 2x + 3} = \frac{(x - 3)(x - 2)}{(x - 3)(x + 1)} = \frac{x - 2}{x + 1} .$$

Hence, $f(x)$ is close to $1/4$.

    Problem   What is $\lim_{x \to -1} f(x)$?

21   The student is correct *if* $m > 0$. For example, to show

$$\lim_{x \to a} (mx + b) = ma + b,$$

suppose $\varepsilon > 0$ is given. If one takes $\delta = \varepsilon/m$, then whenever $0 < |x - a| < \delta$,

$$|(mx + b) - (ma + b)| = m|x - a| < m\delta = m(\varepsilon/m) = \varepsilon.$$

If $m \leqslant 0$, $m = \varepsilon/\delta$ makes no sense since ε, $\delta > 0$.

22   Suppose one would write

$$\lim_{x \to 2} 3x = \frac{1}{2}.$$

In order to show this, one would have to do the following. Given $\varepsilon > 0$, one would have to find a $\delta > 0$ such that $\left|3x - \frac{1}{2}\right| < \varepsilon$ whenever $0 < |x - 2| < \delta$. Now, suppose $\varepsilon < 1$. If one chooses $\delta > 1$, then x = 3 will be in the interval

$$2 - \delta < x < 2 + \delta \quad \text{and} \quad \left|3(3) - \frac{1}{2}\right| = 8\frac{1}{2} > \varepsilon .$$

If one chooses $\delta < 1$, then x = 2 + (δ/2) is in the interval

$$2 - \delta < x < 2 + \delta$$

and $\left|3\left(2 + \frac{\delta}{2}\right) - \frac{1}{2}\right| = \left|5\frac{1}{2} + \frac{3}{2}\delta\right| > 5\frac{1}{2} \not< \varepsilon .$

For additional material, see Answer 14 of this section.

23   The study of limits is preparatory to the study of differential and integral calculus. Once the latter stage is reached one frequently forgets the idea of limit although it is always present.

   A typical example would be to consider an automobile which starts at rest and increases its speed to 60 mph. The speed of the car is obviously not a constant. Suppose one wishes to know the speed of the car two seconds after it starts. If S(t) denotes the distance in miles traveled by the car during t seconds after it starts, then the speed after two seconds is given by

$$\lim_{h \to 0} \frac{S(2 + h) - S(2)}{h} \tag{1}$$

Once a study of the calculus has begun, one simply writes (1) as S'(2).

24   $\lim\limits_{x \to a} f(x) \neq L$ means that for some $\varepsilon > 0$, no matter what $\delta > 0$ one chooses, one can find a value x_0 in the domain of f and in the interval

$$a - \delta < x < a + \delta , \quad x_0 \neq a,$$

such that

$$|f(x) - L| > \varepsilon \quad \text{(See Figures 5.1.6 and 5.1.7.)}$$

FIGURE 5.1.6

FIGURE 5.1.7

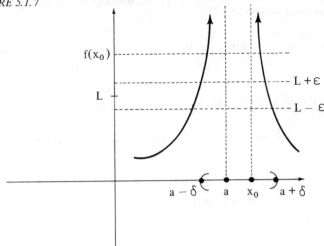

25   It is correct to say that $\lim\limits_{x \to 0} (1/x)$ does not exist. However, instead of writing or saying "does not exist," one frequently uses the symbolism

$$\lim_{x \to 0} \frac{1}{x} = \infty. \tag{1}$$

In other words, the symbols "$= \infty$," which appear in (1), can be translated as "does not exist."

26   To say that a limit (of a function f) does not exist means that there is no *real number* L such that $\lim\limits_{x \to a} f(x) = L$. That is, for any real number L,

$$\lim_{x \to a} f(x) \neq L.$$

From this point, an answer could proceed the same as Answer 25 of this section.

27   Yes, the choice of 1/6 and $\delta \leqslant 1/6$ was arbitrary in the sense that one could have used any number r and $\delta \leqslant 1/r$ for which $(1/3) - r > 0$.

   Problem   Verify the statements made above.

28   In considering $\lim\limits_{x \to a} f(x)$, one is examining the values of f(x) for values of x in the domain of f that are "close" to *a* or approaching *a*, but not equal to *a*. However, if the given function is continuous at x = a, then

$$\lim_{x \to a} f(x) = f(a).$$

That is, one can obtain the limit by simple substitution.

29   No. The student has written

$$(n - 1)! \frac{1}{n} = \left(1 - \frac{1}{n}\right)!$$

Suppose n = 3. The student is then saying that 2!(1/3) = (2/3)! One should ask this student what is meant by (2/3)! Actually,

$$\lim_{n \to \infty} \frac{(n-1)!}{n!} = \lim_{n \to \infty} \frac{1}{n} = 0.$$

(E)   *MAXIMUM AND MINIMUM: APPLICATIONS*

1   The student should not confuse the process of finding an upper bound for

$$\frac{3x^2 + 2x - 5}{7x - 2}$$

with the process of solving an equation such as

$$\frac{3x^2 + 2x - 5}{7x - 2} = 3$$

In the first process, one wishes to find an upper bound u for the numerator and a lower bound l for the denominator. Then we would have

$$\frac{3x^2 + 2x - 5}{7x - 2} \leqslant \frac{u}{l} \quad (u, l > 0)$$

for *every* x in the domain (1, 3). In this example

or $|3x^2 + 2x - 5| \leqslant 3|x|^2 + 2|x| + 5$
      $|3x^2 + 2x - 5| \leqslant 38$

on (1, 3) where x = 3 was used in the computation. That is, 38 is an upper bound for $3x^2 + 2x - 5$ on (1, 3).   However, on (1, 3), $7x - 2 \geqslant 5$ when x = 1 was used in the computation. That is, 5 is a lower bound for $7x - 2$ on (1, 3). Hence

$$\frac{3x^2 + 2x - 5}{7x - 2} \leqslant \frac{38}{5}$$

for every x in the domain (1, 3).

2   Using absolute values is just one standard method of finding a "maximum value" for a function. What one is really finding is an upper bound for the function. That is, if $|f(x)| \leqslant r$ for every x in the domain of f, then r is certainly an upper bound for f; but r need not be a maximum value of f. In the example cited, one might write

$$|3x^2 - 2x + 5| \leqslant 3|x|^2 + 2|x| + 5 \leqslant 3 \cdot 7^2 + 2 \cdot 7 + 5 = 166;$$

i.e., $|3x^2 - 2x + 5| \leqslant 166$

on the interval (2, 7). Thus 166 is an upper bound for the given function on this interval. Observe, however, that for *no* value of x in the given interval is

$$3x^2 - 2x + 5 = 166.$$

The only positive value of x satisfying the latter equation is $7\frac{2}{3}$.

3   The student is assuming that whenever $f'(x) = 0$ a relative maximum or minimum must occur. The example used by the student is a standard one, which is used to show that this need not be the case. If one has a function f defined on R and

$f'(a) = 0$, then x = a is simply a *candidate* for a relative maximum or minimum. The word *candidate* cannot be overemphasized.

    Problem How does one modify the above comments if f is defined on a closed interval or an open interval?

4   Calculus deals with changes and the idea of change is a very natural, and indeed, expected notion. Some typical examples are:

    Physics An object changes it position.
    Biology Changes in blood pressure.
    Economics Changes in prices, costs, demands, and profits.

It is frequently the case that when changes occur, the calculus becomes an important tool in studying those changes. One can find applications to physics in:

    George B. Thomas, Jr., *Calculus and Analytic Geometry*, alt. ed., Addison-Wesley Publishing Co., Reading, Ma., 1972.

For applications to other areas including biology and economics.

    Baxter and Sloyer, *Calculus with Probability*, Addison-Wesley Publishing Co., Reading, Ma., 1973.

5   The student is asking a question that points out a real deficiency in the entire process of mathematical education. Students are usually brainwashed into believing that a *word* problem contains that information and *only* that information which is pertinent to solving a given problem. The problem to which this question refers is an excellent counterexample in which more than enough information is given. A typical solution would involve something similar to Figure 5.1.8.

FIGURE 5.1.8

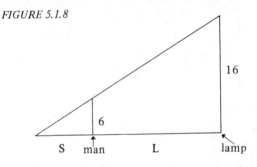

One is given that dL/dt = −5. From similar triangles

$$\frac{6}{S} = \frac{16}{S + L}$$

or   6L = 10S

or $S = \dfrac{3}{5} L$

Hence $\dfrac{dS}{dt} = \dfrac{3}{5} \dfrac{dL}{dt} = \dfrac{3}{5}(-5) = -3.$

That is, the length of his shadow is decreasing at the rate of 3 ft/sec, and this is a constant, which is quite independent of the man's distance from the light.

A5.2   *Elementary Functions and Analysis*

(A)   ASYMPTOTE AND ABSOLUTE VALUE

1   Without further questioning, it is not really clear what the student is asking. The student apparently is suggesting that $.\overline{9}$ does not really equal 1 but only "gets closer and closer to it" as a hyperbola approaches its asymptote. Depending on the student's background, some method should be used to show the student that $.\overline{9} = 1$. (See, for example, Answer 6 in Section A1.2.)

2   The graph of a function f can cross an asymptote. For example, consider

$$f(x) = 2 + \frac{1}{x} - \frac{3}{x^2} .$$

The line $y = 2$ is an asymptote since

$$\lim_{x \to +\infty} f(x) = 2.$$

However, observe that $f(3) = 2$. A graph of $y = f(x)$ is shown in Figure 5.2.1.

FIGURE 5.2.1

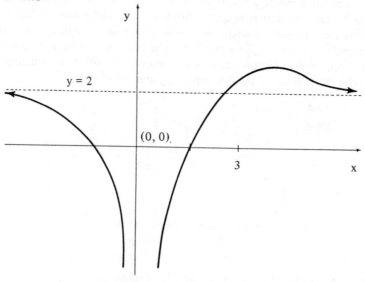

3   A line $x = a$ is a vertical *asymptote* of $y = f(x)$ if

$$\lim_{x \to a^+} f(x) = +\infty,$$

$$\lim_{x \to a^-} f(x) = +\infty,$$

$$\lim_{x \to a^+} f(x) = -\infty, \quad \text{or}$$

$$\lim_{x \to a^-} f(x) = -\infty$$

as illustrated in Figure 5.2.2 on page 261.

FIGURE 5.2.2

(a)

(b)

(c)

(d)

The line y = mx + b is an *asymptote* of y = f(x) if

$$\lim_{x \to \pm\infty} [f(x) - (mx + b)] = 0$$

as illustrated in Figures 5.2.3 and 5.2.4.

FIGURE 5.2.3   FIGURE 5.2.4

4   Yes. The result in this case is that

$$\left|\frac{x+3}{x+1}\right| = \frac{|x+3|}{|x+1|} < \frac{5}{1} = 5 \tag{1}$$

It should be pointed out to the student that the result in (1) must be valid *for every* x such that $0 < x < 2$. When questions of this type arise, the student is frequently confusing (1) with

$$\left|\frac{x+3}{x+1}\right| = 5.$$

In this case, if a solution x were to exist, the same value of x would have to be used in the numerator as in the denominator. Observe that

$$\left|\frac{x+3}{x+1}\right| = 5$$

implies that

$$\frac{x+3}{x+1} = 5 \quad \text{or} \quad \frac{x+3}{x+1} = -5$$

and

$$x = -\frac{1}{2} \quad \text{or} \quad x = -\frac{4}{3}.$$

That is, there is no x, $0 < x < 2$ such that

$$\left|\frac{x+3}{x+1}\right| = 5.$$

The original problem involves finding a bound for

$$\left|\frac{x+3}{x+1}\right|,$$

not solving an equation for a particular value of x. When seeking such a bound, one is free to appropriately use different values of x.

(B)   **AXIOMS AND STRUCTURE**

1   Yes, the student is correct. The element zero acts as both an additive as well as a multiplicative identity. The nonzero elements, being the empty set, vacuously satisfy the property of being a commutative group with respect to multiplication. However, even though the set consisting of zero is a field, it is a trivial field and it is common in books on modern algebra as well as secondary materials to exclude this trivial case by assuming that a multiplicative identity is nonzero.

   Problem Look for secondary materials that include a definition of a field. Is the trivial case excluded?

(C)   **BINOMIAL THEOREM**

1   The student can be told that there is an extension of the binomial theorem where

fractional exponents are used. However, this generalization involves extensive use of the ideas of the calculus, in particular, those involved with power series. Depending on the background of the student, it may be possible to show the student what happens in an extension of the binomial theorem where negative exponents are used. An interesting, but concise, development appears in:

Mosteller, Rourke and Thomas, *Probability with Statistical Applications*, Addison-Wesley Publishing Co., Reading, Ma., 1961, pp. 70-73.

A more extensive development can be obtained from:

James K. Bidwell, "Pascal's Triangle Revisited," *The Mathematics Teacher*, May 1973, pp. 448-52.

(D)   **DETERMINANTS**

1   Determinants really form a class of functions. For example, if we restrict ourselves to 2×2 matrices, then we might consider

$$D_2 \begin{bmatrix} 2 & 1 \\ 3 & 0 \end{bmatrix} = -3$$

$$D_2 \begin{bmatrix} -1 & 3 \\ 2 & 7 \end{bmatrix} = -13$$

etc. Thus D_2 can be considered as a function where the domain is the set of all 2×2 matrices. Similarly, if we restrict ourselves to 3×3 matrices, then we might consider

$$D_3 \begin{bmatrix} 2 & 3 & 1 \\ -1 & 0 & 2 \\ 6 & 1 & -1 \end{bmatrix} = 28$$

$$D_3 \begin{bmatrix} -1 & 2 & 3 \\ 0 & 1 & 1 \\ 2 & 3 & 4 \end{bmatrix} = -3$$

etc. Thus D_3 can be considered as a function where the domain is the set of all 3×3 matrices. In this way, determinants form a class of functions.

$$D_1, D_2, D_3, D_4, \dots$$

2   Yes. Consider the 3×3 determinant given below.

$$\begin{vmatrix} a & a+d & a+2d \\ a+3d & a+4d & a+5d \\ a+6d & a+7d & a+8d \end{vmatrix}$$

Then using properties of determinants, one can add (-1) times row (1) to row (2) and add (-1) times row (2) to row (3) and then get

$$\begin{vmatrix} a & a+d & a+2d \\ 3d & 3d & 3d \\ 3d & 3d & 3d \end{vmatrix}$$

Using the property that if two rows of a determinant are identical, then the value of the determinant is zero, we have the desired result for 3×3 determinants.

Problem 1 Generalize the solution given above for 4 X 4 and, in general, n X n determinants.

Problem 2 Find another proof of the above result.

Problem 3 Does the result in Answer 2 still hold if arithmetic sequence is replaced by geometric sequence; by any sequence, explain?

(E)   ## EQUIVALENCE RELATIONS

1   No, the student is not correct. If the student was correct, then it would follow that any relation $\mathcal{R}$ that is both symmetric and transitive must also be reflexive. However the following example shows that the latter statement is false. Let

$$S = \{a, b, c, d\} \quad \text{and}$$
$$\mathcal{R} = \{(a, a), (c, c), (a, c), (c, a)\},$$

then $\mathcal{R}$ is symmetric and transitive but not reflexive.

The main difficulty here is that in the statement, "If a $\mathcal{R}$ b, then b $\mathcal{R}$ a," how do we know that the hypothesis is valid for all elements a in the set under consideration.

Problem 1 Construct two other examples of relations that are symmetric and transitive but not reflexive.

Problem 2 Show that the following two properties:

(1)   a $\mathcal{R}$ a for each a,
(2)   if a $\mathcal{R}$ b and b $\mathcal{R}$ c, then c $\mathcal{R}$ a,

imply the symmetric and transitive properties.

2   Yes, the student is correct. Besides being an awkward statement, it is incorrect. Consider the following example. Let

$$S = \{a, b, c\} \quad \text{and}$$
$$R = \{(a, b), (b, a), (a, a), (b, b)\}.$$

Thus $(a, b) \in R$ implies that $(a, a) \in R$ and $(b, b) \in R$, but R is still not reflexive in the standard sense.

3   One way of doing this is to go back to the definition of the transitive property and try to clarify what it really means. A definition of the transitive property is as follows.

A binary relation R is said to be transitive if and only if it satisfies the condition that *whenever* $(x, y) \in R$ and $(y, z) \in R$, then $(x, z) \in R$.

The key phrase here is the phrase *whenever* $(x, y) \in R$ and $(y, z) \in R$, then $(x, z) \in R$. Thus this property states what must happen if both ordered pairs, (x, y) and (y, z), are in R and makes *no* statement that if $(x, y) \in R$, then there must be an ordered pair $(y, z) \in R$.

(F)   EXPONENTS

1   For an answer to this question refer to Section A4.4, Answer 1.

2   Although this expression is not ordinarily found in mathematics texts, and even though the notation is not standard, this expression can be defined as given below. A definition that is often used at the high school level is:

> If p denotes an integer, r a positive integer, and b a positive real number, then we define $b^{p/r} = (\sqrt[r]{b})^p$.

One can thus show that $\sqrt[r]{b^p} = (\sqrt[r]{b})^p$. Thus the expression $^-\sqrt[3]{7}$ can be defined either as $(\sqrt[3]{7})^{-1}$ or as $\sqrt[3]{7^{-1}}$ since both expressions are equivalent.

(G)   FUNCTIONS

1   Two functions F and G are the same if and only if they have the same domain and for each x in the domain, F(x) = G(x). Now, when we write

$$F(x) = \frac{x^2 - 9}{x - 3} \, ,$$

the domain is considered to be the set of all real numbers *except* 3. When we write

$$G(x) = x + 3$$

the domain is considered to be the set of all real numbers.
   Since F and G have a *different* domain, F and G are *not* the same function.
   If we *change* F by writing

$$F(x) = \begin{cases} \dfrac{x^2 - 9}{x - 3} \, , & x \neq 3 \\ 6, & x = 3 \end{cases}$$

then F and G have the same domain, and for each x in the domain, F(x) = G(x). Thus, F and G are *now* the same function.

2   No. Consider the function f given by

$$f(x) = \begin{cases} 2x, & x \leqslant 0 \\ 1/x, & x > 0. \end{cases}$$

A graph of f is shown in Figure 5.2.5.

FIGURE 5.2.5

Clearly f is neither strictly increasing nor strictly decreasing. However, f does have an inverse function f^{-1} given by

$$f^{-1}(x) = \begin{cases} \frac{1}{2}x, & x \leqslant 0 \\ 1/x, & x > 0. \end{cases}$$

The converse is true, however, since a strictly increasing or strictly decreasing function is one-to-one and hence must have an inverse. The domain of the inverse will be the image set of the function.

3   Let D_f be the domain of f and D_g be the domain of g. If $D_f \subset D_g$, then one can talk about the function f + g on the domain D_f. Or, if $D_g \subset D_f$, then one can talk about the function f + g on the domain D_g. For example, suppose

$$f(x) = \frac{1}{x}, \quad x > 0$$

and $$g(x) = \frac{1}{x+1}, \quad x > -1$$

Then $D_f = \{x | x > 0\}$ while $D_g = \{x | x > -1\}$. One can talk about f + g on the domain $D_f = \{x | x > 0\}$ and

$$(f + g)(x) = \frac{1}{x} + \frac{1}{x+1}$$

One can talk about f(g(x)) whenever the range (image set) of g is a subset of the domain of f. For example, consider

$$g(x) = x^2, \quad x \in R$$
and $$f(x) = x^3, \quad x \in R$$

Then, the image set of g is R^+ (the set of nonnegative reals), and this is a subset of the domain of f. In particular,

$$f(g(x)) = f(x^2) = (x^2)^3 = x^6, \quad x \in R.$$

However, consider

$$g(x) = x^2, \quad x \in R$$
and $$f(x) = \frac{1}{x-1}, \quad x > 1.$$

In this case the image set of g is *not* a subset of the domain of f. One can, however, consider f(g(x)) for x > 1, in which case,

$$f(g(x)) = f(x^2) = \frac{1}{x^2 - 1}, \quad x > 1.$$

4   Not in general. For example,

$$y = x^2, \quad x \in R$$

gives y as a function of x. However, if one solves for x in terms of y, one obtains

$$x = \pm\sqrt{y}, \quad y \in R^+ \text{ (nonnegative reals)}$$

Hence x is *not* a function of y.

5   There are two "standard" ways of defining a function as in the following.

(1)   Let A and B be sets. By a *function f from A into B*, we mean a rule that assigns to each element of A precisely one element of B. If a ∈ A and the rule f assigns the element b ∈ B to *a*, then we write f(a) = b.

(2)   Let A and B be sets. We say that *f is a function from A into B* if f is a subset of A × B satisfying:

(a)   For each a ∈ A, there is b ∈ B such that (a, b) ∈ f.

(b)   If $(a_1, b) \in f$ and $(a_2, b) \in f$, then $a_1 = a_2$.

If (a, b) ∈ f, then we write f(a) = b.

From a mathematical point of view, Definition 2 is more precise than Definition 1 and does not lead a student to question "What do you mean by a *rule?*". For theoretical purposes, Definition 2 is the better of the two. If one is going to use (2) in the classroom, then there must be a good deal of associated reinforcement including, possibly, an introduction of (1) in addition. Definition 1 is more intuitive and usually requires less reinforcement than (2). There has been a move during the last twenty years to bring Definition 2 into the secondary school classroom and into the (basic mathematics) college classroom. However, the majority of *new* texts designed for such courses and examined by the authors, indicate that Definition 1 predominates.

6   When one writes

$$f(x) = x^2, \quad x \in R,$$

one should really indicate that

$$f(\ ) = (\ )^2 \quad \text{where } (\ ) \in R.$$

The use of the letter x is *immaterial*. For example,

$$f_1(x) = x^2, \quad x \in R \tag{1}$$

$$\text{and} \quad f_2(t) = t^2, \quad t \in R \tag{2}$$

$$\text{and} \quad f_3(u) = u^2, \quad u \in R \tag{3}$$

all indicate the *same* function.

A function is determined by its domain, codomain, and the value assigned to each element of the domain. In the above it should be clear that f_1, f_2 and f_3 determine the *same* function. One could write

$$\{x, f_1(x) | f_1(x) = x^2\} \tag{1}$$

$$\text{and} \quad \{t, f_2(t) | f_2(t) = t^2\} \tag{2}$$

$$\text{and} \quad \{u, f_3(u) | f_3(u) = u^2\} \tag{3}$$

7   As far as we know there is no standard notation for this function. However, it would probably be a good idea for the class to try to invent a suitable notation and then explore what properties this function satisfies. For example, the notation,]x[, might be used and students could be asked to find]3[,]3¼[or]−4[. Would these later symbols have any meaning? That is, what is meant by the smallest integer greater than or equal to 3¼?

Problem 1 Using the suggested symbolism given above or one of your own choosing, investigate what properties the function in Question 7 satisfies: For example, is $]x + y[\ = \ ]x[\ +\ ]y[$, etc.

Problem 2 Is there a notation for the function that is defined as the smallest integer less than or equal to a number? If not, invent a symbolism for this function and investigate its properties. Before you do, however, ask yourself what meaning this function has and if it is a function.

8   In standard usage, there is usually no difference. In specialized areas (normally at the college level or above), however, the word *map* or the phrase *a mapping* is frequently used to designate a single valued *continuous* function. Again, in certain areas, the word *transformation* is used to designate a function from one Euclidean space to another or from one algebraic structure to another, etc. For other uses see:

> W. A. Wickelgren, *How to Solve Problems*, W. H. Freeman and Co., San Francisco, 1974.

9   No. For example, consider the function

$$f(x) = x^2, \quad x \in R$$

so that the domain of f is the set of real numbers. Clearly f is not the zero function. In this case $1/f$ is given by

$$\frac{1}{f(x)} = \frac{1}{x^2}.$$

Thus $f(1/f) = 1$ (the constant function whose value is 1) only for those x such that $x \neq 0$. For any x such that $f(x) = 0$, it is true that

$$f(x)\left(\frac{1}{f(x)}\right) = 1.$$

10   When one writes $f = 0$, one is referring to a function f such that $f(x) = 0$ for *every* x in the domain of f (called the zero function). When one writes $f(x) = 0$, one is normally referrring to an equation (open sentence) that is true for some (possibly no) values of x and false for other values of x.

For example, if $f(x) = x^2 - 5x + 6$, then f is not the zero function. However, $f(x) = 0$ is a true statement for $x = 2$ and $x = 3$, but is a false statement for any other value of x.

11   No. If $f(x) = \cos x$ and $g(x) = \cos \pi x$, then $f + g$ is not periodic. In fact, if f and g are periodic functions with periods p and q, then $f + g$ is not periodic if the ratio p/q is irrational.

Problem 1 Given $f(x) = \cos x$ and $g(x) = \cos \pi x$, show that $f + g$ is not periodic.

Problem 2 Construct an example different from the one given above of two periodic functions whose sum is not periodic. Prove your claim.

Problem 3 If f and g are periodic functions with periods p and q, then $f + g$ is periodic if p/q is a rational number. Prove this.

12   Yes, the student is correct. It is not standard terminology to talk about sets that increase or decrease. However, if there is an *order* on the domain and the range of a function f (as would be the case if both are subsets of the set of real numbers), then one can talk about f as an *increasing function*, provided a ⩽ b implies f(a) ⩽ f(b), and f as a *decreasing function*, provided a ⩽ b implies f(a) ⩾ f(b), where these properties must hold for every a, b in the domain of f.

13   The answer to this question is given by Fourier's Theorem as follows.

      If f is any continuous periodic function of frequency r, then f(x) can be approximated as closely as one desires by a sum of simple harmonic functions of frequencies that are whole number multiples of r.

14   No. For example, $f(x) = x$ and $g(x) = x^3$ have the same domain and range, but f ≠ g.

15   The product f × g or fg is that function that is defined as follows.
      fg: x → f(x) · g(x) where the domain of fg is defined as the intersection of the domains of f and g. That is, if D_f means the domain of the function f and D_g means the domain of the function g, then $D_{fg} = D_f \cap D_g$.

At this point, it should be noted that these two functions, namely, the product of two functions and the composition of two functions, are used in different contexts. The composition of two functions is defined for arbitrary sets under the restrictions given below while the product of two functions is used only when it is meaningful to multiply. The composite function f of g, symbolized by f ∘ g is that function that is defined as follows;

      f ∘ g: x → f[g(x)] where the domain of f of g is all x such that x ∈ Dg and g(x) ∈ Df.

Thus if $f(x) = \cos(x)$ and $g(x) = x^3$, then

      fg: $x → x^3 \cos(x)$

where the domain of fg is the set of real numbers and

      f ∘ g: $x → \cos(x^3)$

where the domain of f ∘ g is again the set of real numbers.

16   If the ordered pair (a, b) ∈ f, then the ordered pair (b, a) ∈ f^{-1}. In order to show that f^{-1} is the reflection of f about the line y = x, it would be sufficient to show that the line y = x is the perpendicular bisector of the line segment between (a, b) and (b, a). Since every point on the line y = x satisfies the condition that the x value equals the y value, then the line y = x intersects the segment containing the points (a, b) and (b, a) in a point with coordinates, say, (x_1, x_1). The slope of the line y = x is 1 while the slope of the line segment containing (a, b) and (b, a) is −1. Also, the distance between (a, b) and (x_1, x_1) is

$$\sqrt{(a - x_1)^2 + (b - x_1)^2}$$

while the distance between (x_1, x_1) and (b, a) is

$$\sqrt{(b - x_1)^2 + (a - x_1)^2};$$

i.e., they are equal. Thus the line y = x is the perpendicular bisector of the segment containing (a, b) and (b, a).

Problem   Explain why it was sufficient to show that the line y = x is the perpendicular bisector of the segment containing (a, b) and (b, a) in order to show that f and f^{-1} are reflections across y = x.

17   If y = f(x) is a function, then x = f(y) is also a function. That is, if y = x^3 is a function, then so is x = y^3 where x is the independent variable in the first case and y is the independent variable in the second case.

However, it might be that the student really does not mean this at all. The student might be asking: If y = f(x) is a function, then suppose that I solve for x; i.e., x = g(y). How do I know if x = g(y) is a function?

In this case there are several different ways to approach the problem. One way is to see if the expression y = f^{-1}(x) satisfies the condition for a function. That is, there is only one y associated with each x. A second way is to graph the expression y = f^{-1}(x) and use the vertical line test. That is, if a vertical line intersects the graph at more than one point, then the graph is not a graph of a function. A third way is to make suitable restrictions on f. That is, if f is one-to-one and onto, then y = f^{-1}(x) will define a function.

18   Yes. A simple example is given by the function f where f(x) = x. The inverse function f^{-1} is also given by f^{-1}(x) = x. Regarded as a function from R onto R, both f and f^{-1} have the same domain and range. Hence we have f = f^{-1}.

A more complicated example is given by the function f where

$$f(x) = \begin{cases} x, & x \leqslant 0 \\ \dfrac{1}{x}, & x > 0 \end{cases}$$

In this case, the inverse function f^{-1} is also given by

$$f^{-1}(x) = \begin{cases} x, & x \leqslant 0 \\ \dfrac{1}{x}, & x > 0. \end{cases}$$

Regarded as a function from R onto R, both f and f^{-1} have the same domain and range. Hence f = f^{-1}.

19   Except in certain cases such as sin (x) and Arcsin (x), one cannot tell whether an expression defines a function or inverse function. In reality it makes little sense to consider these two ideas separately. Normally in mathematics, we work with these notions together since one is defined in terms of the other.   For instance, we would usually see questions such as: "What is the inverse function of ...?" or "Are these two functions inverse functions?"   In fact, even in the special cases cited above, we could say with the suitable restrictions that sin (x) is the function and Arcsin (x) is the inverse function of sin (x) or vice-versa.

20   For an answer to this question, read the following article by Duncan and Litwiller.* The article begins on page 271.

*From *The Mathematics Teacher*, February 1973, pp. 173-74. Reprinted by permission.

TRIGONOMETRIC RATIOS:
Algebraic or Transcendental

By DAVID R. DUNCAN
and BONNIE H. LITWILLER

University of Northern Iowa
Cedar Falls, Iowa

MATHEMATICIANS partition real numbers into two sets: the set of algebraic numbers and the set of transcendental numbers. An algebraic number is defined to be any real number that is a solution of the equation $f(x) = 0$ where $f(x)$ is a polynomial function with integral coefficients. For instance, any rational number $\frac{a}{b}$, where a and b are integers and $b \neq 0$, is algebraic, since $\frac{a}{b}$ is a solution of the polynomial equation $b \cdot x - a = 0$.

A real number that is not algebraic is called transcendental. The proof that a given number is transcendental is usually quite difficult, since the nonexistence of a polynomial equation of the correct form must be proved. However, mathematicians have established the existence of many transcendental numbers, two of them being π and e. In fact, mathematicians have proved that in the sense of infinite cardinality there are more · transcendental numbers than algebraic numbers. From this fact many mathematics students assume that most of the trigonometric ratios represented in a degree-minute-second trigonometric table are transcendental numbers as well as irrational; however, a surprisingly simple argument establishes that any trigonometric function of $r\pi$ where r is any rational number is, if defined, an algebraic number. To aid in our argument we use the following standard theorems from modern algebra.

THEOREM A. *If b is an algebraic number* and $f(x)$ *is a polynomial function with integral coefficients, then $f(b)$ is also an algebraic number.*

THEOREM B. *If b and c are algebraic numbers, then the following numbers are also algebraic:* $b + c$; $b \cdot c$; $b - c$; $\frac{b}{c}$ *if $c \neq 0$;* $\sqrt{b}$ *if b is nonnegative.*

THEOREM C. *If $f(x)$ and $g(x)$ are polynomial functions with integral coefficients, then the following are also polynomial functions with integral coefficients:* $f(x) + g(x)$; $f(x) - g(x)$; $f(x)g(x)$.

In the theorems and proofs that follow we assume that f, g, and h represent polynomial functions with integral coefficients. Our goal is to prove that the six trigonometric functions of $r\pi$, for any rational r, are, if defined, algebraic.

THEOREM 1: *If n is a natural number then $\cos n\theta = f(\cos \theta)$ where f is a polynomial function with integral coefficients.* *Proof (by induction)*

1. By the reflexive property of equality, $\cos \theta = \cos \theta$.

2. Let an integer $k > 1$ be given; for any integer $m \leq k$, assume $\cos m\theta = g(\cos \theta)$ where g is a polynomial function with integral coefficients.

3. Now examine $\cos (k + 1)\, \theta$.

$\text{Cos } (k + 1)\theta = \cos (k\theta + \theta)$

$\qquad = \cos k\theta \cos \theta - \sin k\theta \sin \theta$

$\qquad = g(\cos \theta) \cos \theta$

$\qquad\quad - \tfrac{1}{2}[\cos (k\theta - \theta) - \cos (k\theta + \theta)]$

$\qquad = g(\cos \theta) \cos \theta$

$\qquad\quad - \tfrac{1}{2} \cos (k\theta - \theta) + \tfrac{1}{2} \cos (k\theta + \theta).$

Thus

$\tfrac{1}{2} \cos (k\theta + \theta)$

$\qquad = g(\cos \theta) \cos \theta - \tfrac{1}{2} \cos (k\theta - \theta);$

$\cos (k\theta + \theta)$

$= 2[g(\cos \theta)\cos \theta] - \cos [(k - 1)\theta]$

or

$\cos (k + 1)\theta = 2[g(\cos \theta)\cos \theta] - h(\cos \theta)$. Thus $\cos (k + 1)\theta$ is a polynomial function of $\cos \theta$ by theorem C.

THEOREM 2. *Cos $\dfrac{\pi}{n}$ is algebraic if n is a positive integer.*

Proof. $\cos \pi = \cos \left[n\left(\dfrac{\pi}{n}\right) \right]$, which is of the form $\cos k\theta$ with $k = n$ and $\theta = \dfrac{\pi}{n}$.

Thus $\cos \pi = f\left(\cos \dfrac{\pi}{n}\right)$ where f is a polynomial function with integral coefficients. But $\cos \pi = -1$, so $\cos \dfrac{\pi}{n}$ is a solution of the polynomial equation $f(x) + 1 = 0$; therefore, by definition, $\cos \dfrac{\pi}{n}$ is an algebraic number.

THEOREM 3. *Cos $\dfrac{m\pi}{n}$ is algebraic if m and n are positive integers.*

Proof. $\cos \dfrac{m\pi}{n} = \cos \left[m\left(\dfrac{\pi}{n}\right) \right] = f\left(\cos \dfrac{\pi}{n}\right)$ by theorem 1. By theorem A, $\cos \dfrac{m\pi}{n}$ is algebraic.

THEOREM 4. *Sin $\dfrac{m\pi}{n}$ is algebraic if m and n are positive integers.*

Proof. But $\cos \dfrac{m\pi}{n}$ is algebraic by theorem 3 and by theorem B, $\cos^2 \dfrac{m\pi}{n}$ is algebraic, as is $1 - \cos^2 \dfrac{m\pi}{n}$. Since $\cos^2 \dfrac{m\pi}{n} \leq 1$, then $1 - \cos^2 \dfrac{m\pi}{n} \geq 0$; therefore, $\pm \sqrt{1 - \cos^2 \dfrac{m\pi}{n}} = \sin \dfrac{m\pi}{n}$, which is algebraic by theorem B.

THEOREM 5. *Tan $\dfrac{m\pi}{n}$ is algebraic if m and n are positive integers.*

Proof. Since $\tan \dfrac{m\pi}{n} = \dfrac{\sin \dfrac{m\pi}{n}}{\cos \dfrac{m\pi}{n}}$ and the numerator and denominator of the given fraction are algebraic, by theorem B the quotient is algebraic provided the tangent is defined.

THEOREM 6. *Cot $\dfrac{m\pi}{n}$, sec $\dfrac{m\pi}{n}$, and csc $\dfrac{m\pi}{n}$ are algebraic if m and n are positive integers.*

Proof. Since $\cot \dfrac{m\pi}{n} = \dfrac{1}{\tan \dfrac{m\pi}{n}}$, $\sec \dfrac{m\pi}{n} = \dfrac{1}{\cos \dfrac{m\pi}{n}}$, and $\csc \dfrac{m\pi}{n} = \dfrac{1}{\sin \dfrac{m\pi}{n}}$, by theorem B all of these are algebraic numbers if they are defined.

Since $\cos (-a) = \cos a$ and $\sec (-a) = \sec a$ and since $\cos 0 = \sec 0 = 1$, the above results imply that $\cos r\pi$ and $\sec r\pi$ are, if defined, algebraic for any rational r. Since by theorem B additive inverses of algebraic numbers are algebraic and since $\sin 0 = \tan 0 = 0$, which is algebraic, we conclude as well that $\sin \pi r$, $\tan \pi r$, $\cot \pi r$, and $\csc \pi r$ are, if defined, algebraic for each rational r.

As a special case of the results of this paper, we see that if x, y, and z are nonnegative integers, the sine of x degrees, y minutes, and z seconds is the same as

$$\sin \left(\frac{x\pi}{180} + \frac{y\pi}{180(60)} + \frac{z\pi}{180(3600)}\right),$$

which reduces to

$$\sin \left[\left(\frac{3600x + 60y + z}{180(3600)}\right)\pi \right].$$

By theorem 4, this is algebraic. Similar results follow for the other five trigonometric ratios; the real numbers approximated by the entries in a typical degree-minute-second trigonometry table are thus all algebraic.

21 One reason that the process of finding the zeroes of a function is important is the following. Many problems that do not directly involve zeroes of a function can be changed into problems that do involve such a process. For example, suppose that the temperature T of a certain object, for values of time t over some interval, is given by

$$T = 3t^2 + 6t + 4.$$

One asks whether or not the temperature T is ever equal to 3.16. This is equivalent to asking whether or not the function

$$f(t) = 3t^2 + 6t + .84$$

has a zero for the relevant values of t.

Problem Offer two other examples that illustrate the importance of zeroes of a function.

22 For an answer to this question read:

Haddock and Hight, "Geometric Techniques for Graphing," *The Mathematics Teacher*, January 1966, pp. 2-5.

23 If a, b and c are complex numbers, then in the expression $a^b = c$ it is possible in the complex number system to find the third number if any two are given. The only restriction is that *a* and *c* cannot be zero because of obvious uniqueness problems. Thus it is possible to construct a system of logarithms to any base except 0, but not all such systems would be single-valued functions. (See Section A4.8, Answer 7.) In order to have logarithms that are functions, one must have real numbers to a positive real base other than 1 or 0.*

For example, find x if $\log_{-2} i = x$. By definition, $(-2)^x = i$. Using logarithms

$$x \ln -2 = \ln i$$
$$x = \frac{\ln i}{\ln -2} = \frac{\frac{1}{2}\pi i}{\ln 2 + \pi i} \quad \text{(one answer).}$$

In general, $x = \dfrac{\frac{1}{2}\pi i + 2n\pi i}{\ln 2 + \pi i + 2n\pi i}$.

24 A function, f, is a set of ordered pairs that satisfy certain conditions. That is, no two distinct ordered pairs have the same first component, and every element of the domain must appear as a first coordinate. In most secondary materials, the graph of a function is the set of points on a coordinate system, and each point is located by the components of the ordered pairs of the function. There is a one-to-one correspondence between each point and each ordered pair. Thus one might consider the graph of a function, intuitively, as a *picture* of what the function looks like. However, it should be pointed out that sometimes in advanced mathematics no distinction is made between a set of ordered pairs and the graph of these ordered pairs.

25 Consult Section A3.16, Answers 1 and 2.

*Paraphrased from Howard Fehr, *Secondary Mathematics: A Functional Approach* D.C. Heath & Co., Lexington, Ma., 1951, p. 283.

(H)   *GRAPHS, CURVES AND TANGENTS*

1   Two hyperbolas in which the transverse axis of either one is the conjugate axis of
the other are called conjugate hyperbolas. Thus the pair of hyperbolas given by the
following equations are conjugate hyperbolas.

$$\frac{x^2}{9} - \frac{y^2}{4} = 1 \tag{1}$$

$$\frac{y^2}{4} - \frac{x^2}{9} = 1 \tag{2}$$

The asymptotes for (1) are $y = \pm 2x/3$ while the asymptotes for (2) are $x = \pm 3y/2$; i.e., the asymptotes are the same. It can be shown in general that conjugate
hyperbolas have the same asymptotes.

Problem Show in the general case that conjugate hyperbolas have the same
asymptotes. That is, if

$$\frac{x^2}{a^2} - \frac{y^2}{b^2} = 1 \quad \text{and} \quad \frac{y^2}{b^2} - \frac{x^2}{a^2} = 1$$

are the conjugate hyperbolas, then these hyperbolas have the same asymptotes.

2   The open sentence $ax + by = c$ divides the entire plane into three disjoint sets of
points. These sets of points are:
(1)   The set of points on the line defined by the open sentence $ax + by = c$.
(2)   The set of points in the half-plane defined by the open sentence $ax + by < c$.
(3)   The set of points in the half-plane defined by the open sentence $ax + by > c$.
If one is graphing the set of points that satisfy the open sentence $ax + by < c$, then
one knows that the set of points must be one of the regions depicted above. Thus
if one point whose coordinates satisfy the given open sentence, namely, $ax + by < c$,
can be found, then one knows that this point must be included in the required
region. For a more complete discussion of this problem see:

       Clifford W. Sloyer, *Algebra and Its Applications: A Problem Solving Approach*,
       Addison-Wesley Publishing Co., Reading, Ma., 1970.

3   No, it is not. The restriction is usually made that $a \neq 0$ in the equation $y = ax^2$
when discussing a family of parabolas. If $a = 0$, then one gets the x-axis, which is
a straight line.

4   The student is solving $r = 2 + 4 \sin \theta$ and $r = 2$ simultaneously. The points $A(2, 0)$
and $B(2, \pi)$ are obtained. However, solving such equations simultaneously assumes
that the same value of θ is being used for each equation. In this case the point
$C(0, 2)$, in rectangular coordinates, is obtained with $r = 2$ when

$$\theta = \frac{\pi}{2} \pm 2\pi k, \quad k = 0, 1, 2, \dots$$

while the same point is obtained with $r = 2 + 4 \sin \theta$ when

$$\theta = -\frac{\pi}{2} \pm 2\pi h, \quad h = 0, 1, 2, \dots$$

Hence the point C will *not* be obtained by solving the given equations simultaneously. At this stage, the students should be told to graph such equations in order to discover such points.

5   Not in general. This student is correct if one considers very special classes of curves such as circles or ellipses. However, observe that the tangent to the curve $y = x^3$ at the point $(-1, -1)$ intersects the curve at $(-1, -1)$ *and* at $(2, 8)$ as shown in Figure 5.2.6.

FIGURE 5.2.6

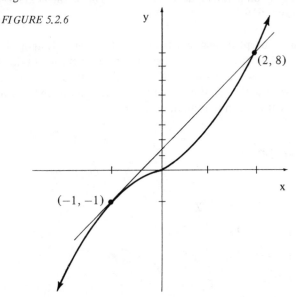

6   No, there is no definite value of n such that x^n becomes the y-axis. However, one might be in a situation where a student says that the y-axis can be viewed as the limiting position of these graphs as n increases without bound. However, this is incorrect since, for any n that is a positive integer, the graph of $y = x^n$ passes through the point $(1, 1)$.

   Problem   On the same axis, construct a few curves for various values of n in the equation $y = x^n$ where n is a positive even integer. Is there a line which might be called the limiting position for these graphs?

(I)   *MATHEMATICAL INDUCTION*

1   Yes. There are two ways in which negative integers can get involved with mathematical induction. For example, suppose P(n) is a statement concerned with a negative integer n. Then, (1) if P(−1) is true and (2) if P(k) is true, then P(k − 1) is true where k is an arbitrary negative integer. The conclusion can be made that P(n) is true for every negative integer n. One can see this by considering P(−n) as a statement concerned with a positive integer n and using the "standard" form of induction.

   For the second case, one should observe that the "starting point" for the standard form of induction is n = 1. However, this need not be the case. Suppose P(n) is a statement concerning positive integers n where n ⩾ 17. Suppose P(17) is true and for any integer k, k ⩾ 17, if P(k) is true, then P(k + 1) is true. The conclusion is that $P(n)$ is true for all integers $n \geqslant 17$. The number 17 used in this example could be replaced by *any* integer including a negative integer. For example, suppose $P(n)$ is a statement concerning integers n where $n \geqslant -30$. Suppose $P(-30)$ is true. If k is an integer such that $k \geqslant -30$ and if $P(k)$ is true, then $P(k + 1)$ is true. The conclusion is that $P(n)$ is true for all integers $n \geqslant -30$. For additional information on mathematical induction, read:

> C. Brumfiel, "A Note on Mathematical Induction," *The Mathematics Teacher.* November 1974, pp. 616-18.

2   No, there is not. The concept of mathematical induction depends upon showing that if a proposition $P(x)$ is true for $x = k$, then it is true for the *next* value $k + 1$. However, the set of real numbers is *not well ordered* and thus there is no *next* value. It is precisely because the set of natural numbers is well ordered that mathematical induction can be used with that number system.

(J)   **SYSTEMS OF NUMBERS**

1   Consider a table of the form:

		Δy	$\Delta^2 y$
x_1	y_1	$y_2 - y_1$	$y_3 - 2y_2 + y_1$
x_2	y_2	$y_3 - y_2$	$y_4 - 2y_3 + y_2$
x_3	y_3	$y_4 - y_3$	$\vdots$
x_4	y_4	$\vdots$	
$\vdots$			

where $x_{i+1} = x_i + 1$, $i = 1, 2, 3, 4, \ldots$

Suppose the points (x_1, y_1), (x_2, y_2) and (x_3, y_3) do not lie on a straight line and that there is a unique quadratic $y = ax^2 + bx + c$ on which these three points lie. Suppose that the second differences are constant. We shall show that (x_4, y_4) also satisfies this quadratic and hence any following "data point" will also. Our assumptions yield

$$y_4 - 2y_3 + y_2 = y_3 - 2y_2 + y_1$$

or
$$
\begin{aligned}
y_4 &= 3y_3 - 3y_2 + y_1 \\
&= 3[a(x_1 + 2)^2 + b(x_1 + 2) + c] \\
&\quad -3[a(x_1 + 1)^2 + b(x_1 + 1) + c] \\
&\quad + [ax_1{}^2 + bx_1 + c] \\
&= ax_1{}^2 + [6a + b]x_1 + [9a + 3b + c].
\end{aligned}
$$

However,
$$
\begin{aligned}
ax_4{}^2 + bx_4 + c &= a[x_3 + 1]^2 + b[x_3 + 1] + c \\
&= a[x_1 + 3]^2 + b[x_1 + 3] + c \\
&= ax_1{}^2 + [6a + b]x_1 + [9a + 3b + c].
\end{aligned}
$$

That is,

$$y_4 = ax_4{}^2 + bx_4 + c,$$

which is what we wished to show.

Problem 1 Does the above process work if $x_2 - x_1 = a_1$, $x_3 - x_2 = a_2$, etc. where a_1, a_2, ..., a_n are greater than zero?

Problem 2 Show that if the data points (x, y) come from a quadratic, then the second differences must be constant.

Problem 3 Show that if the data points (x, y) come from a cubic, then the third differences are constant.

2   One easy way of proving this statement is to use an indirect proof as follows. Suppose that there is a largest integer; then call it n. Look at n + 1. Since n and 1 are integers, then by the closure property of integers, n + 1 is an integer. Also n + 1 is larger than n because $(n + 1) - n = 1 > 0$. However, this fact contradicts our statement that n was the largest integer. Therefore, our conclusion that there is a largest integer is false.

3   No. These two sets of numbers can be placed in one-to-one correspondence and thus they are equivalent sets. That is, they contain the same number of elements. The following example will show how a one-to-one correspondence can be set up between the set of all positive rational numbers and the natural numbers. Imagine that fractional representations of the positive rational numbers are placed in a square array and a path is traced as given:

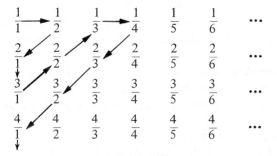

Every symbol in the above array will be crossed just once. If a new symbol a_n is assigned to each symbol in the array as the path is traced (i.e., a_1 to $\frac{1}{1}$, a_2 to $\frac{1}{2}$, a_3 to $\frac{2}{1}$, etc.). then the sequence a_1, a_2, ..., a_n contains one symbol for each of the symbols in the given array. However, there are repetitions for $\frac{1}{1}, \frac{2}{2}, \frac{3}{3}$, etc. If we delete these repetitions so that each positive rational number has just one symbol a_i associated with it, then a new sequence b_1, b_2, b_3, ..., b_n results with no repetitions. If we now make the correspondence that each rational number b_n corresponds to the natural number n, then we have a one-to-one correspondence between the set of positive rational numbers and the set of natural numbers.

Problem 1 Set up a one-to-one correspondence between all rational numbers and the natural numbers.

Problem 2 Set up a one-to-one correspondence between all rational numbers and the integers.

4   The opinion of the authors is that the *real numbers*, which include the rational and irrational numbers, probably received their name because it was thought that these were the only numbers needed to solve real life problems. When numbers such as $\sqrt{-1}$ were first introduced, most people resisted them and said that they were figments of someone's imagination, i.e., imaginary.

We have been unable to really document through our references the reason why the name *real* numbers is used; thus the above is only our "educated" guess, which seems plausible.

5   An algebraic number is a number, real or complex, that satisfies a polynomial equation of the form

$$a_n x^n + a_{n-1} x^{n-1} + \cdots + a_1 x + a_0 = 0,$$

where a_i is an integer. A number that is not algebraic is called *transcendental*.

It can be shown that every rational number is algebraic since every rational number represented by p/q, $q \neq 0$, satisfies the polynomial equation $qx - p = 0$. Thus all transcendentals are irrational. For more information on the topic, consult:

(1)   *Historical Topics for the Mathematics Classroom* (Thirty-First Yearbook), N.C.T.M., Reston, Va., 1969, Capsules 26 and 45.

(2)   L. L. Pennese, "Elementary Proof that e is Irrational," *Selected Papers on Calculus*, ed. Tom A. Apostol, Dickenson Publishing Co., Belmont, Ca., 1969, p. 383.

(3)   Robert Breusch, "A Proof of the Irrationality of π," *Selected Papers on Calculus*, ed. Tom A. Apostol, Dickenson Publishing Co., Belmont, Ca., 1969, p. 386.

(4)   Howard Fehr, *Secondary Mathematics: A Functional Approach for Teachers*, D. C. Heath and Co., Lexington, Ma., 1951, pp. 148-53.

(5)   Gary Masser, "A Transcendental Machine," *The Mathematics Teacher*, May 1973, pp. 407-8.

(6)   Morris Kline, *Mathematical Thought from Ancient to Modern Times*, Oxford University Press, New York, 1972, Chaps. 25 and 41.

Problem Are all irrational numbers transcendental?

6   The number *e* is a transcendental number (see Answer 5 of this section) that is defined as follows:

$$\lim_{n \to \infty} (1 + \frac{1}{n})^n = e \cong 2.71828\ldots$$

The number *e* arises in many useful applications in mathematics such as:

(1)   The term *natural* comes into play because of the way natural logarithms appear in various applications such as laws of growth and decay.

(2)   Continuously compounded interest.

(3)   The cooling of a body.

(4) Radioactivity.

(5) Statistical distributions such as the normal curve.

(6) Catenary curves such as $y = \dfrac{a}{2} (e^{x/a} + e^{-x/a})$

(7) Hyperbolic functions such as $\cosh u = \dfrac{e^u + e^{-u}}{2}$ or $\sinh u = \dfrac{e^u - e^{-u}}{2}$,

which are important in applied and pure mathematics.

The foregoing only represent a small sample of the many ways that e enters into the applications of mathematics. Thus this number is important in our everyday life. For more information regarding e, consult the references given in Answer 5 above and also the following references.

(1) Howard Fehr, *Secondary Mathematics: A Functional Approach for Teachers*, D. C. Heath and Co., Lexington, Ma., 1951, Chap. 8.

(2) J. L. Cosledge, "The Number e," *Selected Papers on Calculus*, ed. Tom A. Apostol, Dickenson Publishing Co., Belmont Ca., 1969, pp. 8-20.

(3) Edna Kramer, *The Nature and Growth of Modern Mathematics*, Hawthorn Books, New York, 1970.

(4) Oliver Bernard, "The Key of e," *The Mathematics Teacher*, January 1972, pp. 5-8.

(5) Meyer Jerison, "Natural Bases of Logarithms," *The Mathematics Teacher*, April 1963, pp. 228-33.

7 For an answer to this question read the following article by May and Tropp.*

Some Algebraic Equations
DO NOT HAVE EXACTLY *N* ROOTS

By **KENNETH O. MAY**

University of Toronto
Toronto, Ontario

and **HENRY S. TROPP**

Smithsonian Institution
Washington, D.C.

THE following dialogue ought to take place one of these days.

Well-Trained Teacher: As you all know, a linear equation has one root, a quadratic equation has two, and in general an algebraic equation of the nth degree with complex coefficients has exactly n complex roots.

Typical Insolent Student: I know that a linear equation always has just one root, but we've solved quadratic equations that turned out to have just one root.

WTT: Can you give an example?

TIS: Sure. $x^2 = 0$ has just one root, zero.

WTT: That's not just one root. That's a double root, a multiple root, so there are really two coincident roots.

TIS: That's not a double root; it's double talk. [After the applause and groans have subsided, he continues.] As far as I can see, the truth set of the equation $x^2 = 0$ has only one member. If we are allowed to say that it really has two

*From *The Mathematics Teacher*, February 1973, pp. 179-82. Reprinted by permission.

coincident members, then we can state some pretty strange theorems. For example, I claim that every wheeled vehicle has exactly 100 wheels. The usual automobile has four repeated wheels, a bicycle has two wheels each repeated 50 times, and a unicycle has a 100-fold wheel.

WTT (silently): Sometimes I wish those teachers in the lower grades wouldn't teach so much of the new math. [To the class] What do you think about this?

(There is much discussion pro and con. Finally one student says: "What's the difference? Say it any way you like as long as we know what's going on.")

WTT: Yes, the most important thing is to know what's going on, but it's also important to express ideas accurately in order to avoid misunderstanding. We try to be very careful about this in mathematics. So let's begin by seeing what we know. In the first place, the fundamental theorem of algebra says that an algebraic equation with complex coefficients has at least one complex root.

TIS: When an equation had only one root, you were ready to say that it had two coincident roots. How do I know that this fundamental theorem doesn't really mean that when an equation has no roots we'll just say it has a nonexistent root and hence at least one root? Can you prove this theorem for us?

WTT: I can't give you a proof, because all proofs are based on ideas that are not familiar to you yet. You should meet a proof in a good first university course in modern algebra or in a course in functions of a complex variable. But I can assure you that it is true and that it involves no double-talk. It really means that for every algebraic equation there is a complex number that satisfies it.

TIS: OK, I'll go along. Every equation has at least one root.

WTT: Also, I think you know that there are equations of degree n with exactly n roots. For example, if we multiply together n different linear factors, like $x - r$, then there will be a root corresponding to each factor. But can an equation of degree n have more than n roots?

(After some discussion, the factor theorem is used to show that if an equation has more than n roots, its left member must be a product of more than n linear factors and hence cannot be of the nth degree.)

TIS: So an equation can't have more than n roots. But as far as I can see an equation of the nth degree can have any number of roots from 1 to n.

WTT: Can you prove this?

TIS: Sure. Just write down as many linear factors as you want. Then raise one of them to a power to make it come out.

WTT (writing on the board): For example, if we want an equation of degree 5 with 3 roots, we write

$$(x - 1)(x - 2)(x - 3)^3 = 0.$$

Everybody write down an equation of degree 6 with the four roots a, b, c, d. (The students write busily, and then the teacher asks for and gets a variety of solutions, depending on the exponents assigned.)

WTT: It looks as though we have a theorem:

THEOREM. *Every algebraic equation of degree n with complex coefficients has at least one and at most n roots. Moreover, for any m between 1 and n inclusive, there is an equation of degree n with exactly m roots.*

WTT (continuing): Do you think it is true? [No objection.] Do you like it better than the statement that every equation has exactly n roots?

TIS: I like it better because it's true, and the other theorem is false, even though it is simpler.

WTT: I have to agree. Nevertheless, you'll find it stated in practically every textbook that there are exactly n roots. Why do you suppose this happens?

(In the discussion it comes out that the fundamental theorem and the factor theorem show that every polynomial can be expressed as a product of linear factors, some of which may be "repeated," i.e., raised to powers greater than one. One student suggests the theorem that every polynomial has exactly n linear factors. This gets shot down immediately by the objections raised to the similar theorem for roots and also by the additional comment that every polynomial has infinitely many linear factors of the form $ax + b$.)

WTT: I think we have another theorem:

THEOREM. *Every polynomial of degree n can be expressed as the product of the coefficient of the leading term times factors of the form $(x - r)^s$, where the sum of the exponents equals n.*

TIS: I still don't see why they talk about exactly n roots.

WTT: When a factor $x - r$ has the power s in the factorization of the polynomial, we call r a root of multiplicity s, or we say that r is an s-tuple root. For example, we say that a root of multiplicity 2 is a double root. The multiplicity appears in solving the equation. When r is found and $x - r$ is divided out, r is found again, and so on. Multiplicity is also reflected in the graph of the polynomial. To help you investigate this I'll give you some polynomials to graph for tomorrow. [Puts some on board with multiple zeros.] Do you think we could modify the statement that every equation has exactly n roots so that it would be true?

(After some discussion there emerges the following theorem.)

THEOREM. *Every algebraic equation of nth degree with complex coefficients has exactly n complex roots if each repeated root is counted according to its multiplicity.*

TIS: I still like better the theorem without any multiple talk.

WTT: I'm going to try to find out why the theorem is usually stated in a way that is wrong when understood literally.

(*WTT* consults the historian of mathematics in the nearest university and reports later.)

WTT: Before all complex numbers were recognized as numbers, algebraic equations did not always have roots within the number system. Not all linear equations with integral coefficients have integral solutions. Not all quadratic equations with rational coefficients have any rational or even real roots. As mathematicians became more familiar with expressions involving the square root of negative one, sentiment began to build up toward recognizing them as numbers, and a few began to guess that if this were done every algebraic equation would "in general" have a number of roots equal to its degree. The first to state this was Albert Girard in his *L'invention nouvelle en l'algèbre* (Leyden, 1629). In fact, his formulation is practically the one that provoked this discussion: "All equations of algebra receive as many solutions as the denomination of the highest term shows, . . ." Girard, in this work, is the first to accept complex numbers on a par with other numbers. This is significant, because it was only in the seventeenth century that negative numbers became sufficiently acceptable to be allowed to assume equal status with positive numbers as valid roots. Girard apparently did not speed up the acceptance of complex roots. Descartes and Newton, for example, said that an algebraic equation could have at most as many roots as its degree. While today this sounds more accurate, their statement was based on indecision as to what kinds of numbers were acceptable as roots. This indecision continued until the beginning of the nineteenth century. The prevailing attitude is clear, for example, in *Principles of Algebra* (London, 1796), where William Frend (later DeMorgan's father-in-law) states that it is absurd to say that even a quadratic equation has two roots. He rejects both negative and complex numbers as possible roots.

The first to approach the problem with precision and clarity was Gauss, in his doctoral dissertation of 1797 (published in Helmstedt, 1799). In Section I of this work Gauss says:

The equation of the mth degree cannot have more than m roots; at the same time it is evident that the equation of the mth degree can have fewer roots, even though X (the equation referred to) is resolvable into m simple (linear) factors: for if some of these factors are identical, the multitude of the many ways of satisfying the equation is less than m.

The laxity with which the theorem is usually stated is a common characteristic of most of the nineteenth- and twentieth-century textbooks. The attitude of "Well, you really know what I mean" is clearly illustrated in George Chrystal's classic *Algebra* (London, 1926, 5th ed., pt. 1, pp. 241–50). On page 241, beneath the title "Fundamental Proposition in the Theory of Equations," Chrystal states:

If $f(z) \equiv A_0 + A_1z + A_2z^2 + \cdots + A_nz^n$ be an integral function of z of the nth degree, whose coefficients $A_0, A_1, \cdots, A_n$ are given complex numbers, or in particular, real numbers, where, of course, $A_n \neq 0$, then $f(z)$ can always be expressed as the product of n factors, each of the first degree, say $z - z_1, z - z_2, \cdots . z - z_n$, $z_1, z_2, \cdots, z_n$ being in general complex numbers.

At this point Chrystal goes on to prove the fundamental theorem, namely, "One value of z, in general a complex number, can always be found which causes $f(z)$ to vanish." He then returns to the original question and concludes with a more careful statement:

If $f(z)$ be an integral function of z of the nth degree, there are n values of z for which $f(z)$ vanishes. These values may be real or complex numbers, and may not be all unequal.

There are many examples of the kind of accuracy *TIS* desires. E. V. Huntington, in his essay "Fundamental Propositions of Algebra" (*Monographs on Topics of Modern Mathematics*, J. W. A. Young, ed., Longmans, Green & Co., 1911, Dover reprint 1955, pp. 151–210) states the theorem as follows (pp. 181–82):

Every algebraic equation of the nth degree:

$$p_0x^n + p_1x^{n-1} + \cdots + p_{n-1}x + p_n = 0$$

can be written as the product of n linear factors:

$$p_0(x - x_1)(x - x_2) \cdots (x - x_n) = 0,$$

where the points $x_1, x_2, \cdots, x_n$ are fixed points depending on the coefficients $p_0, p_1, \cdots, p_n$; each of these points $x_1, x_2, \cdots, x_n$ is a root of the equation, and there are no other roots.

He then adds the footnote:

Since the n factors $x - x_1, x - x_2, \cdots, x - x_n$ are not necessarily distinct from one another, the number of distinct roots may be any number from 1 to n, inclusive; for the sake of brevity, however, it is customary and convenient to say that *an equation of the nth degree always has n roots,* understanding that in special cases some or all of these roots may be coincident.

Nevertheless, the theorem in its original form persists in many textbooks. Why has it continued to be stated in this old way? Perhaps it's because textbook writers seldom read the masters but copy from others whose knowledge is equally second-hand. Also, traditions are slow to change, and often an old inaccurate way of stating things is kept and given a new interpretation. Gauss seems to have recognized this trait. In the section of his doctoral dissertation cited above, he continues:

However, for the sake of brevity the geometers have preferred to say the equation in this case has m roots, only that some turn out to be equal to one another: which is permissible.

TIS: I still prefer to say it like it is. Since we're so fussy about accuracy, why not apply it here?

WTT: Does the class agree?

(They did, and so do we.)

8   Probably the best way to respond is to show the student several examples where part of the set satisfies a certain property but the entire set does not satisfy the property. The main problem here is to get the student to understand this point. Several examples are:

(1)   Let A = {a, b, c, d} and let R be the relation defined as

R = {(a, a), (b, b), (c, c), (d, d), (a, b)} .

Then

$$R' = \{(a, a), (b, b), (c, c), (d, d)\}$$

is symmetric even through R is not.

(2)   In the set of positive real numbers, the property $(a \cdot b)^m = a^m \cdot b^m$ where m is a rational number is a valid property. However, in the set of all real numbers this property is no longer valid; for example,

$$((-1) \cdot (-1))^{1/2} \neq (-1)^{1/2} \cdot (-1)^{1/2}$$

This question brings up an important point. When a mathematician generalizes or extends a given situation, one of the main tasks is to show what properties of the particular situation hold in the generalized situation.

(K)   ### SERIES, SEQUENCES AND PROGRESSIONS

1   This student is having some difficulty with logic. The statement of the theorem that this student wants to use can be written more informally as "nondecreasing and bounded above implies convergence" and "nonincreasing and bounded below implies convergence." The student is saying, however, that "neither nondecreasing nor nonincreasing but bounded implies divergence." This does not follow logically and the example given is an excellent one for showing the student that his statement is, in general, false.

2   A series is convergent when the sequence of partial sums is convergent, not necessarily when the associated sequence is convergent. The examples given offer good illustrations of series that are divergent but where the associated sequences are convergent.

3   A basic theorem in the study of infinite series is:

If

$$\sum_{n=1}^{\infty} a_n \text{ converges then } \lim_{n \to \infty} a_n = 0.$$

Hence it is impossible to find a series that converges in which the associated sequence is a divergent sequence.

4   One should consider the difference between

$$1, \frac{1}{2}, \frac{1}{4}, \frac{1}{8}, \frac{1}{16}, \cdots \tag{1}$$

and

$$1 + \frac{1}{2} + \frac{1}{4} + \frac{1}{8} + \frac{1}{16} + \cdots \tag{2}$$

In (1) there is simply a "list" of numbers. No operation between the numbers is indicated. In (2), there is an "infinite" addition indicated. This is similar to writing

$$2, 3, 4 \tag{3}$$

and writing

$$2 + 3 + 4 .$$ (4)

There is quite a different meaning attached to (4) than to (3).

Returning to (2), a good student in elementary arithmetic would probably not tackle the problem of finding such a sum because the student is aware that one would never finish. However, a poorer student might make an attempt and just start plodding ahead. If one follows the stages of this student's work, one obtains:

$$S_1 = 1$$

$$S_2 = 1 + \frac{1}{2} = 1.5$$

$$S_3 = 1 + \frac{1}{2} + \frac{1}{4} = 1.75$$

$$S_4 = 1 + \frac{1}{2} + \frac{1}{4} + \frac{1}{8} = 1.875$$

$$S_5 = 1 + \frac{1}{2} + \frac{1}{4} + \frac{1}{8} + \frac{1}{16} = 1.9375$$

$$S_6 = 1 + \frac{1}{2} + \frac{1}{4} + \frac{1}{8} + \frac{1}{16} + \frac{1}{32} = 1.96875$$

$$S_7 = 1 + \frac{1}{2} + \cdots\cdots\cdots + \frac{1}{64} = 1.984375$$

$$S_8 = 1 + \frac{1}{2} + \cdots\cdots\cdots + \frac{1}{128} = 1.9921875$$

etc.

It should be clear what is happening and can be shown analytically. Namely, the sequence of the sums (partial sums) obtained is getting closer and closer to 2. It is for this reason that one writes

$$2 = 1 + \frac{1}{2} + \frac{1}{4} + \frac{1}{8} + \cdots$$

5   When one writes $\sum\limits_{i=1}^{5} 2i$ as

$$2 + 4 + 6 + 8 + 10,$$ (1)

the expression in (1) is referred to as a *series*. Now when one writes

$$\sum_{i=1}^{5} 2i = 30,$$

one is *identifying* the series with its sum. From a formal point of view, a teacher should distinguish between a *series* and the *sum* of the series. In practice, however, the indicated identification is usually made so that the formal distinction is of academic importance only.

6   The sequence $s(n) = 1 + (-1)^n$, or more formally 0, 2, 0, 2, 0, 2, ..., is a divergent sequence that is bounded.

7   No. One normally speaks of a sequence *diverging*, such as

2, 4, 6, 8, ...   or   1, −1, 1, −1, 1, −1, ...

or a series *diverging*, such as

$$1 + \frac{1}{2} + \frac{1}{3} + \frac{1}{4} + \frac{1}{5} + \frac{1}{6} + \cdots$$

In calculus courses, one frequently speaks of an integral as *diverging* such as

$$\int_1^\infty \frac{1}{x} \, dx.$$

The symbol ∞ is used in many ways. For example, one frequently writes

$$\lim_{x \to \infty} x^2 = \infty \quad \text{or} \quad \lim_{x \to 0} \frac{1}{x} = \infty.$$

Now, in connection with diverging series, it is normal to say that the series

$$1 + 2 + 3 + \cdots$$

diverges to ∞. However, the series

$$1 + (-1) + 1 + (-1) + 1 + (-1) + \cdots$$

is a series that is diverging. But in this case, one would *not* say that the series " diverges to ∞," but rather that the series "diverges by oscillation."

(L)   *SYNTHETIC DIVISION*

1   First, one need not divide the entire problem by 2 and then multiply the remainder by 2 in order to get the correct solution (see Answer 2 of this section). However, one way of dividing by $2x - 3$ is to divide the dividend by 2 and then multiply the remainder by 2. Why this works is as follows. Let $Q(x)$ and R be the quotient and remainder dividing $P(x)$ by $2x - 3$. Thus one obtains

$$P(x) = Q(x) \cdot (2x - 3) + R. \tag{1}$$

Factoring out a 2, (1) can be written as

$$P(x) = 2 \cdot Q(x) \cdot \left(x - \frac{3}{2}\right) + R. \tag{2}$$

Dividing both sides of (2) by 2, one gets

$$\frac{P(x)}{2} = Q(x)\left(x - \frac{3}{2}\right) + \frac{R}{2} \tag{3}$$

Now from (1), $Q(x)$ is the quotient one is looking for and R is the remainder. Thus by (3), one way of getting these expressions is to divide the dividend, $P(x)$, by 2, using synthetic division. That is, divide by $\frac{3}{2}$ and then multiply the remainder by 2, using the synthetic division process.

   Problem   Generalize the following: when dividing by $ax - b$, what does one do and prove why it works.

2   To divide by a linear polynomial of the form $ax - b$, use $x - \frac{b}{a}$ as the divisor and then divide the quotient obtained, but not the remainder, by a.

Problem Show that the procedure given in Answer 2 leads to a correct solution.

3   For an answer to this question read the following article by Margaret Hutchinson.*

USING SYNTHETIC DIVISION BY QUADRATICS to Find Rational Roots

By MARGARET WISCAMB HUTCHINSON

University of Saint Thomas
Houston, Texas

THERE is a well-known algorithm, synthetic division, for dividing a polynomial $P(x)$ by a linear factor, $x - a$. By the remainder theorem, the remainder obtained is equal to $P(a)$. If $P(a) = 0$, a is a root of the equation $P(x) = 0$. Thus synthetic division can be used to find roots of the equation $P(x) = 0$. In particular, it is used to test for rational roots.

This paper presents a simple algorithm, similar to synthetic division, for dividing a polynomial by a quadratic polynomial. In an interesting application of this algorithm, we can significantly reduce the labor involved in searching for the rational roots of a polynomial equation.

A Modified Synthetic Division Algorithm

Suppose we want to divide a polynomial by a quadratic of the form $x^2 + bx + c$. This can be done quickly and painlessly by a simple modification of the synthetic division algorithm.

Consider the usual long division method:

$$
\begin{array}{r}
2x^3 - x^2 - x + 3 \\
x^2 + 2x + 1 \overline{\smash{\big)}\ 2x^5 + 3x^4 - x^3 \qquad\quad + x - 1} \\
\underline{2x^5 + 4x^4 + 2x^3} \\
-x^4 - 3x^3 \\
\underline{-x^4 - 2x^3 - x^2} \\
-x^3 + x^2 + x \\
\underline{-x^3 - 2x^2 - x} \\
3x^2 + 2x - 1 \\
\underline{3x^2 + 6x + 3} \\
-4x - 4
\end{array}
$$

Our first step in simplifying this process will be to rewrite it, using only the coefficients. If we agree to write the polynomials in order of descending powers of x, inserting zeros when any terms are missing, then our example will look like this:

(1)					2	−1	−1	3	
(2)	1	2	1	⟌ 2	3	−1	0	1	−1
(3)				2	4	2			
(4)					−1	−3	0		
(5)					−1	−2	−1		
(6)						−1	1	1	
(7)						−1	−2	−1	
(8)							3	2	−1
(9)							3	6	3
(10)								−4	−4

Since the first number in lines 3, 5, 7. and 9 needlessly duplicates the number directly above it, we lose nothing by leaving these numbers out. Moreover, the numbers in the quotient are repeated in lines 2, 4, 6, and 8. Thus there is really no need to write the quotient above. Our example is now reduced to the following:

1	2	1	⟌ 2	3	−1	0	1	−1
				4	2			
				−1	−3	0		
					−2	−1		
					−1	1	1	
						−2	−1	
						3	2	−1
							6	3
							−4	−4

Since the divisor will always be of the form $x^2 + bx + c$, the first 1 is unnecessary.

*From *The Mathematics Teacher*, April 1971, pp. 349-52. Reprinted by permission.

Now, since adding signed numbers is simpler than subtracting them, it would be an improvement if we could add at each step instead of subtracting. If we change the sign of the 2 and the 1 in the divisor, we can do this. Now we have:

```
(2)   -2  -1 | 2   3  -1   0   1  -1
(3)                -4  -2
(4)                -1  (-3)  0
(5)                    +2  +1
(6)                    -1  (1)   1
(7)                         2   1
(8)                         3  (2)  -1
(9)                            -6  -3
(10)                           -4  -4
```

Now note that the circled numbers are merely an intermediate sum and are not really useful. To find the -1 in line 6, for instance, we add -1, -2, and $+2$. Since the last number in lines 4, 6, and 8 duplicates numbers in the dividend, they can also be left out.

Eliminating these numbers enables us to write the entire example on just four lines.

The algorithm now takes the form shown below, where the first four numbers in line 4 are the coefficients of the quotient, $2x^3 - x^2 - x + 3$, and the last two numbers are the coefficients of the remainder, $-4x - 4$.

```
(1)  2   3  -1   0   1  -1 | -2  -1
(2)         -2   1   1  -3
(3)      -4   2   2  -6
(4)  2  -1  -1   3  -4  -4
```

Our simplified algorithm is now clear.

1. Write the coefficients of the polynomial in order in row 1, inserting zeros for missing terms. Draw a line between rows 3 and 4.

2. If the divisor is $x^2 + bx + c$, write the numbers $-b$ and $-c$ at one side in row 1.

3. Write the first coefficient in the first column of row 4.

4. Multiply this number by $-b$ and by $-c$, placing the two products above the line in the next two columns, respectively.

5. Add the next column, and write the sum in row 4.

6. Repeat steps 4 and 5 until a number is written above the line in the last column.

7. Add the last two columns, writing the sums in row 4.

This is shown in figure 1 in diagrammatic form. The solid lines indicate addition; the dashed lines, multiplication by -2; and the dotted lines, multiplication by -1.

To divide by a quadratic $ax^2 + bx + c$ whose leading coefficient is *not* 1, we can use

$$x^2 + \frac{b}{a}x + \frac{c}{a}$$

as the divisor and when finished divide the quotient obtained (*not* the remainder) by a.

It is not hard to see why this gives the correct quotient. Dividing $P(x)$ by $ax^2 + bx + c$ gives a quotient $Q(x)$ and a remainder $mx + n$, and

$$P(x) = Q(x)(ax^2 + bx + c) + (mx + n).$$

Fig. 1

Factoring out a, we get

$$P(x) = aQ(x)\left(x^2 + \frac{b}{a}x + \frac{c}{a}\right) + (mx + n),$$

which says that the quotient $Q^*(x)$ obtained on dividing by

$$x^2 + \frac{b}{a}x + \frac{c}{a}$$

is equal to $aQ(x)$, where $Q(x)$ is the quotient we want. Hence to get $Q(x)$ we divide $Q^*(x)$ by a.

For example, to divide

$$3x^5 - x^4 + 6x^3 - 2x + 4 \quad\text{by}\quad 2x^2 - 4x + 8,$$

we divide instead by $x^2 - 2x + 4$:

$$
\begin{array}{rrrrrr|r}
3 & -1 & 6 & 0 & -2 & 4 & \underline{2 \quad -4} \\
  & -12 & -20 & -16 & 48 & & \\
  & 6 & 10 & 8 & -24 & & \\
\hline
3 & 5 & 4 & -12 & -42 & 52 & \\
\end{array}
$$

The correct quotient for the divisor $2x^2 - 4x + 8$ is then

$$\frac{3}{2}x^3 + \frac{5}{2}x^2 + 2x - 6,$$

and the remainder is $-42x + 52$.

How about a synthetic division algorithm for dividing by a cubic? I leave this to the ingenuity of the reader.

An Application

Now let us see how we can use the algorithm developed in the previous section to reduce the labor involved in finding the rational roots of a polynomial equation.

First, we shall need the following theorem:

THEOREM. *Let $P(x)$ be a polynomial whose degree is greater than or equal to two. Let $mx + n$ be the remainder obtained on dividing $P(x)$ by $x^2 + bx + c$, and let r be a root of $x^2 + bx + c = 0$. Then r is a root of $P(x) = 0$ if and only if $r = -(n/m)$.*

Proof. By definition of $Q(x)$,

$$P(x) = Q(x)(x^2 + bx + c) + (mx + n),$$

where $Q(x)$ is the quotient polynomial.

Suppose $r = -(n/m)$. Then

$$P(r) = Q(r)(0) + 0 = 0,$$

and r is a root of $P(x) = 0$.

Conversely, suppose $P(r) = 0$. Then

$$0 = P(r) = Q(r)(0) + mr + n.$$

Thus

$$mr + n = 0,$$

and

$$r = -\frac{n}{m}.$$

Suppose we want to find the rational roots of a polynomial equation $P(x) = 0$. The rational root theorem tells us that the rational roots, if any, are to be found in a certain finite set of rational numbers, $\pm a, \pm b, \ldots, \pm k$.[1] Normally we would proceed to test these possible roots one at a time. Using the synthetic division algorithm and the theorem just proved, we can cut the labor in half and test these numbers *two at a time*.

Consider, for example, the pair $\pm a$. Form the quadratic

$$(x - a)(x + a) = x^2 - a^2$$

and divide this into $P(x)$. The algorithm in this case is particularly simple, since one of the coefficients is zero. We will get

$$P(x) = Q(x)(x^2 - a^2) + (mx + n).$$

By the theorem, if either $+a$ or $-a$ is equal to $-(n/m)$, then this number is a root of $P(x) = 0$. Conversely, if *neither* $+a$ nor $-a$ is equal to $-(n/m)$, then neither is a root and we have eliminated two possible roots in one operation. Of course, if the remainder is zero ($m = n = 0$), then $x^2 - a^2$ is a factor of $P(x)$ and *both* $+a$ and $-a$ are roots.

Consider, as an example, the equation

$$3x^3 - 2x^2 - 5x - 6 = 0.$$

According to the rational root theorem,

---

1. Rational root theorem: Let

$$P(x) = a_n x^n + a_{n-1}x^{n-1} + \cdots + a_1 x + a_0$$

be a polynomial with integral coefficients. Then, if $P(x) = 0$ has a rational root p/q, p divides a_0 and q divides a_n.

possible rational roots are $\pm 1,\ \pm 2,\ \pm 3,$ $\pm 6,\ \pm \frac{1}{3},\ \pm \frac{2}{3}.$

To test the pair ± 1, we divide by $x^2 - 1$.

we conclude that neither number is a root. Next we test the pair ± 2 by dividing by $x^2 - 4$.

$$
\begin{array}{rrrr|rr}
3 & -2 & -5 & -6 & 0 & 1 \\
 & 3 & -2 & & & \\
\hline
 & 0 & 0 & & & \\
\hline
3 & -2 & -2 & -8 & &
\end{array}
$$

Here $m = -2, n = -8, -(n/m) = -4.$ Since this is equal to neither $+1$ nor $-1,$

$$
\begin{array}{rrrr|rr}
3 & -2 & -5 & -6 & 0 & 4 \\
 & & 12 & -8 & & \\
\hline
 & & 0 & 0 & & \\
\hline
3 & -2 & 7 & -14 & &
\end{array}
$$

Here $m = 7, n = -14, -(n/m) = +2,$ hence $+2$ is a root.

(M)   VECTORS

1   The question is somewhat misleading. One can define the vector product of two vectors in a two-dimensional plane. However, the resulting product is generally a vector that is perpendicular to the two given vectors and hence has no meaning unless there is a third dimension available. For example, one *could* consider the vectors $v_1 = (3, 2, 0)$ and $v_2 = (1, 3, 0)$ as vectors in a two-dimensional space. However, the vector product $v_1 \times v_2 = (0, 0, 7)$ is a vector that requires a third dimension.

2   Yes, there is. A definition follows.

> If R and S are nonzero vectors, then the vector product or cross-product or outer product of R and S, denoted by R × S, is the vector T that is perpendicular to the plane determined by R and S. The magnitude of R × S is $|R||S|$ sin θ where θ is the measure of the angle between R and S.

This vector product has useful applications in physics, such as finding the moment of force about a point, and in mathematics itself, such as finding equations for planes perpendicular to two intersecting planes.

3   It is not correct. Consider the following example. Let $v = (1, 3), u = (3, -1)$ and $w = (-3, 1)$. Then $u \cdot v = w \cdot v = 0$, but $u \neq w$. There is no cancellation property for inner product.

> **Problem 1**   Is there a cancellation property for the union of sets, the intersection of sets, the symmetric difference of sets, for example,
>
> $A \triangle B = [A \cup B] - [A \cap B]$?
>
> **Problem 2**   What kind of structure or properties must a system of elements have in order for a cancellation property to be valid?

4   Yes, it is. The linear equation ax + by = c can be derived by taking the following inner product.

> $(x, y) \cdot (a, b) = c$

In addition, the vector (a, b) is perpendicular to the line given by the equation

> ax + by = c.

Problem   Prove the statement given in Answer 4.

5   There are several different ways that the study of vectors can follow. The way that is presented in the question is a geometric and coordinate free approach. That is, the approach used is not committed to a single coordinate system. In this approach vectors are thought of as being represented by arrows. An arrow is an ordered pair (P_1, P_2) of points. Two arrows are then said to be equivalent if and only if they have the same magnitude and direction. Thus one can prove the statement:

> If the points, P_1, P_2, P_3 and P_4 have coordinates $(x_1, y_1), (x_2, y_2), (x_3, y_3)$ and (x_4, y_4), respectively, then the arrows (P_1, P_2) and (P_3, P_4) are equivalent if and only if
>
> $$x_2 - x_1 = x_4 - x_3$$
> $$y_2 - y_1 = y_4 - y_3. \tag{1}$$

Then one makes the statement that a vector is an equivalence class of arrows, that is, the set of all arrows equivalent to a given arrow.

   Problem Prove (1) as given in Answer 5.

A5.3   *Probability*

1   The main difference is that permutations take order into account while combinations do not. For example, suppose that we want to find how many different arrangements can be made of 5 different books on a shelf when 8 different books are available. Since order is considered in this situation, the answer would be

$$_8P_5 = 8 \cdot 7 \cdot 6 \cdot 5 \cdot 4 = 6720.$$

Now suppose that we want to find out how many different selections (order is not important) of five books we can make to put on the shelf if 8 different books are available. Since order is not considered in this case, the answer would be

$$_8C_5 = \frac{8!}{3! \, 5!} = \frac{8 \cdot 7 \cdot 6}{6} = 56.$$

2   The source of difficulty in this problem has to do with the language that is commonly used to explain them. It is common in textbooks on probability to explain independent events as two or more events that have nothing to do with each other. This phrase then suggests that independent events do not overlap and, therefore, are mutually exclusive.

   In order to clear up this situation, precise mathematical notation is needed. Thus, the following definition is given.

   Two events X and Y are independent if and only if $P(X \cap Y) = P(X) \cdot P(Y)$.

Using this definition, one can show that if X and Y are independent events with nonzero probabilities, then $X \cap Y \neq \emptyset$. However, by definition, A and B are mutually exclusive events if and only if $A \cap B = \emptyset$. Thus one can make the following statement.

   If A and B are independent events with nonzero probabilities, then A and B are not mutually exclusive. Or equivalently, if A and B are mutually exclusive events with nonzero probabilities, then A and B cannot be independent.

Problem Prove that if X and Y are independent events with nonzero probabilities, then $X \cap Y \neq \emptyset$.

3   The student is incorrect. The important thing is to get the student to describe the sample space being used. It appears that this student is considering the sample space of eighteen elements shown in Table 5.3.1.

TABLE 5.3.1

First Throw	Second Throw	Third Throw
1	1	1
2	2	2
3	3	3
4	4	4
5	5	5
6	6	6

From these, the student is going to select three elements. This however, leads to an error since the student could select 2, 3 and 4 from the second column. A suitable sample space is to consider the set of all ordered triples where the coordinates are taken, with replacement, from the set $\{1, 2, 3, 4, 5, 6\}$. There are $6 \cdot 6 \cdot 6 = 216$ such triples. In order to find the total number with different entries, observe that there are six choices for the first coordinate, then five for the second, and finally four for the third. Hence there are $6 \cdot 5 \cdot 4 = 120$ ordered triples with different entires. The desired probability is thus $120/216 = .556$ (to three decimal places). Observe that the student's answer is .558 to three decimal places.

4   The student who said ¼ is correct. One way of seeing this is to set up the following sample space. If B stands for boy and G stands for girl, then a sample space would be $\{BG, BB, GB, GG\}$. In a probability section at this level, it would be assumed that each entry above is just as likely as any other and thus has probability of ¼ of occurring.

Problem 1 How did one student come up with the probability of 1/3? How would you help this student?

Problem 2 Find another way of answering Question 4.

5   For an answer to this question, read the following article by Frederick Mosteller.* Article begins on page 292.

*From *The Mathematics Teacher*, May 1962, pp. 332-35. Reprinted by permission.

Understanding the birthday problem

FREDERICK MOSTELLER, *Harvard University,*
Cambridge, Massachusetts.
Comparing and contrasting the birthday problem
and the birthmate problem

THE CLASSICAL BIRTHDAY PROBLEM: What is the least number of people required to assure that the probability that two or more of them have the same birthday exceeds $\frac{1}{2}$?

The usual simplifications are that February 29 is ignored as a possible birthday and that the other 365 days are regarded as equally likely birth dates. The problem and its answer, 23 people, are well known.[1]

Many are surprised at this answer, because 23 is a small fraction of 365. Instead, they feel that a number such as $183 (\approx \frac{1}{2}(365))$ would be more reasonable. Their surprise stems in part from a misunderstanding of the statement of the problem. The problem they have in mind is *the birthmate problem:* What is the least number of people I should question to make the probability that I find one or more birthmates exceed $\frac{1}{2}$?

This problem is known, but not well known,[1] and its answer is 253. The answer exceeds 183 because the sampling of birth dates is done with replacement, rather than without. If we sampled from 365 people with *different* birth dates, 183 is the correct answer to the birthmate problem.

In comparing the birthday and birthmate problems, one observes that for r people in the birthday problem, there are $r(r-1)/2$ pairs or *opportunities* for like birthdays; whereas, if n people are questioned in the birthmate problem, there are only n opportunities for me to find one or more birthmates. It seems reasonable that, approximately, if one is to have about the same probability of success (finding matching birthdays) in the two problems, then $n \approx r(r-1)/2$, because then one has the same number of opportunities in both problems. For example, if the probability of success is to be at least $\frac{1}{2}$, then if $r = 23$, $n = 23(22)/2 = 253$, which happens to be exactly the correct answer. On the other hand, the probabilities of success in the two problems are not identical. For the birthday problem with $r = 23$, $P(\text{success}) \approx 0.5073$, for the birthmate problem $n = 253$, $P(\text{success}) \approx 0.5005$.

Let us generalize the two problems. Let N be the number of equally likely days (or categories), r the number of individuals in the birthday problem, and n the number examined in the birthmate problem. Then for the birthday problem it is easiest to compute first the probability of no like birthdays, and to obtain the probability of at least one like pair by taking the complement.

There are N ways for the first person to have a birthday, $N-1$ for the next so that he does not match the first, $N-2$ for the third so that he matches neither of the first two, and so on down to $N-r+1$ for the rth person. Then applying the multiplication principle, the number of ways for no matching birthdays is

[1] W. Feller, *Probability Theory and Its Applications* (New York: John Wiley & Sons, Inc., 1950 [first edition]), I, pp. 31–32, 112.

$$N(N-1) \cdots (N-r+1), \quad r \text{ factors.} \quad (1)$$

To get the probability of no matching birthdays we also need the number of ways r people can have birthdays without restriction. There are N ways for each person. Then the multiplication principle says that the total number of different ways the birthdays can be assigned to r people is

$$N^r. \qquad (2)$$

The number in expression (1) divided by that in expression (2) is the probability of no like birthdays, because we assume that all birthdays and therefore all ways of assigning birthdays are equally likely. The complement of this ratio is the probability, P_R, of at least one pair of like birthdays in the classical birthday problem.

Thus

$P_R = P$(at least 1 matching pair)

$$= 1 - N(N-1) \cdots (N-r+1)/N^r. \qquad (3)$$

For the birthmate problem the probability that a randomly chosen person does not have my birthday is $(N-1)/N = 1 - 1/N$. If n people are independently drawn, then by the multiplication principle for independent events, the probability that none has my birthday is $(1 - 1/N)^n$. The probability, P_S, that at least one has my birthday is

$$P_S = 1 - \left(1 - \frac{1}{N}\right)^n. \qquad (4)$$

We wish to equate P_S to P_R approximately, and thus approximate n as a function of r. If $P_R = P_S$, then

$$\frac{N(N-1)(N-2) \cdots (N-r+1)}{N^r}$$

$$= \left(1 - \frac{1}{N}\right)^n. \qquad (5)$$

Dividing each factor on the left by an N from N^r, we get

$$1\left(1 - \frac{1}{N}\right)\left(1 - \frac{2}{N}\right) \cdots \left(1 - \frac{r-1}{N}\right)$$

$$= \left(1 - \frac{1}{N}\right)^n. \qquad (6)$$

If we multiply out the left-hand side of Equation (6) to terms of order $1/N$, and expand the right-hand side to two terms we get

$$1 - \left(\frac{1}{N} + \frac{2}{N} + \cdots + \frac{r-1}{N}\right) + \cdots$$

$$= 1 - \frac{n}{N} + \cdots. \qquad (7)$$

Eliminating the 1's shows that, approximately, we want

$$n = 1 + 2 + \cdots + (r-1) = (r-1)r/2. \qquad (8)$$

This result justifies in part our earlier statement about the need for equivalent opportunities.

The approach just given is satisfactory if n is small compared to N, but the following logarithmic approach leads to a more refined relation between n and r if $P_R \approx P_S$.

Recall that if $|x| < 1$, then

$$\log_e (1-x) = -\left(x + \frac{x^2}{2} + \frac{x^3}{3} + \cdots\right). \qquad (9)$$

Taking the logarithm of both sides of Equation (6) gives us

$$\log\left(1 - \frac{1}{N}\right) + \log\left(1 - \frac{2}{N}\right) + \cdots$$

$$+ \log\left(1 - \frac{r-1}{N}\right) = n \log\left(1 - \frac{1}{N}\right). \qquad (10)$$

We use Equation (9) to expand each logarithm in Equation (10) to get (after multiplying both sides of the equation by -1) Equation (11). Each line on the left side of Equation (11) corresponds to one logarithmic expansion in the left of Equation (10).

$$\left.\begin{array}{l} \dfrac{1}{N}+\dfrac{1}{2N^2}+\dfrac{1}{3N^3}+\cdots \\[2mm] +\dfrac{2}{N}+\dfrac{2^2}{2N^2}+\dfrac{2^3}{3N^3}+\cdots \\[2mm] +\dfrac{3}{N}+\dfrac{3^2}{2N^2}+\dfrac{3^3}{3N^3}+\cdots \\[2mm] +\cdots \\[2mm] +\dfrac{r-1}{N}+\dfrac{(r-1)^2}{2N^2}+\dfrac{(r-1)^3}{3N^3}+\cdots \end{array}\right\} =n\left(\dfrac{1}{N}+\dfrac{1}{2N^2}+\dfrac{1}{3N^3}+\cdots\right). \tag{11}$$

Now we sum the left side of Equation (11) column by column, using the usual formulas for the sum of the integers, the sum of the squares of the integers and so on to get

$$\frac{r(r-1)}{2N}+\frac{r(r-1)(2r-1)}{6(2N^2)}+\frac{r^2(r-1)^2}{4(3N^3)}+\cdots$$

$$=n\left(\frac{1}{N}+\frac{1}{2N^2}+\frac{1}{3N^3}+\cdots\right). \tag{12}$$

To get a refined estimate of n in terms of r, we divide both sides of Equation (12) by

$$\frac{1}{N}+\frac{1}{2N^2}+\frac{1}{3N^3}+\cdots,$$

and by ordinary but arduous long division we find

Thus factoring $r(r-1)/2$ out of the quotient gives

$$n\approx\frac{r(r-1)}{2}\left[1+\frac{r-2}{3N}+\frac{r(r-2)}{6N^2}\right]. \tag{13}$$

It is amusing to note that the coefficient of $1/N$ is the number of triple birthdays, but I have not found an intuitive rationale for this.

Thus for $N=365$, $r=23$, to equate probabilities for the two problems, $n\approx258$. And for these numbers $P_R\approx0.5073$ and $P_S\approx0.5073$.

In the Table for the Birthday Problems, we give in column 1 a target probability. Column 2 gives for the birthmate problem the smallest value of n that provides a probability of success larger than the tar-

$$\frac{\dfrac{r(r-1)}{2}+\dfrac{r(r-1)(r-2)}{6N}+\dfrac{r^2(r-1)(r-2)}{12N^2}+\cdots}{\left.\dfrac{1}{N}+\dfrac{1}{2N^2}+\dfrac{1}{3N^3}+\cdots\right)\dfrac{r(r-1)}{2N}+\dfrac{r(r-1)(2r-1)}{12N^2}+\dfrac{r^2(r-1)^2}{12N^3}+\cdots}$$

$$\frac{r(r-1)}{2N}+\frac{r(r-1)}{4N^2}+\frac{r(r-1)}{6N^3}+\cdots$$

$$\frac{r(r-1)(r-2)}{6N^2}+\frac{(r+1)r(r-1)(r-2)}{12N^3}+\cdots$$

$$\frac{r(r-1)(r-2)}{6N^2}+\frac{r(r-1)(r-2)}{12N^3}+\cdots$$

$$\frac{r^2(r-1)(r-2)}{12N^3}+\cdots$$

$$\frac{r^2(r-1)(r-2)}{12N^3}+\cdots$$

$$+\cdots$$

TABLE FOR THE BIRTHDAY PROBLEMS: $=N365$

(1) TARGET P	(2) n	(3) P_S	(4) r	(5) P_R	(6) n_1	(7) P_1	(8) n^*	(9) n_{13}
.01	4	.01091	4	.01636	6	.01633	6	6
.05	19	.05079	7	.05623	21	.05598	21	21
.10	39	.10147	10	.11695	45	.11614	45	45
.20	82	.20146	14	.22310	91	.22093	92	92
.30	131	.30190	17	.31501	136	.31141	138	138
.40	187	.40132	20	.41144	190	.40623	193	193
.50	253	.50048	23	.50730	253	.50048	258	258
.60	334	.60001	27	.62686	351	.61824	359	359
.70	439	.70013	30	.70632	435	.69682	447	447
.80	587	.80020	35	.81438	595	.80454	614	614
.90	840	.90019	41	.90315	820	.89456	851	851
.95	1092	.95001	47	.95477	1081	.94848	1128	1128
.99	1679	.99001	57	.99012	1596	.98746	1683	1682

get probability. Column 3 gives the corresponding probability of success, P_S. Column 4 gives the smallest value of r that produces a probability of success for the birthday problem greater than the target probability shown in column 1. The actual probability of success, P_R, is shown in column 5. The 6th and 7th columns show $n_1 = r(r-1)/2$, for the r given in column 4, together with the probability of success, P_1, in the birthmate problem, with n_1

people. Column 8 gives n^*, the value of n for the birthmate problem that makes the probability of success in the birthmate problem nearest to the probability of success, P_R, in the birthday problem. Column 9 gives n_{13}, the value of n obtained from the approximation of Equation (13). Over the range of target probabilities considered in the table, n, n_1, n^*, and n_{13} are rather close. Also the probabilities P_R and P_1 are close, though $P_R > P_1$.

6   The student is correct. Consider the following example. A lot of ten items contains eight perfect and two defective items. If a sample of three items is taken, what is the probability P that the sample will contain precisely one defective item. Now, a standard method would be to consider the sample as unordered and to use combinations as in

$$P = \frac{\binom{2}{1}\binom{8}{2}}{\binom{10}{3}} = \frac{7}{15} \ .$$

In one considers order in the sample and uses permutations, one obtains

$$P = \frac{3(2 \cdot 8 \cdot 7)}{10 \cdot 9 \cdot 8} = \frac{7}{15} \ .$$

Problem Offer two other examples that will illustrate to the student that in many problems one can use either combinations or permutations.

7   One reason for the definition is as follows. Since

n! = n · (n − 1)!

then when n = 1, we get

1! = 1 · 0!

Since we would like to have this latter statement be valid, it seems reasonable that we should define 0! to be equal to 1.

Problem Find another reason why it is reasonable to define 0! to be 1.

8   See Answer 5 of this section.

9   Suppose that the objects are letters, say r A's and (n − r) B's. In order to get a permutation of these letters, one can think of filling n slots, r of them with A and n − r with B. Once the r slots for A are selected, one has *no* choice but to put a B in those that remain. There are

$$\binom{n}{r} \quad \text{or} \quad {}_nC_r$$

ways of selecting the r slots for A. Hence the number of permutations of these letters must also be

$$\binom{n}{r} \text{ or } {}_nC_r.$$

A5.4   *Trigonometry*

1   In some texts there is no difference; the terms are used interchangeably. However, in some texts there is a difference. In deriving an identity, one has to discover or find the identity while in verifying an identity, the identity is given.

For example, one might be given a problem such as "Derive an identity that expresses sin ((π/3) + x) in terms of sin x or cos x or both." In this case, one has to find or discover an intended identity. In a problem such as "Verify that $\cos^2 (x) = 1 − \sin^2 (x)$," one is given the identity and proceeds from this point.

2   Although the method used is often given in trigonometry books, if nothing more is said then logically speaking it is incomplete and thus incorrect. What the student has proved is the following. If

$$\frac{1}{\cos \theta} - \cos \theta = \tan \theta \cdot \sin \theta \quad \text{for} \quad \theta \neq \frac{\pi}{2} + k\pi,$$

then

$$1 - \cos^2 \theta = \sin^2 \theta .$$

That is, the student has assumed that the expression, which he is trying to derive, is true. He is really trying to show the converse of the statement given above. Thus if the student makes some kind of statement at the end that one must now reverse the given steps for the proof, then he would be correct.

It should be pointed out that one should not discourage the student from doing what he has done in this problem since this is a valid problem solving technique (working backwards using an analytic method). However, if left in this form it is not complete and is incorrect. One simply cannot assume that the hypothesis of a conditional is true simply because the conclusion is a true statement. In fact, using a truth table, one can see that the hypothesis could be either true or false.

The following "proof" might help in seeing that even though the conclusion of a conditional is true that the hypothesis could be false. If this method was valid, then one can prove that π is any real number as follows:

$$\pi = 5 \Rightarrow \pi + 2 = 5 + 2$$
$$\Rightarrow \frac{\pi + 2}{7} = \frac{5 + 2}{7}$$
$$\Rightarrow 0\left(\frac{\pi + 2}{7}\right) = 0\left(\frac{5 + 2}{7}\right)$$
$$\Rightarrow 0 = 0.$$

Since $0 = 0$ is a known identity, then $\pi = 5$. The fallacy here is that one cannot proceed backwards to prove that if $0 = 0$, then $\pi = 5$.

3 See Answer 2 of this section.

4 No, one cannot. One can only conclude that the replacement set for the identity is the subset of R of values for which the expressions in the identity are defined. That is, one must exclude from R those values for which any expression in the identity is not defined. For example, in the identity given, one must exclude those values x of R for which $\csc^2 x = 0$.

5 See Answer 2 of this section.

6 See Answer 2 of this section.

7 One way of showing the student that he is incorrect is to have the student substitute values in his expression to see if he gets correct results. Thus let $x_2 = \pi/2$ and $x_1 = 0$. Then

$$\cos\left(\frac{\pi}{2} - 0\right) = \cos\frac{\pi}{2} - \cos 0$$
$$\cos\frac{\pi}{2} = \cos\frac{\pi}{2} - \cos 0$$
$$0 = 0 - 1$$
$$0 = -1,$$

which is not correct. After substituting a few more values the student should be convinced that his formula is not correct. It should be pointed out to the student that $\{(x, y)|y = \cos x\}$ is a function; if one replaces cos by the symbol f for a function, then what the student is trying to say is that $f(x_1 - x_2) = f(x_1) - f(x_2)$.

However, not all functions have this particular property, and, in particular, the cosine and sine functions do not have this property.

Problem Find a "fairly simple" function f, which could be used to show a student that it is not always the case that $f(x_1 - x_2) = f(x_1) - f(x_2)$.

8 Consider Figure 5.4.1. In this diagram, $OD = \sec \theta$. Thus, if the segment $\overline{OD}$ is extended to a line through O, then there is a line which intersects the circle in two distinct points, that is, a secant line. See Figure 5.4.1 on page 298.

Problem Can the tangent be similarly interpreted?

FIGURE 5.4.1

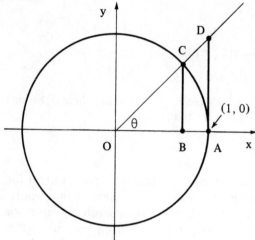

9   The correct answer should be

log K = log ½ + log a + log b + log sin C.

In the answer given in the problem, the student is finding K if K = (a · b sin C)$^{1/2}$, which is not correct.

10   The student made a mistake in the second line, i.e.,

$$y = \frac{1}{\sin} \, x = \frac{x}{\sin} \, .$$

One might ask the student what the expression "sin" in the above stands for. Does it represent a function or does it represent an element in the range of the sine function? The teacher can then show the student that whichever choice the student makes will then lead to some result inconsistent with what he has already done.

Problem 1   Suppose that the student says that "sin" refers to a function. How would you show the student that this choice leads to a result inconsistent with what he has previously done.

Problem 2   Answer the question given in Problem 1 if the student says that "sin" refers to an element in the range.

11   The tangent function defined by $\{(x, y)|y = \tan x\}$ is not defined when x = 90°. Therefore, x = 90° is not a solution of the expression tan x cos x = 1. One might reinforce this by showing the student that when x = 90°, then cos x = 0. This indicates that, in the expression $\frac{\sin x}{\cos x} \cdot \cos x$, the student is dividing by zero. The student made a mistake by not restricting the values of x in the domain to those values for which the expressions in tan x cos x = 1 are defined.

12   Suppose that it was true that sin^{-1} (x) = (1/sin x). We know that sin (sin^{-1} x) = x since sin and sin^{-1} are inverse relations. If sin^{-1} (x) = (1/sin x), then

$$\sin \, (\sin^{-1} \, x) = \sin\left(\frac{1}{\sin x}\right),$$

which is not always equal to x. For example let $x = \pi/6$, then

$$\sin\left(\frac{1}{\sin(\pi/6)}\right) = \sin 2, \text{ which is not equal to } \frac{\pi}{6}.$$

The symbol "$\sin^{-1} x$" for the inverse sine relation, although conventional, is misleading because of the confusion that it may create as illustrated in this question. Since we are dealing here with a conventional notation used with a number of relations, the student should be aware of the difference between a property of numbers and the use of such notation.

13   See Section A3.3, Answer 2 and Section A5.4, Answer 8.

14   Yes, $y = A\cos(bx + c_1) + B\sin(bx + c_2)$ can be written either in terms of a cosine function or a sine function or as $y = 0$. Let

$$y = A\cos(bx + c_1) + B(\sin bx + c_2). \tag{1}$$

Then using appropriate addition formulas, one gets

$$y = A(\cos bx \cos c_1 - \sin bx \sin c_1)$$
$$+ B(\sin bx \cos c_2 + \sin c_2 \cos bx)$$

or $$y = \cos bx \,(A\cos c_1 + B\sin c_2)$$
$$+ \sin bx \,(B\cos c_2 - A\sin c_1) \tag{2}$$

Let $X = A\cos c_1 + B\sin c_2$ and $Y = B\cos c_2 - A\sin c_1$.

then (2) becomes

$$y = X\cos bx + Y\sin bx \tag{3}$$

Consider

$$X^2 + Y^2 = A^2 + B^2 + 2AB\sin(c_2 - c_1).$$

If $A^2 + B^2 + 2AB\sin(c_2 - c_1) = 0$,

then $X^2 + Y^2 = 0$, which implies that $X = Y = 0$. That is $y = 0$ in (1). If

$$A^2 + B^2 + 2AB\sin(c_2 - c_1) \neq 0.$$

then $X^2 + Y^2 \neq 0$ and (3) can be written as

$$y = \sqrt{X^2 + Y^2}\left(\frac{X}{\sqrt{X^2 + Y^2}}\cos bx + \frac{Y}{\sqrt{X^2 + Y^2}}\sin bx\right) \tag{4}$$

Since

$$\left(\frac{X}{\sqrt{X^2 + Y^2}}\right)^2 + \left(\frac{Y}{\sqrt{X^2 + Y^2}}\right)^2 = 1,$$

then the point

$$\left(\frac{X}{\sqrt{X^2 + Y^2}}, \frac{Y}{\sqrt{X^2 + Y^2}}\right)$$

is on the unit circle. Thus

$$\frac{X}{\sqrt{X^2 + Y^2}} = \cos c_3 \quad \text{and} \quad \frac{Y}{\sqrt{X^2 + Y^2}} = \sin c_3 \,.$$

If we let $Z = \sqrt{X^2 + Y^2}$, then (4) becomes

$$y = Z (\cos c_3 \cos bx + \sin c_3 \sin bx)$$

$$y = Z \cos (bx - c_3). \tag{5}$$

Problem Can you write the equation

$$y = A \cos (bx + c_1) + B \sin (bx + c_2)$$

in terms of a sine function?

15   The student is quite right. The correct way of doing this should be as follows.

$$\sin [m°(\theta)] = \tfrac{1}{2}$$

where in this particular case

$$m°(\theta) = 30.$$

However it is customary, although not quite accurate, for both historical and reasons of simplicity, to use the notation $\sin [30°] = \tfrac{1}{2}$; that is, replace $m°(\theta)$ by $\theta°$, with the understanding that the first interpretation is meant.

Thus in writing $\sin 30° = \tfrac{1}{2}$, we really have a composite function. That is, we have $f[g(x)]$ where $g(x)$ is a measure function, the domain is the set of angles, the range is the set of real numbers and $f(x)$ is the trigonometric function sine.

16   No, it is not. The student is trying to use the identity

$$\sec x = \frac{1}{\cos x} \,.$$

Therefore,

$$\sec 38° = \frac{1}{\cos 38°} \,,$$

not $\cos \dfrac{1}{38°}$.

17   In right triangles, the following definition is usually given.

If θ is an *acute angle* of any right triangle, then

$$\cos \theta = \frac{\text{length of side adjacent to } \theta}{\text{length of hypotenuse}}.$$

Thus the definition is used only on *acute angles*. Since a right angle is not acute, then the definition is not used in this case.

It is possible, however, to consider the angle whose measure is 90° as a "limiting case" in which one takes zero as the length of the side adjacent to *a* shown in Figure 5.4.2. One difficulty here is that the "limiting figure" is a line segment and not what is generally accepted as a triangle.

FIGURE 5.4.2

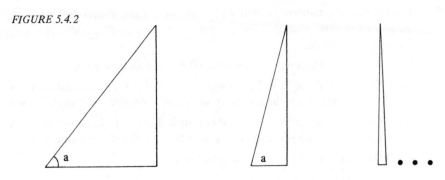

18   This is simply a matter of convention. Historically, a choice had to be made. It would have been entirely correct to call *rotation in the clockwise direction* positive if one had so desired.

19   For an answer to this question, read:

> J. C. Biddle, "The Square Function," *The Mathematics Teacher*, February 1967, pp. 121-23.

20   One way of helping the student see the pattern in this situation is to ask the student to graph both $y = \sin x$ and $y = \sin (x + \pi/3))$ on the same set of axes. After the graphs are completed, then the teacher might point out that the graph of

$$y = \sin (x + (\pi/3))$$

has the same shape as the graph of $y = \sin x$ but it is shifted $\pi/3$ units to the left. A good set of problems to give the student at this point would be the following:

Graph each of the following and try to find out how the graphs in each of the groups are related.

I	II
(a) $y = x^2$	(a) $y = |x|$
(b) $y = (x - 1)^2$	(b) $y = |x - 1|$
(c) $y = (x - 2)^2$	(c) $y = |x - 2|$
(d) $y = (x - 3)^2$	(d) $y = |x - 3|$
(e) $y = (x + 1)^2$	(e) $y = |x + 1|$
(f) $y = (x + 2)^2$	(f) $y = |x + 2|$
(g) $y = (x + 3)^2$	(g) $y = |x + 3|$

Problem 1 How are the graphs $y = \sin x$ and $y = \sin x + b$ (where b is a non-zero real number) related. That is how can you graph the second function if you know the graph of the first?

Problem 2 How are the graphs $y = \sin x$ and $y = A \sin x$ (where A is a non-zero real number) related?

Problem 3 Does the relation that you found in Problem 1 hold for the functions $y = x^2 + b$ and $y = x^2$; for $y = |x| + b$ and $y = |x|$, $(b \neq 0)$.

Problem 4 Does the relation you found in Problem 2 hold for the functions $y = x^2$ and $y = ax^2$; for $y = |x|$ and $y = a|x|$, $(a \neq 0)$.

Problem 5 Generalize the properties that you have discovered in Problems 1-4.

21   The inverse of cotangent, secant and cosecant are not always defined in the way mentioned in this question. For example, one "standard" calculus text offers the following definitions.

(1)   Arccot x is the number y for which $0 < y < \pi$ and cot y = x.

(2)   For $x \geq 1$, Arcsec x is the number y such that $0 \leq y < \pi/2$ and sec y = x. For $x \leq -1$, Arcsec x is the number y such that $-\pi \leq y < -\pi/2$ and sec y = x.

(3)   For $x \geq 1$, Arccsc x is the number y such that $0 < y \leq \pi/2$ and csc y = x. For $x \leq -1$, Arccsc x is the number y such that $-\pi < y \leq -\pi/2$ and csc y = x.

In general, with suitable restrictions, one wants

csc (Arccsc x) = x.

If one accepts the definition used in the question, then

$$\text{csc (Arccsc x)} = \text{csc} \left(\text{Arcsin} \frac{1}{x} \right)$$
$$= x \quad \text{(why?)}$$

Problem Show that with the definitions given in Question 21 that

cot(Arccot x) = x   and   sec(Arcsec x) = x.

22   The trigonometric functions have the same names as the related circular functions; only the domains are different. The trigonometric functions have domains that are sets of angles and ranges that are sets of real numbers. In reality, however, the trigonometric functions are composite functions. That is, sin 30° means sin $[m°(\phi)]$ where ϕ is an angle whose degree measure is 30 and m is a measure function. The circular functions have domains that are sets of real numbers and ranges that are sets of real numbers However, the functions are related by the following:

If ϕ is an angle whose radian measure is y, then

$$\cos [\phi] = \cos [m^R(\phi)] = \cos y$$

where $m^R(\phi)$ is the measure of ϕ in radians.

$$\sin [\phi] = \sin [m^R(\phi)] = \sin y$$
$$\tan [\phi] = \tan [m^R(\phi)] = \tan y,$$

etc. for the remaining trigonometric functions. For example,

$$\sin [30°] = \sin [\pi/6].$$

There could be extensions of this idea such as hyperbolic trigonometric functions and parabolic trigonometric functions, but these functions are usually defined for domains of real numbers and are thus closer in meaning to circular functions than to trigonometric functions.

23   No, the student is not correct. Consider $\text{Cos}^{-1} \left(\cos \dfrac{7\pi}{6} \right)$. Then

$$\cos \frac{7\pi}{6} = \frac{-\sqrt{3}}{2} \quad \text{and} \quad \text{Cos}^{-1} \left(\frac{-\sqrt{3}}{2} \right) = \frac{5\pi}{6}.$$

Thus, $\text{Cos}^{-1} \left(\cos \dfrac{7\pi}{6} \right) \not\equiv \dfrac{7\pi}{6}$ mod π.

> **Problem 1** Is there a way of fixing up the student's statement so that the result would be a valid statement?

> **Problem 2** Can a statement similar to the student's statement be made for $\text{Sin}^{-1}(\sin x)$?

24 It should be pointed out that the following notation is frequently used.

arcsin x (lower case *a*) refers to a *relation* (1)

Arcsin x (capital *A*) refers to a *function* (2)

If the student meant (1), then the student is correct. However, if the student meant (2), then the student is not necessarily correct. The range of Arcsin is the set of all numbers a, $-\dfrac{\pi}{2} \leqslant a \leqslant \dfrac{\pi}{2}$. If x is in this range then

Arcsin (sin x) = x (3)

Otherwise, (3) is false. Let $x = 2\pi$, then $\sin 2\pi = 0$ and Arcsin $(0) = 0$. Therefore, Arcsin $(\sin 2\pi) = 0$, not 2π.

25 Yes, the student's method will work. If $\tan \theta = \sqrt{5}/6$, then

$$\frac{\sin \theta}{\cos \theta} = \frac{\sqrt{5}}{6} = \frac{\sqrt{5}/r}{6/r}.$$

Since $\sin^2 \theta + \cos^2 \theta = 1$, then

$$\left(\frac{\sqrt{5}}{r}\right)^2 + \left(\frac{6}{r}\right)^2 = 1,$$

i.e., $\dfrac{41}{r^2} = 1$ or $r^2 = 41$.

Thus $r = \sqrt{41}$. Therefore $\sin \theta$ and $\cos \theta$ can be found with their appropriate signs.

26 One way to help would be as follows. Consider a circle with a radius of one unit and its center at the origin. Divide the circle into 360 equal pieces as partially illustrated in Figure 5.4.3. Each angle indicated has a measure of one degree $(1°)$.

FIGURE 5.4.3

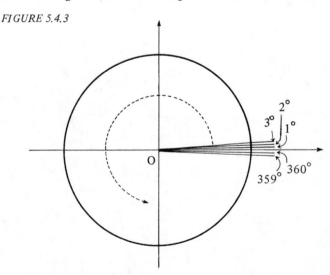

Now consider the same circle. Beginning at point P in Figure 5.4.4 measure one unit (same as used for the radius) along the circle as indicated. The resulting angle has a measure of one radian (approximately 57.3 degrees).

FIGURE 5.4.4

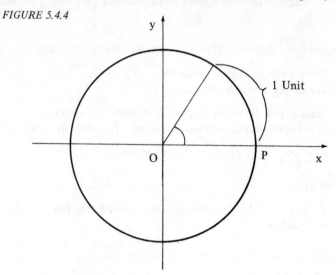

An intuitive approach might be to have the student draw a circle in a rectangular coordinate system with its center at (0, 0). Have the student approximate (by shading or some other means) one-sixth of the circumference. The angle formed (subtended) is about one radian.

Index